Youth Culture and the M

This expansive, lively introduction charts the connections between international youth cultures and the development of global media and communication.

From 1950s drive-ins and jukeboxes to contemporary social media, the book examines modern youth cultures in their social, economic, and political contexts. Exploring the rise of young people as a distinct media market, the book examines the relation of youth to modern consumerism, marketing, and digital technologies. The chapters are packed with analysis of media representations of youth, debates about the media's 'effects' on young audiences, and young people's use of the media to elaborate identities and negotiate social relationships. Drawing on a wealth of international examples, the book explores the impact of globalisation and new media technologies on youth cultures around the world. Assessing a profusion of worldwide research, the book shows how modern youth cultures can only be understood as part of an international web of connections, exchanges, and experiences.

With an ideal balance between detailed examples and engaging analysis, this book is a must-read for anyone interested in youth cultures and the modern media.

Bill Osgerby is Emeritus Professor of Media, Culture, and Communication at London Metropolitan University, UK. He has published widely on British and American cultural history.

Youth Culture and the Media

Global Perspectives

Second edition

Bill Osgerby

Routledge
Taylor & Francis Group

LONDON AND NEW YORK

Second edition published 2021
by Routledge
2 Park Square, Milton Park, Abingdon, Oxon OX14 4RN

and by Routledge
52 Vanderbilt Avenue, New York, NY 10017

Routledge is an imprint of the Taylor & Francis Group, an informa business

© 2021 Bill Osgerby

First edition published by Routledge 2004

British Library Cataloguing in Publication Data
A catalogue record for this book is available from the British Library

Library of Congress Cataloging-in-Publication Data
Names: Osgerby, Bill, author.
Title: Youth culture and the media : global perspectives / Bill Osgerby.
Description: Second Edition. | new york : routledge, 2020. | Includes
bibliographical references and index.
Identifiers: LCCN 2020017833 (print) | LCCN 2020017834 (ebook) | ISBN
9780415621656 (hardback) | ISBN 9780415621663 (paperback) | ISBN
9781351065269 (ebook)
Subjects: LCSH: Youth–Social aspects. | Mass media and youth.
Classification: LCC HQ796 .O7164 2020 (print) | LCC HQ796 (ebook) | DDC
302.23083–dc23
LC record available at https://lccn.loc.gov/2020017833
LC ebook record available at https://lccn.loc.gov/2020017834

ISBN: 978-0-415-62165-6 (hbk)
ISBN: 978-0-415-62166-3 (pbk)
ISBN: 978-1-351-06526-9 (ebk)

Typeset in Bembo
by Taylor & Francis Books

Contents

Preface and acknowledgements

An earlier incarnation of this book appeared as *Youth Media*, part of Routledge's Introduction to Media and Communications series, published in 2004. It seems like a long time ago now. Back in 2004, US TV audiences had just seen the launch of a new reality game show, *The Apprentice*, presented by a bombastic businessman. And, working from his dorm bedroom, a young Harvard student was busy setting up 'Facemash', a computer network that linked up his college friends. Clearly, a lot has changed since then. Major events have impacted on the world (not least the financial crisis of 2007–8 and the Covid-19 pandemic of 2020). And the landscape of global media has undergone a huge transformation. A wealth of new academic research, furthermore, has charted and analysed the developments. Hence, while this book is ostensibly a new edition of *Youth Media*, very little of the original remains. While the original book's key themes and some of its structure still feature, pretty much everything else has been revised, updated and rewritten to take account of the major changes in the realms of youth culture and the media, along with the wealth of scholarship these changes have engendered.

I would like to say a big thank you to Jennifer Vennall and Natalie Foster at Routledge for their amazing patience and support. I would also like to thank my mum, dad and brother George for their enduring love and support. And I would especially like to thank Liz Davies for not just reading through the manuscript but for all her wonderful help. Finally, I would like to thank Puss the cat for her furry contribution.

1 Introduction

Youth culture and the media: global perspectives

Youth culture, the media, and 'seismic' social change

'Youthquake' was a hot phrase in 2017 when it was chosen as 'word of the year' by Oxford Dictionaries (the dictionary branch of Oxford University Press). Defined as 'a significant cultural, political or social change arising from the actions or influence of young people', 'youthquake' was selected partly for its prevalence. The term had been widely used by the British media to describe a surge in young people's support for the political opposition during the 2017 general election. But the term's pertinence had also influenced the Oxford lexicographers. As the head of Oxford Dictionaries explained, 'youthquake' had been chosen because, during a 'difficult and divisive year', it was 'a rare political word that sounds a hopeful note' (quoted in Cain, 2017). But the term could equally describe the more general impact young people and their cultures have had, since the early twentieth century, on patterns of social, economic, and political change around the world.

Indeed, 2017 was not the first time commentators had used the term 'youthquake' to describe the way young people seemed to be a driving force in 'seismic' social change. In 1965 Diana Vreeland – the editor-in-chief of fashion magazine *Vogue* – had originally used the phrase in an editorial that trumpeted the way youngsters seemed to be reconfiguring the world's cultural landscape:

> Youth ... is surprising countries east and west with a sense of assurance serene beyond all years ... under 24 and over 90,000,000 strong in the US alone. More dreamers. More doers. Here. Now. Youthquake, 1965.
>
> (Vreeland, 1965: 112)

And, two years later, *Look* – the American features magazine – used the term as the title for a special volume chronicling young people's prominence in tumultuous times. As the book's promotional blurb explained, youth seemed to be key protagonists in events that had shaken up US society:

> This is their age – the age of the teeny-bopper and the long hair, of the Peace Corps worker and the peace marcher, of the mod and the mini, of the under 25er.
>
> (*Look*, 1967)

Outside America the same theme also surfaced. In Britain, for example, the 1970s saw an array of cultural commentators use the phrase 'youthquake' to denote the way young people had been central to the shifts transforming British society since the Second World War. According to Richard Neville, a 'youthquake' had divided the country into two generational 'armed camps' (1970: 13), while Peter Lewis argued Britain had been the epicentre of an 'explosive discovery of teenage identity' (Lewis, 1978: 118), and Kenneth Leech observed how a 'youthquake' had transformed the 1950s into 'supremely the decade of the teenager' (1973: 1).

More recent 'youthquakes' have also registered on the Richter scale of worldwide change. In 2003, for instance, the term was emblazoned across the cover of *Egypt Today*, as the English-language Egyptian magazine spotlighted the way the nation's youngsters were 'rocking the world of movies, music and TV' (November 2003). And in 2018 US futurologist Rocky Scopelliti used the term 'youthquake' for the title of his account of the way a new industrial era was being globally forged through a confluence of demographic change and technological development. For Scopelliti, the world's growing youth population was at the cutting edge of the technological advancements transforming every facet of social life – a position, Scopelliti argued, made explicit by young people's immersion in the realms of digital media and communications:

> … their voice and influence is global through the social media they continue to fuel. It's instantly delivered to their smartphones, and that's become as natural to them as the air they breathe, efficiently consumed through the artificially intelligent, personalised, platform-based, exponential models serving them.
>
> (2018: 6)

Scopelliti's views exemplify the way youth have invariably been configured as the vanguard of technological change and, especially, the emergence of new forms of media and communications. And, undoubtedly, young people have played a key role in the proliferation of digital media in the early twenty-first century. Most obviously, youth has been a key market for the new forms of communication and entertainment unleashed by digital technologies, but young people have also been in the forefront of the way these technologies are used for new forms of cultural expression and self-representation. Symbolic configurations of youth, moreover, have invariably figured in the way the media itself has interpreted these changes, with young people represented as both the epitome of the social benefits afforded by technological innovation, and the embodiment of their malignant consequences. These relationships between youth and the media, however, are not unique to the age of digital communication. As this book demonstrates, throughout the twentieth and early twenty-first centuries, close connections have existed between developments in youth culture and changes in the fields of media and communication.

Primarily, this book explores the complex relationships that exist in the production, circulation, and consumption of media and cultural texts geared towards markets and audiences of young people. It analyses the historical development and contemporary configuration of the commercial youth market, highlighting its relation to both the broader development of modern media institutions and to wider shifts in social, economic, and political relations. Attention is given to the impact of increasing conglomeration in the media industries, the shift towards niche marketing and the growing importance of 'cultural intermediaries' in modern business practice. But consideration is also given to youth's relationship with the media and the various ways young people make commercial texts and products 'meaningful'. Recognition is given to young people's ability to be 'active consumers' who create their own identities through their practices of consumption, but issues of institutional power, control, and inequality are also stressed. Generally, emphasis is placed on the way cultural meanings are always dynamic – continually formed and reformed as they circulate through (and feed back into) the various sites of production, representation, and consumption.

As well as exploring the symbiotic relationships that exist between young people's cultural formations and commercial industries, this book also analyses media representations of young people and the way configurations of 'youth' have featured within wider media and political discourse. Here, attention is given to the various ways the media have constructed 'ideologies of youth' through the deployment of specific representational codes and modes of address. The constitution of ideologically-charged representations of youth, it is argued, has functioned as an important medium through which fundamental shifts in social boundaries and cultural relationships have been historically explored, made sense of and interpreted – not only by the media, but also by legislators, institutions of social control and a wide spectrum of cultural commentators.

The book also seeks to place these issues within a 'global' context. In a world characterised by growing social, economic, and political connections, local youth cultures cannot be understood in isolation but only as part of an international web of connections, exchanges, and experiences. As David Buckingham and Mary Jane Kehily explain, the early twenty-first century has seen many young people's lives transformed by the forces of globalisation:

> Young people are now growing up with significantly greater access to globalized media: media companies are increasingly constructing and targeting global markets, and young people are using new media to form and sustain transnational connections. Growing numbers of them have also experienced global migration, and inhabit communities in which a wide range of global cultures mix and cross-fertilize.
>
> (Buckingham and Kehily, 2014: 8–9)

The flows of globalisation, however, have not subsumed differences between the experiences and expressions of young people around the world. Indeed, rather than speaking of youth culture (singular), it is probably more accurate to think in terms of youth culture*s* (plural), and this book highlights the way local histories and circumstances still play a crucial role in defining and determining young people's lives. At the same time, however, local experiences are embedded in international networks of interaction and influence, and so this book stresses the way *global* perspectives are essential for understanding the relationships between youth culture(s) and the media.

'"Anywhere, anytime" connectivity': media and communication in young people's lives

It has become something of a cliché to observe that contemporary young-sters are immersed in the media. Nevertheless, the media clearly play a major part in young people's lives. The TV shows they watch, the music they listen to, the video games they play, the websites they visit, and the social networks they use; all of them offer young people a stream of differ-ent experiences, ideas, and knowledge. And, year on year, surveys attest to the significant amount of time young people spend engaging with media technologies and content. For example, in their 2019 survey of US young-sters' media use, the independent research agency Common Sense Media found that teenagers aged between 13 and 18 spent an average of over 7 hours a day using screen media of some kind.[1] And, while teenagers were watching half an hour less of shows on a TV set than they did in 2015, the numbers watching online videos 'every day' had more than doubled – from 34 per cent in 2015 to 69 per cent in 2019 – and the amount time spent watching online material had risen from half an hour a day to about an hour (Rideout and Robb, 2019: 3). And, while the amount of time spent using social media had remained fairly steady across the four-year period, it still accounted for over an hour of the average teenager's day (Rideout and Robb, 2019: 6). One of the most noticeable shifts was the way smartphone ownership among 13–18-year-olds had grown substantially since 2015, increasing from 67 per cent to 84 per cent in 2019 (Rideout and Robb, 2019: 5). The trend testified to the way mobile phones had become deeply embedded in the daily lives of most American teenagers, a 2018 study by the Pew Research Center finding that 42 per cent of US teens reported feeling 'anxious' when they did not have their phones, while around a quarter said they felt lonely (25 per cent) or upset (24 per cent) (Anderson and Jiang, 2018: 6).

European research also testified to the omnipresence of media in young peo-ple's lives. In 2018, for example, Rinaldo Kühne and Susanne Baumgartner reported that German adolescents watched television for an average of 105 minutes and listened to radio for 79 minutes every day, while they spent an average of around 200 minutes a day online (Kühne and Baumgartner, 2018: 8). In Britain, meanwhile, the Office of Communications (Ofcom – the body responsible for regulating broadcasting) reported that in 2016 young people aged between 16 and 24 were the country's most active media and communications users. On average, members of this group spent nearly 9 hours a day using various forms of media and communications. Furthermore, through multi-tasking (using several media forms at the same time), Ofcom estimated the youngsters crammed just over 13 hours' worth of media and communications activity into their daily routine (Ofcom, 2016: 20–21). And in 2020 the multinational research network EU Kids Online reported that, while there was variation across the 19 European countries it surveyed, media and communications usage was deep-rooted in young people's lives. Compared to 2010, the study found, the amount of time youngsters spent online each day had almost doubled in many countries – for example, from about one to three hours per day in Spain, and from about two to three-and-a-half hours in Norway (Smahel et al., 2020: 6). Smartphones, moreover, were 'always at hand, providing an "anywhere, anytime" connectivity', the majority of youngsters surveyed reporting they used their smartphones almost all the time, several times each day or at least daily – although this ranged between 65 per cent (France) and 89 per cent (Lithuania) (Smahel et al., 2020: 6).

Media and communication, therefore, occupy a central place in young people's social and cultural lives. Moreover, the wealth of research undertaken on youth's relationship with the media demonstrates the way young people are seen as being separate and distinct from the wider, 'adult' world, and are considered a focus for particular issues and concerns. Across the variety of international studies, however, 'youth' is bracketed as an age group in diverse ways. This testifies to the way the period in the life course encompassed by the term 'youth' has varied significantly between different societies. Indeed, while the United Nations defines 'youth' as 'those persons between the ages of 15 and 24 years', it acknowledges there 'is no universally agreed international definition of the youth age group' (United Nations, nd). While 'youth' is generally conceived as a period of semi-dependence that divides the full dependency of childhood and the complete independence of adulthood, its precise boundaries are relative and contingent.

The developing concepts of 'youth' and 'youth culture'

'Youth', therefore, is not an inherent period in the life course, but is a social construct; an age category created through the interaction of social, economic, and political forces. Of course, the experience of aging is a fundamental biological process and the physical transformations associated with puberty represent a tangible moment of transition from childhood to mature adulthood. But the social characteristics ascribed to the generational category labelled 'youth' have varied between different historical and cultural contexts. As David Sibley has argued, the boundary separating childhood and adulthood is imprecise and 'the act of drawing the line in the construction of discrete [age] categories interrupts what is naturally continuous' (Sibley, 1995: 35). Rather than being a consistent and unvarying stage in human physical and psychological

development, therefore, the distinguishing features of 'youth' are the product
of wider judgments made by specific societies. As Walter Heinz explains:

> The coordinates of this period of life vary according to the economy and
> the educational and social policies of the state: the life course and its
> component 'youth' are path-dependent social structures. Modern societies
> differ in their institutional arrangements concerning life transitions: educa-
> tion and training provisions, labour market regulations, exclusion
> mechanisms, social assistance rules, and the extent to which there is an
> explicit youth policy.
>
> (Heinz, 2009: 6)

The precise demarcations of 'youth' as an age group vary considerably, but a
general concept of 'youth' as a period of life dividing childhood and adulthood
first became established in Europe and North America during the late nineteenth century. According to John Gillis (1974), this period saw modern
notions of youth delineated as a consequence of a growing apprehension
among legislators and reformers that the teenage years were a life stage distinguished by social and psychological vulnerability. As a result, there ensued a
flood of protective legislation which – coupled with a new range of specialised
welfare bodies and employment practices – marked out youth as a distinct
social group associated with particular needs and social problems. Claire Wallace and Sijka Kovatcheva (1998) also see processes of industrialisation and the
development of state agencies as central factors in the emergence of youth as a
clearly defined stage in the life course. For Wallace and Kovatcheva, concepts
of youth developed as a facet of Western modernity and 'the development of
the modern world associated with professional bureaucratic power, industrial
society and enlightenment rationality' (1998: 10). From this perspective, the
modern configuration of distinct age groups was the product of state bureau-
cracies, who developed age as a precise method of calibration in administrative
practices that worked to define and control subordinate populations, an institutional formalisation of life stages that reached a high point with the expansion
of state welfare and education systems after the Second World War.[2]

Modern notions of 'youth' as a discrete life stage demanding special attention
and supervision were particularly associated with the concept of 'adolescence'
developed in psychology and pedagogy during the late nineteenth and early
twentieth centuries. Studies such as G. Stanley Hall's rambling opus, *Adolescence: Its Psychology and Its Relations to Physiology, Anthropology, Sociology, Sex,
Crime and Education* (1904) popularised the notion of adolescence as a distinct
phase of bio-psychological transformation that began with puberty and ended
in mature adulthood. Hall's view of adolescence as an innately volatile period
of identity formation (inevitably troubling for both young people and wider
society) retains influence in branches of psychology. More generally, however,
this approach fell from favour during the mid-twentieth century as empirical
investigation cast doubt on notions of adolescence as an intrinsically traumatic

phase of personal development.[3] In place of inherent bio-psychological characteristics, theorists increasingly focused on the social characteristics that were
believed to set youth apart as a discrete social group. During the early 1940s,
for instance, the American sociologist Talcott Parsons coined the term 'youth
culture' to denote what he saw as a distinct generational cohort subject to
common processes of socialisation. For Parsons, this 'youth culture' was a
transitionary experience that performed a positive function for the social whole
by 'easing the difficult process of adjustment from childhood emotional
dependency to full "maturity"' (Parsons, 1943: 30).

Other American researchers also contributed to the developing theories of
youth as a distinctive life stage. In *Childhood and Society* (1950), for example,
Erik Erikson presented adolescence as a confusing (though not especially deviant) phase of identity formation, while in *Generation to Generation* (1956) S.N.
Eisenstadt emphasised the way adolescent peer culture eased young people into
their adult roles. James Coleman's *The Adolescent Society* (1961) was also influential, portraying a teenage culture whose attitudes and interests were markedly
different to those of the wider adult world. In these terms it was not any innate
biological or psychological 'storm and stress' that set young people apart as a
generational group, but their distinctive social experiences, values, and
behaviour.[4]

Mid-twentieth century perceptions of 'youth' as a distinct social group were
bolstered by a convergence of social and economic developments. On both
sides of the Atlantic a postwar 'Baby Boom' ensured a burgeoning youth
population throughout the 1950s, 1960s, and 1970s, while the expansion of
consumer industries and the reconfiguration of traditional labour markets
ensured buoyant levels of youth employment and boosted young people's
spending power. In turn, the growth of youth's disposable income underpinned a huge expansion of the commercial youth market, so that by the late
1950s the range of products geared to the young was virtually boundless. The
media and consumer industries scrambled to capitalise on youth's enhanced
economic muscle, with filmmakers, record companies, magazine publishers,
and fashion firms all jostling to cash-in on the growth of teen spending. This
exponential growth of the youth-oriented leisure and entertainment industries
added force to notions of a distinctive adolescent peer culture. Indeed, intrinsic
to Parsons' concept of 'youth culture' and Coleman's account of the 'adolescent society' was the assumption that the new fads, fashions and media pitched
at the young were catering to a generational culture denoted by its preoccupation with leisure, style, and conspicuous consumption. Increasingly,
then, the characteristics that seemed to set 'youth' apart as a distinct cultural
group were not their bio-psychological attributes, but their distinctive patterns
of media use and practices of consumption.

With the explosion of youth-oriented media and entertainment during the
1950s and 1960s, notions of a new, hedonistic and distinctly 'teenage' form of
consumption became prevalent in accounts of social change. In both the US
and Britain, 'teenage' culture was configured as the harbinger of a modern

consumerism in which the 'old' boundaries of class and economic inequality were perceived as steadily disappearing. The media and social theorists alike presented newly affluent 'gilded youth' as the vanguard of a liberated, exciting, and pre-eminently classless modern society. In reality, however, inequalities of wealth and status remained (as they still remain) crucial determinants of young people's social experiences and life chances. Indeed, while notions of an integrated and homogeneous 'youth culture' dominated the sociology of youth during the 1950s and early 1960s, the influence of social class was never entirely disregarded. In America, for example, August Hollingshead's study of *Elmstown's Youth* (1949) described the activities of generationally-based cliques, but also acknowledged the ways social behaviour was still shaped by family and community background. In Britain researchers gave even greater recognition to the influence of socio-economic structures on young people's experiences. David Downes' (1966) study of youths from London's East End, for instance, highlighted the way social class affected young people's attitudes and aspirations, while Graham Murdock and Robin McCron found that teenagers' tastes in pop music and style were influenced by their class background, earlier researchers having 'seriously underestimated the importance of class inequalities in shaping adolescents' lives and in limiting their responses' (Murdock and McCron, 1973: 692).

Class emerged as a pre-eminent theme in analyses of British youth culture during the late 1970s. Especially influential in this respect was work produced by members of the Centre for Contemporary Cultural Studies (CCCS) at the University of Birmingham. Edited by Stuart Hall and Tony Jefferson, *Resistance through Rituals* (1976) drew together work by various members of the CCCS team who elaborated a neo-Marxist reading of youth style (encompassing dress, music, language, and attitudes) as a form of class-based resistance against a dominant culture. Crucially, the CCCS contribution underscored the way young people did not share a common 'youth culture' or an 'adolescent society'. Instead, the CCCS clearly demonstrated how socio-economic inequalities and their attendant conflicts generated a range of very different cultural identities among young people. The CCCS approach was a huge influence on subsequent research worldwide, though its emphasis on issues of social class was increasingly criticised for overshadowing other systems of power relations. And, from the 1980s onwards, the study of youth culture was steadily recast through interventions inspired by developments in feminism, post-structuralism, postcolonialism, and queer theory – all of which helped frame young people as a heterogeneous group whose diverse identities were elaborated in response to complex sets of power structures and social experiences.

At the same time, many theorists have argued that since the late twentieth century the boundaries demarcating 'youth' as a distinct period of life have become increasingly blurred. At one end of the scale, consumer culture has increasingly stretched down to a 'tween' market in which pre-teen children emulate 'teenage' tastes and identities. At the other end, many commentators have observed how youth, as a life stage, has extended further into adulthood.

For many young people the shift from education to work has become a more protracted process, while the lack of stable jobs and affordable, independent housing mean that transitions to adulthood have become longer, less predictable, and more precarious. As a consequence, Andy Furlong observes, 'many researchers have begun to appreciate the inadequacy of the term "youth" for under-standing processes that may shape the lives of individuals well into their twenties and beyond' (Furlong, 2009: 2). For some, the changes amount to the emergence of a whole new stage in the life course – 'emerging adulthood' – though critics argue that such categorisation can be too sweeping, ignoring marked differences between the life experiences of young people, both globally and within the same country.

Some theorists, however, have argued that at particular historical moments there is sufficient commonality between the experiences of young people to mark them off as a distinct 'generational' group. In the early twenty-first century, for example, many accounts presented young people as a unique generation, set apart from their predecessors through their experience of growing up immersed in new digital technologies. Such ideas won widespread popularity, but for critics such 'generational' perspectives were often too simplistic and woefully over-generalised.

'The problem of generations': cohorts of youth and historical shifts

The idea of identifiable 'generations' and socially significant 'generation gaps' runs deep in perceptions of youth and young people's relation to wider society. Put most simply, a 'generation' is a cohort of individuals born within a particular time frame. In these terms, generations are almost organic phenomena that 'naturally' emerge as years go by. But, from a more analytic perspective, distinct 'generations' are not inevitably constituted through the passing of time. Instead, they are actively created through processes of historical change. As June Edmunds and Bryan Turner observe in their analytic history of the concept, a 'generation' is best seen as 'an age cohort that comes to have social significance by constituting itself as a cultural identity' (2002: 7). In these terms a 'generation' is not simply a chronological age group, but is a cohort of individuals who have been categorised and defined in a particular way as 'a consequence of their specificity, that is their particular location in the development of a society or culture' (ibid.). A distinct generation, then, is not naturally imbued with characteristic features. Rather, it is constituted and identified as a collective entity through processes of historical development and transformation.

The notion of distinctive generational groups has its intellectual origins in the work of theorists such as the French philosopher Auguste Comte and the Hungarian sociologist Karl Mannheim.[5] First published in 1853, Comte's book *Cours de Philosophie Positive* (translated as *The Positive Philosophy*) saw generational conflict as a key motor of social change, as the conservatism of an older generation is steadily challenged by the new ideas of an emerging cohort.

For Mannheim, too, distinct generations were a key feature of modern societies. Mannheim's essay '*Das Problem der Generationen*' ('The Problem of Generations'), first published in 1923, argued that groups of people who grow up during specific historical periods share a common set of formative experiences and this leads to the development of a distinctive consciousness and collective 'modes of behaviour, feeling and thought' (Mannheim, 1952: 291). Mannheim's views were at least partly indebted to the traumatic experience of the First World War and the sense that those who experienced the horrors of the conflict first-hand were set apart as a distinctive generation. And, indeed, landmark events have commonly been the cue to heightened generational awareness, British sociologist Jonathan White noting how 'generational consciousness and social trauma have tended to go hand-in-hand' (White, 2013: 219).

Many contemporary scholars, however, are wary of the concept of generation. As David Buckingham points out, the study of generational differences 'inevitably runs the risk of essentialising those differences' (2006: 3). In these terms, the notion that particular generational groups are intrinsically distinguished by shared characteristics can produce simplistic stereotypes that are overly homogenising, and gloss over important social divisions and economic differences *within* a generational cohort. Nevertheless, the notion of distinctive generational groups remains an influential concept, and has been especially prominent in journalistic and popular accounts of young people and social change. In this respect the work of American authors William Strauss and Neil Howe stands out. In books such as *Generations* (1991), *The Fourth Turning* (1997) and *Millennials Rising* (2000), Strauss and Howe popularised the idea that social shifts in the US have been linked to the recurring characteristics of successive generations who 'collectively possess a common persona' (Howe and Strauss, 2000: 4). From this perspective, historical developments are associated with successive generational archetypes – dubbed by Strauss and Howe the 'Hero', 'Artist', 'Prophet', and 'Nomad' generations – that have arisen cyclically and have swung America towards distinctive kinds of social, political, and economic change. For example, those who grew up during the 1950s and 1960s are seen by Strauss and Howe as an archetypal 'Prophet' generation – a cohort that are typically born after a great war or crisis and come of age as passionate, young crusaders in an age of rejuvenated community life and consensus (Strauss and Howe, 1997: 84).

Strauss and Howe's ideas have attracted much interest and have been widely cited by journalists, politicians, and market researchers. The authors' arguments, however, have drawn considerable scholarly criticism, journalist Jeremy Peters observing how many academic historians dismiss their books as being 'about as scientific as astrology or a Nostradamus text' (Peters, 2017). Indeed, Andy Furlong argues that Strauss and Howe's work is akin to 'pop-psychology' insofar as it is 'light on theory and lacks the sort of rigour normally found in academic discussions' (Furlong, 2013: 16). For critics, popular accounts of a 'generational' essence or mindset are invariably poorly evidenced and simplistic, and deliver sweeping and over-generalised narratives that ride roughshod over social, economic, and cultural complexities.

More sophisticated accounts, however, highlight the way discrete generational identities are forged by social and economic forces operating in a particular historical context. For the French theorist Pierre Bourdieu, for example, generations are socially and culturally defined by their distinct 'habitus' – their characteristic tastes, attitudes, and lifestyles – which are partly a result of the historical circumstances in which they are born, but which also emerge through struggles between generations over cultural and economic resources (Bourdieu, 1991). And, in the sociology of childhood, scholars such as Leena Alanen (2001) have developed the concept of 'generationing' to denote the way contextual factors play a key role in the way generations are negotiated and constructed as social formations. As the Swedish media theorist Göran Bolin explains, 'generationing' as a process implies that people are not destined to be specific generations by birth, but that certain cohorts over time receive a generational consciousness and self-understanding that make them understand themselves as members of a specific generation' (2017: 125). According to Bolin, moreover, along with wider social and cultural factors, the media play an important role in this process. From this perspective, the broad media 'landscape' – the media's developing technologies, formats, and content, along with the uses to which they are put – is an important feature in the formation of generational identity, and plays a key role in the way generations are not only perceived by wider society but also perceive of themselves (2017: 130). In the early twenty-first century these issues were highlighted by the rise of digital technology and the impact of new forms of communication and entertainment on young people's lives. But, as this book shows, dimensions of 'generationing' have been pronounced since youth first emerged as a distinct consumer market.

Approaching youth culture and the media

This book charts the developing relationship between youth and the media, and the different ways this association has been interpreted, represented, and responded to by politicians, social scientists, and the media itself. There is a distinct historical dimension to the discussion, and the book can be seen as contributing to what Christine Feldman-Barrett (2018) sees as a 'historic turn' in youth-oriented scholarship, with researchers giving increased attention to both the experiences of young people in the past, and the way these experiences relate to contemporary issues and debates. This trend towards historicisation, Feldman-Barrett observes, has seen 'youth culture, events and activities ... appraised and analysed for how they sit within a timeline and/or how, on a micro-level, they symbolize or relate to greater cultural forces afoot in a particular era' (Feldman-Barrett, 2018: 741). Such an approach is vital because, as Mary Celeste Kearney (2014) contends, it is only through attention to historical context that we can understand the continuities and discontinuities that characterise the development of youth culture. 'We must', Kearney cogently counsels, 'reflect critically on the current moment as a specific temporal location that, while unique, is necessarily shaped by, and shaping of, the past' (Kearney, 2014: 66).

Global themes and issues are also, of course, prominent throughout the book. This, however, does not imply that developments in *every* region of the world will be examined. Such a task is well beyond the scope of the present volume. Rather, the book considers internationally-relevant themes and relationships, providing global and local case studies that bring out the geopolitical interconnections and tensions that characterise the fields of youth culture and the media. Consideration, for example, is given to the way digital media technologies have offered new possibilities for transnational connectedness and dialogue, but emphasis is given to the way these new opportunities are framed by profound global inequalities in terms of power, ownership, and control.

These disparities are particularly pronounced in relationships between the 'Global North' and the 'Global South' – a distinction increasingly used by social scientists to discuss geopolitical relations of power. The Global North refers broadly to the US, Canada, the UK, the European Union, Israel, Japan, Singapore, South Korea, as well as Australia and New Zealand; while the Global South encompasses the regions of Latin America, Asia, Africa, and Oceania. This book teases out the way relations between the Global North and Global South are played out in the fields of youth culture and the media, and it charts the way such relations have been accounted for by different theories and perspectives. To some extent, however, these theories themselves are constituent in the broader patterns of global inequality. As Adam Cooper and his associates observe, the field of contemporary youth studies is characterised by the poignant paradox that '90% of the world's youth live in Africa, Latin America or developing countries in Asia', but 'the overwhelming majority of research occurs at institutions in the global North' (Cooper, Swartz and Mahali, 2019: 30). Moreover, there is a tendency in some research to make generalisations based solely on the experiences of youngsters in the Global North. As Herman Cuevo and Ana Miranola argue, ideas developed in a particular context have sometimes been carelessly universalised, so that a theory 'is developed to address young people's concerns and experiences within a specific place but is afterwards utilised as placeless' (Cuevo and Miranola, 2019: 6). These oversights and assumptions, however, will be increasingly challenged and rectified with the appearance of more research that works towards what Cooper and his colleagues envisage as a 'Youth Studies for the global South' – a shift which, they argue, would contribute to a 'disentangled, decentred and more democratic field' (Cooper, Swartz and Mahali, 2019: 31).

Another key theme in this book is attention to what might be termed the 'political economy' of youth culture. Political economy is defined, in a very general way, by media theorist Vincent Mosco as the 'study of the social relations, particularly power relations, that mutually constitute the production, distribution and consumption of resources, including communication resources' (2009: 2). Put more simply, political economy is a critical approach rooted in the analysis of production, business, and trade. Beyond this, however, the combination of the terms 'political' and 'economy' underscores the way the organisation of production is invariably seen as embedded in a wider context of political issues and relationships. In these terms, therefore, a political economy of the media focuses on the way media forms are produced, distributed, and consumed, with political economists of the media often giving particular attention to changing patterns of media ownership and control, and their relation to the shifting contours of political life.

Political economy has long been a facet of the study of media and communications. While it has been a presence in these fields, however, Jonathan Hardy observes how its role has often been 'relatively marginal', with 'greater attention devoted to "texts" and "audiences" than either "production" or the wider contexts in which communication takes place' (Hardy, 2014: 3). Indeed, this is especially true in the case of studies of youth culture and the media, where interest in texts and young people's use of them has often overshadowed a consideration of the structures of economic organisation that underpin the production, circulation, and consumption of youth-oriented media. This book seeks to go some way to addressing this oversight by examining the economic conditions and commercial dynamics fundamental to the development of media targeted at the young.

The book begins by charting the development of the modern youth market. Chapter 2 outlines the first appearance of a commercial youth culture during the nineteenth century, then shows how young people became a more distinctive consumer group during the mid-twentieth century as shifts in demography and labour markets pushed youth to the centre of a postwar consumer boom in both North America and Western Europe. During the late twentieth and early twenty-first centuries economic recession, industrial restructuring and the global financial crisis of 2007–8 eroded the labour markets that had been the foundation for the explosion of 'teenage' consumption during the 1950s and 1960s. Despite this, Chapter 3 shows how young people continued to represent a key consumer group that underpinned the proliferation of new, digitally-based communications and entertainment industries. The chapter surveys these developments, and critically appraises claims they marked the arrival of a new, 'millennial' generation of uniquely media-savvy youngsters.

Chapter 4 considers representations of young people. Attention is given to the way media and politicians alike have made recurring use of the themes and images of 'youth' as a symbol for broader social and political issues. The chapter explores the way representations of 'youth' have served as an 'ideological vehicle' where understandings of wider social changes are encoded, with young people *both* celebrated as the exciting precursor to a prosperous future *and* (sometimes simultaneously) vilified as the most deplorable benchmark of cultural decline.

The heated controversies surrounding the media's influence on young audiences are examined in Chapter 5. The history of 'effects' research is critically surveyed, along with the challenges made by its critics, and the chapter assesses how far fears of 'violent media' and 'video game addiction' mark meaningful responses to dangerous 'media effects', or represent recurring episodes of moral panic.

In Chapter 6 the focus shifts to young audiences' engagement with popular media, and the different ways this has been understood by social theorists. The chapter surveys the way 'mass culture' theories that saw young people as the passive victims of exploitative cultural industries have, since the late twentieth century, given way to accounts that emphasise the capacity of young people to be active agents in the creation of their own identities and cultures. Particular regard is given to the contribution of subcultural theory, together with the range of 'post-subcultural' approaches that seek to address what are seen as the former's shortcomings and misconceptions.

Chapter 7 explores issues of business conglomeration and globalisation in relation to the youth market and young people's cultures. While recognition must be given to the way processes of internationalisation have delivered vast power to global media corporations, it is argued that crude notions of 'cultural imperialism' are unable to capture the complex nature of international media flows, nor the variety of ways young people have integrated 'global' media and products within distinctively local youth cultures and identities. These themes are continued in Chapter 8, which examines in more detail the way contemporary youth cultures and their associated media are forged through processes of global interconnection and local transformation. Here, particular attention is given to the way the multifaceted flows of globalisation have generated modern youth cultures characterised by complex mixtures of ethnicity and identity.

Chapter 9 gives attention is to the way young people engage with the media to negotiate their sense of identity, manage their social relationships, and engage in processes of cultural creativity. It begins by considering how the virtual spaces of the Internet may have fed into a wider 'decentring' of identity, with individuals articulating an ever-widening range of identities and selves. Attention is also given to the way new technologies such as Web 2.0 and smartphones have impacted on young people's lives. Youngsters' use of social media to elaborate identities and relationships is examined, along with the ways they navigate through the complex online realms of public and private life. The chapter concludes by considering how far young people's wealth of online creativity amounts to a new era of 'participatory' media engagement.

The book concludes with an overview of the relationship between youth culture and the media. Particular attention is given to the notion of 'circuits of culture' and the way the meanings of media texts and cultural artefacts are generated through an intersection of processes of production, identity formation, representation, consumption, and regulation. If young people's relationship with the media is to be adequately understood, it is argued, attention must be devoted to each of these processes and the ways they interact with the other aspects of the cultural circuit. As Douglas Kellner has cogently emphasised, 'in order to grasp fully the nature and effects of media culture, one needs to develop methods to analyse the full range of its meanings and effects' (Kellner, 1997: 109). In these terms, issues of political economy, textuality, and audience reception are not antithetical, but can be constructively combined in a 'trans-disciplinary' and 'multiperspectival' analysis of young people's relationships with the modern media.

Notes

1 There were, however, important disparities within this group. According to the Common Sense Media survey, teenagers from higher-income homes used screen media much less than those from lower-income households – 6:49 hours per day compared to 8:32 hours per day (Rideout and Robb, 2019: 5). The variation underscores the way young people's experiences should not be homogenised – recognition must always be given to important social, economic, and cultural differences.
2 A detailed account of the evolution of modern conceptions of youth in Western Europe can be found in Mitteraurer (1992), while Chudacoff (1989) and Baxter (2008) both show how the modern system of age stratification in the US emerged during the late nineteenth and early twentieth centuries.
3 See, for example, the criticisms advanced in Rutter et al. (1976). A critical survey of competing theories of adolescence is provided in Coleman (1992).
4 Influenced by developments in US sociology, accounts of a homogeneous 'culture of youth' also surfaced in Britain. See, for instance, Rowntree and Rowntree (1968) and Turner (1969).
5 A critical account of the development of 'generation' as an analytic category within the social sciences can be found in Jaeger (1985).

2 The rise of the teenage media market

Youth, consumption, and entertainment in the twentieth century

'I'm a business, man!': The economic significance of youth culture

For Jay-Z, 2019 saw a career landmark. That year *Forbes* magazine, America's leading business journal, announced the rapper had become hip-hop's first billionaire. His success was certainly impressive. Raised in Brooklyn's housing projects, Jay-Z (real name Shawn Carter) had started out hustling a living on the mean streets of New York. But his musical career took off in 1995 when, aged 26, he established his own label, Roc-A-Fella Records, to release his 1996 debut album, *Reasonable Doubt*. A critical and commercial coup, the album was followed by a string of triumphs over the ensuing decades, Jay-Z releasing no fewer than 14 albums that hit No. 1 in the *Billboard* chart (Caulfield, 2018). His achievements, moreover, stretched well beyond music. In 1999, for instance, he founded the clothing line Rocawear, followed in 2003 by the upmarket sports-bar chain 40/40 Club – both of which grew into multi-million-dollar corporations. In 2008, meanwhile, he formed the entertainment company Roc Nation, and in 2015 acquired the tech company Aspiro, taking charge of their media streaming service – Tidal – which became one of the world's largest online streaming companies. By any measure, it was an illustrious rise to the top; and in 2005 Jay-Z could quip, with complete justification, 'I'm not a businessman, I'm a business, man!'[1]

Jay-Z's commercial feats were testimony to the star's business acumen. But his success also had broader significance. Jay-Z's status as the first 'billionaire rapper' was indicative of the way hip-hop had been transformed. During the late 1970s it had emerged as the sound of 'rebellion' on the margins of the music industry, but by the early twenty-first century hip-hop represented a global, multi-million-dollar enterprise. More broadly, however, Jay-Z's success also demonstrated the huge economic importance of youth culture and its attendant industries. Rather than being a frivolous sideshow, the commercial youth market has grown to be a vast international business sector. The pop music, films, and fashions associated with young people have all become economic powerhouses, generating billions of dollars every year. This chapter, therefore, explores the rise of the youth market as a leading area of commerce.

The chapter identifies the early stirrings of a commercial youth culture amid the trends towards urbanisation and consumerism that characterised North America and Western Europe during the late nineteenth and early twentieth centuries. The growth of a distinctive youth market is then traced through the 'Baby Boom' years of the 1950s and 1960s, to its subsequent development amid the shifting economic landscape of the 1970s, 1980s, and 1990s. Throughout, emphasis is placed on the relation between the youth market and wider patterns of social, economic, and political change – the development of modern youth culture being constituent in the broader transformation of production, distribution, and consumption in industrialised societies. While broad commercial trends are highlighted (for example, the emergence of youth-oriented media and marketing during the 1950s), recognition is also given to the unique characteristics of national experience (for example, the contrasting forms of 'teenage' market that appeared in postwar America and Britain) as different countries entered the age of modern consumerism.

The youth market takes shape: the late nineteenth and early twentieth centuries

The origins of the modern youth market lie in the industrialisation and urbanisation of North America and Western Europe during the late nineteenth century. *Fin de siècle* cities were becoming bustling centres of entertainment and consumption, and youth was a significant force in the transformation. In the US, for example, historian Kathy Peiss (1987) shows how young, working women were pivotal to the development of commercial leisure during this period, young women representing a major segment of the audience for dancehalls, amusement parks, and movie houses. Young men were an equally significant consumer market. Indeed, by the end of the century groups of working-class youths – both white and African-American – were making a virtue of conspicuous consumption. Flamboyantly promenading in broad-brimmed hats, embroidered shirts and frock-coats, these 'b'hoys' (as they were known in New York) were a distinctive feature of life in urban America (Swiencicki, 1998: 786). Their middle-class peers, too, were an important market, Howard Chudacoff (1999) showing how an extensive 'bachelor subculture' developed around the network of eating houses, barber shops, city bars, and theatres that thrived on the patronage of affluent, young 'men about town'.

Europe saw comparable trends. During the late nineteenth century European cities became hubs for mass entertainment industries geared to an urban working class whose disposable income and leisure time were gradually being extended. Constituent in these developments was the rise of working youngsters as a distinct cultural group and, as Jon Savage (2007) shows, they were increasingly targeted by a wide variety of social movements and commercial businesses. In Britain, for example, young workers' spending power had, by the turn of the century, laid the basis for an embryonic youth market for particular goods and entertainments. Indeed, writing in 1905, an observer in the industrial city of Manchester described how a 19-year-old, semi-skilled youth earned a pound a week in an iron foundry and, after surrendering 12 shillings to his parents for board, was free to spend the remainder on clothes, gambling, and the music halls (C.E.B. Russell, cited in Springhall, 1980: 89).

The youth market steadily flourished during the 1920s and 1930s. In Britain youth unemployment was a problem in some regions, but generally demand for young workers remained high since their labour was relatively inexpensive (compared to that of adults) at a time when employers were cutting costs. Interwar Britain, therefore, saw a steady increase in working youngsters' income, historian David Fowler estimating that youth's money wages rose by between 300 and 500 per cent. Retaining around 50 per cent (or more) of this income, Fowler argues, young wage-earners 'invariably enjoyed a standard of living higher than that of the rest of the family' and represented an increasingly attractive market for entrepreneurs and manufacturers (Fowler, 1995: 95; 101). For Fowler, then, a 'hard-sell youth market' began to blossom in Britain during the 1920s and 1930s as cinemas, dancehalls, and magazine publishers all courted the spending power of young workers (Fowler, 1995: 170).

In interwar America the youth market also blossomed. Generally, the 1920s saw the US economy boom, gross domestic product rising by nearly 40 per cent between 1922 and 1929. Amid this age of prosperity, a fully formed, commercial youth market came into view. Stanley Hollander and Richard Germain (1993), for example, show how a substantial number of businesses began to direct their efforts towards youth spending during the 1920s. 'Entrepreneurs, consultants and marketing scholars', they argue, 'expounded the significance of the youth market', while 'special youth promotion, special youth pricing, and special youth distribution [was] applied to a wide range of products such as automobiles, apparel items, personal hygiene products, typewriters, and cigarettes, and services provided by such establishments as hotels, inns, dancehalls and barber shops' (Hollander and Germain, 1993: 114; 55).

The rise of this market was, to a large part, predicated on the proliferation of a new 'campus culture'. This stemmed from the thriving American middle-class, whose affluence brought a huge expansion in higher education during the Jazz Age. Once the preserve of a small elite, colleges and universities saw a threefold increase in enrolments between 1900 and 1930, with nearly 20 per cent of the college-age population attending some kind of educational institution by the end of the 1920s. Young, relatively well-to-do, and free of family responsibilities, these students were an attractive market for businesses, and attempts to court youth spending were invariably focused on the college sector (Hollander and Germain, 1993: 24–5). In turn, the products of the youth market fed into the rise of what historian Paula Fass identifies as 'the first modern American youth culture' – a collegiate universe that formed around student fraternities, dancehalls, cinemas, cafeterias and other campus hangouts (1978: 122).

The student culture chronicled by Fass weathered the lean years that followed the Wall Street Crash of 1929. More widely, however, American youth were hit hard by the Depression of the 1930s, and numbers of unemployed youngsters spiralled. During the 1940s, however, the American youth market was revitalised by the labour demands of the wartime economy. The economic pressures of the war drew increasing numbers of young people into the workforce, US Census Bureau statistics showing that in 1944 more than two in five young men aged between 16 and 17 were gainfully employed (Modell, 1989: 165–166). As a consequence, greater disposable income was delivered into young hands, and by 1944 American youth wielded a spending power of around $750 million (Adams, 1994: 127). This growing economic muscle renewed businesses' interest in the youth market and helped foster a developing belief that young people constituted a consumer group of exceptional independence and influence – trends that became increasingly pronounced amid the prosperity of the 1950s and 1960s.

'The teen-age tide': Baby Boomers and the birth of the teenager

The explosion of the youth market during the 1950s and 1960s was especially pronounced in the US. This was partly indebted to demographic trends. A growth in the birth rate had begun during the 1930s, but after the Second World War the new confidence of peacetime, coupled with growing economic prosperity, brought a shift towards earlier marriage and a postwar 'Baby Boom'. The number of births leapt from 2.9 million in 1945 to 3.4 million in 1946, cresting at 4.3 million in 1957 and remaining high until 1964 (Colby and Ortman, 2014: 2). As a consequence, subsequent decades saw the US teen population surge – from 10 million to 15 million during the 1950s, eventually hitting a peak of over 20 million by 1970 (Eggebean and Sturgeon, 2006: 6). Widely dubbed the 'Baby Boomer' generation, this group was pivotal to the growth of the commercial youth market, but also became the focus for developing theories of 'youth' and youth culture. And, while crude notions of discrete generational groups should be avoided (see Chapter 1), it is important to recognise the way a nexus of social, economic and cultural factors combined to mark out the experience of postwar Baby Boomers as distinct to that of preceding generations.

Alongside the demographic trends, an expansion of education also helped accentuate the social profile of postwar youth. Between the wars, the US high school system had already grown significantly and expansion continued after 1945 – the proportion of US teenagers attending high school rising from around 60 per cent in the 1930s to virtually 100 per cent during the 1960s (Modell, 1989: 225–226). At the same time, college and university enrolment soared. In 1950 about 41 per cent of high school graduates went on to college, but by 1960 this had risen to 53 per cent, the trend giving a new lease of life to the campus culture that had surfaced between the wars (West, 1996: 306). These changes played an important role in increasing young people's social prominence, but probably even more important were the economic changes that boosted American youth's spending power throughout the 1950s and

1960s. The late 1940s had seen a decline in full-time youth employment, but the wartime increase in young people's earnings was sustained in peacetime by a combination of part-time work and parental allowances – some estimates suggesting youngsters' average weekly income rose from just over $2 in 1944 to around $10 by 1958 (Macdonald, 1958: 60). Indeed, the perceived scale of the increase spurred the addition of a new term to the popular lexicon – the 'teenager'.

Since the 1600s it had been common to refer to an adolescent as being someone in their 'teens', but it was only in 1941 that an article in *Popular Science* magazine featured the first published use of the word 'teenager', and the term increasingly leaked into popular usage (Hine, 1999: 8–9). The advertising and marketing industries were especially crucial in popularising the concept, marketers using the term 'teenager' to denote what they saw as a new breed of affluent, young consumer who prioritised freedom and fun. A *Business Week* feature of 1946 exemplified the trade enthusiasm. 'Teen-Age Market: It's "Terrif"', proclaimed the journal, as it trumpeted 'the jackpot market' that had 'come into its own during the war'.[2] Whetting commercial appetites, *Business Week* described how 'the going is high, wide, and handsome with this market whose astounding responsiveness and loyalty endear it to any manufacturer's heart' (*Business Week*, 8 June 1946).

Throughout the following decades teenagers' increased spending power impressed commentators. In 1959, for example, *Life* announced the arrival of 'A New $10-Billion Power: the US Teenage Consumer', the magazine explaining how youth had 'emerged as a big-time consumer in the US economy', with 'the youngsters and their parents shelling out about $10 billion this year, a billion more than the total sales of GM [General Motors]' (*Life*, 31 August 1959). Similarly, in 1964, an awe-struck edition of *Time* magazine profiled the surge of 'The Teen-Age Tide' – America's 22 million teenagers, whose disposable income of $12 billion a year made them 'the coolest customers in the US' (*Time*, 9 October 1964: 58). And by 1965 a special 'Teen Time' edition of *Esquire* magazine profiled a burgeoning youth market worth $13 billion a year. 'In the time it takes to read these lines', *Esquire* advised its readers, 'the American teen-ager will have spent $2,378.22' (Hechinger and Hechinger, 1965: 65).

Rather than being the product of a wholesale, 'generational' shift, however, it is important to recognise the way America's postwar teenage market had a distinct social and economic make-up. As sociologist Jessie Bernard observed in 1961, youngsters immersed in 'teen-age culture' were 'disproportionately from the higher socioeconomic class background', while 'youngsters of lower socio-economic classes are in the teen-age culture only in their early teens' (Bernard, 1961: 2). Moreover, as historian Grace Palladino argues, embedded racism and economic inequality ensured that throughout the 1950s 'black teenagers remained invisible as far as mainstream society was concerned' (Palladino, 1996: 175–176). Postwar enthusiasm for the youth market, therefore, obscured the way the 'teen-age tide' was, to a large part, the preserve of the white middle-class. Nevertheless, the economic influence of this group was unmistakable, and the postwar increase in their spending power spurred a spectacular growth in the scope and scale of the US youth industries.

'Shake, Rattle and Roll': the explosion of US teen media

Throughout the 1950s and 1960s US businesses scrambled to stake a claim in the teenage goldmine. The range of media and products geared to the young was legion, consumer industries interacting with and reinforcing one another as they wooed young consumers. Of the $10 billion in discretionary income wielded by American youth in 1959, *Life* estimated that 16 per cent (roughly $1.5 billion) went to the entertainment industries, the remainder being spent on everything from fashion and grooming products to cars and sporting goods (*Life*, 31 August 1959).

An index of the growing scale of the American youth market was the runaway success of *Seventeen* magazine. Conceived as a publication geared to young women at college, *Seventeen* was launched in 1944. Its premier edition selling out within two days, *Seventeen*'s circulation had rocketed to over a million a month by 1947, and by 1949 was touching two-and-a-half million (Schrum, 1998: 139). More widely, teenage girls were increasingly targeted by a range of fashion and entertainment industries. As Kelly Schrum (2004) notes, during the 1940s the US media coined the phrase 'bobby-soxer' to denote adolescent girls who sported a new style of sweaters, full skirts, bobby-socks and saddle shoes, and who jitterbugged to the sounds of big band swing or swooned over showbusiness stars such as Mickey Rooney and Frank Sinatra. The 'Swoonatra' phenomenon (as it was dubbed) attracted particular attention. Though already in his mid-20s, Sinatra was promoted as the boyish kid from Hoboken, the singer capturing thousands of young hearts in 1942 as he sold out a month-long residency at New York's Paramount Theater – his return to the venue, two years later, bringing Manhattan to a standstill as thousands of amorous fans besieged Times Square.

During the 1950s the teenage market had even greater impact on American music with the rise of rock 'n' roll – a new genre of popular music tied especially closely to youth demand.[3] The roots of the new music lay in black rhythm and blues (R'n'B),[4] where the phrase 'rock 'n' roll' was coined as a euphemism for sex. With African-American migration during the 1940s, the popularity of rhythm and blues had spread to northern and western cities where black radio shows regularly featured R'n'B records produced by Atlantic, Chess, Sun, and a growing number of independent labels. The music was geared to an African-American audience, but it also picked up a significant white market as young radio listeners tuned in to late-night shows. The crossover of R'n'B into the white youth market was further galvanised by entrepreneurs such as Alan 'Moondog' Freed, a Cleveland disc jockey whose playlists began to feature R'n'B records during the early 1950s. Moving to a bigger station in New York in 1954, Freed continued to champion the original

R'n'B performers but, in being pitched to a more mainstream youth market, the music was steadily 'whitened' and reconfigured as 'rock 'n' roll'.

In a process of 'hybridisation' that was to become a recurring feature of modern youth culture (see Chapter 8), rock 'n' roll fused (black) R'n'B with elements of (white) country and western music. Rock 'n' roll' retained a rebellious aura, but the sexual overtones characteristic of rhythm and blues were toned down as the major labels recruited white performers to produce 'acceptable' covers of R'n'B standards. Decca, for example, enjoyed early success with 'whitened-up' interpretations of R'n'B by Bill Haley, who scored hits with 'Shake, Rattle and Roll' in 1954 and 'Rock Around the Clock' the following year. A bigger commercial triumph, however, came in 1956 with RCA Victor's signing of Elvis Presley. The singer had enjoyed moderate success on Sam Phillips' independent Sun label but, with the backing of a major company, Elvis became a national phenomenon – selling over 8 million records within six months and representing a $20 million industry within a year (figures that were then mind-boggling) (Stuessy and Lipscomb, 2009: 30). More broadly, teen-oriented rock 'n' roll was soon dominating the American music industry, Rebee Garofalo estimating that the genre's share of the pop market jumped from 15.7 per cent in 1955 to a whopping 42.7 per cent by 1959 (Garofalo, 1999: 336).

The growing teenage market also impacted the film industry. As Thomas Doherty comprehensively shows, a new 'teenpic' industry was spawned as moviemakers developed concerted strategies to 'attract the one group with the requisite income, leisure, and gregariousness to sustain a theatrical business' (Doherty, 2002: 2). The new teenpics, Doherty argues, began with a wave of movies that capitalised on the 1950s rock 'n' roll boom, heralded by Columbia Pictures' release of *Rock Around the Clock* (1956); a film Doherty regards as 'the first hugely successful film marketed to teenagers *to the pointed exclusion of their elders*' (57, orig. emphasis). But the teenpic was a diverse species, and Doherty identifies a wide variety of subgenres, stretching from delinquency pictures such as MGM's *High School Confidential* (1958) and Warner's *Untamed Youth* (1957), to syrupy romantic comedies (or 'clean teenpics') such as singer Pat Boone's pictures for 20th Century Fox, *Bernardine* and *April Love* (both 1957).

Hollywood's major studios conjured with images of wayward youth in movies such as Columbia's *The Wild One* (1953) and Warner's *Rebel Without a Cause* (1955). The two films promoted, respectively, Marlon Brando and James Dean as icons of teenage culture, though both films were essentially sober melodramas aimed at a general audience. Rather than the major studios, it was the independent sector that most successfully zeroed-in on teen demand. Independent companies such as Marathon and Fairway International made bold plays for young cinemagoers, but it was always American International Pictures who led the way. Founded in 1954, AIP was the brainchild of Samuel Arkoff (a cigar-chewing business lawyer) and James H. Nicholson (a hotshot promotions man). AIP was in the vanguard of a new wave of 'exploitation' studios whose pictures were churned out as quickly and cheaply as possible, were promoted with spectacular ballyhoo, and – as Arkoff explained in his memoirs – were targeted at the sensibilities of 'the gum-chewing, hamburger-munching adolescent dying to get out of the house on a Friday or Saturday night and yearning for a place to go' (Arkoff, 1997: 4).

The rise of the teenage market also fuelled a proliferation of drive-in cinemas. 'Ozoners' (as drive-in were fondly known) had first appeared during the 1930s, but their numbers mushroomed during the 1950s. In 1946 the US boasted only 102 drive-in theatres, but by 1949 there were nearly 1,000 (Segrave, 2006: 37). Five years later there were more than 3,000, and in 1957 *Newsweek* hailed the drive-in as 'the biggest single development in the movie industry in years' (1957: 86). A large part of the drive-in audience were young, suburban families but, as Doherty argues, the youth market was also crucial; drive-in operators courting teenagers with open-air dance-floors, fixed-price-per-carload admission and special 'teen-targeted' late-night shows – which helped cement the drive-in's reputation as a 'passion pit' for amorous adolescents (Doherty, 2002: 91–92).

Young audiences were also addressed by the budding medium of television. During the 1950s teenage life was a firm feature in many American TV soap operas and family-based sitcoms. Shows such as *The Adventures of Ozzie and Harriet* (1952–66), *Father Knows Best* (1954–62) and *Leave It to Beaver* (1957–63) all featured teenage characters who became increasingly central to storylines over the course of the 1950s. The launch of the sitcom *The Many Loves of Dobie Gillis* (1959–63), meanwhile, saw the arrival of the first prime-time TV show directly focused on teenage characters, the series chronicling the hapless adventures of Dobie Gillis (Dwayne Hickman) and his beatnik buddy, Maynard G. Krebs (Bob Denver).

The rise of American teen TV was the result of broadcasters' attempts to pull in advertisers through developing new programme formats that would appeal to young audiences. This was especially true of the ABC network. Since its bigger, more established rivals (CBS and NBC) were best placed to exploit the mass TV audience, the younger and smaller ABC network sought to compete by courting more specialised markets – the network developing a reputation for programming aimed at youth and young families with children. During the 1950s local stations also played their part in the growth of teen TV. Shows featuring pop performers and their fans became a staple of local TV stations' afternoon and Saturday morning schedules, examples including *Teen Twirl* (WNBK-Cleveland, 1955) and *Teen Club Party* (WGN-Chicago, 1957). Most famous, however, was *American Bandstand*. Launched by WFIL-Philadelphia in 1952, the show's success ensured that in 1957 it transferred to the ABC network, where its audience figures regularly touched 20 million (Sanjek, 1988: 444).

A host of market research strategies were also developed to target adolescents' wallets. During the 1950s agencies such as Teen-Age Survey Incorporated and the Student Marketing Institute tracked the vagaries of teenage taste, while *Seventeen* magazine collated data from surveys of its readership and packaged the information in the form of a composite teenager – named

'Teena' – that was then sold to retailers and manufacturers. The field was led, however, by Eugene Gilbert. Working as a 19-year-old shoe-store clerk in 1945, Gilbert had noticed how, despite stocking the latest styles, the shop attracted few young customers. Persuading the owner to advertise more directly to young buyers, Gilbert was struck by the sudden rise in sales and began to develop market research among his peers as a viable business. Deploying what was then an innovative research strategy, Gilbert eschewed 'number-crunching' and quantitative surveys in favour of a more qualitative approach. Recognising that young people themselves were best placed to gauge the attitudes of the teenage market, Gilbert recruited an army of students to interview their friends, canvassing opinions and providing feedback on their consumer preferences. It was a winning formula, and by 1947 Gilbert's research firm – Youth Marketing Co. – had plush offices in New York and was working with such prestigious clients as Quaker Oats, Studebaker, and United Airlines.

Gilbert himself was celebrated as a figurehead of youth consumption. Profiled by magazines such as *Newsweek* and *Harper's*, he was hailed as a leading authority on modern youth. Pronouncements in his syndicated newspaper column – 'What Young People Think' – charted the caprices of the young, while his book *Advertising and Marketing to Young People* (1957) became a manual for those chasing adolescent cash. Moreover, Gilbert's enterprise neatly illustrated the way the marketing business does not simply provide a neutral description of trends in youth spending. Instead, advertisers play an active part in identifying, constructing, and promoting specific notions of the teenage market. Gilbert, for example, regularly evangelised youth as a commercial market of unprecedented importance, explaining to the marketing journal *Advertising Age* in 1951:

> Our salient discovery is that within the past decade teenagers have become a separate and distinct group within our society, enjoying a degree of autonomy and independence unmatched by previous generations.
>
> (*Advertising Age*, 26 February 1951: 1)

Gilbert was sceptical, however, about the commercial possibilities of European teens. Visiting Britain in 1954, and again in 1956, he decided no potential existed for a permanent marketing office in London. But the marketing guru's doubts soon proved ill-judged.

'A distinctive teenage world': the international growth of the youth market

The greater destruction wrought on European economies by the Second World War ensured that the development of modern consumerism in Europe was slower, partial, and more uneven than in the US. As a consequence, the rise of young people as a discrete consumer group was more hesitant than in

America. Nevertheless, by the late 1950s the growth of a distinctive 'teenage' market for products and entertainments was being identified across Western Europe.

As in the US, developments were partly indebted to demographic trends. While the precise character varied, most Western European countries experienced some kind of postwar Baby Boom.[5] The rises in birth rates, like those in America, had begun during the 1930s, but they accelerated during the late 1940s and 1950s amid a period of economic growth and rising living standards. The consequence was a steady 'bulge' in teenage populations from the late 1950s to the mid-1970s. At the same time, changes in education bolstered the social profile of youth. Again, there were national differences but, broadly, Western European countries saw a steady expansion of secondary education after the Second World War. In Britain, for example, the 1944 Education Act brought a major extension of Britain's secondary school system, while the school-leaving age was raised from 14 to 15 in 1947 and, as a consequence, the bracketing of 'youth' as a distinct social group was made more concrete and clear-cut.[6]

Though slightly behind the US, then, many European countries saw the postwar social profile of youth enhanced by the combination of a Baby Boom and an expansion of secondary education. As in America, however, it was economic changes and an increase in young people's spending power that was fundamental to a significant surge in European youth markets. In Britain, for example, the widely-cited work of Mark Abrams highlighted the growing commercial importance of young people since the Second World War. Undertaken during the late 1950s for the London Press Exchange (an advertising agency), Abrams' research suggested British youngsters' real earnings had risen by 50 per cent since 1945 (roughly double the increase for adults) while their 'discretionary' spending had grown by as much as 100 per cent – representing an annual expenditure of around £830 million (Abrams, 1959: 9). Abrams maintained, moreover, that this spending was concentrated in particular consumer markets (representing, for example, 44 per cent of total spending on records and 39 per cent of spending on motorcycles) which, he concluded, represented the rise of 'distinctive teenage spending for distinctive teenage ends in a distinctive teenage world' (Abrams, 1959: 10).

Abrams' choice of phrase was indicative of the way the term 'teenager' had been imported into Europe as a term to denote an apparent upsurge in young people's spending power. And, as in the US, the word 'teenager' was often used by journalists and advertisers to project an image of a new, homogeneous generation of young consumers. But (as in America) the reality was that 'teenage' spending power was concentrated among specific socio-economic groups. European developments, however, did not simply replicate those in the US. Instead, the youth markets that emerged in Europe had a distinct character, shaped by each country's specific course of economic development. For example, while the American teenage market of the 1950s and 1960s was largely a feature of the suburban middle-class, that which emerged in Britain was

understood to be a more working-class phenomenon. Indeed, this was something underscored by Abrams' studies. While he highlighted the rise of a 'distinctive teenage world', for example, Abrams still emphasised that 'teenage
demand' was 'largely without appeal for middle class boys and girls' (Abrams,
1961: 10). The 'teenage market', Abrams insisted, was '... almost entirely
working class', with '... not far short of 90 per cent of all teenage spending
conditioned by working class taste and values' (Abrams, 1959: 13).

   The increase in British youth's spending power was largely the outcome of
shifts in working-class labour markets. After 1945 the British workforce as a
whole felt the impact of a decline in heavy industry, the movement of capital
into lighter forms of production (especially the manufacture of consumer
goods), the expansion of production-line technologies and trends towards
'de-skilling'. But these changes had particular consequences for young workers.
Labour market shifts created demand for flexible, though not especially skilled,
labour power and young people (because they were cheaper to employ than
adults) were ideally suited to the role.[7] As a consequence, the 1950s and early
1960s saw buoyant levels of youth employment and a concomitant rise in
earnings. The statistics produced by Abrams probably exaggerated the scale of
young people's economic muscle – and they certainly obscured some significant regional variations[8] – but the broad tenor of his claims was accurate.
The wage packets of Britain's working youngsters were certainly not bulging,
but they were tangibly enhanced – and underpinned a conspicuous expansion
of the commercial youth market.

   By the late 1950s the range of products geared to young people seemed
boundless. Popular music, in particular, became closely tied to the young's
spending power. The growing youth market, for example, fuelled the meteoric
rise of the 7-inch, vinyl single after its launch in 1952. In Britain vinyl singles
surged in popularity, and the success of releases was gauged in new, sales-based
record charts – the first appearing in *New Musical Express* in 1952, followed by
Record Mirror's 'Top Fifty' in 1954. And, as in the US, rock 'n' roll also
emerged as a pop genre entwined with the youth market. In Britain the initial
wave of American rock 'n' rollers (Bill Haley, Chuck Berry, Elvis Presley) was
soon joined by home-grown talent such as Cliff Richard, Tommy Steele, and
Marty Wilde. And, with the 1960s boom in beat groups, British bands such as
The Beatles and The Rolling Stones soon presided over global pop.

   The Beatles, in particular, were a spectacular media phenomenon. In 1962
the Fab Four already enjoyed modest success, but during 1963 Beatlemania
exploded. By the end of the year, seven Beatles' records had dominated Britain's Top Twenty, the band had headlined a Royal Variety Performance and
their every appearance was besieged by screaming fans. The following year the
band became a worldwide sensation. In early 1964 The Beatles played their
first concerts in America and were showcased on television's *Ed Sullivan Show*.
At each event they were swamped by ecstatic crowds and, in 1964 alone,
American stores sold an estimated $50 million worth of Beatles merchandise
(Davies, 1978: 219).

The British film industry, too, made overtures to youth. Europe had nothing to match the huge American 'teenpic' industry, but British filmmakers made a concerted pitch to young cinemagoers with films featuring domestic pop stars such as Tommy Steele, Cliff Richard, and The Beatles.[9] In contrast, British radio reacted slowly. During the 1950s rock 'n' roll could be heard only by tuning in to the American Forces Network or Radio Luxembourg. At the BBC (a public service broadcaster, then with monopoly control of Britain's radio services) rock 'n' roll was largely ignored as a consequence of restrictions on the amount of recorded music that could be broadcast,[10] combined with officialdom's disdain for a music it deemed crassly commercial. Radio stations specifically geared to a youth audience appeared in Britain only during the early 1960s, with the rise of unlicensed, 'pirate' stations such as Radio Caroline and Radio London; while the BBC finally responded in 1967 with the launch of its own pop music station, Radio One.[11]

The younger medium of TV responded more swiftly. Initially, pop music shows such as the BBC's *Hit Parade* (launched in 1952) and *Off the Record* (1956) were low-key in their youth appeal. By the later 1950s, however, competition between the BBC and ITV (their new commercial rival, launched in 1955) helped generate a TV genre targeted more specifically at youth. Pop programmes such as the BBC's *Six-Five Special* (1957–8) and *Juke Box Jury* (1959–67) still made concessions to an adult audience through the inclusion of dinner-jacketed compères, but the launch of ITV's *Oh Boy!* (1958–9) – a show broadcast live from the Hackney Empire – heralded the rise of a quick-fire format aimed squarely at youth. And, in a similar fashion, ITV carried the day during the early 1960s with the hit pop series *Ready, Steady, Go!* (1963–6). For a while the BBC struggled to compete, but finally developed a winning formula with the launch of its long-running flagship pop show, *Top of the Pops* (1964–2006).[12]

Across Western Europe, the teenage market seemed in full-flood by the early 1960s. Imports of US music, fashion, and films were hugely popular, but most countries also developed indigenous equivalents. In France, for example, historian Susan Weiner shows how the growing tide of youth consumption was marked by the rise of American-style rock 'n' roll singers dubbed *copains* (buddies) or *yé-yés* (in reference to the typical, American-influenced refrain of their songs – 'yeah, yeah') (Weiner, 2001: 146).[13] Especially successful was Johnny Hallyday, who leapt to stardom in 1960 after he appeared on TV, aged 17, singing '*T'Aimer Follement*' (his French version of Elvis Presley's 'Makin' Love'). Singers like Hallyday were popularised on radio shows such as *Salut les Copains*, a two-hour pop show launched by French radio station Europe 1 in 1959. Broadcast five nights a week, the show spawned an associated magazine, *Salut les Copains*, in 1962,[14] along with a profusion of merchandise. As Weiner points out, 'teens who tuned in to "Salut les Copains" could buy postcards, key chains, cups, and bowls featuring the show's mascot, Chouchou, a figure clad in jeans and a T-shirt and sporting a Beatles haircut' (147). Indeed, more generally, Weiner observes how 'the alliance of music and consumer products targeting youth was unabashed', and in France during the early 1960s 'manufacturers had only to associate a product with the words "copain" or "jeune" to signify its desirability' (149).

As historian Uta Poiger (2000) demonstrates, West Germany also developed its own teenage industries. In 1956, for example, *Bravo* was launched with the subtitle 'the magazine for film and television', but within a year this was ditched in favour of 'the magazine with the young heart', as the publication focused more determinedly on the youth market. And, in the world of German pop music, singers Peter Kraus and Conny Froboess were systematically marketed as 'teenager ideals' (Poiger, 2000: 190). Kraus was originally promoted as the 'German Elvis', but elements of rebelliousness were soon played down and he was predominantly portrayed as 'a nice German boy' as he appeared alongside Froboess in frothy pop movies such as *Wenn die Conny mit dem Peter* (1958) and *Conny und Peter Machen Musik* (1960). And, as Poiger shows, the stars' popularity was exploited by canny clothes retailers, with the launch of 'Conny sweaters' (for girls) and 'Peter Kraus pulls (vests)' for boys, as the German fashion industry set its sights on youth spending (191).

Outside Europe – in countries experiencing growing levels of industrialisation, urbanisation, and consumer spending – a distinctive youth market also steadily flourished. In Australia and New Zealand, Jon Stratton (1992) and Chris Brickell (2017) respectively show how a recognisable youth culture had existed in cities such as Melbourne, Sydney, Auckland, and Wellington since the late nineteenth century, when the term 'larrikin' was applied to young, distinctively-dressed ruffians.[15] And, after the Second World War, Australia and New Zealand both saw the emergence of a burgeoning commercial youth market akin to those in the US and Europe. While the youth-oriented film, music, and publishing industries were less developed in Australia and New Zealand, imports from America and Britain were widely available and there was a steady profusion of consumer goods targeted at youth. As elsewhere, the term 'teenager' was imported to denote what many took to be a new generation of young, affluent consumers. Again, however, notions of a distinctive 'teenage' culture obscured important divisions. Stratton, for example, demonstrates how the growing youth market of postwar Australia was (like that in Britain) largely indebted to a rise in the earning power of specifically working-class youngsters; a trend that was (as in Britain) a facet of wider improvements in working-class living standards. Indeed, the class character of the youth market emerging in Australia and New Zealand during the 1950s was suggested by the pejorative labels applied to youngsters who embraced the new, American- and British-influenced styles of fashion and music – with the colloquial term 'bodgie' applied to young men, while 'widgie' denoted their female associates.[16]

'The new generation': young consumers during the late twentieth century

Across North America, Western Europe, and other economically developed countries, therefore, previous levels of youth consumption were thrown into the shade by the 'teenage' markets that emerged during the 1950s and 1960s. As changes in labour markets delivered greater economic power to the young, the media and leisure industries (serviced by a new army of advertisers and marketers) scurried to exploit the lucrative potential of youth spending.

The 'youth' market was also creeping up the age scale. Increasingly, more mature consumers – adults in their 20s, 30s, and older – adopted the outlooks and interests associated with youth culture. Indeed, Ron Eyerman and Andrew Jamison argue that during the 1960s youth 'became the model and set standards for the rest of society in many spheres of culture, from the most superficial like clothing and hair-styles, to the most deeply rooted like the basic social inter-actions of men and women and blacks and whites' (Eyerman and Jamison, 1998: 113). During the 1960s the affluent and upwardly-mobile middle class, especially, embraced products and media whose 'youthful' connotations seemed to guarantee a hedonistic, free-wheeling lifestyle. Advertisers worked hard to foster this association, Thomas Frank (1997) showing how a 'creative revolu-tion' in American advertising saw marketers habitually mobilise 'youth' as an aphorism for fun, freedom, and consumer fulfilment. The trend registered across a wide range of products and advertising campaigns of the 1960s, but was encapsulated by the success of the Ford Mustang. First rolling off assembly lines in 1964, the sporty Mustang was designed to be a 'youth' car. As such, it exploited the profitable Baby Boomer market, but it was also pitched to older customers who sought to identify with 'youthful' themes of adventure and fun. And, indeed, the Mustang was a major hit in older markets, 16 per cent of first-year sales going to men in the 45 to 55 age bracket (Kochan, 1996: 113).

From the mid-1960s to the early 1970s, in both the US and Europe, the emergence of new consumer groups also ensured the continued buoyancy of the youth market. In Britain, for example, the expansion of higher education increased the market potential of middle-class youngsters. Overall, participation in higher education increased from 3.4 per cent in 1950, to 8.4 per cent in 1970, reaching a figure of over 500,000 (Bolton, 2012: 14) – an expansion that was intended to improve working-class students' access to higher education, but was exploited most successfully by the middle class. Compared to their working peers, students commanded smaller disposable incomes, but the experience of studenthood offered other compensations; not least, greater amounts of leisure time and (usually) the independence of living away from the parental home. And, as a result, students were increasingly targeted by the media and consumer industries.

In the US, African-American youth became a more prominent consumer market. Although white racism and economic inequality remained entrenched, by the early 1960s the combination of civil rights activism and greater employment opportunities had improved living standards for many African-Americans, who gradually emerged as a significant consumer group. This was reflected in the realm of youth culture by the soul music boom of the 1960s. The success of Detroit's Tamla-Motown record labels was indicative. Founded by musician and producer Berry Gordy, Jr. in 1959, Motown broke into the commercial mainstream in 1962, scoring six Top-Ten hits in the *Billboard* chart. Further success followed, with 14 hits in 1966, 13 in 1967, and 10 in 1968. Motown emerged as the most successful independent record company in the US, and by 1973 Gordy was Chairman of Motown Industries – a multi-million-dollar company that boasted record, motion picture, TV, and publishing divisions.[17] Motown's output appealed to a multiracial audience, but the success of other soul labels (for example, Atlantic and Stax) was based more squarely on the African-American market, while the early 1970s saw most major record companies introduce divisions to deal specifically with 'Black music' (Negus, 1998: 369). TV executives and advertisers also began to pay more attention to African-American audiences. In 1970, for example, the Chicago TV station WCIU, launched *Soul Train* as a black counterpart to *American Bandstand*, and the show's success led to its syndication the following year. And youth-oriented TV dramas such as *Room 222* (1969–74) and sitcoms such as *What's Happening!* (1976–9) also began to focus on the experiences of young African-Americans.

The youth market remained a cornerstone of the media and consumer industries in both America and Europe throughout the 1970s and 1980s. Nevertheless, from the mid-1970s, a combination of demographic trends and economic downturn began to shake the commercial confidence that had characterised the 'jackpot' days of the 1950s and 1960s. As the postwar Baby Boom passed its zenith, decreasing birth rates brought a decline in the size of teenage populations on both sides of the Atlantic. In the US, for example, the proportion of the national population aged under 18 rose from 31 per cent in 1950 to 36 per cent in 1960, but then dropped to 28 per cent by 1980 (Department of Health and Human Services, 1998: 16). In Britain, too, falling birth rates were significant. The UK's Baby Boom crested in 1964, the drop in births bringing a steady decline in the youth population from the late 1970s (Office of National Statistics, 2015).

At the same time, the favourable economic conditions that had paved the way for the postwar explosion of youth consumption – economic growth, full employment, and rising living standards – steadily unravelled. Advanced capitalist economies slid into a long downturn punctuated by severe recessions in the mid-1970s, the early 1980s, and the early 1990s. And youth employment was a major casualty. As economists David Blanchflower and Richard Freeman observe, young workers lack the training or seniority that often buffer older workers from swings in the market, so the young are especially vulnerable to changes in economic conditions. As a consequence, in both the US and most of the European Union, the relative employment rates and earnings of young people declined (Blanchflower and Freeman, 2000ii). In the US the jobless rate for teenagers hovered at around 15 per cent throughout the late 1980s (Stern et al., 1995: 5), while in Britain the labour markets that had buoyed-up youth employment during the 1950s and 1960s steadily contracted so that by 1986 the number of unemployed aged between 16 and 24 had reached 727,000 – nearly a third of Britain's jobless total (International Labour Office, 1988: 651).

Generally, young people's routes into employment became extended and more unpredictable. Labour market shifts saw many youngsters channelled into low-paid and part-time jobs, while others were displaced into a proliferation of training schemes.[18] As sociologists Phil Cohen and Pat Ainley explained, young people entering this new economic environment found themselves pioneering:

> ... a life cycle paradigm which entails moving from education to part-time work interspersed with periods of education and training. Many young people find themselves moving from one scheme and training course to another without ever entering full-time, secure employment.
>
> (Cohen and Ainley, 2000: 83)

In this context, many young people faced bleak prospects. In the US, for example, researchers such as Donna Gaines (1991) revealed the existence of a 'teenage wasteland' – an alienated sub-stratum of American youth who struggled with the hardships of social and economic disfranchisement. In Britain a similar picture unfolded, Robert MacDonald (1997) arguing that increases in unemployment and homelessness during the 1990s had created a youth 'underclass' that was marginalised (both culturally and economically) from mainstream society. And, more widely, Cindi Katz argued that profound shifts in the global economy had 'cut a swathe' through the everyday environments of young people all over the world – with movements of capital, the decline of manufacturing economies and the transformation of labour markets combining to shatter the social and economic certainties that young people had once taken for granted (Katz, 1998: 130).

During the 1980s and early 1990s the shifts in demography, coupled with the rise in youth unemployment, prompted pessimism about the youth market's continued potential. Reflecting on American trends, Hollander and Germain observed that 'emphasis on the youth market declined somewhat' during the 1980s with 'fewer marketing research and advertising agencies claim[ing] to specialize in the youth market during that decade than was true during the 1960s' (Hollander and Germain, 1993: 110). In Britain, too, many commentators were uncertain about the youth market's future. Fiona Stewart, for example, speculated that the 1990s might see 'the commercial and cultural centre of gravity ... shift up the age spectrum to the middle age group', with the consequence that '"young people" will no longer be the drivers of change that they have been perceived to be over the past thirty years' (Stewart, 1992: 207; 225).

But reports of the youth market's death were – to paraphrase Mark Twain – an exaggeration. Indeed, despite rising levels of youth unemployment, the 1980s were a time of relative prosperity for many youngsters. In America, for example, Dennis Tootelian and Ralph Gaedeke calculated that, although the teenage population had dropped by 15.5 per cent during the 1980s, teens' collective spending power actually increased by nearly 43 per cent, with individual spending rising from $1,422 to $2,409 per capita (Tootelian and

Gaedeke, 1992: 35). Those British youngsters lucky enough to be in full-time employment (or who could rely on well-heeled parents) also enjoyed a measure of affluence – and were even fêted by marketers and advertisers as the embodiment of a wider spirit of thrusting entrepreneurialism and hectic consumerism. For example, in their 1988 report, *Youth Lifestyle*, market analysts Mintel claimed to have discovered among British youth a 'new consumption and success ethic' that had been generated by 'the sustained economic growth of the enterprise culture' (Mintel, 1988: 23). In a similar vein, McCann-Erickson's international survey, *The New Generation*, identified a 'New Wave' of 'post-permissive' youngsters who exhibited 'the most highly developed form of the new multi-profile consumption in our society' (McCann-Erickson Worldwide, 1989: 25).

Generally, the youth market survived as a mainstay of media and consumer industries throughout the 1980s. While some youth-oriented media forms withered away, others quickly took their place. In the US, for example, the era of the classic 'teenpic' had passed, and the drive-in movie circuit (already struggling by the 1970s) virtually disappeared. But, as the drive-in waned, the shopping mall emerged as a key site of teen congregation and provided Hollywood with a ready market of young consumers who, Tim Shary argues, 'formed the first generation of multiplex moviegoers' (Shary, 2014: 7). And a new flood of teen-oriented movies were spearheaded by the 'Brat Pack' – a term coined by the press for a troop of young actors who were rising stars in Hollywood's new youth films.[19] Especially influential were the teen movies either written, produced, or directed by John Hughes – most obviously, *Sixteen Candles* (1984), *The Breakfast Club* (1985) and *Pretty in Pink* (1986). For the TV industry, too, youth remained a crucial audience. Indeed, from the moment it began broadcasting in 1986, the Fox TV network was candid in its intention to go after the youth market, and across American TV the 1980s and 1990s saw the appearance of a legion of new 'teen-oriented' dramas such as *21 Jump Street* (1987–1990), *Beverley Hills 90210* (1990–2000) and *Dawson's Creek* (1998–2003).

The 1980s also saw the emergence of new media formats that ultimately eclipsed older systems. Launched by Sony in 1982, for example, the Compact Disc (CD) quickly developed as an internationally accepted standard, steadily shunting vinyl records into specialised markets and heralding the dawn of the age of digital technology. The launch of MTV in 1981, meanwhile, not only initiated cable and satellite TV programming aimed at youth but also provided the impetus for the rise of music videos as an important adjunct to the record industry.

Despite the recessions of the 1980s and early 1990s, then, youth continued to be a significant consumer market. By the beginning of the new millennium, moreover, demographic shifts and economic trends seemed to signal a return to the 'golden' era of the 1950s and 1960s. Although the long-term decline in birth rates continued, the youth populations of the US and many European countries were set to grow during the early twenty-first century as the 'echo' of the Baby Boom worked its way through each nation's demographic profile. In the US, the late 1990s saw social commentators talk of a new 'Baby Boomlet' (Gabriel, 1995) as the children of the original Baby Boomers matured and the number of American teenagers steadily grew – the US teenage population reaching 31.6 million by 2000, nearly 6 per cent higher than the Baby Boomer peak of 29.9 million in 1976 (US Census Bureau, 2001). Predictably, marketers were energised at the prospect of this 'Teen Dream for Investors' (*Business Week*, 15 July 2002). A PBS TV special aired in February 2001, for example, spotlighted the army of market analysts and advertisers eagerly chasing 'the hottest consumer demographic in America' – the 'largest generation of teen-agers ever' who 'last year … spent more than $100 billion themselves, and pushed their parents to spend another $50 billion on top of that'.[20]

Market researchers elsewhere were also excited by the prospect of the Baby Boom's generational 'echo'. In Britain, for instance, Market Assessment International (MAI) hailed the arrival of 'Millennium Youth', or the 'M-Genera-tion'. According to MAI's research, the first teenagers to come of age in the twenty-first century were 'richer than any previous generation – if measured in terms of possession of consumer durables and personal disposable income', with 80 per cent of the country's 11–16-year-olds owning their own television and 83 per cent possessing their own bank account (MAI, 1999: 4).

The recessions and industrial restructuring of the 1970s, 1980s, and early 1990s, then, undermined the economic conditions that had been the basis of the boom in teenage consumption during the 1950s and 1960s. Nevertheless, in both the US and Europe, the youth market continued to represent a lucra-tive business sector. The late 1990s, in fact, saw a combination of economic, demographic, and cultural trends come together to re-energise youth-oriented media and marketing, with 'youthful' tastes and values coming to define desirable consumer lifestyles. The trend continued into the early twenty-first century, and was given added impetus by the rise of digital technology and the impact of new forms of communication and entertainment. These are areas considered in more depth in the following chapter.

Notes

1 Jay-Z originally made the wisecrack in 'Diamonds From Sierra Leone', a colla-borative track featured on Kanye West's 2005 album, *Late Registration*.
2 The novelty of the term 'teen-ager' is suggested by the way the word was often hyphenated during the late 1940s and 1950s. By the 1960s, however, the term was commonplace and it was usual to refer to 'teenagers' (without a hyphen).
3 Innumerable books chronicle the development of rock 'n' roll, though Gillett (1996) provides one of the fullest accounts.
4 The term 'rhythm and blues' is now often used to denote a fusion of soul and hip-hop. From the late 1940s to the early 1960s, however, 'rhythm and blues' had a more specific meaning, denoting a pre-eminently African-American musical genre that fused southern (rural) blues styles with newer (urban) swing and boogie-woogie. Luminaries of the genre included Muddy Waters, B.B. King, and Howlin' Wolf.

5 International overviews of the mid-twentieth century Baby Boom can be found in Greenwood et al. (2005) and Reher and Requena (2015).

6 In several European countries, the profile of youth as a distinct social group was further accentuated by the experience of national service. In France, for example, from 1944 all young men were expected to serve for a year in the armed forces, while West Germany introduced two years' military conscription in 1956. And in Britain, from 1948, healthy males aged 17–21 were expected to serve in the armed forces for 18 months. Britain had phased out national service by 1963, while France suspended peacetime military conscription in 1996, followed by Germany in 2011.

7 A concise overview of the impact of economic change on patterns of British youth employment is provided in Roberts (1995).

8 Indeed, less widely publicised, locally based studies – for example, those conducted by Jephcott (1967) and Smith (1966) – suggested levels of youth spending much lower than Abrams had estimated.

9 The story of the British pop film is entertainingly charted in Medhurst (1995).

10 Since the 1930s an agreement between the BBC, the record industry and the Musicians Union had set limits on the amount of music that could be broadcast on the radio.

11 Accounts of the development of British pop radio during this period are furnished in Barnard (1989: 32–49) and Hind and Mosco (1985: 7–18).

12 A chronicle of British TV's early forays into the field of pop music can be found in Hill (1991).

13 Briggs (2015: 14–43) also provides an effective overview of *les copains*.

14 Published until 2006, the magazine's success prompted the launch of German, Spanish, and Italian editions.

15 An extensive history of the 'larrikin' is also provided in Bellanta (2012).

16 According to the Australian National Dictionary Centre (https://slll.cass.anu.edu.au/centres/andc), the name 'bodgie' probably stemmed from the British slang term 'bodge', meaning 'to work clumsily'. In Australia during the 1940s this phrase had come to mean 'something (occasionally someone) which is fake, false, or worthless'. The origins of 'widgie' are more obscure, though the term may have derived from a blend of the words 'woman' and 'bodgie'.

17 A history of the rise of Tamla-Motown and its cultural significance is provided in Early (2004).

18 For more detailed accounts of these developments, see Adamski and Grootings (eds) (1989), Ashton, Maguire and Spilsbury (1990), Blanchflower and Freeman (2000ii) and Furlong and Cartmel (2007: 34–51).

19 The 'Brat Pack' comprised actors such as Emilio Estevez, Anthony Michael Hall, Andrew McCarthy, Judd Nelson, Ally Sheedy, and Molly Ringwald.

20 'The Merchants of Cool', a documentary in the PBS *Frontline* TV series, was originally screened on 27 February 2001.

3 Millennials and the media

Youth, communication, and consumption
in the early twenty-first century

Youth culture and the new world of digital media

Swedish gaming vlogger Felix Kjellberg – better known as 'PewDiePie' – was an
Internet sensation. His beginnings were relatively humble, Kjellberg registering a
channel on the video-sharing platform YouTube in 2010 to present his 'Let's
Play' commentaries on video games. But his goofy, energetic delivery won a
budding following, and his endeavours diversified into music videos, comedy clips
and vlogs (a video blog, or diary-style clip). Relentlessly hyped by his catch-
phrase – 'Subscribe to PewDiePie' – his output proved a hit, attracting over
2 million subscribers within two years and rising to be YouTube's most viewed
channel by 2014. Named by *Time* magazine as one of the world's most influential
100 people in 2016, PewDiePie's success continued, and by 2019 his channel had
chalked-up a staggering 102 million global subscribers (Spangler, 2019). The figures were impressive, and testified to the huge changes that characterised youth-
oriented communication and entertainment in the early twenty-first century.

Above all, PewDiePie's triumphs pointed to the impact of digital technology
on modern youth culture. Generally, the Internet and digitally-based technologies transformed everyday life, but it often seemed young people were in the
forefront of the changes. Indeed, this seemed borne out by PewDiePie's following, 44 per cent of whom were aged between 18 and 24 (Genova, 2018).
Moreover, PewDiePie's success highlighted the vast economic potential of
online media geared to youth. With reported earnings of $12 million in 2015,
PewDiePie headed *Forbes* magazine's first list of the world's richest YouTube
stars, and by 2019 it was estimated he generated monthly revenues of nearly $8
million (Czarnecki, 2019). The precise way PewDiePie raked in such sums was
also significant. His biggest venue streams came from merchandising and
advertising (played before or during his videos), but brand endorsements were
also important.[1] This illustrated the way 'branding' – cultivating a brand's distinctive identity – had become a central pillar in the world of marketing;
developments which had, in turn, spawned a burgeoning industry of online
influencers and social media marketing.

This chapter examines the impact of such developments on contemporary
youth culture. It begins by considering the way that – despite the global

financial crisis of 2007–8 – young people continued to represent a key commercial market, with the term 'millennials' coined to denote what some observers saw as a new generation of young, relatively affluent consumers. These developments took place alongside the upsurge of digital technology and the huge growth of video games, online media, and social networks. The chapter surveys these changes, and critically reviews theories which cast the shifts in terms of a *generational* transformation – that is to say, as a shift marked by the rise of a new cohort of youngsters who are uniquely immersed in new media technologies. Similar views were expounded in the world of marketing, where the epithets 'Generation X', 'Generation Y' and 'Generation Z' were coined for successive markets of youngsters who were conceived as exceptionally discriminating, technically adept and 'media-savvy'. Again, the chapter reviews and critically evaluates such ideas. Consideration is also given to developments in advertising and marketing geared to youth. Specific attention is paid to the rise of branding and social influencers – promotional strategies regarded as particularly suited to a world where mass markets have steadily given way to a multitude of 'niche' market segments. The chapter concludes by considering how far these changes have taken place alongside the emergence of a new, distinctive period in the life course – 'emerging adulthood' – that separates adolescence and full adulthood. Throughout the chapter, it is argued that readings of social and economic change framed in terms of 'generational' shifts tend to be over-generalised. Such claims fail to recognise both significant national variations and the huge diversity of young people's experience. They obscure, especially, the way young people's lives remain profoundly affected by inequalities in terms of class, ethnicity, and gender.

'Millennials rising': the youth market rejuvenated?

Many countries saw young people hard hit by the global financial crisis of 2007–8. Youth employment is especially vulnerable during periods of economic downturn (see Chapter 2), and in both America and Europe the number of jobless youngsters grew. In the US the youth unemployment rate rose from 11.5 per cent in 2008 to 18.2 per cent in 2010 (Bell and Blanchflower, 2011: 13). And, according to the European Commission, the unemployment rate for those aged between 15 and 24 in the EU28 area rose from 15.1 per cent in 2008 to a peak of 23.9 per cent in 2013, before receding to 19.7 per cent by the end of 2015 (European Commission, 2017). In some countries, however, rates remained depressingly high. In May 2017, for example, market analysts Statistica calculated that the youth unemployment rate in Spain had reached 38.6 percent, while that for Greece stood at a colossal 46.6 per cent (Statistica, 2017).

Even in countries less blighted by youth unemployment, commentators were often gloomy about young people's economic prospects. In Britain, for example, 2010 saw a spate of popular books that blamed Baby Boomers for squandering the fortunes of a young generation who consequentially faced a life of lower earnings, higher education expenses, and rising housing costs.[2] And in

2016 the Resolution Foundation – an independent social research agency – attracted a flurry of publicity when it launched a commission to explore growing inequality between generations. 'In contrast to the taken-for-granted promise that each generation will do better than the last', the Foundation warned, 'today's 27-year-olds (born in 1988) are earning the same amount that 27-year-olds did a quarter of a century ago' (BBC News, 2016). Despite this, however, marketers remained buoyant about youth's economic potential. Indeed, many enthused at the prospect of what they saw as a new, burgeoning market of young 'millennials'.

The first use of the term 'millennials' is widely credited to the US authors William Strauss and Neil Howe, who coined the term in their books *Generations* (1991), *The Fourth Turning* (1997) and *Millennials Rising* (2000) (see Chapter 1). For Strauss and Howe, 'millennials' were the cohort of youngsters born between 1982 and 2003. Mapped onto the authors' over-arching model of 'generational cycles', millennials represented an archetypal 'Hero Generation' – a cohort who come of age at a time of crisis, but rise to address and resolve the challenges (Strauss and Howe, 1997: 84). Strauss and Howe's depiction was, in fact, positively radiant. Millennials were, the authors averred, 'more numerous, more affluent, better educated, and more ethnically diverse' than 'any other generation in living memory'. Arguing that a 'can-do youth revolution' was set to 'overwhelm the cynics and pessimists', Strauss and Howe suggested the early twenty-first century would see the millennial generation 'entirely recast the image of youth from downbeat and alienated to upbeat and engaged – with potentially seismic consequences for America' (Howe and Strauss, 2000: 4).

As *Millennials Rising* became a bestseller, the term 'millennials' passed into popular usage as a general moniker for those entering young adulthood during the early twenty-first century. The term proved especially popular among marketers and advertisers. Indeed, as the world economy staggered to its feet in the wake of the 2007–8 financial crisis, many business commentators effused about what they saw as the auspicious commercial possibilities offered by young millennials. Writing in *Advertising Age* in 2012, for example, E.J. Shultz acknowledged that US millennials had been hard hit by unemployment, but insisted they still represented 'a force to be reckoned with', and estimated they would account for consumer spending worth $65 billion over the ensuing decade (Shultz, 2012). Others were equally upbeat. Advertising experts Jeff Fromm and Christie Garton, for instance, argued that millennials represented 'the largest and most influential generation of consumers ever' (Fromm and Garton, 2013); while *Forbes* contributor Micah Solomon declared 2015 to be 'The Year of the Millennial Customer'. Counselling eager entrepreneurs, Solomon advised that America's 80 million millennial consumers were 'about to become the most important customers your business has ever seen':

> In spite of the clichés you see in the media about this generation (ramen-eating, impecunious, underemployed, and so forth), Millennials are not only the largest generation in U.S. and world history, they're on the cusp

of commanding the largest wallet power as well. It's estimated they'll be spending $200 billion annually by 2017 and $10 trillion over their lifetimes as consumers, in the U.S. alone.

(Solomon, 2014)

Millennial consumers outside North America and Europe also attracted interest. With the relentless globalisation of media and consumer industries (see Chapter 7), businesses increasingly turned attention to China, India, the Middle-East, and south-east Asia – regions experiencing rapid economic development, but which also boasted huge (and growing) youth populations. Here, millennial markets seemed to offer rich pickings. In 2017, for example, the blog of market researchers Daxue Consulting advised clients that 'Chinese Millennials have emerged as a key consumer group in the world's second-largest economy', and had 'demonstrated themselves to be confident, discerning spenders; frugal and yet less price sensitive, particularly with regard to luxury and high-quality goods' (Daxue Consulting, 2017). And, for global financial services firm Morgan Stanley, the Indian youth market was equally attractive. Writing in *Forbes* magazine, Morgan Stanley explained that India was 'on track to become the youngest country in the world by 2020, with a median age of 29', while the country's more than 400 million millennials accounted for a third of its population and 46 per cent of its workforce. 'In India', Morgan Stanley concluded, 'millennials will certainly make an economic mark, and investors and industry players who are ready to meet their needs – and offer them more – stand to benefit' (Morgan Stanley, 2017).

The idea of a rising, economically propitious 'millennial' youth market was, however, open to question. According to their detractors, for instance, Strauss and Howe's concept of a new, 'millennial' generation – together with their over-arching theory of 'generational cycles' – lacked intellectual rigour, and was overly impressionistic and generalised (see Chapter 1). Moreover, like the excitement that had surrounded the rise of 'teenage' spending 50 years before, much of the marketing enthusiasm for 'millennials' was hyperbolic and sometimes facile. Certainly, *some* young people were relatively prosperous, and the youth market could sometimes offer big returns. But any notion of a uniform generation of 'millennial' consumers overlooked the complex differences and inequalities – in terms of, for example, class, gender, and ethnicity – that characterised young people's lives, both within and between societies. Nevertheless, the concept of generationally distinctive 'millennials' was widely espoused, and often found a ready audience. In part, this was indebted to the huge social changes wrought by the explosive growth of digital and online technologies – trends in which young people were often seen as torchbearers.

New horizons of digital media: video games, streaming, and social networks

The development of youth culture in the early twenty-first century went in tandem with the growing impact of digital technologies on the worlds of entertainment and communication. The market for video games, in particular, had come a long way since its primitive beginnings during the 1970s. In 2019, for example, Newzoo (leading games market analysts) estimated that in 2019 the world's 2.5 billion gamers would spend around $152.1 billion on games, a figure likely to grow to $196 billion by 2022. And, while 2019 saw the US generate the greatest gaming revenues for an individual country ($36.9 billion), the Asia–Pacific (APAC) region was also important, accounting for 47 per cent of global revenues ($72.2 billion) (Wijman, 2019). Moreover, as China emerged as an economic powerhouse, it also became a key player in the games industry. Indeed, between 2015 and 2018 China represented the world's largest gaming market, a position it lost only after sales were hit by a government freeze on new game licences amid a bureaucratic reorganisation and concerns about the social impact of gaming (see Chapter 5) (Wijman, 2019). And, while demand for console games remained strong (generating global revenues of $47.9 billion), other market sectors were in the ascendant, most obviously mobile gaming – on tablets and smartphones – which represented the largest market segment in 2019, with worldwide revenues of $68.5 billion (Wijman, 2019). And, with the arrival of Stadia – a 'cloud-based' gaming platform, launched by Google in 2019 – mobile gaming was set for new horizons of growth.

Along with video games, the spread of online file-sharing and streaming services was also significant. Early forms of online file-sharing had quickly followed the launch of the World Wide Web in 1991. But it was the arrival of Napster that first highlighted the significance of the technology. Launched in the US in 1999 by 19-year-old Shawn Fanning, Napster was a pioneering Internet peer-to-peer (P2P) file-sharing site that allowed users to freely exchange digital audio files – typically pop songs – encoded in MP3 format. The service was a quick hit and, at its peak, Napster boasted 80 million registered users worldwide (Jowitt, 2017). The transfer of copyrighted material, however, met with anger from the recording industry, and subsequent lawsuits for copyright infringement – dubbed 'music piracy' by critics – brought Napster to an end in 2001.[3] But myriad imitators followed, competing against officially licensed music download platforms such as Apple's iTunes, launched in 2001. A particular success was The Pirate Bay, founded in 2003 by the Swedish anti-copyright organisation, Piratbyrån (The Piracy Bureau). The site was an online index that allowed visitors to freely download entertainment media and, by 2014 reportedly had 40 million active users (Kottasova, 2014). Again, however, issues of copyright infringement resulted in numerous legal cases, and in 2015 The Pirate Bay's Internet domain was seized by a Swedish court.[4]

Alongside the legal battles, the music industry also responded to 'music piracy' by supporting the growth of licensed online streaming platforms. These provide access to recorded material usually through a 'freemium' business model – whereby basic services are free, while additional features are offered via paid subscriptions. Founded in 2006 in Sweden, Spotify proved especially popular, boasting 248 million monthly active users (MAUs) and 113 million subscribers by 2019 (De Silva, 2019). Other streaming services also saw success, with the Berlin-based SoundCloud (launched in 2007) attracting around 175 million users and Apple Music (launched in 2015) about 60 million by 2018 (McIntyre, 2018). But even these figures were put in the shade by the rise of YouTube. Launched in California in 2005, YouTube began life as a video hosting platform, but it also developed into a popular site for music streaming. This boosted the site's appeal, and by 2017 YouTube was available in localised versions in 102 countries, the platform attracting 1.5 billion monthly users worldwide (Shinal, 2017).

Eclipsing even the rise of video gaming and streaming services, was the phenomenal growth of online social networks.[5] Internet platforms that allow users to create a public profile and interact with fellow users, social network sites are defined more comprehensively by communication theorists danah boyd and Nicole Ellison as:

> ... web-based services that allow individuals to (1) construct a public or semi-public profile within a bounded system, (2) articulate a list of other users with whom they share a connection, and (3) view and traverse their list of connections and those made by others within the system.
>
> (boyd and Ellison, 2008: 211)

Generally credited as the Internet's first social media site, Six Degrees was launched in the US in 1997. Taking its name from the aphorism of 'six degrees of separation' – which posits that everyone in the world is connected to everyone else by no more than six degrees of separation – the site's innovation lay in the way it allowed users to create personal profiles and add friends to a personal network. The site, however, was probably ahead of its time and, while its user numbers peaked at around 3.5 million, Six Degrees struggled with the fact that many users still did not have a large number of friends online, consequently it folded in 2001 (boyd and Ellison, 2008: 214). Nevertheless, other sites quickly followed. Launched in 2002, for example, Friendster allowed users to save contacts as part of a personal network, but it also allowed them to share messages, photos, and videos with other members. Within months Friendster had over 3 million users, but it struggled with technical difficulties. As a result, its appeal in the US waned. Friendster's popularity elsewhere, however, skyrocketed – especially in the Philippines, Singapore, Malaysia, and Indonesia – and its user numbers peaked at around 100 million (boyd and Ellison, 2008: 216).[6] Even more successful, however was MySpace.

Launched in 2003, the Californian-based MySpace began life as a file-storage platform, but it quickly transitioned into a social network that was a major hit with young users. Quickly gaining a reputation as a hub for rock bands and their fans, MySpace was attracting teenagers *en masse* by 2004 (boyd and Ellison, 2008: 217), and by 2006 it had 47.3 million members (Goff, 2013: 32). MySpace, however, was dogged by technical glitches and many users were alienated by the increased presence of advertising. As a consequence, users drifted away to the new social media success – Facebook.[7]

Originally founded in 2004 by Harvard student Mark Zuckerberg and four friends, Facebook began as 'Facemash', a social media site exclusive to Zuckerberg's Harvard peers. Renamed 'The Facebook', the site was opened to other colleges, then high schools, before being made available to the general public (aged over 13) in 2006. By the end of that year membership had risen to 12 million, and was growing rapidly as users shifted away from MySpace. By 2011 MySpace membership was still 63 million, but Facebook's exponential growth had seen it become the world's biggest social network site, with over 500 million members (Goff, 2013: 32). As MySpace declined, Facebook's rise seemed relentless. In 2012 Facebook became the first social network to surpass 1 billion registered accounts, and by 2019 it boasted almost 2.38 billion monthly active users (Statistica, 2019i).

But other social networks also found success through their distinctive features. Twitter, for example, was launched as a micro-blogging and social networking service in 2006. Distinguished by limiting users to only 140 characters in their messages or 'tweets' (raised to 280 in 2017), it had attracted 321 million monthly active users by the end of 2018 (Statistica, 2019ii). The WhatsApp messenger service, meanwhile, was launched in 2009 and ten years later boasted around 1.6 billion active users (Statistica, 2019iii). Instagram also rose rapidly. Launched as a photo and video-sharing social networking service in 2010, by 2018 Instagram's active users numbered more than 1 billion (Statistica, 2019iv). And the multimedia messaging service Snapchat – whose distinguishing feature is that it allows users to send photos that self-delete shortly after opening – was launched in 2011, and by 2018 was reporting 186 million daily active users worldwide (Statistica, 2019v).

Most social networks with more than 100 million users originated in the US. Nevertheless, these are usually available in multiple languages, and enable users to connect with others across the world. But regionally-based social networks have also thrived through addressing local contexts and content. In Russia, for example, VKontakte (also known as VK.Com) was founded in 2006 as an online social media service akin to Facebook. It proved especially popular among Russian speakers but was available in several languages and, by the end of 2019, was the largest European social network with more than 100 million active users (SimilarWeb, 2019).

In China, meanwhile, access to foreign social networks such as Facebook, Twitter and YouTube is blocked by the 'Great Firewall of China' – as the Chinese government's Internet censorship is often dubbed. Instead, homegrown sites flourished. In 2005, for example, the Chinese conglomerate Tencent (the world's largest gaming company – see Chapter 7) launched Qzone, a social networking website which laid claim to 645 million users by 2014 (Bischoff, 2014). Meanwhile, the Renren Network (formerly known as the Xiaonei Network), was launched in 2005. A social networking service sometimes dubbed the 'Chinese Facebook', it became especially popular among Chinese students and, though its appeal was waning, it recorded around 257 million active users in 2017 (Statistica, 2019vi). Perhaps the biggest success, however, was WeChat. Originally launched by Tencent in 2011, WeChat began as a simple mobile messaging app but subsequently evolved into a multi-faceted platform encompassing e-commerce, gaming, and shopping services. Alongside its functionality, WeChat's userbase also rapidly climbed, growing to over 1 billion monthly active users by 2018 as the company steadily pushed into overseas markets (Iqbal, 2019).

Clearly, then, digital technologies have transformed the worlds of communication, media, and entertainment. But they have also altered media *relationships*, with a trend towards the 'convergence' of various media forms.[8] This has entailed greater degrees of integration and interconnection, so that there is a 'blending' between the worlds of online media, TV, movies, music, print, and mobile devices. We might, for example, watch a movie or read a newspaper on a mobile phone or tablet. And, for some theorists, this amalgamation of media platforms has been paralleled by a convergence of media ownership (see Chapter 7), along with a blurring between the roles of media producers and consumers (see Chapter 9).

Changes wrought by digital and online technologies have impacted across society, but young people are often seen as being in their forefront. Indeed, communications researchers John Carey and Martin Elton argue that age is a key factor determining the early adoption of new media technologies, with younger people most likely to be 'early adopters' of media innovations (2010: 42). And the growth of social media networks, certainly, seems to have been spearheaded by young users. In 2014, for example, 38 per cent of worldwide users of Tumblr (a micro-blogging and social network site, launched in 2007) were aged between 16 and 24, while a further 32 per cent were aged between 25 and 34. Instagram's global users were also markedly young, with 37 per cent being aged between 16 and 24 and 30 per cent aged between 25 and 34. Facebook's users were generally older but still relatively young, with 25 per cent of worldwide users being aged between 16 and 24, while 29 per cent were aged between 25 and 34 (Statistica, 2014). Snapchat users, meanwhile, were especially young. In 2017, for example, 50 per cent of Snapchat users were under 25 years old, while and 23 per cent were still in high school (LSE, 2017).

In some regions, moreover, the youth of social network users has been particularly pronounced. In Russia, for example, over 77 per cent of VKontakte's users were aged under 34 in 2018 (Statistica, 2019viii). And in China 50 per cent of the nation's social media users were aged under 30 in 2013 (Go-Globe, 2013); while in 2017 more than 69 per cent of Chinese people aged between 15 and 19 were social media users compared to around 34 per cent of those aged between 50 and 59 (Statistica, 2019vii). Some Chinese platforms, moreover, had particular youth-appeal. Launched in 2016, for instance, Douyin billed itself as 'a destination for short-form mobile videos', and was a digital app that allowed users to create and share short video clips (of 3 to 15 seconds) on mobile devices. A quick sensation, Douyin had garnered 100 million users within a year, with more than 1 billion video clips viewed every day (Graziani, 2018). But the app was especially popular among the young, with 75 per cent of its users being aged between 18 and 35 in 2018 (Nanjing Marketing Group, 2018). The youth of its userbase was sustained when Douyin's Chinese owners, ByteDance, launched the app for international markets in 2017. Renamed TikTok, the app was – again – rapidly a success, and had been downloaded nearly 800 million times worldwide within a year (Yurieff, 2018).[9] But, as in China, the app had particular appeal for the young, with around 41 per cent of its global users being aged between 16 and 24 in 2019 (Beer, 2019).

Undoubtedly, then, new developments in entertainment and communication technologies had come to play a big role in the lives of many young people. And, for some theorists, the affinity between young people and digital technologies was so significant it represented nothing less than a *generational* transformation. Like Strauss and Howe, these theorists saw young people in the early twenty-first century as qualitatively different to earlier generations. In this case, however, the difference was configured as a 'digital generation gap' – with young people set apart from their forbears by what was seen as their confident engagement with the world of new digital technologies. Such views were widely promoted, and often gained popular traction. But they were also open to criticism.

'Digital natives'?: Assessing the digital generation gap

Canadian business consultant Don Tapscott was an early proponent of the 'digital generation gap' thesis. For Tapscott, young people on the cusp of the new millennium were set apart from their parents. Dubbing them the 'Net Generation', Tapscott argued that contemporary youngsters thought and learned differently as a consequence of their immersion, since birth, in digital technologies. 'For many kids, using the new technology is as natural as breathing', Tapscott enthused (1998: 4). 'Boomers, stand back', he cautioned, 'these kids are already playing, communicating, working, and creating communities very differently than their parents' (1998: 2).

Marc Prensky (2001) advanced similar arguments. For Prensky, young people born roughly between 1980 and 1994 were 'digital natives'. They were, he argued, indigenous to the world of digital technologies and had lived their whole lives 'surrounded by and using computers, videogames, digital music players, video cams, cell phones, and all the other toys and tools of the digital age' (2001: 1). As a consequence, Prensky argued, young people were distinguished by their high levels of technological literacy and confident engagement with digital media. In contrast, Prensky deemed older groups 'digital immigrants'. Cast as lacking the technological fluency of the new generation, the older 'immigrants' were presented as often being bewildered by the dexterous skills of the young. And, for some theorists, the shift demanded fundamental educational changes to accommodate the new skillsets of 'digital natives' who, it was held, were experiential learners, proficient in multi-tasking and reliant on communications technologies for accessing information.[10] Such ideas won considerable interest among journalists, politicians, and policy-makers but, for critics, they were open to question.

Writers like Tapscott and Prensky (like Strauss and Howe) were criticised for providing little in the way of empirical evidence to substantiate their case. Instead, it was argued, they had relied on anecdotes, conjecture, and speculation. Moreover, some critics pointed to the way their arguments were underpinned by a high measure of 'technological determinism'. That is to say, they tended to see technology as an autonomous force that develops somehow independently from human society. Or, as David Buckingham puts it, 'technology is seen to emerge from a neutral process of scientific research and development, rather than from the interplay of complex social, economic, and political forces. It is then seen to have effects – to bring about social psychological, and political changes – irrespective of the ways in which it is used, and of the social contexts into which it enters' (Buckingham, 2006: 9). In contrast, influential media scholars such as Raymond Williams (1974) have long challenged the reductionism of such an approach and its tendency to neglect the way technologies are, themselves, shaped by human activity in a pre-existing social context. Certainly, technologies possess their own, inherent qualities. But the 'digital natives' thesis tended to ignore the way the rise of technologies is indebted to an interplay of social, economic, and political factors. Moreover, it disregarded the way the uses of technology are largely shaped by those who control its production and distribution.

The ideas of writers such as Tapscott and Prensky also side-lined the continuity and interdependency that existed between 'new' (digital) media and 'old' (analogue) media (for example, TV, films, or radio). Their approach exemplified what Gabriele Balbi and Paolo Magaudda (2018) see as a 'newness ideology' common in much writing about the media, which sees the newest media as the most evolved and best outcome of a historically linear process of development. In reality, however, media development is often incremental and full of conflicting pathways. 'The most recent medium', Balbi and Magaudda explain, 'is not always the best one and media histories are often a process of trial and error, forms of *metabolization* and rejection by potential users' (20). Furthermore, there is rarely any sudden leap from an 'old' media epoch into a dazzlingly new one. Rather, Balbi and Magaudda argue:

> … it is almost impossible to distinguish between old and new media because the latter often imitate or are, at least, inspired by older forms and these are then in turn subjected to a process of remediation and meaning transfer prompted by new technologies … In any specific historical period, in other words, the various media are all interrelated and reciprocal according to an intermedia logic.
>
> (Balbi and Magaudda, 2018: 20)

Notions of a new generation of 'digital natives' were also flawed by their tendencies to overstate and homogenise young people's relationship with new technologies. Tapscott and Prensky, for instance, both overlooked the relatively pedestrian character of much digital media usage by young people. Indeed, empirical studies suggest that young people's use of the Internet is hardly spectacular, but is characterised by fairly mundane forms of information retrieval – visiting websites, listening to music, messaging friends, watching YouTube videos and so on.[11] Moreover, writing in 2008, the Australian educationalist Sue Bennett and her associates criticised ideas of a new 'digital' generation' for being woefully over-generalised (Bennett, Marton and Kervin, 2008). Supporting their case, Bennett et al. cited empirical research in the US which had found that, while ownership and use of digital technologies was widespread among young people, the degree of technical skill they possessed was variable, with only a small minority (21 per cent) actively engaging with the creation of multimedia content (Kvavik, Caruso and Morgan, 2004). This was supported by studies of Australian university students undertaken by Beverley Oliver and Veronica Goerke (2007), and Gregor Kennedy et al. (2008). Both studies found that digital media may have been widely used by young people, but their degree of skill and expertise was variable. As Kennedy and his associates put it, 'there are clearly areas where the use of and familiarity with technology-based tools is far from universal or uniform' (2008: 115). And similar findings have been produced by studies of students from Britain, China, and South Africa.[12]

Overall, then, empirical research finds little evidence that young people have adopted learning styles radically different to those of adults. Moreover, while studies show that young people certainly use a wide range of digital technologies for education and entertainment, their degree of technical expertise is variable, and is significantly affected by issues such as gender, ethnicity, and class. So, as Bennett and her associates astutely concluded, 'It may be that there is as much variation *within* the digital native generation as *between* the generations' (Bennett, Marton and Kervin, 2008: 779).

Such variations become especially stark when seen in the context of the global 'digital divide'. The term 'digital divide' denotes forms of inequality of access to digital media, communication technologies and, in particular, the Internet. Such inequalities can take a variety of forms – between different social groups, for example, or between different geographical regions. But particular concern has focused on the 'digital divide' between rich nations (generally with high Internet coverage) and poor nations (with more limited access). As Balbi and Magaudda argue, global institutions such as the International Telecommunication Union (ITU) and the United Nations Educational, Scientific and Cultural Organization (UNESCO) have long promoted economic policies to combat this digital divide in the belief that the spread of the Internet will 'naturally' lead to progressive social democratisation, while private firms such as Facebook have also made significant investments designed to extend worldwide Internet access (Balbi and Magaudda, 2018: 108). But, while these initiatives have met with a measure of success, the digital divide remains pronounced. For example, data suggests that by the end of 2017 nearly half the world's population did not use the Internet. And, while 95 per cent of people in North America had access to the Web, this compared to just 32 per cent of people in Africa (Balbi and Magaudda, 2018: 109).

The global digital divide, moreover, is particularly pronounced among the young. In 2017 the United Nations Children's Fund (UNICEF) reported that young people aged between 15 and 24 were the world's 'most connected age group' – with 71 per cent online, compared to 48 per cent of the world's general population (UNICEF, 2017: 1). But this still left about 29 per cent of youth worldwide – around 346 million youngsters – who were *not* online, and nearly 9 out of 10 of these lived in Africa or Asia and the Pacific (UNICEF, 2017: 45). Additionally, there was a pronounced gender gap – with, globally, 12 per cent more men than women using the Internet, while in India less than one-third of Internet users were female (UNICEF, 2017: 1).

Digital divides, furthermore, do not simply result from different levels of physical access. Inequalities in terms of technical skills and experience are also important. In her (2014) study of young people in Sri Lanka, for example, Dinuka Wijetunga found that, even though economically underprivileged youngsters often had access to mobile phones with sophisticated communication capabilities, their ability to use these features was much less than their economically advantaged peers. For the most part, she found, the poorer youngsters relied on the phones' talk and text features, and made little use of any Internet capabilities (despite being keen to access them). This, Wijetunga argued, was a consequence of social and cultural inequalities. The poorer youngsters, she explained, may have had access to phones with advanced features, but the instructions to use them (as well as the services themselves) were only available in English – which the youngsters could not understand. Furthermore, the more economically advantaged groups had prior experience of using services like Facebook on computers at home and at school, and could transfer this familiarity to their use of mobile phones. Poorer youngsters, however, had no comparable experience, so struggled to use such features on their phones. Rather than simply inequalities of access, then, Wijetunga concluded that it was 'certain design characteristics of the phone [that] prevented underprivileged youth from using many of the features that their privileged counterparts routinely make use of in their daily communication activity' (Wijetunga, 2014: 713).

Marketing concepts of young consumers: Generations X, Y, and Z

Empirical research, therefore, consistently points to the diversity of young people's media experiences. And issues such as gender, ethnicity, and socio-economic inequality are clearly a major influence on youngsters' relationships with media and communication. Nevertheless, notions of a new, relatively homogeneous, generation of 'media-savvy' youngsters have been widespread. Such themes have been especially pronounced in the world of marketing, where successive cohorts of youth – dubbed, sequentially, 'Generation X', 'Generation Y' and 'Generation Z' – have been configured as a new group of young consumers, made exceptionally elusive through their high degree of media literacy. The premise has a long history. Indeed, since the 1950s teenage spending has been presented as a singularly tough market, difficult both to analyse and tap into (see Chapter 2). During the 1990s, however, the elusiveness of youth's spending power became an increasingly central theme in marketing discourse.

The term 'Generation X' was taken from Canadian author Douglas Coupland's (1991) novel chronicling the lives of quirky and anomic youngsters.[13] During the 1990s it was adopted by the US marketing industry to denote what was seen as a rising cohort of young consumers whose 'media-savvy' and cynical outlook contrasted with the idealism and relative naivety of earlier Baby Boomers. Karen Ritchie (1995: 11), for example, warned advertisers they would 'have to learn new methods to cope with the changing markets'. 'Media, marketing, and advertising were simpler sciences when Boomers were young', Ritchie counselled (1995: 64), while the new 'Xers' were distinguished by 'a healthy scepticism about advertising and a love/hate relationship with the media' (1995: 87). Outside the US, the theme also caught on. In Britain, for instance, commentators also spoke of a new 'Generation X', characterised by a suspicion of advertising and the media. Illustrative was David Cannon's depiction of a generation of young people who were 'highly individualistic' and had 'sophisticated knowledge of consumer products' (Cannon, 1994: 2). Having grown up in an age of uncertainty and rapid developments in media technology, Cannon explained, Generation X had become wary, fiercely independent and were 'highly aware and critical of appearances' (1994: 10).

By the end of the 1990s the original Generation X-ers were well on their way to adulthood. Taking their place, however, were a new cohort seen by marketers as *even more* media literate and advertising-wary. They were sometimes dubbed 'millennials' (the term taken from Strauss and Howe's work), but *Business Week* also christened them 'Generation Y' – partly because they succeeded 'Generation X', and partly because they had, it was argued, a propensity to question everything (Newbourne and Kerwin, 1999). Indeed, while lucrative, the Generation Y / millennial market was deemed uniquely challenging as a consequence of youngsters' media expertise and mistrust of traditional, 'hardsell' advertising strategies. As Thomas Pardee put it in a 2010 article for *Advertising Age*, 'Millennials are … perhaps the most analytical and media-savvy consumers ever' (Pardee, 2010).

The view became virtually a credo in the marketing industry. And a new wave of specialist research agencies proliferated, all touting their abilities to help businesses penetrate what they presented as a uniquely fickle consumer market. Writing in *New Yorker* in 1997, Malcolm Gladwell coined the term 'coolhunters' to describe the growing legion of consultants who specialised in keeping their finger on the pulse of the youth market, using a mixture of quantitative surveys, qualitative interviews, and clued-up intuition to link-up big business with young people's attitudes and tastes. And, into the twenty-first century, the ranks of 'coolhunting' professionals proliferated, accompanied by a mountain of marketing manuals purporting to be incisive guides to the youth market's mindset. For those interested in tapping into millennials' spending power, for example, the welter of 'how to' guides included Johnson (2006), Yarrow and O'Donnel (2009), Livingston (2010), Wells (2011) and Benjamin et al. (2011). And, while much of this material originated in the US, its themes were reproduced in market research that appeared across Europe (Ferrer, 2018), Africa (Liquid Telecom, 2018) and Asia (Brandative, 2016).

The marketing industry's analyses of 'millennial' consumers often sounded impressively clued-up. Invariably, however, there was little substance behind the promotional spiel. Much of it amounted to unsubstantiated blather from market analysts with a vested interest in depicting the youth market as treacherous commercial waters. Indeed, as David Buckingham notes, the way categories such as 'Generation X' and 'Generation Y' were chronologically defined could vary enormously between different marketing experts, and sometimes it seemed distinctly arbitrary (Buckingham, 2014: 209). Moreover, many of the market 'guides' offered little in the way of hard data. As Buckingham observes:

> ... rather than providing unprecedented or novel insights, these books provide copious amounts of sweeping generalizations, much of it repetitive, self-confirming and banal. Most of the evidence provided is anecdotal, taken from journalistic sources, or simply unsupported – perhaps most clearly in the case of Livingston (2010), whose primary point of reference (and source of authority) is his own experiences and preferences as a self-declared member of 'Generation Y'.
>
> (Buckingham, 2014: 209)

Moreover, as Buckingham argues, marketing discourse does not provide a neutral account of 'reality'. Instead, it has an 'illocutionary force' that can 'actively conjure into being the market of which it speaks' (Buckingham, 2014: 203). In these terms, advertisers and marketers do not simply describe the youth market, they play an active role in its creation by popularising specific ideas about young consumers' attitudes and tastes. In the 1950s, for example, advertising experts such as Eugene Gilbert and Mark Abrams did not detachedly chronicle the budding teenage market, but gave it form and substance through their pronouncements (see Chapter 2). Marketers' subsequent claims about the proclivities of Generation X and Generation Y did much the same. And, as Generation Y reached adulthood, they were succeeded by 'Generation Z'. Born in the late 1990s and early 2000s, Generation Z were yet another cohort of youth configured by the marketing industry as *even more* media-savvy and capricious than their predecessors.

The tradition, moreover, was set to continue. Originally popularised in the book *The ABC of XYZ: Understanding the Global Generations* by Australian authors Mark McCrindle and Emily Wolfinger (2010), the term 'Generation Alpha' was increasingly coined by marketers to denote a new age cohort born between 2011 and 2025. And – in a conspicuous echo of the rhetoric that surrounded millenials and digital natives – market researcher McCrindle predicted that this emerging generation would be 'the most technology-supplied generation ever, and globally the wealthiest generation ever' (cited in Williams, 2015).

Selling to youth in the digital age: advertising, branding, and social influencers

The growing role of market researchers in consumer industries geared to the young is constituent in broader business trends since the late twentieth century. As British cultural theorist Sean Nixon argues, the 1980s and 1990s saw an increased 'aestheticization' of consumer industries as advertising, design, and marketing became more central to the selling of goods and services. In their attempts to zero-in on their desired markets, Nixon argues, businesses relied more heavily on 'cultural intermediaries' – design, marketing, and advertising practitioners – to 'articulate production with consumption', imbuing products with values and meanings that would prompt consumers to identify more closely with a particular product or brand (Nixon, 1997: 181). Market analysts emerged as especially important cultural intermediaries. As businesses sought economic advantage by 'getting close to the customer', market researchers and forecasting agencies were increasingly relied upon to monitor subtle shifts in consumers' attitudes. Justin Wyatt, for example, has shown that while market research always had a place in Hollywood's economic strategies, from the late 1970s studios' marketing departments wielded greater power and prestige (Wyatt, 1994: 155). Parallel changes have been identified by Keith Negus in the recording industry, with a move away from 'inspired guess work, hunches and intuition' towards the wide-ranging use of advanced quantitative and qualitative methods of market research (Negus, 1999: 53). And, in the youth market, the trend was especially prominent, as ever-more sophisticated methods of analysis were deployed in attempts to monitor the attitudes of young consumers.

The techniques of marketing pioneered by Eugene Gilbert in the 1950s (see Chapter 2) were an early move in this direction. With his army of young market researchers reporting on their peers' tastes, Gilbert's attention to consumers' feelings was a foretaste of the attitudinal research that became commonplace during the 1960s and 1970s.[14] Indeed, during the 1980s and 1990s such approaches were still central to the work of 'coolhunting' analysts such as Teenage Research Unlimited (TRU). Founded in 1982, TRU emerged as one of America's foremost research agencies specialising in the youth market. With a client base of more than 150 major companies, TRU boasted that its combination of quantitative and qualitative research cut to 'the essence of what being teen means. From the meaning of "cool" to the truths about brand loyalty and age aspiration, it shows ... the world of teens – in vivid color and exciting detail' (TRU, 2002).

During the early twenty-first century, however, market research was transformed by the new opportunities for gathering consumer data made available via the explosive growth of digital media. The huge amount of information users input to social media platforms, along with the general proliferation of 'online chatter', made it possible for businesses to tap into a vast repository of information chronicling consumers' habits, attitudes, and lifestyles. 'Web scraping' (sometimes called 'Web harvesting', or 'Web data extraction'), for example, sees automated software used to extract colossal quantities of online data which can then be used to scrutinise consumers' behaviour. And, perhaps more significantly, the economic model of social networking platforms such as YouTube, Facebook, and Twitter relies on the storage and analysis of data about users and their online activity, which can then be sold to advertisers. As media theorist Christian Fuchs explains, with online networks becoming an increasing part of people's everyday lives, 'more and more precise user data and aggregated data can be sold to advertising clients who, armed with information about potential consumption choices, provide users with personalized advertising that targets them in all of these everyday situations' (Fuchs, 2011: 291). As a consequence, audiences are no longer simply consumers of media products. Instead, through the collection of their online data, audiences have become commodities in their own right. This can be seen as a trend towards 'surveillance capitalism' (a term popularised by social psychologist Shoshana Zuboff (2019)), a commercial practice in which digital technologies are used to collect, collate, and monetise personal data.

Clearly, this is an advantage to advertisers, who are able to zero-in on target markets, sometimes with considerable accuracy. But, for critics, the practice raises concerns about the acquisition and distribution of users' data – especially when websites' privacy policies and terms of service can be less than transparent. Indeed, such issues were thrown into the spotlight in 2018 when it was revealed that the personal data of up to 87 million Facebook users had been acquired by a British political consulting firm, Cambridge Analytica, without the users' consent, and was subsequently used in political advertising campaigns (*New York Times*, 2018). As a consequence, Facebook CEO Mark Zuckerberg was grilled by politicians in the US and UK and, in 2019, the company was fined around $5 billion by the US Federal Trade Commission (*Guardian*, 2019).

Techniques for analysing the youth market, then, have undergone significant development. So, too, have strategies for advertising to young consumers. During the 1990s, for example, a vogue for 'guerrilla marketing' saw businesses eschew high gloss, hard-sell promotion strategies in favour of 'hip and edgy' campaigns that relied on stencilling, stickering, and flyposting, as well as engineering outrageous PR stunts aimed at causing a stir.[15] In 2005, for instance, Sony launched its new PlayStation Portable game by hiring graffiti artists to spray-paint walls around major US cities with images of kids playing with the new gadget. Increasingly, however, business turned to the Internet and social media as avenues to access the youth market. The shift was manifest in the rise of promotional tools such as 'adver-gaming' (which blends advertising with video games), branded applications (that build a brand through a digital app that offers users entertainment or information) and viral marketing (that prompts consumers to promote products through their social media contacts). Social network sites have become particularly important in these strategies. As Tracy Tuten explains, such sites are especially attractive to advertisers because they 'encourage interaction between consumers and brands', and can 'enhance perceptions of the "brand as a person", thereby strengthening a brand's personality, differing a brand from its competitors, and setting the stage for a perceived relationship' (Tuten, 2008: 19–20). This attention to the development of a brand's 'personality' was indicative of the more general focus on 'branding' – developing a brand's identity and symbolic associations – a practice increasingly seen as vital in the operation of media and consumer industries.

During the 1980s and 1990s corporations increasingly viewed a brand's 'identity' as a strategic economic asset. In the youth market, especially, a brand's image came to be seen as a key commercial resource, with the symbolic associations of a brand name or logo – for example, the Nike 'swoosh' or the Stüssy 'signature' – allowing products to be linked with distinct values and lifestyles. Fashion companies were in the forefront of trends towards a more systematic exploitation of brand image, Paul Smith (1997) showing how the clothing company Tommy Hilfiger developed a particularly vigorous approach in the licensing of its brand name. And in 2011 the importance of 'branding' and 'brand identity' was underscored when US leisurewear firm Abercrombie & Fitch offered a 'substantial payment' to Mike 'The Situation' Sorrentino – an irrepressible star of *Jersey Shore*, MTV's reality-TV show – if the celebrity would agree to *stop* wearing their clothes. 'We are deeply concerned', an Abercrombie & Fitch spokesman explained, 'that Mr Sorrentino's association with our brand could cause significant damage to our image' (*Guardian*, 2011).[16] In itself, the episode was insignificant, but it drew attention to the crucial importance credited to 'brand identity' in the contemporary market.

This close attention to 'branding' was also key to the increasing importance of social media influencers (SMIs) as a form of marketing. SMIs are online 'opinion leaders' who use social media platforms – for example, YouTube, Twitter, Facebook and, especially, Instagram – to share posts with their followers about their personal lives and preferences for particular products and services. And, for businesses, SMI's became an important means of accessing markets. As Allison Hearn and Stephanie Schoenhoff explain:

> The SMI works to generate a form of 'celebrity brand' via social networks, which can subsequently be used by companies and advertisers for consumer outreach.
>
> (Hearn and Schoenhoff, 2016: 194)

The attraction of SMIs for businesses is that they are seen as an especially direct and 'organic' way of connecting with consumers. Influencers are people regarded as carrying significant credibility with their followers, and their endorsements are perceived as candid and 'authentic'. For businesses, then, SMIs are seen as an ideal way of investing a brand with an engaging and trustworthy 'identity'. First flourishing in the fashion and beauty markets, they became increasingly common in the food, travel and entertainment industries; and by 2012 most major brands were incorporating SMIs into their promotional strategies (Kumar and Mirchandani, 2012).

Some SMI's endeavours are small-scale, reaching relatively few followers. But others have tremendous reach. For instance, in 2019 Huda Kattan – a Dubai-based beauty blogger – boasted over 32 million followers on Instagram (Izea, 2019), while in the gaming world PewDiePie was facing hot competition from gaming influencers such as Mark Fischbach who (as 'Markiplier') had attracted over 6 million Instagram followers and more than 19 million subscribers to his YouTube channel (InfluencerDB, 2018). And, whereas 'low-level' influencers are usually incentivised by receiving free products or a token payment for their endorsements, Instagram influencers with around a million followers could, by 2018, command around £10,000 ($13,000) for a one-off post (cited in Mackay, 2018). SMIs, and online marketing more generally, have become especially valued for the ability to reach 'niche' markets. Traditional marketing strategies mostly targeted undifferentiated 'mass' audiences; but the new, digitally-based advertising techniques are regarded as better able to target more specific market segments. This was seen as a critical capability given the increased 'fragmentation' of the modern media audience, a trend that was constituent in broader economic shifts.

For many theorists, capitalist economies have undergone a fundamental transformation since the late 1960s – moving from a 'Fordist' era of mass production for mass consumer markets, into a new, 'post-Fordist' epoch of flexible production for a profusion of differentiated market segments.[17] In contrast to the mass production of standardised goods characteristic of Fordist enterprise (a term derived from the mass production processes pioneered by the Ford motor company), post-Fordist business practice is characterised by the deployment of sophisticated technology in the production of smaller batches of goods geared to a plurality of market segments. Style, image, and marketing are also seen as playing a more important role in post-Fordist economic life, as businesses strive to invest their products with values and meanings that appeal to buyers associated with specific market niches and 'lifestyles'. For the media, these trends are also manifest in the splintering of mass audiences into a plethora of different segments. The rise of digital technology was central to these processes since it multiplied the number and variety of media channels available to consumers, who could increasingly choose between an abundance of digital TV, radio, websites, streaming services, and social media. As a consequence, audiences have become more fragmented and diverse. The age of *mass* media and *mass* audiences has not entirely disappeared, but trends are towards formats that eschew a general market in favour of smaller, more nuanced targets.

According to Stanley Hollander and Richard Germain (1993), such developments have been evidenced especially clearly in the field of youth marketing. For Hollander and Germain, contemporary appeals to an array of 'niche' groups of young consumers are a marked contrast to the approach taken during the 1950s, when products were pitched to a more homogeneous youth market:

> True, the products, services, and marketing appeals that were being aimed at youth [during the 1950s] were differentiated from those designed for younger and older groups. But whether we look at apparel or popular music or some other youth-oriented category of offerings, we see things that were intended for *masses* of youths.
>
> (Hollander and Germain, 1993: 107)

In some ways, however, the production of 'teenage' media and consumer goods during the 1950s could, itself, be seen as a pioneering move away from concepts of a monolithic 'mass' market. Indeed, the very practice of appealing to youth as a discrete consumer group, associated with particular tastes and interests, could be seen as an early form of 'post-Fordist' marketing strategy. Increasingly, however, the boundaries demarcating the 'youth' market have extended into a wider range of age groups.

Changing transitions to adulthood: a 'golden age of youth'?

Rather than being an inherent life stage with intrinsic qualities and meanings, 'youth' has always been a socially constructed concept (see Chapter 1). This is especially evident in the history of 'youth' as a marketing category, where the symbolic values of youth culture – independence, energy, excitement – have been shaped, to a large part, by advertisers and marketers. And, in the early twenty-first century, the marketing industry steadily extended this category and its associated values to embrace a greater range of demographic groups. At the younger end of the age-scale, pre-teen children – especially girls – were increasingly configured as a lucrative consumer market aspiring to escape the constraints of childhood and embrace 'teenage' tastes and identities. In the US, particularly, this 'tween' market of 8- to 14-year-olds was viewed as a valuable commercial prize, market analysts Youth Market Alert estimating that in 2010 America's 20 million 'tweens' already wielded an annual spending power of $43 billion (Krotz, 2010).[18]

Older age groups were also configured as a new 'youth' market. In a 2005 cover story for *Time* magazine, journalist Lev Grossman spotlighted what he called 'the twixters' – 'young adults who live off their parents, bounce from job to job and hop from mate to mate' (Grossman, 2005: 42). And in 2006 author Christopher Noxon coined the term 'rejuvenile' for what he saw as 'a new breed of adult, identified by a determination to remain playful, energetic, and flexible in the face of adult responsibilities' (Noxon, 2006: 2). Commercial interests, meanwhile, quickly latched onto the potential of the protracted 'youth' market. For example, in its 2008 report *The Golden Age of Youth*, Viacom Brand Solutions International identified a distinct 25–34-year-old

'Golden Youth' market of consumers who were still actively and emotionally connected to youth culture, but were largely ignored by marketers and advertisers. Characterised by a lack of responsibilities but a relatively high disposable income, the group presented money-spinning possibilities. As Viacom's report explained:

> The traditional demographic definition of 'youth' is no longer applicable in today's society, and marketers should target consumers based upon their engagement and participation with youth culture rather than their chronological age.
>
> (Viacom Brand Solutions International, 2008: 1)

The idea of an older 'youth' market was prominent in pronouncements from the marketing industry, but the concept touched on some realities of social change. During the 1980s and 1990s young people in many countries were already experiencing less stability in their transitions to 'adult' life, with an increased complexity of pathways (in terms of educational courses, training, temporary and part-time jobs, and social relationships) into the roles and responsibilities traditionally associated with adulthood (see Chapter 2). The economists David Blanchflower and Richard Freeman, for example, argued that in North America and Europe young people were responding to a more challenging economic environment by enrolling in higher education in greater numbers, staying longer in their parents' homes and postponing setting up their own families. 'Taken together', they concluded, 'increased schooling and residence in parental homes have elongated the period of youthful preparation for the job market and family formation. The "young" are older than they were several decades ago' (2000i: 7). The trends continued into the early twenty-first century[19] and, for some theorists, amounted to a profound shift in the lifecycle of industrialised societies. From this perspective a new, distinctive phase had appeared, separating adolescence and adulthood − 'emerging adulthood'.

The term 'emerging adulthood' was originally coined by Jeffrey Arnett in an article published in the journal *American Psychologist* in 2000, and Arnett subsequently developed the concept in a number of books, anthologies, and journal articles.[20] For Arnett, trends in industrialised societies during the late twentieth century − specifically, the extension of education and the delay of marriage and parenthood − had altered the life experiences of young people aged between 18 and 25. Rather than being a time when young people settled into long-term adult roles, Arnett contended, the late teens and early 20s had more typically become 'a period of frequent change and exploration' (2000: 469). Basing his arguments on 300 interviews with Americans, aged between 18 and 29 (Arnett, 2004: 24), Arnett asserted that 'emerging adulthood' had come to constitute a new, distinct phase in life that separated the dependency of childhood and adolescence from the enduring responsibilities of adulthood. This new developmental stage, Arnett explained, was characteristically a time of 'independent exploration' in the areas of love, work and worldview:

> Emerging adulthood is a time of life when many different directions remain possible, when little about the future has been decided for certain, when the scope of independent exploration of life's possibilities is greater for most people than it will be at any other period of the life course.
>
> (2000: 469)

According to Arnett, 'emerging adulthood' was characterised by five key themes. It was, he suggested, a period of significant identity exploration in which young people were searching to find a meaning in work, relationships, and beliefs. It was a time of instability, when young people had a tendency to change their residence, job, and relationships more frequently. It was also a time of self-focus and relative freedom from obligations to parents, spouses, and children. Additionally, it was time of relative optimism, as young people looked forward to a future of opportunities and possibilities. Moreover, young people during this period of life were conscious that they were between adolescence and adulthood – they felt they were no longer adolescents, but also not quite adults (Arnett, 2004; Tanner and Arnett, 2011: 15). Taken together, Arnett maintained, these features marked out 'emerging adulthood' as 'a new life stage that opened up when transitions in love and work that previously took place in the late teens or early 20s moved into the late 20s or early 30s' (Tanner and Arnett, 2011: 15).

Arnett's ideas garnered considerable academic and popular attention. The concept of 'emerging adulthood' was widely referenced by journalists and policy-makers and, in 2013, even spawned a dedicated academic journal. While it undoubtedly struck a popular chord, however, the theory also attracted criticism.[21] Indeed, the notion that 'emerging adulthood' could be identified as a distinct phase in the life course was strongly questioned. Doubts were raised not only about how far this period constituted a discrete developmental phase (rather than simply being part of a continuous developmental process) but also about the precise nature of the developments that supposedly took place. As Leo Hendry and Marin Kloep observed, 'in classifying emerging adulthood as a developmental stage, there should be "something" that develops during this time, and Arnett never clarifies what exactly that might be' (2010: 178). Perhaps more damaging, however, were the criticisms of Arnett's tendency to see 'emerging adulthood' as a relatively universal experience in young people's lives.

To be fair, Arnett sometimes signposted limits to his claims. 'Is emerging adulthood a period of life that is restricted to certain cultures and certain times?', he rhetorically asked in his original article. 'The answer', he replied, 'appears to be *yes*' (2000: 477, orig. emphasis). As he went on to explain, emerging adulthood was a period that 'exists only in cultures that postpone the entry into adult roles and responsibilities until well past the late teens. Thus, emerging adulthood would be most likely to be found in countries that are highly industrialised or postindustrial' (478). For his critics, however, Arnett's claims remained too sweeping and over-generalised. Sociologist James Côté was especially withering, pointing to a raft of studies that suggest the idea of 'emerging adulthood' was at best overextended, and at worst a flawed myth (Côté, 2014; Côté and Bynner, 2008). For example, Jennifer Silva's (2012) qualitative research on working-class Americans aged in their 20s and 30s uncovered a variety of 'coming of age narratives', several very different to that outlined by Arnett. Similarly, US-based quantitative research such as that produced by D. Wayne Osgood and his associates (2005) pointed to a diverse range of pathways to adulthood, none of which suggested the rise of a new 'developmental stage'. Moreover, while Arnett tended to see young people's frequent movement between different employment as a facet of their freely chosen 'identity exploration', Côté observed how, for many youngsters, this was actually a consequence of 'coping with precarious, ambiguous, and exploitative job situations' (Côté, 2014: 184).

Beyond the US, studies also cast doubt on the universality of 'emerging adulthood'. Of course, Arnett, had always painstakingly qualified his claims and recognised that emerging adulthood 'is a period of the life course that is culturally constructed, not universal and immutable' (2000: 270). Nevertheless, evidence from around the world suggested notions of emerging adulthood as a new developmental stage were unduly presumptive. Indeed, while Arnett argued that emerging adulthood was a life stage most likely to be found in societies that were 'highly industrialised or postindustrial', even in such contexts studies pointed to a great diversity in young people's lives. Hendry and Kloep's (2010) qualitative study of Welsh youngsters aged 17–20, for example, found a highly diverse range of life experiences and attitudes, many very different to those outlined by Arnett. Furthermore, the majority of their sample (25 of their 38 subjects) self-identified as 'adults', while about half did not optimistically view the future in terms of possibilities (as Arnett had conjectured). Instead, they felt trapped by a decided *lack* of opportunities, and were resigned to their fate.

And, while John Bynner's (2005) analysis of three longitudinal studies of British youngsters found elements of support for Arnett's model, it also suggested that socio-economic inequalities ensured marked differences between young people. The most common feature to emerge from the research, Bynner concluded, was 'growing polarization between the advantaged and the disadvantaged'. 'Emerging adulthood' was prominent among the former, but 'the traditional accelerated routes to adult life were still as common as ever among the rest' (Bynner, 2005: 377). Similarly, in their quantitative analysis of the transitions to adulthood made by two cohorts of youngsters from the US, UK, and Finland, Ingrid Schoon and John Schulenberg found marked differences and disparities. 'There is', they concluded, 'a growing polarization of fast versus slow transition prevalences', with:

> … those from less privileged backgrounds making the transition to employment and parenthood earlier than others, potentially due to

insufficient resources to take advantage of educational opportunities and to support an extended period of education.

(Schoon and Schulenberg, 2013: 55)

Some theorists, nevertheless, maintain that the concept of emerging adulthood is applicable to a range of international contexts. Rita Žukauskienė, for example, assembles a variety of European studies which, she argues, provide 'substantial evidence that many of the features of emerging adulthood, as conceptualized by Arnett … can be observed among youth in Europe' (Žukauskienė, 2016: 6). Reviewing these studies, however, Arnett himself acknowledges that, while many European countries share similar demographic trends, 'Europe is highly diverse in other aspects of emerging adulthood' – with transitions to adulthood differing between national contexts, and important differences existing between the experiences of working-class and middle-class youngsters (Arnett, 2016: 210–211).

In China, too, young people's life experiences seem rather different to the model posited by Arnett. In their (2004) study of students at a Beijing university, for example, Larry Nelson and his colleagues found that the attitudes of their 207 respondents showed some similarities to Arnett's concept of emerging adulthood. At the same time, however, the specific values and expectations of the young people's culture also ensured important differences, with the majority of the students believing they had already reached mature adulthood (Nelson, Badger and Wu, 2004: 30).

Undoubtedly, the social and economic changes of the early twenty-first century had significant impact on young people's life experiences. And there is certainly some evidence to show that transitions to adulthood have become extended and more complex. But whether these changes represent the rise of a new, relatively universal, condition of 'emerging adulthood' is moot. 'As it stands', Côté shrewdly observes, 'it is a leap of logic to conclude that because it takes people longer to pass certain social markers of adulthood they are experiencing a new developmental stage' (2014: 183). Moreover, while there may be many new twists, turns, and detours in young people's pathways to adulthood, empirical research suggests that not only are these pathways characterised by a significant degree of difference, but that these differences remain – to a high degree – resolutely determined by 'old' social and economic inequalities.

Along with terms like 'millennials', 'digital natives' and 'Generation X', 'Y' and 'Z', therefore, the notion of 'emerging adulthood' may, to a degree, point to real changes in the lives of young people. Indeed, the rise of digital technologies has clearly transformed many youngsters' cultural landscape while, for many, transitions to adulthood have become complex and protracted. Configuring these developments in terms of a *generational* change, however, can be over-generalised and reductive; and glosses over the continued importance of structural factors in determining young people's life experiences. Indeed, notions of an ascending cohort of new, technologically clued-up and media-savvy millennials can be seen as just the latest instalment in a long history of 'generational symbolism' in which representations of youth are used to elaborate a very particular – and ideologically loaded – view of social change. The next chapter looks more closely at these symbolic constructions of 'youth', and assesses the ways shifting representations of young people have been related to wider patterns of social, economic, and political change.

Notes

1 While the number of PewDiePie's endorsements were relatively few, those he made were for major brands such as Mountain Dew and Legendary Pictures – so they were high profile and reputedly well-paid (PMYB, 2017). At times, however, PewDiePie's own 'brand' struggled to maintain positive associations. In 2017, for example, Disney ended a partnership with the star after it was alleged some of PewDiePie's videos had featured anti-Semitic jokes and neo-Nazi imagery (Solon, 2017).

2 The collection included Beckett (2010), Howker and Malik (2010) and Willets (2010).

3 The Napster brand-name, however, survived as the company was bought up and reconfigured as a licensed music subscription service.

4 Nevertheless, The Pirate Bay continued to operate via new Internet domains and other technical manoeuvres.

5 Overviews of the early development of social network sites can be found in boyd and Ellison (2008) and Goff (2013).

6 In 2009 Friendster was acquired by Malaysian owners and, from 2011, was reconfigured as a gaming site. It struggled against rivals, however, and finally closed in 2019.

7 The decline of MySpace was inexorable, but the site continued to operate and in 2019 was still attracting around 8 million visits per month (Armstrong, 2019).

8 Surveys of theories of media convergence are provided in Grant and Wilkinson (eds) (2009) and Dwyer (2010).

9 TikTok and Douyin are effectively the same, but are run on different Internet servers to comply with Chinese censorship restrictions.

10 See, for instance, Frand (2000) and Oblinger and Oblinger (2005).

11 Examples include Facer, Furlong, Furlong and Sutherland (2003), Holloway and Valentine (2003), Livingstone and Bober (2005), and Livingstone and Haddon (eds) (2009).

12 From Britain, the studies included Helsper and Eynon (2010), Jones et al. (2010) and Margaryana, Littlejohn and Vojtb (2011). Research on Chinese students was undertaken by Li and Ranier (2010), and on South African students by Thinyane (2010).

13 Coupland's title was taken from a UK punk rock band of the 1970s who, in turn, had poached their name from Hamblett and Deverson's (1964) sociological study of British youth.

14 See Brierly (2005: 35–38) and Fox (1985: 183–187).

15 The term 'guerrilla marketing' was originally popularised in Levinson's (1984) marketing manual.

16 Sorrentino's nickname – 'The Situation' – was derived from his talent at fermenting troublesome social scenarios. Indeed, in 2018 Sorrentino faced an especially troublesome scenario when he was sentenced to 8 months in prison for tax evasion. On release, in 2019, he resumed his reality-TV role (Cohen, 2019).

17 Michel Aglietta (1979) was one of the first theorists to suggest the structures of 'Fordist' capitalism were transforming. From the late 1960s, Aglietta argued, declines

in productivity and demand prompted American industries to move into more flexible forms of production and business organisation. Subsequently, other authors (for example, Murray (1990)) coined the term 'post-Fordism' to denote what they saw as a new economic order based on practices of flexible production and market segmentation.

18 A more detailed analysis of 'tween' media and marketing can be found in Mitchell and Reid-Walsh (eds) (2005).

19 In the UK, for example, 2019 saw the Office of National Statistics (ONS) report that (probably as a consequence of increasing housing costs) the preceding two decades had seen a 46 per cent rise in the number of young people aged between 20 and 34 living with their parents. According to the ONS, 32 per cent of men in this age group and 21 per cent of women lived in their parental home (ONS, 2019).

20 See, for instance, Arnett (2004), Arnett and Hughes (2012), Arnett, Kloep, Hendry and Tanner (eds) (2011), Arnett and Tanner (eds) (2006) and Murray and Arnett (eds) (2019).

21 An overview of Arnett's theories, together with a summary of key criticisms, is provided in Syed (2016).

4 Media representations of youth
Pathologies, panaceas, and moral panics

Symbolic dimensions to representations of youth

Between 2016 and 2018 local media and politicians depicted the Australian city of Melbourne as overrun by gangs of young Africans. Concerns were roused in 2016 by events at Melbourne's Moomba festival. Australia's largest community festival, Moomba was usually a time of family fun, but that year brawling youths spilled onto the streets. For *The Age*, Melbourne's daily newspaper, young immigrants were to blame. As the paper recounted:

> Hundreds of hooligans, of African, Pacific Islander and other backgrounds, swarmed into the city on Sunday evening intent on wreaking havoc ... people have been hurt and traumatised, after businesses have been wantonly damaged.
>
> (*The Age*, 15 March 2016)

And ensuing months saw media reports depict Melbourne, the state capital of Victoria, as a city gripped by a crime wave wrought by African gangs. Youngsters from Melbourne's Sudanese migrant community were singled out as a particular menace, and tabloid newspapers dubbed Victoria the 'State of Fear' as Peter Dutton, the Federal Home Affairs Minister, insisted:

> We need to call it for what it is. Of course, this is African gang violence ... people are scared to go out to restaurants of a night-time because they're followed home by these gangs.
>
> (cited in Karp, 2018)

Others, however, were more reassuring. Victoria's deputy police commissioner argued that stories of 'gang violence' were misleading. And Tim Pallas, the state's acting premier, responded to claims residents were too scared to visit restaurants by sardonically suggesting they try his favourite brasserie (Karp, 2018). In fact, official crime data indicated Melbourne was not a city laid waste by young Africans. Overall, crime rates in Victoria actually fell by 4.8 per cent in 2017, and across the preceding decade the proportion of crimes committed by young people had fallen from 52 per cent of recorded offences in 2007–8 to 40 per cent in 2015–16 (CSA, 2016; Whalquist, 2018). Statistics showed, moreover, that young offenders were much more likely to have been born in Australia than overseas (MacDonald, 2017: 1185; Majavu, 2018: 8). Rather than being a rational response to a quantum leap in youth crime, therefore, some commentators saw Melbourne's 'African gangs' crisis as disproportionate and distorted. For sociologists such as Fiona MacDonald, the episode was better understood as a facet of a wider backlash against immigration in which 'reporting of ethnic youth gangs as the perpetrators of public violence [had] merged with the "fear" of refugees and asylum seekers, creating a complex landscape of social exclusion' (MacDonald, 2017: 1183).

Anxieties about Melbourne's 'African gangs', then, pointed to many other dimensions of social and political conflict in contemporary Australia. But it also exemplified the symbolic dimensions to media images of youth. The notion of lawless, 'alien' youths running amok were illustrative of the way representations of young people often condense wider themes, functioning as a 'metaphorical vehicle' that encapsulates society's more general hopes and fears. This chapter explores these 'mythic' dimensions to youth, and the way they serve as a symbolic focus for wider social debates. Specific consideration is given to negative representations of young people and their role in 'moral panics' that escalate popular anxieties through the exaggeration of real or imagined threats. The place of gender and ethnicity in moral panics is discussed, and reasons for their increasing prominence are reviewed. Attention is also given to the way recent changes in society and the media have impacted on contemporary moral panics, with particular attention given to what some theorists see as the rise of a 'risk society' and a broadly-based 'culture of fear'.

But media representations of youth have never been entirely negative. The chapter concludes by considering the way youth has sometimes been configured as a totem of economic growth and social progress. Here, consideration is given to the way configurations of the 'teenager' during the 1960s served to promote visions of liberating consumerism and national renewal on both sides of the Atlantic. Attention is also given to the revival of such constructions during the early twenty-first century in a discourse that casts young people – especially young women – as the embodiment of neoliberal values of individualism and enterprise.

'Idealizations and monstrosities': the mythic qualities of youth

Media representations of young people often possess a significant symbolic dimension. An enduring, evocative emblem, 'youth' is an example of what the French cultural theorist Roland Barthes termed 'mythologies'. For Barthes, 'mythologies' – or 'myths' – were an overarching 'metalanguage' that organises our perceptions by conveying cultural meanings beyond the surface level of representation. As the pioneering semiotician put it, a myth is not a particular object, but is 'the way in which [an object] utters a message' (Barthes, 1972: 117).

From this perspective, myths are vehicles for expressing ideas and feelings. They are resonant motifs that work to connote emotions, meanings, and concepts. And 'youth' abounds in 'mythic' qualities.

Many theorists have observed how representations of youth often condense broader themes of change. Given their close association with ideas of growth and the passage of time, it is perhaps inevitable that conceptions of 'youth' and 'generation' possess such allegorical qualities. And, as numerous authors observe,[1] youth's symbolic function is powerfully extended at moments of profound social transformation – for instance, during the twilight years of the nineteenth century or the period of social and economic realignment that followed the Second World War. This symbolic capacity is highlighted by US historians Joe Austin and Michael Willard, who explain how 'public debates surrounding "youth" are an important forum where new understandings about the past, present, and future of public life are encoded, articulated and contested', so that 'youth' functions as 'a metaphor for perceived social change and its projected consequences' (Austin and Willard, 1998: 1).

Representations of youth, moreover, are characterised by a recurring duality. Young people have been cast as *both* totems of social prosperity *and* as deplorable benchmarks of national decline. These contrasting images – termed 'youth-as-fun' and 'youth-as-trouble' by Dick Hebdige (1988i: 19) – are often contrived stereotypes that bear tenuous relation to the experiences of young people themselves. But, historically, these tropes have wielded significant connotative power and have often served as motifs around which dominant interpretations of social change are elaborated. As Austin and Willard explain, young people have been widely constructed as both 'angels of history' and 'demons of culture'; viewed alternatively (and sometimes simultaneously) as both 'a vicious, threatening sign of social decay' and '"our best hope for the future"' (Austin and Willard, 1998: 2).

The point is also eloquently expressed by anthropologists Jean and John Comaroff. 'Youth', they argue, 'are complex signifiers, the stuff of mythic extremes, similarly idealizations and monstrosities, pathologies and panaceas':

> In short, 'youth' stands for many things all at once: for the terrors of the present, the errors of the past, the prospect of a future. For old hopes and new frontiers.
>
> (Comaroff and Comaroff, 2005: 20)

The Comaroffs stress the 'mythic bipolarity' that has characterised representations of young people, but they also highlight the way 'youth' has often been configured as the stuff of nightmares. '"Youth"', the Comaroffs argue, 'is a collective noun that 'has all too often indexed a faceless mass of persons who were underclass, unruly, male, challengingly out of place – and, at once physically powerful and morally immature, always liable to seize the initiative from their elders and betters' (2005: 24). This depiction of youth as the repository of respectable fears has a long, angst-ridden history.

The 'fifth horseman of doom': youth, media, and moral panics

In the US, youth has often been cast in a critical light. During the late nineteenth century America's developing cities could be seen as breeding grounds for crime and violence, and their working-class denizens – especially the young – were habitually configured as dissolute and dangerous. Concerns continued into the following century, and by the 1920s fears of juvenile delinquency had prompted a flurry of investigations. But an even greater sense of alarm came during the 1950s, when America was gripped by the perception that juvenile crime was spiralling out of control. The fears seemed borne out by a relentless rise in crime statistics, which fuelled a tide of exposés in magazines, newspapers, and newsreels that depicted a form of delinquency frighteningly new in its severity. The mood was captured in 1953 by Clymer Hendrickson, a New Jersey Senator, who contended delinquent youth represented the 'fifth horseman of doom', and that US youngsters were 'harder, fiercer, more shocking than ever before in our Nation's history' (*Washington Post*, 12 April, 1953).

As historian James Gilbert shows, Gallup surveys suggest public concerns about delinquency saw a brief peak in 1945, followed by a more sustained period of alarm between 1953 and 1958 (Gilbert, 1986: 63). In response, that year saw the appointment of a Senate Subcommittee on Juvenile Delinquency to investigate the problem's cause. Headed by Estes Kefauver (Senator for Tennessee), the enquiry continued until the early 1960s, and its very existence helped confirm views that juvenile delinquency – or the 'J.D'. problem, as it was often dubbed – was a major social issue. According to Gilbert, however, the anxieties were exaggerated. The 'juvenile crime wave', he argues, was largely a statistical phenomenon produced by new strategies of law enforcement and changes in the collation of crime data (Gilbert, 1986: 66–70). Moreover, Gilbert suggests, there was a significant 'symbolic' dimension to the concerns, with the alarm about youth crime serving as a focus for a broad sense of unease. In these terms, rather than being a response to a genuine eruption of adolescent vice, the postwar fears surrounding delinquency served as 'a symbolic focus for wider anxieties in a period of rapid and disorienting change', with the fears about juvenile crime articulating 'a vaguely formulated but gnawing sense of social disintegration' (Gilbert, 1986: 77).

Other countries have seen similar responses unfold. Historian Geoffrey Pearson, for example, argues that since the nineteenth century Britain has seen as 'a long and connected history of fearful complaint and controversy' in which 'each succeeding generation has understood itself to be standing on the brink of some radical discontinuity with the past, and in which the rising generation has been repeatedly seen as the harbinger of a dreadful future' (Pearson, 1984: 102). Victorians, for example, were preoccupied with an apparent explosion of street crime associated with packs of young thugs, christened 'hooligans' by the newspapers (Pearson, 1983, 1984: 74–118). And 1950s Britain was haunted by the spectre of Teddy boy gangs – youngsters with a taste for rock 'n' roll and

American style, who the press associated with an unprecedented wave of crime and violence (Pearson, 1983, 1984: 12–24).[2] According to sociologists Paul Rock and Stanley Cohen (1970), however, the welter of negative publicity was significantly overstated, and presented relatively minor incidents as though they were a problem running out of control.

By the early 1960s the Teddy boy's image had been displaced by the chic, Italian-inspired styles associated with a new group of youngsters – the mods. Media responses to mod style, however, often reproduced the overwrought treatment given to the Teds. The mods' appearance was often presented as a symbol of national decline, an approach that peaked in press responses to a series of 'battles' between the mods and their motorcycle-riding rivals, the rockers, in 1964. But in *Folk Devils and Moral Panics*, his classic analysis of the events (first published in 1972), Cohen highlighted the dimensions of sensationalism endemic to the press coverage. According to Cohen, the total amount of violence in the disturbances was actually slight, but the events were presented as wholesale havoc by the media in an episode of overblown alarm he termed a 'moral panic'.[3]

For Cohen, the concept of 'moral panic' denoted processes through which the media contributed to the escalation of social events through misrepresenting and magnifying the activities of real or imagined deviant groups, or what he referred to as 'folk devils'. In the case of the mods/rockers 'battles', for example, hyberbolic press coverage of the initial events sensitised the police and the public, so that future trouble was anticipated and vigilantly watched for. And – in an archetypal case of self-fulfilling prophecy – more 'mods and rockers violence' was duly spotted and vigorously dealt with by the police. The over-dramatic press reports, therefore, had fanned the sparks of an initially trivial incident, creating a self-perpetuating 'amplification spiral' which had steadily escalated the phenomenon's significance. The media coverage, moreover, 'breathed life' into the folk devils. The 'mods and rockers', Cohen argued, had initially been fairly ill-defined youth styles, but were given greater form and substance by the sensational news stories. And the two groups steadily polarized as youngsters began to identify themselves as members of either faction – the mods or the rockers.

Cohen's ideas have been widely influential, and the concept of moral panic has been applied to a broad range of social phenomena.[4] But youth culture, especially, has been a prominent focus for episodes of moral panic. As Cohen himself observed, since 1945, youth groups have 'occupied a constant position as folk devils', with a ceaseless demonology of young terrors lining up in the 'gallery of types that society erects to show its members which roles should be avoided and which should be emulated' (Cohen, 2002: 1–2).

Galleries of young folk devils also appeared beyond Britain and the US. Indeed, in 1960 the scale of concern prompted a World Health Organization report to the United Nations that spotlighted the 'New Forms of Juvenile Delinquency' seemingly sweeping the world (World Health Organization, 1960). In Australia and New Zealand anxieties focused on 'bodgies' and 'widgies' (see Chapter 2), while Katie Mooney (2005) shows how 'ducktail' youths (known for their distinctive 'ducktail' hairstyle') provoked alarm in 1950s South Africa. Across Europe the media also conjured with images of rebellious youth as it reported on groups of young people with a taste for American-style rock 'n' roll, jeans and black leather jackets. In Holland they were dubbed '*nozem*' (derived from '*penzone*', Dutch slang for 'underworld'), in Sweden '*skinnknutte*' ('leather-jackets') and in Italy '*teppisti*' ('thugs'), while historian Efi Avdela shows that in Greece fears coalesced around the spectre of young '*tediboismos*' (the English term 'Teddy boy' adapted to Greek grammar) (Avdela, 2008).

In Austria, Switzerland, and West Germany, meanwhile, the leather-jacketed '*halbstarken*' ('half-strong') were blamed for a wave of violent disorders.[5] And in France alarm surrounded the '*blousons noirs*' ('black jackets') – young, leather-clad motorcyclists who were branded by the press as dangerously delinquent due to their provocative style and raucous gatherings. Anxiety was also prompted by the large groups of young people who congregated at French coastal resorts. Perceived as antisocial gangs, they attracted considerable press coverage, as did the growing following for indigenous rock 'n' roll stars such as Johnny Hallyday and Eddy Mitchell. Matters peaked in 1963 when crowds of youngsters clashed with police after an open-air rock 'n' roll concert in Paris, events that sparked a deluge of sensational newspaper headlines.[6]

Moral panics about youth culture were, then, legion during the 1950s and 1960s.[7] In a period of profound change 'youth' became, in many countries, a symbolic focus for a broader sense of postwar apprehension. The 'youth debate' articulated widespread concerns about the direction of social change; and anxieties about the rise of consumerism, changing moral standards, and shifting class relations were all projected into visions of menacing youth. Issues of gender also loomed large. Historically, moral panics about crime and violence have tended to focus on young men. But young women have been prominent in moral panics about sexual behaviour. Marilyn Heggarty (2008), for instance, shows how wartime America saw a press outcry about 'Victory-girls' or 'V-girls' – young women whose 'free and easy' liaisons with servicemen were presented as evidence of a breakdown in national morality. And Amanda Littauer (2003) shows how similar concerns arose in the 1950s as 'Bar-Girls' or 'B-Girls' were configured as prime-movers in an upsurge of shocking vice.

And moral panics about young women and morality remain a feature of the contemporary media. Sharon Mazzarella (2020), for instance, presents a series of modern-day case-studies in which the US media has constructed girls' sexuality, sexual expression, and sexual identity as troublesome and in need of adult policing. Such episodes are, as Shayla Thiel-Stern argues, part of a long history of moral panics that 'are often tied to the feeling that the adolescent girls are not performing gender in a way that is consistent with the dominant understanding of girlhood in their own community, and this has often fostered a cultural crisis that journalists might not necessarily start but do certainly foster and perpetuate' (Thiel-Stern, 2014: 7). In these episodes of concern, issues of violence have been relatively rare, but are far from unknown. Christine Barron and Dany Lacombe (2005), for example, analyse the way the Canadian media configured a series of incidents of female violence during the late 1990s as a new, threatening 'Nasty Girl' phenomenon in a moral panic that was constituent in a broader backlash against feminism. Indeed, on occasions when young women are involved in violent crime, the media coverage is often especially damning. This intensity derives from the way female 'folk devils' are presented as – to use a phrase coined by criminologist Ann Lloyd (1995) – 'doubly deviant'. That is to say, they are condemned not only because they have broken the law but also because they have transgressed social expectations of feminine behaviour.

The 'transnational folk devil': youth, moral panic, and 'racialised others'

While Cohen highlighted the relation of moral panics to wider processes of social change, his attention to their broader political context was more limited. But an attempt to incorporate his ideas in a broad analysis of political change was elaborated in Britain during the 1970s by researchers based at Birmingham University's Centre for Contemporary Cultural Studies (CCCS). Originally founded in 1964, and headed by Stuart Hall from 1968, the CCCS produced research spanning a formidable array of themes – including the form and meaning of media texts, the structures of working-class culture, power and gender relations, and the political dimensions of racism. And, in their study *Policing the Crisis* (1978), Hall and his colleagues integrated Cohen's notion of moral panic in an expansive, Marxist-influenced analysis of shifts within British social, economic, and political life since 1945.

The 1950s and early 1960s had been, the CCCS argued, a time when Britain's steady economic growth laid the basis for a period of social and political consensus. By the mid-1960s, however, the country's economic situation had nosedived, and the basis for the postwar consensus steadily unravelled. As social and political conflict intensified, the CCCS contended, 'consensus politics' gave way to more coercive governments that were willing to rule through force. For the CCCS team, the media played a key role in securing popular acceptance of this move to a more authoritarian political order by generating a succession of moral panics – about permissiveness, vandals, student radicals, trade union agitators, and so on – that culminated in 1972 with a major furore about street crime. The news media, Hall and his colleagues argued, drew on images of the New York ghetto to construct the idea that street robberies in Britain's inner-cities represented the outbreak of a 'new' kind of violent crime – 'mugging'. For the CCCS theorists, the hysteria about 'mugging' was a classic moral panic, where the magnitude and intensity of the reaction was 'at odds with the scale of the threat to which it was a response' (Hall et al., 1978: 17). Crucially, however, they saw this panic as serving a political purpose in the way it was employed not only to justify tougher policing and more punitive sentencing, but to legitimise a more general political shift towards authoritarianism.

Policing the Crisis was an ambitious study. And, for some, it represents a landmark analysis of crime, the media, policing and the state (McLaughlin, 2008). But the study has also attracted criticism. Detractors have seen it, for example, as a superficial examination of criminal statistics and police practices (Waddington, 1986), an over-politicised and excessively deterministic model of 'moral panic' (Barker, 1992), and an over-simplification of processes of news production (Schlesinger et al., 1991). Certainly, there is room to question some of the grander claims Hall and his colleagues made for their analysis of British postwar history. Nevertheless, they made a valuable contribution in highlighting the way moral panics are often woven into a broader tapestry of shifting political relations. Moreover, the CCCS shrewdly pointed to the way issues of 'race' and racism are often prominent in moral panics. As Hall and his colleagues observed, the 'folk devils' in the 1970s mugging panic were presented not just as urban youth, but – more specifically – as *Black*, urban youth. As such, the panic drew much of its symbolic power from a long history of 'racialised Othering'. This has seen white, Western culture stigmatise ethnic 'difference' as an 'Otherness' that is configured as not only inferior and socially subordinate, but also as threatening, savage and dangerously 'alien'. And, as the CCCS team explained, the mugging moral panic gained much of its potency from the way it plugged into Britain's rich vein of racist discourse:

> The symbolization of the race-immigrant theme was resonant in its subliminal force, its capacity to set in motion the demons which haunt the collective subconscious of a superior race; it triggered off images of sex, rape, primitivism, violence and excrement.
>
> (Hall et al., 1978: 244)

And Britain is hardly alone in this respect. In the US, for example, elements of racism have figured prominently in the country's catalogue of moral panics about youth. Craig Reinarman and Harry Levine (1989i; 1989ii; 1997), for instance, argued that a deep strain of racism ran through America's drug scares of the 1980s and 1990s. While drug abuse has undoubtedly been a significant problem in the US, Reinarman and Levine suggested that media and political responses to the issue were often orchestrated attempts to engender moral panic. They contended, for instance, that concerns about 'crack' cocaine during the 1980s and 1990s were 'concocted by the press, politicians, and moral entrepreneurs to serve other agendas' (1989ii: 127). Asserting that the US crusade against 'crack' represented an exercise in scapegoating, Levine and Reinarman argued that the campaign not only appealed to 'racism, bureaucratic self-interest, economics, and mongering by the media' (1989ii: 258), but also 'allowed conservative politicians to be law-and-order minded ... [and] permitted them to give the appearance of caring about social ills without committing them to do or spend very much to help people' (1989ii: 255).[8]

The cultural critic Henry Giroux (1996, 1997, 2012) has been particularly critical of the US media's demonisation of youth – especially black youth – as a font of urban America's problems. For Giroux, media representations of African-American youth have helped promote 'a white moral panic' (1996: 97) which has not only 'reproduce[d] racist stereotypes about blacks by portraying them as criminals and welfare cheats', but has also 'remove[d] whites from any responsibility or complicity for the violence and poverty that has become so endemic to American life' (1996: 66). Moreover, like Levine and Reinarman, Giroux sees this racist stereotyping as not simply the result of prejudice, but as part of wider political strategies. Representations of African-American youth as predatory and violent, Giroux explains, have fed into 'the increasing public outcry for tougher crime bills designed to build more prisons and legislate get-tough policies with minorities of color and class' (Giroux, 1996: 67).

More recently, many researchers have highlighted the way a racialised 'Muslim Other' has become – as George Morgan and Scott Poynting put it – the preeminent 'transnational folk devil' in the Global West (2012: 1). For postcolonial theorists, the basis of this process of Othering lies deep in an imperialist past. Rather than simply referring to the period after the colonial era, the concept of postcolonialism denotes the way colonialism's discourses, power structures and social hierarchies are seen as continuing (albeit through different or new relationships) in the present day. In this respect the ideas of the Palestinian-American theorist Edward Said have been especially influential. According to Said, Western colonialism characteristically operated through 'discourses of power' that saw the non-Western world configured as the binary opposite of the West, as its Other. The West, he argued, constructed the East as its antithesis, so the East – or 'the Orient' – was defined as stagnant and unchanging, or as erotic and uncontrolled, or as oppressive and authoritarian; whereas the West presented itself as dynamic and innovatory, rational and tolerant. This discourse of 'Orientalism', Said contended, existed as a Western style of 'dominating, restructuring, and having authority over the Orient' (Said, 1978: 11).

Said's original thesis was based on an analysis of Western art during the nineteenth and early twentieth centuries, but he later (1981) discussed how modern-day Western media reproduced many Orientalist tropes in their representations of Islam, Muslims, and the Arab world. And, following events such as the first Gulf War and (especially) the 9/11 terror attacks of 2001, many other theorists pointed to the way Orientalist themes not only became more prolific in Western media, but were also more hostile and belligerent.[9] From this perspective, while incidents of terrorist violence are obviously appalling, responses from the Western media have often been highly distorted, and their constructions of Islam and Muslims – particularly *young* Muslims – have been characterised by significant elements of racialised Othering and 'Islamophobia'.

In the wake of the 9/11 terrorist attacks, Morgan and Poynting argue, the West saw the development of 'a globally constructed "radical Muslim" folk demon' (2012: 5). This, they suggest, was constituent in 'a long-term and large-scale process of Islamic moral panic' which circulated worldwide, though was given specific 'conjuncture, peculiarities and distinctiveness' in national contexts as it melded with local fears (5). Illustrative were events in Holland where, as Abdessamad Bouabid shows, a series of urban disorders in 2007 and 2010 were blamed on Moroccan-Dutch youngsters who then 'became the prime symbol of nuisance, crime and Islamic radicalization' (2016: 718). Linking with general fears about crime and youth, Bouabid argues, concerns about the disorders developed into the general perception of a 'Moroccans problem', a discourse which constructed social problems as being rooted in the culture of an ethnic Other (722).

Similar processes unfolded in Australia. Between 2000 and 2003, Martin Humphrey (2007) argues, Sydney saw a series of high-profile criminal cases involving murder and rape that were configured as an epidemic of crimes committed by Muslim youth. In the media and public debate, Humphrey contends, the crimes were constructed as a problem specifically related to young, Lebanese-Australian immigrants whose Muslim culture was presented as 'trapped by tradition' and 'incompatible with the secular West' (21). The episode, Humphrey suggests, reflected 'a convergent moral panic drawing on the global script of cultural conflict' (20). But it was a moral panic, he argues, that had particular resonance in Australia given the way immigration policy has been a key instrument in the country's traditions of nation-building and national identity. 'Becoming Australian', Humphrey suggests, means 'subordinating all minority or cultural identities to national identity' (12), and there exists a '"good migrant" / "bad migrant"' discourse that 'judges migrants according to their ability to fit in with the dominant society and achieve success' (10). In these terms, he contends, the Lebanese-Australian crime 'epidemic' was blamed on the offenders' culture and their strong attachment to Islamic values. Muslims, consequently, were judged to be 'bad migrants', and were made to symbolise the margins of Australian citizenship.

The same '"good migrant" / "bad migrant"' discourse was also pivotal to Australia's 'African gangs' scare of 2016–18 (see above). Indeed, the 'African gangs' furore can be seen as the latest instalment in a longstanding narrative that, David Nolan and his associates argue, has seen the Australian media 'focusing on African migrant communities as a "problem group" that is represented through racializing tropes and discourses' (Nolan et al., 2016: 260). While constituent in a long tradition of racist demonisation, however, the 'African gang' panic was given particular impetus by its historical context. The established prejudices and stereotypes, as Fiona MacDonald observes, merged with new fears engendered by 'the global displacement crisis' and 'increasing politicisation and backlash against immigration and multiculturalism' (2017: 1183). As MacDonald explains:

> In contemporary western societies, national and local concerns around youth violence and the formation of youth gangs have merged with global prejudices of refugees, creating new stereotypes of young male refugees as the key perpetrators of racial violence. This is particularly evident in

Australia, where the violence of ethnic youth gangs is considered more of a threat to public safety than extremist violence.

(MacDonald, 2017: 1183)

For many commentators, moreover, these fears have often served as a pretext for the introduction of more coercive measures of policing. Mandisi Majavu, for instance, argues that the Australian media's narrative of 'African gangs' has been used 'as justification for heavy surveillance, harsh sentencing … and it is further used to rationalize the vociferous calls to deport to Africa young Black Africans who break the law' (2018: 28). More generally, Morgan and Poynting argue that escalating concerns about terrorism and the threat of 'alien' Others has brought worldwide moves towards authoritarianism:

> In the post-9/11 world … the idea of collective insecurity has been used throughout the 'West' to justify the erasure of base-line national civil and cultural liberties, on the presumption that such communities indulge a sort of 'fifth column', a danger to 'our way of life', and that their communities give succour to enemies within the nation and support to enemies outside.
>
> (Morgan and Poynting, 2012: 8)

In Western societies, then, there is a long history of moral panics underpinned by constructions of racialised Others. Representations of youth have clearly figured prominently in such discourses, but the symbolism has also been distinctly gendered. As Australian sociologist Anita Harris observes, dimensions of gendered and racialised Othering have often overlain one another. While female adolescence has typically been represented as 'risky business that must be carefully negotiated', Harris argues, within this general configuration 'particular kinds of young women have been constructed as a problem for society, namely young mothers, the sexually active, and Black and Indigenous girls' (Harris, 2004: 15).

Dimensions of gendering were, indeed, apparent in constructions of the 'radical Muslim' folk devil that followed the 9/11 terror attacks. As Shiva Zarabadi and Jessica Ringrose (2018) show, in the UK a moral panic ensued in 2015 after three UK Muslim schoolgirls absconded to join Islamic State camps in Syria. And, in the media coverage that followed, there was a shift in dominant constructions of Muslim femininity. While Muslim women and girls had previously been prevalently represented as docile, submissive and 'perennially oppressed by the mass of Muslim men/Islam/culture', Zarabadi and Ringrose argue that media treatment of the runaway schoolgirls saw the emergence of a 'new category of religioned femininity' – the 'Jihadi Bride' (Zarabadi and Ringrose, 2018: 85). The media's representation of the 'Jihadi Bride', they contend, represented the affective birth of a 'new "risky sexualized other"':

> … a potentially suspicious and risky figure, salacious to the public appetite as news headlines debate whether jihadi brides are willing participants or hapless victims. Are they 'desiring subjects' or 'seduced' subjects?

This ambiguity is horrifying, as both signify desire and agency in relation to the radicalization panic, enabling the mobilization of powerful desires to unveil and uncover the truth of Muslim femininity and sexuality.

(Zarabadi and Ringrose, 2018: 102)

Moral panics updated

Since the 1970s many authors have sought to update and refine Cohen's original moral panics thesis. The contribution of Erich Goode and Nachman Ben-Yehuda is especially noteworthy. In *Moral Panics: The Social Construction of Deviance* (2011) Goode and Ben-Yehuda make an important differentiation between moral panics, social problems, and moral crusades. Social problems, they argue, differ to moral panics because they lack folk devils or wild fluctuations of concern, while moral crusades are distinct campaigns initiated by particular interest groups or moral entrepreneurs. And, for Goode and Ben-Yehuda, moral panics are specifically defined by five clear criteria. Concern, hostility, consensus, and volatility are all important attributes but, they suggest, a dimension of *disproportionality* is especially crucial – by definition, they argue, moral panics are disproportionate reactions to perceived threats.

Critics such as criminologist Peter Waddington (1986), however, suggest the way moral panic theorists use notions of 'disproportionality' can be highly selective. From this position there is room to question the basis on which societal reactions to an event are judged to be 'disproportionate'. Such pronouncements, critics argue, might simply reflect the personal values of a theorist. Additionally, while Cohen's analysis neatly highlighted the media's role in creating social phenomena and escalating their impact, it had less to say about what the events meant for those involved. Indeed, Cohen was well aware of this omission. In the introduction to his study of the 1960s mods and rockers, Cohen acknowledged that the youngsters themselves were 'hardly going to appear as "real, live people" at all'. 'They will be seen', he explained, 'through the eyes of societal reaction and in this reaction they tend to appear as disembodied objects, Rorshach blots onto which reactions are projected' (Cohen, 2002: 15).

Subsequently, however, a wealth of research has focused on the experience of the 'Rorshach blots', many researchers exploring the meanings and attitudes held by groups of young people configured by the media as 'folk devils' (see Chapter 6). Sarah Thornton, however, is critical of moral panic theorists' tendency to present 'folk devils' as simply the 'innocent victims of negative stigmatisation' (Thornton, 1995: 136). Instead, Thornton shows how the opprobrium of a moral panic 'baptizes transgression', with folk devils often 'relish[ing] the attention conferred by media condemnation' (Thornton, 1995: 181). Some folk devils, she argues, actually embrace their lawless reputation, lapping up the infamy, so that 'although negative reporting is disparaged, it is subject to anticipation, even aspiration' (Thornton, 1995: 135).[10]

Other criticisms have also been levelled at the notion of moral panic. Writers such as Ian Taylor (1981), for example, have warned that simply dismissing fears of crime and violence as spurious 'moral panics' not only devalues 'ordinary' people's experiences of these phenomena, but also creates a political vacuum open to exploitation by a reactionary 'law and order' lobby. And historian John Springhall (1998) voices reservations about attempts to 'debunk' sensational crime stories by stressing historical precedent along the lines of 'there's nothing really new about all this'. Such responses, he argues, risk sliding into an academic condescension that shows insufficient regard for genuinely held fears and concerns (Springhall, 1998: 8). While sensitive to these issues, Cohen himself argued that highlighting the media's role in constructing a social problem does not necessarily question the problem's existence; nor does it dismiss issues of causation, prevention, and control. Rather, he suggested, it reveals the way media discourse gives particular meanings to the problem and 'draws attention to a meta debate about what sort of acknowledgement the problem receives and merits' (Cohen, 2002: xxxiv).

Since the 1970s, however, shifts in the structure and operation of the media have led some theorists to suggest Cohen's original theories require major revision. Both Angela McRobbie (1994) and Sarah Thornton (1994; 1995), for example, have suggested that the classic moral panics model operates with an excessively monolithic view of the media. Compared to the 1960s and 1970s, they argue, the modern media have become more diverse and fragmented, and are composed of a 'multiplicity of voices, which compete and contest the meaning of the issues subject to "moral panic"' (McRobbie and Thornton, 1995: 560). In their analyses of the moral panics surrounding Britain's dance music and 'acid house' scenes of the late 1980s and 1990s, for example, McRobbie and Thornton contended that account needed to be given to the 'plurality of reactions, each with their different constituencies, effectivities and modes of discourse' (McRobbie and Thornton, 1995: 564). The 'classic' notion of moral panic, they argued, failed to distinguish the array of different media responses to the 'acid house' scene. And they especially highlighted the way the mainstream media's scare-mongering was challenged by alternative accounts offered in the 'micro' and 'niche' media that had mushroomed during the 1980s and 1990s – grass-roots fanzines, for example, that had 'tracked the tabloids' every move, reprinted whole front pages, analysed their copy and decried the *misrepresentation* of Acid House' (McRobbie and Thornton, 1995: 568).

Written in the 1990s, McRobbie and Thornton's account obviously predates the rise of the Internet and the explosion of social media. Developments which have meant, as Morgan and Poynting argue, 'moral panics have become compressed both temporally and spatially, so that they are now global and virtually instantaneous' (Morgan and Poynting, 2012: 5). At the same time, however, the proliferation of online news sources has extended the universe of 'micro' and 'niche' media identified by McRobbie and Thornton. Indeed, new legions of Internet bloggers, activists and 'citizen journalists' can now engage with a moral panic and contest the narrative of events presented by politicians and mainstream media.

By the same token, however, the spread of social media has also opened the gates for a flood of crackpot scare-stories and conspiracy theories, along with a wealth of 'fake news' propagated by both governments and interest groups. All of which may work to instigate and intensify moral panics in a time characterised by some commentators as the era of 'post-truth'.[11] Moreover, according to some theorists, the use of news derived from social media can, for some audiences, simply act as a 'bubble' or 'echo chamber'. That is to say, rather than engaging with a plurality of different news sources, some users of social media may simply seek out information that reinforces their preconceived views.[12] So, while some forms of online 'niche' media might work to dispute and dissipate episodes of exaggerated alarm, others can reinforce existing prejudices and fuel moral panics. Furthermore, as Charles Critcher has ruefully observed, despite the cacophony of different voices heard in the contemporary media, some remain considerably louder and more powerful than others, and '[w]hen the police, the tabloid press and the governing party conjoin in the concerted campaign, the weak power base of the alternative media is revealed' (Critcher, 2000: 154).

Nonetheless, with the proliferation of different news sources, greater space is often given to agencies, experts and pressure groups to challenge moral panics and 'folk devil' stereotypes. And the concept of 'moral panic' has, itself, begun to inform journalistic discourse and public debate. For instance, amid the variety of views and perspectives that circulated around Melbourne's 'African gangs' furore of 2018 (see above), journalist Calla Wahlquist recounted how a local community worker voiced concern that the episode was becoming 'a racialised moral panic' (Wahlquist, 2018). The remark neatly illustrates the way that, as Cohen himself observed in 2002, contemporary episodes of moral panic have seen the media become more self-reflective in their coverage, so that 'the same public and media discourse that provides the raw evidence of moral panic [also] uses the concept as first-order description, reflexive comment or criticism' (Cohen, 2002: vii).[13]

Uncertainty, risk, and the 'culture of fear'

Moral panics have, for some theorists, become a more prevalent feature of modern life. Kenneth Thompson (1998), for example, has suggested that moral panics should no longer be seen as isolated, sporadic incidents, but as part of a wider, more integrated social and political condition of sustained anxiety. In a similar vein, Angela McRobbie and Sarah Thornton argued that, far from occurring from 'time to time', moral panics have become:

> … a standard response, a familiar, sometimes weary, even ridiculous rhetoric rather than an exceptional emergency intervention. Used by politicians to orchestrate consent, by business to promote sales in certain niche markets, and by the media to make home and social affairs news-worthy, moral panics are constructed on a daily basis.
>
> (McRobbie and Thornton, 1995: 560)

This escalation of moral panics may be constituent in what some critics see as an increasingly pervasive sense of uncertainty and risk in contemporary societies. Indeed, while threats and danger have always been a factor in human experience, theorists such as Anthony Giddens (1999) and Ulrich Beck (1992; 1999) argue that a more heightened awareness of real and perceived risk has become a pronounced feature of modern life. For Giddens, the erosion of Western traditions and religion, combined with the technological, political-economic, and social changes associated with globalisation, has fundamentally altered the appreciation of risk. This is not to say that life has become inherently 'more risky' but, Giddens argues, risk has increasingly become a strategic organising principle that guides both individual and institutional thinking as society becomes more preoccupied with the future and its safety.

Ulrich Beck also drew attention to the collapse of certainty and stability in the modern world. In *Risk Society* (published in German in 1986 and translated into English in 1992), Beck argued that the West was undergoing an epochal transformation, with the certainties of industrial modernity giving way to a new, less predictable era. In this context, Beck suggested, people had been confronted by the pervasive risks unintentionally generated by the processes of modernisation – these risks operating not only at a global level (for instance, the threat of nuclear war or environmental disaster) but also at the level of everyday personal life. Beck acknowledged these hazards were unequally spread among social groups (their distribution arranged in a fashion similar to the inequalities of a class society), but he argued that class ties had steadily weakened. In a more 'individualised' world, Beck contended, people increasingly had to rely on themselves as they negotiated the challenges of day-to-day living. Arguably, these changes have registered particularly on the young, and many commentators have pointed to the way young people face a world in which their life experiences – in terms of family structure, educational opportunities, and routes to employment – have become beset by uncertainty and risk.[14]

And, for some observers, a corollary to growing perceptions of social unpredictability has been an increasingly pervasive sense of fear. British-Hungarian theorist Frank Furedi, for example, argues that fear now virtually represents a pathology in itself. In his book *Culture of Fear* (originally published in 1997 and revised in 2006), Furedi draws on Beck's ideas of the 'risk society' to argue that, with the growing prevalence of uncertainty, fear has become one of the most distinctive features of contemporary society. Where once fear had a tangible quality and clear sense of focus, Furedi argues, it now has 'an unpredictable and free-floating character':

> One day we fear gun-crime, a week later our attention is drawn to carjacking only to be distracted the next month by the epidemic of happy slapping. In contemporary times, fear migrates freely from one problem to the next without there being a necessity for causal or logical connection.
>
> (Furedi, 2006: 4)

A similar condition is charted by US sociologist Barry Glassner in his book *The Culture of Fear* (2018). For Glassner fear has become ubiquitous in modern

America, with a growing perception that dangers are everywhere. For Glassner, however, these dangers are often exaggerated by a media desperate to attract audiences, and by politicians eager for public support and voter-appeal. As a consequence, Glassner argues, social attention focuses on 'unlikely but sensational threats', while more widespread problems – for example, poverty and economic inequality – go unaddressed (Glassner, 2018: i).

Originally published in 1999, Glassner's book was revised and updated in 2018. Overall, he found that relatively little had changed and 'Americans remain inordinately fearful of unlikely dangers' (Glassner, 2018: ii). Yet, in the wake of the 9/11 terror attacks and the election of President Trump in 2016, Glassner noted how the culture of fear had seen a few key shifts. Most notably, he observed, 'foreign terrorists and immigrants have replaced domestic bogeymen as the principal figures in fearmongering by politicians and in much of the media' (2018: ii). But youth, he added, had become an especially enduring bogeyman. While the reality of youth crime is often unspectacular, Glassner explained, it is routinely magnified to nightmare proportions:

> We have managed to convince ourselves that just about every young American male is a potential mass murderer – a remarkable achievement, considering the steep downward trend in youth crime throughout the 1990s. Faced year after year with comforting statistics, we either ignore them – adult Americans estimate that people under eighteen commit about half of all violent crimes when the actual number is 13 per cent – or recast them as 'The Lull Before the Storm' (*Newsweek* headline).
>
> (Glassner, 2018: 3)

Modernity's 'panacea': positive archetypes of youth

Representations of youth, however, have never been exclusively negative. Alongside the moral panics and malevolent stereotypes, there have always co-existed more positive media constructions in which young people are presented as the vibrant vanguard of a prosperous future. Indeed, at certain historical moments, media images of youth as a social 'panacea' have eclipsed the darker, more apprehensive iconography of youth as a 'pathology'. In the US during the early 1960s, for example, positive images of youth came to the fore as young people were celebrated as an invigorating social force. Ideals of 'youth', for instance, were powerfully mobilised by President Kennedy in both his public persona and in his vision of America's 'New Frontier' of progress and optimism.[15] And, as earlier concerns about juvenile crime diminished, young people were fêted by the media and consumer industries and 'youth' became enshrined as the signifier of a newly prosperous age of freedom and fun.

Above all, it was the concept of the 'teenager' that embodied this positive, uplifting iconography. In some quarters 'teenage' culture was derided as the worst example of commercial massification (see Chapter 6). But, more widely, the teenager was cast in radiant terms. The trend began in the 1950s, but picked up pace in the early 1960s as teenagers were configured as harbingers of a new consumer culture – a social group distinguished not simply by their youth, but by a particular style of conspicuous, leisure-oriented consumption. This, of course, was a 'mythic' construction – and 'real' teenagers' lives remained characterised by marked inequalities of wealth and power (see Chapter 2). But in media and advertising rhetoric, the 'teenager' was promoted as an essentially classless avatar of pleasure and abundance. Here, historian Kirse May (2002) shows, images of Californian youth culture took the lead. During the early 1960s, the Golden State – home to surfing, hot rods, and bouncy pop groups like the Beach Boys – set the pace for America's 'New Frontier' in teenage leisure and pleasure. These, then, were archetypes of 'well-behaved, well-meaning, middle-class teenagers', with films, TV series, and pop records all packaging California's kids as 'a beautiful and wholesome generation living it up on the coast' (May, 2002: 119).

In Britain, too, the early 1960s saw the media project a positive imagery of youth. Newspapers, magazines, and films all popularised notions of young people as a vibrant contrast to the tired conventions of the past. And, as in America, the term 'teenager' did not simply denote a generational age group, but signified a new brand of liberated, hedonistic consumption. As writer Peter Laurie contended in his taxonomy of *The Teenage Revolution*, published in 1965:

> The distinctive fact about teenagers' behaviour is economic: they spend a lot of money on clothes, records, concerts, make-up, magazines: all things that give immediate pleasure and little lasting use.
>
> (Laurie, 1965: 9)

Consumer pleasure in an age of swinging modernity, then, was the central theme in configurations of the 1960s 'teenager'. It was hardly surprising, therefore, that politicians sought to capitalise on youth's dynamic aura. In 1964, for example, The Beatles were acclaimed by Sir Alec Douglas Home, Britain's prime minister, as 'our best exports' and 'a useful contribution to the balance of payments' (Davies, 1978: 222). Harold Wilson, his successor, was not to be outdone and in 1965 invested The Beatles as Members of the Order of the British Empire (a prestigious honour).

Even the mod 'folk devils' could be embraced in the 1960s celebration of youth. Indeed, at the same time as they were reviled as the *bête noire* of the affluent society (see above), Britain's mods were also hailed as stylish consumers *par excellence*. Superficially clean-cut and well-dressed, mods were often treated as the pace-setters of 1960s élan, the press eagerly charting changes in the minutiae of their fashion and music. Even in 1964, at the height of the moral panic about the mods and rockers 'battles', the *Sunday Times Magazine* (then an arbiter of fashionable chic) featured a sumptuous photospread spotlighting the mods' sartorial flair.[16] The association between youth and liberated modernity reached its apex in the mid-1960s when the image of 'Swinging London' – with its throbbing nightclubs and fashionable boutiques – encapsulated ideas of thrilling consumer freedom. The images resonated in both Europe and

America, where British cultural exports such as Beatlemania, mod style, and Mary Quant's fashion designs won an enthusiastic reception, and *Time* magazine's 1966 cover story on 'London: The Swinging City' captured the sense of excitement. 'Youth is the word and the deed in London', *Time* enthused, 'seized by change, liberated by affluence ... everything new, uninhibited and kinky is blooming at the top of London life' (*Time*, 15 April 1966).

By the end of the decade, however, the positive vibe was faltering. In the US, the mid-1960s saw the economy start to stumble, and liberal optimism gradually crumbled in the face of urban disorder and the quagmire of the Vietnam War. Against this backdrop, the iconography of youthful high-spirits began giving way to more negative representations of youth – with students and countercultural radicals attracting particular media venom. At the same time, however, the counterculture was also a source of fascination. Indeed, its libertine ethos of self-expression proved widely attractive at a time when cultural values were rapidly changing. Hence the fashions and attitudes of the counterculture all percolated into the social mainstream. In fact, rather than representing the antithesis of modern consumerism, the 1960s counterculture is better seen as playing a part in its evolution. As writer Thomas Frank suggests, the counterculture was not the nemesis of the consumer society but 'may be more accurately understood as a stage in the development of the values of the American middle class, a colorful instalment in the twentieth century drama of consumer subjectivity' (Frank, 1997: 120). For advertisers, especially, the countercultural scene offered images of 'youthful' pleasure and freedom commensurate with consumerist agendas. As one American adman affirmed in a 1968 editorial for *Merchandising Week*: 'Everywhere our mass media push psychedelia with all its clothing fads, so-called "way-out" ideas etc. Youth is getting the hard sell' (cited in Frank, 1997: 120).[17]

In Britain, as in the US, the 1960s counterculture attracted its share of opprobrium. The counterculture's overtly political elements attracted particular ire. Responses, however, were not uniformly negative. As in America, the counterculture's aesthetics and lifestyles elicited fascination, sympathy, even a degree of media admiration. The attitude was exemplified by reactions to The Rolling Stones' drugs trial of 1967. Amid a blaze of publicity, the Stones' frontmen, Keith Richards and Mick Jagger, were convicted and sentenced to three months' imprisonment for possession of illegal drugs (though both walked free after an appeal). Rather than denouncing the Stones, however, significant sections of the media rallied to their defence. Famously, *The Times* published an editorial asking 'Who Breaks a Butterfly on a Wheel?' – the newspaper defending Jagger and Richards and attacking their prison sentences as draconian (*The Times*, 1 July, 1967).

And a similar enthusiasm for youth resurfaced in Britain 30 years later. In the 1990s the buzzing phrase 'Cool Britannia' was coined by the media to denote what was seen as a renaissance in British art, fashion, design, and music. But the term also encapsulated the broader sense of a nation newly invigorated in the wake of the election of Tony Blair's ('New') Labour government in 1997.

In this imagery of a revitalised Britain, notions of 'youth' had particular reso-nance. National rejuvenation had been a key theme in Blair's electioneering, the Labour leader promising that his government would 'make this the young country of my generation's dreams'. And, as prime minister, Blair – much like Harold Wilson during the 1960s – strove to attach himself to the upbeat cachet of youth culture. Blair, for example, enjoyed photo opportunities with the all-girl pop group the Spice Girls, while Noel Gallagher (boisterous singer with the rock band Oasis) was invited to a reception at Downing Street, and Alan McGee (founder of Creation Records, a leading indie label) was appointed as a special advisor to the government's Creative Industries Task Force (CITF) – a body where government ministers and leading media figures joined forces to map out the economic potential of Britain's creative industries.[18]

'Girl power' as the epitome of enterprise

During the early twenty-first century positive symbolic codings of youth were also conspicuous. Notions of a new generation of tech-savvy 'digital natives', for instance, were often characterised by positive stereotypes that cast youth as the cutting-edge of technologically-driven progress (see Chapter 3). Some theorists also highlighted the way representations of youth were prominent in discourses of neoliberalism and capitalist enterprise. Mayssoun Sukarieh and Stuart Tannock, for example, argued that in the wake of the global financial crisis of 2007–8 concerns about a jobless 'lost generation' were accompanied by a more positive configuration of youth as the essence of economic recovery. Agencies such as the World Bank, they suggested, mobilised images of 'youthful' creativity and entrepreneurialism in their promotion of neoliberal agendas. 'The competence, strengths and maturity of youth', Sukarieh and Tannock contended:

> … are emphasized and celebrated, as grounds for pulling young people into the workforce, opening up the spheres of education and youth development to market forces and business interests, promoting the ideol-ogy of neoliberalism among the young and undermining the traditional entitlements of welfare state provision.
>
> (Sukarieh and Tannock, 2015: 24)

For many researchers, moreover, contemporary archetypes that posit youth as a positive social force are distinguished by a pronounced gendering. Angela McRobbie, for instance has suggested that, rather than youth in general, it is increasingly young women who have become 'a metaphor for social change' (McRobbie, 2000: 201). Anita Harris concurs, arguing that since the early 1990s media representations of young femininity have been dominated by two key tropes – the '"at risk" girl' and the '"can-do" girl'. The '"at risk" girl' is conceived as a font of social problems, with an errant lifestyle that undermines her career opportunities and leaves her vulnerable to personal harm. Crucially, however, this situation is configured as the consequence of the individual's life decisions rather than of a wider socio-economic context so that, Harris argues, 'structural disadvantage is recast as poor personal choices, laziness and poor family practices' (2004: 25). This representation of young femininity, furthermore, is often simplistically correlated with issues of class and ethnicity, so that 'Blackness and poverty ... are seen to somehow cause young women to be willful, wanton and stupid' (2004: 30). Against this, however, stands the positive configuration of the '"can-do" girl'. Here, femininity is represented in terms of 'successful, individualized girlhood' (20), with archetypal '"can-do" girls' being distinguished by their 'commitment to exceptional careers and career planning, belief in their capacity to invent themselves and succeed, and their display of consumer lifestyle' (14).

Harris, moreover, argues that these dual constructions of young femininity 'stand for a number of hopes and concerns about late modernity' (14). The prevalence of these media archetypes, she suggests, is linked to the rise of a 'risk society' (see above) in which success and failure is dominantly presented as not the outcome of structural inequalities but as the outcome of an individual's own abilities to navigate their way through a world of increasing uncertainty. For Harris, then, the image of the '"can-do" girl' epitomises 'the ideal late modern subject ... one who is flexible, individualized, resilient, self-driven, and self-made and who easily follows nonlinear trajectories to fulfillment and success' (16).

A similar theme is explored by Marnina Gonick (2006). Again, Gonick argues that representations of young femininity during the early twenty-first century have become dominated by two contrasting tropes – dubbed by Gonick 'Reviving Ophelia' and 'Girl Power'. 'Reviving Ophelia' is akin to Harris's archetype of the '"at risk" girl'.[19] Here, young femininity is represented as a problematic cause of moral concern, with girls configured as 'vulnerable, voiceless, and fragile' (199). 'Girl Power', on the other hand, denotes a more positive version of girlhood, one that is 'assertive, dynamic, and unbound from the constraints of passive femininity' (199). For Gonick, this 'Girl Power' motif first proliferated in popular culture during the early 1990s, exemplified by the models of independent femininity elaborated in movies such as *Charlie's Angels* (2000) and *Crouching Tiger, Hidden Dragon* (2000), and TV series such as *Buffy The Vampire Slayer* (1997–2003) and *Xena: Warrior Princess* (1995–2001). But, for Gonick, the theme was especially exemplified by the Spice Girls, the British, all-girl group who scaled the heights of pop stardom as their 1996 single, 'Wannabe', topped the charts of 27 countries. Recruited, modelled, and marketed by record company moguls, in many respects the Spice Girls were a conventional product of the pop industry. But, under their feisty slogan 'Girl Power', the group recast many of the qualities of pop femininity and elaborated a version of feminine identity that (in some respects, at least) seemed independent and empowered. According to Gonick, however, the 'Girl Power' and 'Reviving Ophelia' archetypes effectively worked in tandem to promote an identity commensurate with the demands of an increasingly 'individualised' neoliberal society. As Gonick puts it:

> My argument is that both Girl Power and Reviving Ophelia participate in the production of the neoliberal girl subject with the former representing the idealized form of the self-determining individual and the latter personifying an anxiety about those who are unsuccessful in producing themselves in this way.
>
> (Gonick, 2006:199)

McRobbie (2004, 2008) also highlighted the way notions of agency and 'Girl Power' were effectively depoliticised in a popular, 'post-feminist' discourse which, she argued, presented gendered inequalities as a thing of the past and cast successful young women as the standard-bearers of neoliberal individualism. And a similar link between idealised archetypes of young femininity and the values of neoliberal capitalism was identified by Ofra Koffman and Rosalind Gill in their (2014) analysis of the rhetoric surrounding global development. For Koffman and Gill, a prominent feature of global development discourse of the early twenty-first century was the 'Girl Effect'. That is to say, global charities and development agencies such as UNESCO, UNICEF, and the WHO, along with many transnational corporations, have increasingly shifted their investment strategies in order to improve the economic opportunities of young women in developing countries (242). Regardless of the actual impact such schemes may have, Koffman and Gill argue, what stands out is the way they borrow and mobilise the discourses of 'girl power' and popular feminism that have circulated in the West since the early 1990s. This 'girl-powering' of development discourse, they suggest, has seen a set of contrasting constructions in which of girls of the Global North are presented as 'empowered, postfeminist subjects', while those in the Global South as are configured as 'downtrodden victims of patriarchal values' (243). This duality, Koffman and Gill suggest, not only elaborates a racist caricature of the developing world as 'a homogeneous sphere plagued by harmful cultural practices' (254), but also – by promoting individualism and entrepreneurialism as the solution to poverty – obscures the way inequality is rooted in social, economic, and political power structures. In these terms, then, the idealised representations of young femininity that underpin the 'Girl Effect' are marked by a very selective uptake of feminism that:

> ... yokes discourses of girl power, individualism, entrepreneurialism and consumerism together with rhetorics of 'revolution' in a way that – perhaps paradoxically – renders invisible the inequalities, uneven power relations and structural features of neoliberal capitalism that produce the very global injustices that the Girl Effect purports to challenge.
>
> (243–244)

Clearly, then, representations of youth continue to serve as an important symbolic register for wider social and political discourses. Often, young people are reviled as the incarnation of malevolent forces menacing established ways of life – but, in some contexts, they are also lauded as the embodiment of growth and progress. At the same time, however, it is possible to overplay this polarity. Indeed, sometimes – perhaps increasingly – the two configurations have overlapped and co-existed in media representations of youth that seem blurred and contradictory. This ambivalence has been especially evident in debates about the media's possible 'effects' on young audiences, where young people have been cast as *both* innocent victims *and* potential villains. This debate is examined in detail in the following chapter.

Notes

1 See, for example, Clarke et al. 1976; Davis, 1990, Lesko, 2001 and Smith et al. 1975.
2 Teddy boys were so-called because their style of tapered trousers and long jackets seemed redolent of Edwardian fashions – 'Ted' being a diminutive version of 'Edward'.
3 Cohen credits his colleague, Jock Young with the first published use of the term 'moral panic', and suggests that they both drew inspiration for the concept from the ideas of Canadian media theorist Marshall McLuhan (Cohen, 2002: xxxv).
4 A thorough review of the concept of moral panic and several case-studies of its application can be found in Krinsky (ed.) (2013).
5 See Poiger (2000: 71–105) and Grotum (1994).
6 Warne (2006) provides a historical survey of moral panics about youth culture in postwar France.
7 For anthologies of studies dealing with more recent moral panics about young people, see Critcher et al. (eds) (2013), Hier (ed.) (2011), and Krinsky (ed.) (2008).
8 Reeves and Campbell (1994) also provide an incisive account of the political dimensions to moral panics about drug abuse in the US during the 1980s.
9 See, for example, Ahmed and Matthes (2017), Bonn (2010), Poole and Richardson (2006), Poynting et al. (2004) and Welch (2006).
10 Motorcycle gangs, for example, have long delighted in their 'folk devil' reputation. See Osgerby (2020).
11 For critical overviews of the concepts of 'fake news' and 'post-truth' see Farkas and Schou (2019) and McIntyre (2018). Corner (2017) also provides a valuable review of related literature.
12 Studies of social media's 'echo chamber' effect include Bakshy et al. (2015) and Lawrence et al. (2010). Some researchers, however, are critical of the concept of the social media 'echo chamber'. See, for example, Baberá et al. (2015) and Dubois and Blank (2018).
13 See also Altheide (2009).
14 See, for instance, Ceislik and Pollock (2002), Davis (1999), Furlong and Cartmel (1997) and Williams et al. (2003).
15 For a discussion of the aura of 'youthful' idealism that surrounded the Kennedy Presidency, see Hellmann (1997: 105).
16 Robert Freeman and Kathleen Halton, 'Changing Faces', *Sunday Times Magazine*, 2 August, 1964, 12–19.
17 Heath and Potter (2004) also highlight the way counterculture figured in the development of modern consumerism.
18 By the end of the 1990s, however, the 'Cool Britannia' bubble had burst. Disillusioned with what they saw as the Labour Party's failure to deliver on promises to help young people and the poor, the grandees of British pop turned on the

government. Noel Gallagher professed shame at having accepted his invitation to Downing Street, while Alan McGee angrily quit the CITF.

19 Gonick derives the term 'Reviving Ophelia' from *Reviving Ophelia: Saving the Selves of Adolescent Girls* (1994) – a best-selling book by US psychologist Mary Pipher, which deployed the character of Ophelia (from Shakespeare's play, *Hamlet*) as a personification of what Pipher saw as a generalised crisis in contemporary girlhood.

5 Media effects and youth
A crucible of controversy

Young people and the 'media effects' debate

On 16 April 2007, Virginia Polytechnic Institute became the site of what was then the worst school shooting in US history. That morning 23-year-old student Seung-Hui Cho began a killing spree by shooting dead two young women in a college dorm. He then mailed a rambling 'manifesto' to the TV station NBC, and enclosed a collection of videos of himself ranting and posing with weapons. Two hours later, armed with two pistols, he entered the university. Chaining the exit doors shut, he then stalked the rooms, leaving a trail of 30 dead faculty and students, and 17 wounded. Within nine minutes police had arrived on the scene but, as they entered the building, Cho killed himself with a gunshot to the head.

What became known as the 'Virginia Tech' shooting was indicative of the way mass killings had become a depressingly regular feature of American life. But the event was also significant for the way it became a focus for the general controversy surrounding the media's impact on young audiences. Indeed, within hours of the Virginia Tech massacre (even before the name of the perpetrator had been released), several pundits had suggested violent video games were an influence on the killer. For example, Jack Thompson, a Florida lawyer and anti-video game campaigner, blamed video games for teaching children to kill, while Dr. Phil McGraw (better known as 'Dr. Phil' on his long-running TV talk-show) asserted that video games and other violent media were turning young people into mass murderers (Ferguson, 2013i: 121).

Others, however, were more circumspect. Indeed, the report of the panel commissioned by the Virginia state governor to investigate the killings seemed to exonerate video games. Cho, the report found, had not been a keen video gamer. He had sometimes played the (fairly benign) game *Sonic the Hedgehog*, but he had relatively little interest in 'violent' media. As the review panel explained, Cho 'was enrolled in a Tae Kwon Do program for a while, watched TV and played video games like *Sonic the Hedgehog*. None of the video games were war games or had violent themes' (Virginia Tech Review Panel, 2007: 32). What may have played a bigger part in Cho's behaviour, some commentators suggested, was his long history of mental illness. Nevertheless, in some quarters, the notion remains entrenched that 'violent' media are an important cause of aggression and real-world violence. In 2018, for example, none other than President Trump told reporters that he was 'hearing more and more people say the level of violence on video games is really shaping young people's thoughts', and the following year (in the wake of a spate of horrific mass shootings) the President opined, 'We must stop the glorification of violence in our society ... This includes the gruesome and grisly video games that are now commonplace' (cited in Griffin, 2019).

This chapter examines the controversies surrounding the media's impact on young audiences. It begins with a survey of the history of popular fears that cast the media as a negative influence on young people – from Victorian 'penny dreadful' novels to the Internet. These popular fears have been paralleled by an extensive body of social scientific research suggesting a causal relationship between 'violent' media and aggressive behaviour by the young, and the chapter charts the development of this tradition of 'media effects' research. This tradition has many proponents, but it has also been challenged by numerous theorists, and the chapter surveys the chief criticisms made of 'effects' research, its assumptions, methodologies, and conclusions. Discussion then proceeds to the concept of 'media panics', and the way recurring alarm has surrounded new developments in media technology and their impact on the young. Such episodes, it is argued, are rooted in fear of challenges to existing power structures and relationships, and represent attempts to define social values and impose cultural authority. The chapter concludes with a review of growing anxieties about young people's apparent 'addiction' to video games. Focusing on the development of this discourse in South Korea and China, the chapter considers how far concerns about 'video game addiction' mark a meaningful response to dangerous 'media effects', or represent the latest wave of 'media panic'.

'Your kids might be ready to explode': popular fears of media influence on the young

Anxieties about the perceived negative impact of popular culture on young people have a long history. Successive scares have cited different forms of commercial entertainment as a corrupting influence on the young. In Britain, as John Springhall (1998) shows, the Victorian era saw moral crusaders link an apparent rise in juvenile crime to the popularity of sensationalist 'penny gaff' theatres and 'penny dreadful' novels. In the US lurid 'dime' and 'half-dime' novels attracted similar criticism during the late nineteenth century. Consequently, they were targeted by campaigners such as Anthony Comstock who ensured the passage of the Federal Anti-Obscenity (or 'Comstock') Law of 1873, which suppressed the circulation of popular fiction and allowed for the arrest of publishers of 'pernicious literature'.[1] During the 1920s and 1930s gangster films attracted similar controversy. Hollywood was accused of delivering impressionable youth into a career of crime through depicting mobsters as glamorous and exciting, and in both America and Europe many gangster movies were either censored or banned outright.

In the US, anxieties about the 'corruption' of youth by popular entertainment reached a crescendo during the 1950s. In 1953 concerns about rising levels of juvenile crime prompted the appointment of a Senate Subcommittee to investigate the causes of delinquency (see Chapter 4). The Subcommittee considered the role of various factors, though the possible influence of the media was a recurring preoccupation. Testimony was heard from a parade of moral campaigners, including the influential psychologist Frederic Wertham, whose 1954 study, *Seduction of the Innocent*, presented popular 'horror' and 'crime' comics as a wellspring of juvenile depravity. The Subcommittee's findings, however, were inconclusive. Scrutinizing the comics industry, followed by TV and Hollywood, the Senate hearings found little evidence of a clear link between the media and juvenile crime. Nevertheless, while the clamor for federal censorship was resisted, the Subcommittee demanded the media exercise stricter self-supervision and the call was generally acceded to. Hence comic publishers adopted a severe, self-regulatory Comics Code in 1954 that proscribed any content dealing with 'shocking' or 'sensational' subjects. Concerns about the negative impact of comics on young readers also circulated worldwide. And, throughout the 1950s, fears similar to those in the US melded with local anxieties to fuel anti-comics crusades in at least 20 countries across 4 continents.[2]

Fears that comics were a cause of youth crime dissipated during the 1960s. But a succession of anxieties about other media took their place. In Britain, for example, the early 1980s saw the tabloid press spearhead a campaign against what were dubbed 'video nasties' – a loosely defined group of gory, low-budget, American and Italian horror films that included *The Texas Chainsaw Massacre* (1974), *I Spit on Your Grave* (1978) and *Cannibal Holocaust* (1980). Available via (then new-fangled) video rental stores, the accessibility of such movies on VHS tapes was relatively unregulated, and critics construed their popularity would lead inexorably to a rise in violent crime. As a consequence, the introduction of the 1984 Video Recordings Act made British film censorship laws some of the toughest in Europe.[3] In 1993, however, fears revived after a 2-year-old boy, James Bulger, was murdered in Liverpool by two 10-year-olds, Robert Thompson and Jon Venables. The murder was horrific, and made all the more shocking by the youth of the perpetrators. Subsequent accounts suggested the killers' troubled childhoods lay at the root of their behaviour[4] but, at the time, the press speculated that the young killers had been influenced by violent horror movies – especially *Child's Play 3* (1991), a film depicting a malevolent doll's spree of cruelty. There was, it later transpired, little evidence to show the young killers had ever seen the film. But the campaign against 'video nasties' was recharged, with tabloid newspaper *The Sun* organising a public burning of copies of *Child's Play 3* and urging its readers: 'For the Sake of ALL Our Kids: BURN YOUR VIDEO NASTY' (26 November, 1993).

In response to the episode, the British government commissioned child psychologist Elizabeth Newsom to investigate the media's influence on the young. Subsequently published as *Video Violence and the Protection of Children* (1994), Newsom's study seemed to be a watershed in debates about the media's effects on youth. Her report purported to demonstrate conclusively that 'violent' media caused young people to behave violently. Newsom's analysis claimed to be based on considerable empirical evidence, and to draw on a wealth of scholarly expertise – and it prompted a further tightening of Britain's (already relatively strict) censorship laws. On close inspection, however, Newsom's study proved less than convincing. In systematic critiques, media theorists Martin Barker (2001) and Guy Cumberbatch (2002) both showed Newsom's work to be largely speculation based on an uncritical survey of assorted press stories, while none of the 25 'experts' she cited had actually published work in the field of media analysis.

In the US a comparable controversy unfolded following the tragedy at Columbine High School in Colorado on 20 April, 1999. Armed with an arsenal of pistols, shotguns and pipe-bombs, 18-year-old Eric Harris and 17-year-old Dylan Klebold went on a deadly rampage through classrooms, killing 12 of their fellow students and a teacher, before turning the weapons on themselves. In the wake of what became known as the 'Columbine High School Massacre', attention soon focused on the possible role of popular entertainment. The press quickly conjectured that 'gothic' rock music might be a factor in the killings, since Harris and Klebold had been members of a loose group of friends who supposedly shared a taste for 'goth' music and style. As a consequence, *The New York Post* ran a feature titled 'Telltale signs your kids might be ready to explode', alongside a picture of Adolf Hitler and photographs of teenagers in 'goth' make-up (cited in Ferrell et al., 2004: 145). Rock musician Marilyn Manson, already a target for moral crusaders, was also singled out for criticism – many commentators citing the dark imagery of Manson's songs and performance as an influence on the Columbine killers.[5] Computer games were also blamed. Harris and Klebold had been keen on games such as *Doom* and *Final Fantasy VII*, and the games' violent content was cited as contributing to the murders. In 2001 relatives of the Columbine victims even filed a $5 billion lawsuit against 25 computer companies (including Sony and Nintendo), claiming the firms' products had triggered the killings. In 2002, however, the lawsuit was dismissed after a court ruling that the computer games firms had no case to answer. Notions that rock music had been a factor in the murders also lacked foundation, as it subsequently emerged that neither Harris nor Klebold had been fans of Marilyn Manson. And, rather than finding evidence of media effects, subsequent research on the Columbine shooting has highlighted the contribution of a collection of cultural and environmental factors, together with the mental illnesses from which both killers probably suffered.[6]

Nevertheless, concerns about possible links between the media and youth violence continued to punctuate the late twentieth and early twenty-first centuries. Along with the Virginia Tech killings of 2007, for example, video games were cited as an influence on 20-year-old Adam Lanza who, in 2012, used a (legally purchased) assault rifle to kill 26 people (including 20 children aged between 6 and 7 years old) at Sandy Hook Elementary School in Connecticut, before killing himself with a pistol. Following the slaughter, a renewed debate ensued about the effects of violent video games on young people. And, according to Wayne LaPierre, Executive Vice President of the National Rifle Association (NRA – the biggest gun rights advocacy group in America), the relative ease with which powerful firearms can be obtained in the US was of little importance to the shooting. Instead, LaPierre contended, responsibility for the tragedy lay at the door of 'vicious, violent video games', along with:

> … blood-soaked slasher films like *American Psycho* and *Natural Born Killers* that are aired like propaganda loops on 'Splatterdays' and every day, and a thousand music videos that portray life as a joke and murder as a way of life.
>
> (*Guardian*, 21 December 2012)

As in the case of other mass shootings, however, there was scant evidence of any causal link between violent video games and the killer's behaviour. Indeed, while the State Attorney's final report into the Sandy Hook shooting noted that Lanza often played video games, it observed how his particular favourite was not a violent shooting game, but *Dance Dance Revolution* – a dance-exercise game (Office of the State's Attorney Judicial District of Danbury, 2013: 31–32). And, instead of the influence of video games, it was Lanza's significant record of mental illness that the State Attorney highlighted as a key factor in events.

There is, then, a long history of popular fears regarding a possible causal link between 'violent' forms of media and violent behaviour by young people. Evidence for such an influence, however, is scarce. Official investigations, for example, have repeatedly refuted the idea of a causal connection between video games and mass shootings. At the same time, however, these popular fears have been paralleled by an extensive tradition of social scientific research that has claimed to reveal a *general* relationship between 'violent' media and aggressive behaviour by the young. This tradition, though, is a site of heated controversy and has both ardent advocates and fervent critics.

From the 'talkies' to video games: the development of 'media effects' research

One of the first systematic attempts to analyse the media's effects on audiences was a series of studies of cinemagoers undertaken in the US between 1929 and 1933. The research was financed by the Payne Study and Experiment Fund, a body established in 1927 by Frances Payne Bolton (a wealthy politician) to investigate the media's influence on children and adolescents. Backed by the

Payne Fund, the investigation was led by W.W. Charters and comprised 13 separate studies of the impact of movies on the young.[7] Ultimately, the studies' findings were inconclusive. Films, Charters averred, could be 'a potent medium of education', but at the same time they were 'one among many influences which mould the experience of children' (Charters, 1933: 60–61). Despite such qualified conclusions, however, the Payne research was sensationalised in the press. And the studies' most inflammatory findings were selectively seized upon by moral crusaders and used to justify a stricter system of film censorship. This was manifest in a firmer enforcement of the Production Code introduced by the industry-sponsored Motion Picture Association of America (MPAA) in 1930. The Production Code (also known as the Hays Code after Will Hays, the first President of the MPAA) was a strict system of censorship that spelled out what was – and what was *not* – considered morally acceptable in US filmmaking, and it dominated Hollywood until it was replaced by a new, more liberal, Ratings System in 1968.

Similar developments took place outside the US. As historian Sarah Smith shows, throughout the world the arrival of cinema during the early twentieth century was met with concern about its social impact. These anxieties intensified with the development of the 'talkies' from 1927 and, as Smith observes, during the 1930s 'literally hundreds of surveys and reports were generated worldwide' investigating the possible influence of films on their audiences (Smith, 2005: 7). Usually centred on children and young people – who were viewed as especially susceptible to the cinema's 'negative' influence – this research was customarily followed by the introduction of stricter measures of film censorship and regulation.

During the 1950s, 1960s and 1970s the growing reach of the media – combined with the rapid spread of new media technologies, such as TV – spurred further investigation. In the US, especially, studies proliferated in the field of psychology where there developed a significant tradition of 'effects' research that examined the impact (usually conceived as negative) of the media on audiences' social behaviour. And it was invariably children and adolescents who were the focus of such studies.[8]

Research undertaken by the psychologist Albert Bandura at Stanford University in California during the early 1960s is regarded as a particular landmark in the 'media effects' tradition. Sometimes dubbed 'the Bobo doll experiments', Bandura's work was based on a series of laboratory-based tests that examined children's behaviour after they watched an adult act aggressively towards a Bobo doll – a doll-like toy with a rounded bottom, that rocked back to an upright position after being knocked down. The experiment had several versions, but generally Bandura found that children who had watched the adults behaving aggressively towards the Bobo doll were more likely themselves to act aggressively towards the doll than children who had not watched the adults' aggression. Later configurations of the experiment saw children shown a film of an adult punching and screaming aggressively at the Bobo doll. Again, Bandura concluded that the children tended to imitate the aggressive behaviour they

had seen (Bandura et al., 1961; Bandura et al., 1963). The research was intended as a general examination of the way individuals learn through processes of
observation and imitation. Subsequently, however, the Bobo doll studies were
widely cited as evidence of the negative influence of 'violent' media on young
people's behaviour, and they have been followed by innumerable 'effects'
experiments claiming to show just such a link.

Longitudinal studies also purported to show a connection between 'violent'
media and aggression. Beginning in the 1960s, psychologists Rowell Huesmann
and Leonard Eron studied more than 800 children aged under 10, and –
through conversations with parents, teachers, and the children themselves –
assessed how much violence the children watched on TV and how aggressive
they were in daily life. There was, the researchers found, a tendency for those
children who watched higher amounts of TV violence also to demonstrate
higher levels of aggressive behaviour. Collecting further data when the children
were 19, and then collating information on their criminal records when they
were aged 30, the researchers found that subjects who had watched more violent TV when they were children tended to be those who became involved in
serious crimes in later life. 'If a child's observation of media violence promotes
the learning of aggressive habits', Huesmann concluded, 'it can have harmful
lifelong consequences' (Huesmann, 1986: 129–130).

In 2003 Huesmann, Eron and their colleagues reported similar findings from
a further longitudinal study that followed children from the ages of ages 6 to 10
into adulthood. Longitudinal research produced elsewhere also supported their
view. In Britain, for example, William Belson's (1978) study interviewed 1,565
London boys aged between 13 and 17 across the period 1959–71, and concluded that those exposed to high levels of TV violence in childhood went on
to commit 49 per cent more acts of serious violence than those who had been
exposed to much less. More recently, German researchers Barbara Krahé and
Ingrid Möller measured exposure to media violence and self-reported aggressive behaviour by 1,200 seventh and eighth grade students over a year. Across
this time, they found the students' initial reports of high exposure to media
violence correlated significantly with their later reports of aggressive behaviour
(Krahé et al.: 2004). And, in a later study of 1,700 high school students, Krahé,
Möller and their associates found that students' consumption of media violence
predicted their levels of both self-reported and teacher-rated aggressive behaviour two years later (Krahé et al. 2011).

At the same time, however, other longitudinal studies have challenged
notions of such a relationship. In the US, for instance, one of the largest studies
of its kind saw Ronald J. Milavsky and his associates survey 3,200 young people
over the period 1970–73, and concluded from their work that watching acts of
violence on TV had relatively little influence on youngsters' behaviour
(Milavsky et al., 1982). Moreover, simply because aggressive people have watched 'violent' media, this does not necessarily mean it is this experience that has
caused them to behave aggressively. Any number of social, cultural, and economic factors might also play a part – indeed, perhaps a more significant part.

Additionally, it may be quite likely that individuals who *already* have a pro-clivity for aggression also gravitate towards violent media. *Correlation* and *causation* are quite different matters, and demonstrating a statistical correlation does not – in itself – prove any causal relationship.

Nevertheless, during the 1990s a new wave of 'effects' research focused on video games. For some theorists, the immersive and interactive nature of video games meant they were potentially more influential than 'traditional' forms of media such as books, music, or films.[9] Again, this research was dominated by (largely American) psychological researchers whose laboratory-based experiments, they argued, showed a causal relationship between children and young people's playing of 'violent' video games and subsequent aggressive behaviour. An early (1988) contribution came from Nicola Schutte and her colleagues. In a study reminiscent of Bandura's Bobo doll experiments, Schutte and her team worked with children aged between 5 and 7 years old, and found that those who played 'violent' video games tended to exhibit more aggressive behaviour afterwards (Schutte et al., 1988). Working with college students, meanwhile, Craig Anderson and Catherine Ford (1986) split their subjects into a group who played either a 'high aggression' video game (*Zaxxon*), a group who played a 'mild aggression' video game (*Centipede*), and a control group who played no game at all. Their results showed that players of *both* games exhibited higher levels of hostility than the control group, while those assigned to the 'high aggression' game reported much higher levels of anxiety than the other two.

A flurry of academic studies of the 'effects' of video games followed throughout the 1990s, though it was a book by David Grossman that attracted the greatest publicity. A former army lieutenant colonel and a professor of Military Science at Arkansas State University, Grossman emerged as a leading critic of video games following the publication of *On Killing* (1995). The book saw Grossman identify marked parallels between the simulation training used to prepare soldiers for combat and the immersive experience of 'first-person-shooter' video games. Such games, Grossman concluded, not only enhanced young people's weapons skills but also broke down the psychological barriers that prevented youngsters from killing.[10]

Grossman's views attracted considerable press attention, but they were based chiefly on his own convictions rather than any substantive research. In contrast, academic studies often painted a more complex picture. In 2001, for example, John Sherry attempted to summarise the findings of 30 existing studies of 'violent' video games using a process of 'meta analysis' – that is to say, a synthesis of results from a large number of individual studies to produce a single, 'over-arching' conclusion. Reviewing the assembled literature, Sherry's findings were mixed. The research, he concluded, demonstrated how 'there is a small effect of video game play on aggression, and the effect is smaller than the effect of violent television on aggression' (2001: 427). More important, he argued, was the *kind* of violence contained in the game. When the violence was related to sports or fantasy themes, Sherry concluded, the effect on aggression was much smaller than when the violence involved depictions of aggression towards human beings.

Other studies, however, claimed there was a much clearer relationship between violent video games and aggression. In 2003, for example, a meta-analysis produced by Craig Anderson and his associates suggested Sherry's survey had underestimated the effects of 'violent' media. More recent studies with better forms of methodological design, they argued, showed a pronounced link between exposure to 'violent' media and aggression. 'Research on violent television and films, video games, and music', Anderson and his colleagues averred, 'reveals unequivocal evidence that media violence increases the likelihood of aggressive and violent behavior in both immediate and long-term contexts' (2003: 81). 'The scientific debate over whether media violence increases aggression and violence', they declared with clear-eyed confidence, 'is essentially over' (81).

In the wake of such assertions, 2005 saw the American Psychological Association (APA – a scientific and professional body representing US psychologists) adopt a 'Resolution on Violence in Video Games and Interactive Media'. According to the resolution, the APA took the view that the available evidence demonstrated how 'exposure to violent media increases feelings of hostility, thoughts about aggression, suspicions about the motives of others, and demonstrates violence as a method to deal with potential conflict situations' (APA, 2005). In the case of video games, moreover, the APA argued that 'the practice, repetition, and rewards for acts of violence may be more conducive to increasing aggressive behaviour among children and youth than passively watching violence on TV and in film' (2005). As a solution, the APA proposed the promotion of greater levels of media literacy among the public, together with a reduction of violence in videogames marketed to children and youth, as well as the stricter regulation of the content of video games and interactive media.

In 2010, Anderson and his colleagues produced a further, updated meta-analysis of research on the effects of video games. The new study took into account what the authors described as 'an explosion of research on violent video games since the last comprehensive analysis was published' (Anderson et al., 2010: 153); and it incorporated a 'larger sample of higher quality studies', along with work from a growing body of Japanese research (156). From a synthesis of this work, Anderson et al. painted a picture similar to their previous assessment. 'Regardless of research design or conservativeness of analysis', they explained, 'exposure to violent video games was significantly related to higher levels of aggressive behaviour' (162). Moreover, taking the research from Japan into account, they surmised that the effects of exposure to 'violent' video games 'are significant in Eastern as well as Western cultures' (167).

Concerns were sustained by the growing prevalence of video games. In America, for example, nearly 97 per cent of children aged between 12 and 17 played video games by 2008 (Lenhart, 2008: 1). And, by 2017, video games were played either sometimes or often by 72 per cent of men and 49 per cent of women aged under 30 (Brown, 2017). Legal rulings in the US also stoked the controversy. In 2005 the California State Legislature passed a law – sponsored by State Senator Leland Yee, a former child psychologist[11] – which banned the sale of violent video games to anyone aged under 18, and enforced a stricter system of ratings to control games' availability. In 2011, however, the Californian law was ruled unconstitutional and struck down by the US Supreme Court. Video games, the Supreme Court judged, should have the same 'free speech' protection under the First Amendment as that afforded to other media. The court, moreover, found that the psychological research on violent video games was 'unpersuasive' and noted that much of it contained methodological flaws (Ferguson, 2013iii: 61).

The continuing controversy prompted the APA to convene a team – the APA Task Force on Violent Media – to consider fresh studies in the area, and to review the APA's 2005 Resolution on violent video games. Launched in 2013 and chaired by psychologist Mark Appelbaum, the Task Force comprised seven academics considered experts in the area. It assessed research on violent video games published between 2005 and 2013, along with four meta-analyses that reviewed more than 150 studies produced before 2009. Published in 2015, the APA team's report conceded there was insufficient evidence to demonstrate whether playing violent video games had a physiological or neurological impact, or whether playing such games led to violence or delinquency (APA Task Force on Violent Media, 2015: 16). At the same time, however, the Task Force were unequivocal that the existing research 'demonstrates a consistent relation between violent video game use and increases in aggressive behavior, aggressive cognitions, and aggressive affect, and decreases in prosocial behavior, empathy, and sensitivity to aggression' (APA Task Force on Violent Media, 2015: 11).

In view of such findings, 2015 saw the APA update its position in a fresh 'Resolution on Violent Video Games'. The new document acknowledged the degree of controversy surrounding the relationship between violent video games and aggressive behaviour, but the 2015 Resolution was effectively a reiteration of the APA's earlier position. 'Scientific research', it averred, 'has demonstrated an association between violent video game use and both increases in aggressive behavior, aggressive affect, aggressive cognitions and decreases in prosocial behavior, empathy, and moral engagement' (2015). And, again, the APA recommended greater levels of public education and a stricter system of games regulation.

Not everyone, however agreed. In October 2013 American psychologist Christopher Ferguson sent an open letter – co-signed by an international group of 228 media scholars, psychologists, and criminologists – to the APA expressing concerns about the Task Force's review process. The APA's original 2005 Resolution, the signatories argued, had come to 'several strong conclusions on the basis of inconsistent or weak evidence', while research produced after the APA's 2005 statement had 'provided even stronger evidence that some of the assertions in it cannot be supported'. 'Policy statements based on inconsistent and weak evidence', the letter concluded, 'are bad policy and over the long run do more harm than good, hurting the credibility of the science of psychology' (Ferguson, 2013ii). Ultimately, the letter fell on deaf ears. But it clearly demonstrated the heated academic controversy surrounding the 'influence' of violent video games, and was indicative of the wide body of criticism that has been levelled at 'media effects' research.

'An easy scapegoat': the critique of 'media effects' theories

The social impact of video games – indeed, of the media in general – has always been an area of intense disagreement. And, in the case of the 'effects' of violent video games, research findings are much more conflicted than the APA's pronouncements suggest. Indeed, many studies suggest violent video games have no negative effects on young players. In Britain, for example, a (2019) study by Andrew Przybylski and Netta Weinstein found no evidence to link violent video games with real-world aggression. Based on a survey of the gaming habits and behaviour of a representative sample of 1,000 14- and 15-year-olds, Przybylski and Weinstein found no evidence that violent gaming relates to aggressive behaviour. The study's results, they concluded, 'provide confirmatory evidence that violent video game engagement, on balance, is not associated with observable variability in adolescents' aggressive behaviour' (Przybylski and Weinstein, 2019: 14).

Some research suggests, in fact, that video gaming can have a *positive* impact on young people.[12] Several studies, for example, show that video gaming can improve youngsters' visuospatial cognition (Green and Bavelier, 2007; Spence and Feng, 2010), some suggest it can boost social interaction and civic involvement (Lenhart et al., 2008), and others argue that video games can be a valuable platform for education (Durkin, 2010). The research of Matthew Grizzard and his colleagues (2014), meanwhile, suggested that playing violent video games might lead to increased levels of moral sensitivity. Their study of 185 students attending a US Midwestern university found that subjects who repeatedly played violent video games as immoral characters experienced feelings of guilt that could heighten the importance they gave to issues of care and fairness. 'Contrary to popular belief', Grizzard et al. concluded, 'engaging in heinous behaviors in virtual environments can lead to an increased sensitivity to moral issues' (Grizzard et al., 2014: 5).

Criticisms have also been levelled at meta-analyses claiming a link between violent video games and aggression. Christopher Ferguson (2007i; 2007ii), for example, has argued that a significant publication bias underpins such meta-analyses' selection of research and – once this issue is adjusted – no support is found for the hypothesis that violent video game playing is associated with higher levels of aggression. Working with John Kilburn, Ferguson was especially critical of Anderson et al.'s meta-analysis of 2010 (see above), arguing that its biased selection of research sources had led to an overestimation of the influence of violent video games on aggressive behaviour (Ferguson and

Kilburn, 2010).[13] Indeed, in their own (2009) meta-analysis of existing research, Ferguson and Kilburn found little evidence to support any link between media violence and aggressive behaviour, conclusions that were supported by Ferguson's later (2015) study. Moreover, as Ferguson and Kilburn observed, at the same time as violent video games exploded in popularity, violent crime rates among youths and adults in the US, Canada, Britain, Japan and most other industrialised countries declined to lows not seen since the 1960s (Ferguson and Kilburn, 2010: 176). This, in itself, cast doubt on notions of a causal link between video games and aggression. Indeed, surveys of available research produced for the governments of Australia (Australian Government, 2010), Britain (Harris, 2001; Buckingham et al., 2007) and Sweden (Swedish Media Council, 2011) have all concluded there is no substantial evidence that aggressive behaviour results from playing video games.

Considerable criticism has also been levelled at the methodologies employed by many 'media effects' studies. The laboratory-based nature of much of this research, for example, has been criticised for being far removed from 'real-life' social conditions. As a consequence, it is argued, the artificiality of the research setting undermines the validity of any findings. As David Gauntlett points out, such research 'rests on the mistaken belief that children's behaviour will not be affected by the fact that they know they are being manipulated, tested and/or observed' (Gauntlett, 2001: 56). For instance, in the case of Bandura's famous Bobo doll experiments (see above), Ferguson argues that it is unclear whether the children who bashed Bobo were acting agressively per se, or were mimicking *specific* aggressive acts believing this was expected of them:

> In other words, overall aggressive behaviors may not have changed much, but the style of the aggressive behaviors might have been altered due to the novel kinds of aggressive behaviors presented. It is also unclear that the children were necessarily motivated by aggression, as opposed to aggressive play or even the desire to please the adult experimenter.
>
> (Ferguson, 2010: 71)

The validity of such experiments might also be undermined by the fact that the kind of texts subjects encounter in the laboratory (along with the manner of their presentation) is unlikely to be representative of what they would normally choose to view, nor of the way they would actually use media texts in their daily lives. Moreover, as Theresa Cronin observes:

> ... in the real world acts of violence have myriad consequences for both the victim and perpetrator, and individuals also have a range of more or less legitimate ways of dealing with their aggression, like phoning a friend or hitting a pillow, which are simply not available to them in the laboratory.
>
> (Cronin, 2014: 94)

Additionally, 'effects' studies invariably give scant regard to the meaning of media 'violence'. The quality of 'violence' is treated as though it is objective and self-evident, and free of any value judgement by the researchers. Few studies offer definitions of 'violence' beyond 'acts of hurting or harming', so they largely ignore the extent to which different *kinds* of violence set in different *contexts* (for example, 'violence' depicted in a cartoon, presented in a news report, or featured in a horror movie) might be interpreted and understood by audiences in very different ways. In these terms, a video game might be deemed 'violent' by some people, but considered mild and innocuous by others. As David Morrison and Andrea Millward (2007) argue, definitions of what is judged to be 'violent' media content will vary according to the attitudes, values, and life experience of the person making the judgement. Martin Barker and Julian Petley make this point especially succinctly:

> … claims about the possible 'effects of violent media' are not just false, they range from the daft to the mischievous … different kinds of media use different kinds of 'violence' for different purposes … without asking where, when and in what context they are used … it is stupid simply to ask 'what are the effects of violence?'
>
> (Barker and Petley, 2001: 1–2)

Media 'effects' research can also be criticised for the way it customarily sees audiences as passive and uncritical. The 'effects' model tends to conceive the relationship between media and audience as a simple question of stimulus and effect, with little attention to the way audiences actively engage with the media. In contrast, researchers informed by perspectives developed in the fields of cultural and media studies argue that audiences are not passive 'empty vessels' that receive 'input' from the media in a direct and straightforward manner. Instead, audiences are seen as active agents who consciously engage with, interpret and respond to media texts (see Chapter 6). In these terms, audiences draw on their pre-existing ideas, attitudes, and social experiences to think about and understand the media, actively creating meanings around the texts they consume. As a consequence, cultural studies theorists such as Buckingham see 'effects' research as inherently flawed by its lack of regard to the social process through which the meanings of media texts are produced and circulated:

> Meaning is seen to be inherent in the 'message', and to be transmitted directly into the mind and thence the behaviour of the viewer. As a result, it becomes unnecessary to investigate what viewers themselves define as violent, or the different ways in which they make sense of what they watch.
>
> (Buckingham, 1993: 7)

From this perspective, laboratory experiments and quantitatively-based research are ill-suited to uncovering the way people make sense of media texts and give meaning to their social behaviour. Instead, theorists working within the disciplines of sociology, media, and cultural studies have argued that a better approach is to use qualitative research methods (for example, ethnography, interviews, and focus groups) to explore the various meanings and interpretations different audiences give to the media (see Chapter 6). Moreover, critics suggest, blaming media 'effects' for society's problems deflects attention from the way such problems may actually have their roots in wider social, economic, and political failings. As Buckingham puts it:

> ... the media routinely serve ... as an easy scapegoat, which may actively prevent a more considered, and more honest, appraisal of the issues. To blame the media provides a convenient means of displacing the concern away from questions which are much harder to examine, and which we may actively wish to avoid.
>
> (Buckingham, 1993: 5–6)

Youth, communication technologies, and 'media panics': from the telegraph to 'sexting'

Modern controversies about the influence of computer games are the latest instalment in the long history of anxieties about the media's influence on youth. Each new media technology has been surrounded by concerns about its impact on the young. For Danish media theorist Kirsten Drotner (1992; 1999), these successive moments of alarm represent examples of 'media panic'. Drawing on theories of moral panic (see Chapter 4), Drotner argues that, since the nineteenth century, the development of new media forms has been accompanied by a fever of social anxiety – a media panic – that perceives the new technologies as a unique danger to public morality and well-being.[14]

In such media panics, Drotner explains, 'the mass media are both the source and the medium of public reaction' (1992: 44). And, focusing particularly on popular fiction and film, she traces a history of media panics across a number of countries. As each new medium has been introduced, Drotner suggests, there has been a kind of historical amnesia about previous panics. While earlier media achieve social acceptance, the new form becomes a focus for a fresh wave of concern. Media panics, however, are underpinned not so much by a fear of the new technologies per se as by an apprehension that they contribute to broader challenges being made to dominant power structures and social relationships. From this perspective, then, media panics (like moral panics) reflect wider political agendas and are constituent in broader social struggles.[15] According to Drotner, moreover, media panics have generally focused on the young because children and young people have often been in the vanguard of new media developments. And calls for greater media censorship and regulation, she suggests, represent attempts to reinstate control of young people's cultural independence and restore traditional structures of cultural authority. As Drotner explains:

> On a social level, media panics basically attempt to reestablish a generational status quo that the youthful pioneers seem to undermine. This tacit generational struggle is demonstrated in the adult strategy of externalising the problem: it is the young and their media uses that are targeted as evils.
>
> (Drotner, 1999: 614)

The 'generational' dimension to media panics is, to some extent, demonstrated by the social make-up of those who believe strongest in a causal link between playing video games and real-world aggression. Research in this area is limited, but Przybylski's (2014) US-based survey of over 1,000 adults suggested that those who ardently believe video games are a source of aggression are older, and have little experience of gaming themselves. Belief in a causal link, Przybylski found, was strongest among groups aged over 45, and who had minimal gaming experience. This group, his study suggested, were 'between four and six times more likely to believe that electronic games contributed to human aggression compared to younger adults' (Przybylski, 2014: 232).[16]

Media panics, like moral panics, can also have a pronounced dimension of gendering. Indeed, there is a long history of social fears casting women as especially vulnerable to 'threats' posed by new media technologies. Rather than responding to genuine dangers, these fears have invariably been provoked by suspicion of the greater independence the new technologies may afford to women, and their potential challenge to traditional models of femininity. Literary historian Jacqueline Pearson, for example, shows how reading novels was criticised as an unhealthy and 'dangerous' pastime for women in Britain during the late eighteenth and early nineteenth centuries (Pearson, 1999). And Justine Cassell and Meg Cramer (2008) show how the arrival of the telegraph and telephone in the US during the late nineteenth century was accompanied by fears that young women might use the new technologies to make contact with inappropriate romantic partners or dangerous strangers. These fears, Cassell and Cramer suggest, have many parallels with modern-day concerns about the vulnerability of young women to sexual predators on the Internet and social media.

Of course, there are some well-documented cases of young people falling victim to sexual abuse and violence by strangers they meet online – and such events are clearly abhorrent. It is, though, misleading to see the Internet itself as the cause of such tragedies. As Cassell and Cramer observe, concurrent with the rise of the Internet in the US, the proportion of crimes committed against girls where the offender was an adult stranger actually *declined* rather than increased (2008: 54). The most common offender in such crimes, they point out, is a family member or acquaintance, and the focus on online danger runs the risk of obscuring 'the real danger posed to young people by those close to them' (58). Moreover, Cassell and Cramer argue, from the telegraph to the Internet, fears about the vulnerability of women to the dangers of new communications technologies has been underpinned by anxieties regarding the potential disruption of traditional sexual values and the challenge of new models of femininity. As they explain, a review of the history of panics about women and new communications technologies shows how:

> ... it is less the technology per se that turns out to be the culprit (or even the kinds of relationships made possible by the technology), and more the potential sexual agency of young women, parental loss of control, and the specter of women who manifest technological prowess.
>
> (Cassell and Cramer, 2008: 70)

For some authors, similar concerns have surrounded mobile phones. The growing prevalence of mobile phones among young people, Gerard Goggin (2006) has argued, spawned a series of 'mobile panics', or episodes of overblown alarm about the threat mobile phones posed to, variously, youngsters' health, literacy, and cultural values. In particular, Goggin highlighted the way attention in Australia had increasingly focused on mobile phones' imaging capabilities and the practice of 'sexting' – in which young people send nude or semi-nude pictures of themselves via their mobile phone. The ensuing media panic about sexting, Goggin suggested, not only stoked public anxieties about youth and new technologies, but also met with a legal response that was overzealous and authoritarian.

Nora Draper (2012) suggests sexting met with a similar response in the US. Analysing coverage of sexting in US TV news during 2008–9, Draper found that, alongside a tendency to exaggerate the occurrence of teen sexting, the TV coverage was dominated by three key themes. Firstly, there was a tendency to cite mobile technologies themselves as a cause of sexting, with 'technologically deterministic' explanations that were suffused with 'the notion that "good kids" are seduced by the accessibility of digital technologies into deviant activities' (225). Secondly, there was a marked gendering in representations of sexting – with a distinct 'focus on girls as vulnerable to technological seduction' (227). Thirdly, Draper argued, the TV coverage generally promoted increased surveillance of young people's media use as the most effective tool for discouraging teen sexting. Sexting, Draper acknowledged, should be viewed as possibly risky behaviour, given the potential loss of control over something as powerful as a sexually explicit image. But, she suggested, the TV coverage of sexting was akin to Drotner's notion of 'media panic' in the way it delivered an exaggerated, distorted – and highly gendered – view of the practice.

A similar account of sexting is offered by Amy Hasinoff (2012; 2015). In the US, Hasinoff argues, the early twenty-first century saw sexting widely presented as 'a technological, sexual and moral crisis' (2012: 450). While there was certainly some truth to media stories of teenage girls being traumatised by unauthorised distribution of their private images, Hasinoff suggests the severity of the problem was often overstated. She also notes how policies meant to curb sexting – primarily criminalisation and abstinence – often failed to account for distinctions between consensual sharing and malicious distribution. The social responses to sexting, moreover, were highly gendered, with girls who create sexual images either demonised as 'deviant and dangerous' or stigmatised as helpless victims. In contrast, Hasinoff challenges the idea that sexting inevitably victimises young women. Instead, she suggests that sexting can sometimes be a site of active media production, and a site for sexual expression and exploration. 'Even though a sexual image might be created for an audience of only one person – or just for yourself', Hasinoff contends, 'such mediated practices of self-representation may facilitate media critique, creativity, and self-reflection' (Hasinoff, 2012: 457).

'An opium of the spirit'?: Video games, youth, and the question of 'addiction'

Media panics focused on young people, therefore, continued into the early twenty-first century. Older demons – comics, film, TV – slipped into the background, but were replaced by new areas of concern. Video games remained a site of anxiety but, rather than their possible links to aggression, a fresh wave of fears focused on their 'addictive' potential. Such concerns were especially pronounced in South Korea and China.

In South Korea the start of the century saw the number of video gamers explode. The growth was partly indebted to the quick spread of high-speed broadband which, since the late 1990s, greatly boosted the popularity of online games – especially Massive Multiplayer Online Games (known as MMOGs or, more commonly MMOs) – that were often played in a burgeoning number of Internet cafés known as 'PC Bangs'. Increasingly, however, the popularity of video gaming attracted concern, critics arguing that young players were becoming addicted to the games and this was leading to social and psychological problems. The issue was given prominence by a series of high-profile cases, including that of an unemployed 24-year-old who reputedly died in a PC Bang after an 86-hour binge of gaming (Kim, 2019). In response, hundreds of private clinics opened specialised units where patients could detox from their gaming addiction and receive counselling for their disorder, and in 2006 the Korean government opened a dedicated telephone hotline for gaming addicts (Cain, 2010). Disquiet, however, continued to mount and in 2011 the government passed what was known as the 'Shutdown Law' – legislation that introduced a curfew blocking access to online games for those aged under 16 between midnight and 6.00 a.m.[17]

In China, too, alarm surrounded a perceived epidemic of gaming addiction. As in Korea, online video gaming had mushroomed in China from the late 1990s, its growth facilitated by the increased availability of high-speed broadband (and a relatively relaxed attitude to software piracy). China's flourishing games industry was a jewel in the crown of the country's rapid economic development, but the popularity of video gaming among the young was also seen as a font of social problems. Particular anxiety surrounded the proliferation of illegal Internet cafés or '*hei wangba*' ('Black Net Bars'), which became popular gaming centres for young people throughout China. Concerns peaked in 2002 when a fire – started by two disgruntled teenagers – broke out in a Beijing *wangba*, killing 24 youngsters enjoying an all-night gaming session. The incident has been dubbed the 'Chinese Columbine' by US media theorist Henry Jenkins (2006), who observes how the tragedy was followed by a storm of media criticism of video games comparable to that which followed the 1999 Columbine school shooting in America (see above). The Chinese press featured a catalogue of reports where crime, violence and suicide appeared to be linked to video gaming, and stories increasingly portrayed 'Internet addiction' as a serious problem among the young. Online games were commonly referred to as 'opium for the spirit' – a metaphor that, as Marcella Szablewicz notes, holds enormous rhetorical power in China through its allusion to a period of colonialism and national humiliation (2010: 460).

As a consequence, China saw a flood of new clinics and hospitals geared to remedy the problem, and treatment for addiction to gaming and the Internet became a billion-dollar industry (Zhang, 2013: 2404). The authorities also responded. Many *wangba* were shut down, and 'Internet addiction' ('*wanglou chengyin*') was officially designated a clinical disorder by the government in 2008. New measures were also introduced to combat the problem. In 2007 an Online Game Addiction Prevention System (or 'fatigue system') sought to deter extensive gaming sessions by limiting game rewards after a certain amount of time. The scheme, however, was deemed ineffective and was succeeded by stricter controls. In 2010 'real-name registration' was enforced in games, linking players' games accounts to their ID cards, and in 2019 new regulations for Internet service providers effectively banned gamers aged under 18 from playing online between 22.00 and 08.00, while they were also restricted to 90 minutes of gaming on weekdays and 3 hours on weekends and holidays (Cuthbertson, 2019).

Elsewhere, similar concerns took hold. In the US a growing number of hospitals began to treat young patients for their apparent addiction to video gaming, while in Britain 2019 saw the National Health Service (NHS) open its first specialist unit to treat children and young adults who seemed addicted to video games. The moves reflected the growing scientific attention directed to the issue of gaming addiction. In 2013 a condition dubbed 'Internet gaming disorder' was discussed in the American Psychiatric Association's *Diagnostic and Statistical Manual of Mental Disorders (DSM-5)* – a guide used by mental health professionals to diagnose mental disorders – but the Association concluded there was, as yet, insufficient evidence to determine whether the problem represented a unique mental disorder (Parekh, 2018). Nonetheless, in 2017, the World Health Organization (WHO) announced it would soon officially identify 'gaming disorder' as a new medical condition. Consequently, in 2018, the eleventh edition of the WHO's *International Classification of Diseases (ICD-11)* – a list of diseases and medical conditions used by health professionals to make diagnoses and treatment plans – included a classification for 'gaming disorder'. According to the WHO, the condition was characterised by 'a pattern of persistent or recurrent gaming behaviour ("digital gaming" or "video-gaming"), which may be online (i.e., over the Internet) or offline'; and it was manifested by 'impaired control over gaming', 'increasing priority given to gaming to the extent that gaming takes precedence over other life interests' and 'continuation or escalation of gaming despite the occurrence of negative consequences' (World Health Organization, 2018). This was only the second time the WHO had recognised the existence of a behavioural addiction, the first being gambling which had been included in the 1990 revision of the *ICD*.

The WHO's inclusion of 'gaming disorder' in *ICD-11*, however, obscured the degree of controversy that surrounds the issue. Generally, the idea that people can be clinically addicted to *behaviours* – rather than *substances* like alcohol or heroin – remains contentious. And the notion of 'gaming addiction' has been the focus for a scholarly debate every bit as heated as that which earlier surrounded the purported relationship between violent video games and aggression (see above). On one hand, there are many researchers who see clear evidence for the existence of gaming addiction as a distinct medical disorder. For example, following the American Psychiatric Association's discussion of the problem in *DSM-5*, psychologist Nancy Petry headed a group of 12 researchers from 9 different countries who argued there now existed 'an international consensus for assessing Internet gaming disorder' (Petry et al., 2014). On the other hand, however, many researchers hotly contested such claims. For instance, responding to Petry et al., another international group of 28 researchers headed by British psychologist Mark Griffiths argued there was no consensus on the issue, and the existence of 'Internet gaming disorder' remained a matter of debate (Griffiths et al., 2016).[18] Moreover, in a large study of gamers aged 18 to 24 in the US, Britain, Canada, and Germany, Andrew Przybylski and his colleagues found that, while a relatively small number might meet the criteria for 'Internet gaming disorder' proposed in *DSM-5*, there was no evidence these had particularly poor emotional, physical or mental health (Przybylski, Weinstein and Murayama, 2017).

Many researchers were also critical of the WHO's decision to declare 'gaming disorder' a new medical condition. Responding to the WHO's initial proposal, an international group of 26 renowned social scientists wrote to the WHO expressing concern at the organisation's stance on gaming addiction. 'Some gamers', the group acknowledged, 'do experience serious problems as a consequence of the time spent playing video games'. At the same time, however, they argued that 'it is far from clear that these problems can or should be attributed to a new disorder' (Aarseth et al., 2017: 268). According to these critics, the decision to recognise 'gaming disorder' as a new medical condition was flawed in a number of respects. The quality of available evidence about the problem was, they argued, poor – the field was fraught with contradictions and the existing research was tentative or speculative. Moreover, the critics observed, there was no consensus around the symptoms of the condition, with some studies suggesting that 'problematic gaming' might be a 'coping mechanism' that develops as a consequence of a *different* underlying problem (269). Furthermore, the group suggested, the notion of 'gaming disorder' leaned too heavily on models based on substance use and gambling, consequently it 'over-pathologized ... thoughts, feelings and behavior that may be normal and unproblematic in people who regularly play video games' (268).[19]

For the critics, the formalisation of 'gaming disorder' as a distinct condition would have a range of negative medical, scientific, and social consequences. It would, they warned, stigmatise the millions of children and young people who played video games as 'part of a normal, healthy life', and provide justification for authoritarian intervention in young people's leisure (269). It would also, they suggested, lock future research into a 'confirmatory approach' – that is to say, researchers might see the WHO's decision as formal validation of a new disorder, and so would stop undertaking studies that could challenge the established orthodoxy (269). Additionally, the group cautioned, the WHO risked contributing to a moral panic about the 'harm' of video gaming by pathologising the normal behaviour of millions of young gamers on the basis of ambiguous research evidence (269).[20]

Clearly, the global audience for online games is vast. And few would dispute that a small part of this audience experience problems as a consequence of extensive playing. Whether this represents a serious issue, however, remains a matter of debate. Social scientific opinion, furthermore, is divided over whether 'gaming addiction' constitutes a separate medical condition in its own right, or is behaviour that develops as a consequence of other underlying social or mental problems. In South Korea, for example, media theorists such as Yoon Tae-jin, argue that many studies identifying 'gaming addiction' in the country are overly broad, failing to distinguish between particular games or genres, and tend to assume from the outset that 'gaming addiction' is a distinct condition (Kim, 2019). Even the South Korean government has feuded over the matter, 2019 seeing Prime Minister Lee Nak-yeon set up an arbitration committee to deal with the issue after the culture ministry refused to join a consultative body led by the health ministry. And, for some commentators, South Korea's 'video gaming problem' is not a result of spiralling levels of clinical addiction, but the outcome of family pressures, overbearing parenting and the notorious pressures of the country's education system (Kim, 2019). In other contexts, too, it is possible that video games have become both a scapegoat for broader social problems, and the object of an alarmist 'media panic' that serves as a vehicle for more general cultural and political fears.

In the case of China, particularly, several authors point to the way contemporary concerns about 'Internet addiction' articulate more general anxieties about modernisation and cultural change. The Chinese government, Alex Golub and Kate Lingley observe, has always viewed the country's growing access to the Internet with ambivalence. On one hand, the government has enthusiastically embraced the Internet as 'both a symbol and a means of modernization key to China's development' (Golub and Lingley, 2008: 61–2). But, on the other hand, the Internet has also been viewed as a cultural and political challenge. 'The Internet', Golub and Lingley explain, 'provides access to material the Chinese government deems unsuitable and creates a new "public sphere" in which activists can communicate and organize' (62). As a consequence, the Chinese government has sought various means to control and censor the Internet – most obviously the launch of the 'Great Firewall of China' in 1995. During the early twenty-first century, however, these tensions were further exacerbated by the massive scale and pace of socio-economic transformation, especially the rise of consumerism and its attendant lifestyles. As a consequence, general fears about the impact of technology and the Internet on Chinese society intensified – and were articulated especially strongly in the flurry of media stories that reviled 'Internet addiction' and the negative influence of video games. As Golub and Lingley explain:

> Chinese reportage expresses a profound sense that Internet addiction is emblematic of socioeconmic change in China and underlying moral tensions. As such, this articulates awareness and concern with fear of a threatened moral order in the face of social change, medicalization of social relationships, the rise of new forms of self-fashioning enabled by new media that are not socially sanctioned, the growth of consumerism as a lifestyle, and the dilemmas of child rearing and family structure in a changing country.
>
> (Golub and Lingley, 2008: 60)

In these terms, then, Chinese fears of 'Internet addiction' represented, to a large part, a media panic fuelled by a general set of anxieties about the course of social change and the cultural realignment of modern China. Moreover, this panic was given significant impetus by the Chinese government's longstanding fear of the Internet as a potential source of political challenge. As Szablewicz keenly observes, 'it should not come as a surprise that many suspect the government of using Internet addiction to divert attention from their ulterior motive of censoring and controlling the Internet for political reasons' (Szablewicz, 2010: 457).

Generally, therefore, claims about the 'effects' of the media (whether it be comics, films, music, TV or video games) remain contentious. Moreover, concerns about the 'influence' of the media on the young are best understood in their wider social, economic, and political context – where they often articulate more general concerns about shifts in social relationships and the transformation of cultural life. It would, of course, be erroneous to claim the media have no cultural impact whatsoever. To be sure, the media play a key role in organising people's understandings of the world, afford resources through which cultures are shaped and identities forged and, as media theorist Douglas Kellner puts it, 'provide symbolic environments in which people live' (1995: 151). At the same time, however, Kellner emphasises the way the media are always a 'contested terrain in which different groups inflect its meanings in different ways' (ibid). From this perspective, the media are not simple vehicles for a pre-determined 'message' that is delivered straightforwardly to the audience. Instead, media texts are riddled with ambiguities and inconsistencies, and their 'effects' on audiences are invariably complex, contradictory, or – in some cases – negligible.

Nor should we overlook the way audiences actively engage with the media. Audiences appropriate, reconfigure, and sometimes challenge a text's meanings. And they can also resist the forces of opprobrium and control. In the case of the Chinese 'Internet addiction' panic, for example, some gamers actively contested the rhetoric and stereotypes of the anti-games campaign. In 2009, for instance, Tao Hongkai – China's 'Number One Internet Addiction Specialist' – appeared on national TV to criticise 'unhealthy Internet gamers'. And, in response, irate gamers unleashed a *'renrou sousmo'* ('human flesh search') by posting Hongkai's personal details (along with many slanderous comments about him) across the Web (Szablewicz, 2010: 463). In 2010, meanwhile, over 100 fans of the online game *World of Warcraft* (*WoW*) worked to produce an hour-long animated film, *War on Internet Addiction*, a political satire that depicted *WoW* gamers struggling to save their beloved game from malevolent addiction experts and an authoritarian government. Posted on video-sharing sites, within days the film had attracted millions of viewers and comments (Szablewicz, 2010: 463, Zhang, 2013: 2403). Such episodes highlight the way young people are often sophisticated cultural agents who engage actively and creatively with the media. It is these processes of creative engagement and active meaning-making that are the focus of the next chapter.

Notes

1 West (1988) provides an overview of early anxieties prompted by American youngsters' penchant for dime novels, rock 'n' roll and other popular entertainment.
2 A detailed account of the US horror comic controversy of the 1950s is provided in Hajdu (2008). Lent (ed.) (1999) collects histories of the period's worldwide campaigns against comics, while Barker (1984) chronicles Britain's anti-comics crusade.
3 Critical accounts of Britain's 'video nasties' controversy of the1980s can be found in Barker (ed.) (1984) and Petley (2013).
4 Background to the case, outlining the problematic childhoods of Bulger's murderers, is provided in Smith (1994).
5 Wright (2000) offers a perceptive critique of the social anxieties that surrounded Marilyn Manson, his songs and performance.
6 See, for example, the accounts presented by Brown and Merritt (2002) and Larkin (2007).
7 A full account of the Payne Fund studies is contained in Jowett, Jarvie and Fuller (1996).
8 Effective overviews of the 'media effects' research tradition can be found in Carter and Weaver (eds) (2006), Oliver et al. (eds) (2020) and Potter (2012).
9 Concise histories of debates about the effects of video games can be found in Ferguson and Colwell (2017) and Kowert and Quandt (eds) (2016).

10 Four years later a crusading follow-up appeared in the form of *Stop Teaching Our Kids to Kill: A Call to Action against TV, Movie and Video Game Violence* (Grossman and DeGaetano, 1999).

11 Somewhat ironically, in 2015 Senator Yee (a vocal critic of violent video games) pled guilty to charges of (real-world) gun-running, along with bribery, extortion and money-laundering (Federal Bureau of Investigation, 2015). He was subsequently sentenced to five years in prison.

12 Debates about the positive impact of playing video games are, however, as contentious as those surrounding the negative effects. An overview of 'positive effects' research is provided in Ferguson (2010).

13 Similar criticisms are also raised in Hilgard, Engelhardt and Rouder (2017).

14 The successive fears surrounding new media forms are also identified by, among others, Ferguson and Colwell (2017), Gauntlett (2005), Livingstone (2002) and Springhall (1998).

15 It should be remembered, however, that many of the criticisms levelled at the concept of moral panic (see Chapter 4) also apply to the idea of media panic. For a critique of theories of media panic, see Buckingham and Jensen (2012).

16 Ferguson and Colwell (2017) found similar results in their study of academics' beliefs about the impact of video games on young people's aggression. Their survey of 175 criminologists, psychologists and media scholars found that it was primarily older academics, with little direct experience of gaming, who endorsed more negative views of video games and their effects.

17 Subsequent investigation by Lee, Kim and Hong (2017) suggested the impact of the Shutdown Law was relatively inconsequential.

18 The argument is developed further in Ferguson and Colwell (2019).

19 See also the critique provided in Markey and Ferguson (2017).

20 Rejoinders came in the form of several responses, sometimes with overlapping authorship, published in a dedicated edition of the *Journal of Behavioural Addictions*. See, for example, Griffiths et al. (2017) and Saunders et al. (2017). There followed a response from the original authors (van Rooij et al., 2018).

6 Young people and media consumption

From mass culture to subcultures, 'resistance' … and beyond

Sticking it to Putin: the political and creative energies of youth culture

In 2012 the Russian anarcho-feminist punk band, Pussy Riot, became a global cause célèbre. Staunch critics of Russian President Vladimir Putin and his government, the group made worldwide headlines when they performed an incendiary 'Punk Prayer' in Moscow's Cathedral of Christ the Saviour as a protest against the Orthodox Church's support for Putin's election campaign. Subsequently arrested, members of the group were sentenced to two years in prison for 'hooliganism motivated by religious hatred'. But international politicians and celebrities rallied to their defence. In Britain *The Times* spoke for many when it denounced Pussy Riot's imprisonment as evidence of Putin's 'determination to crush popular opposition', and the newspaper hailed the band as 'true and important figures of political protest' (*Times*, 29 December 2012).

Pussy Riot's protest was an episode of political importance. The event pointed to a groundswell of concern about a Russian regime sliding into autocracy. Beyond this, however, the *mode* of the group's dissent was also significant. Pussy Riot's embrace of punk music and attitude testified to the way distinctive styles, fashions, and music can pulsate with political and cultural energy. And, more generally, their protest was indicative of the way young people can actively engage with the media, using its forms, texts, and spaces to create their own cultures and identities.

This chapter explores debates about young people's capacity to be creative and innovative media-users. It begins by considering the 'mass culture' critique of popular culture which – in its various liberal and radical incarnations – presented young people as passive consumers, helplessly manipulated by commercial industries. The various criticisms made of this approach are outlined, before discussion moves to accounts that see young people as more active cultural agents. Here, particular attention is given to the 'subcultural' theories developed in Britain during the 1970s, and their depiction of youth style as a strategy of 'resistance' to dominant power structures. Subcultural theory is critically appraised, together with the range of 'post-subcultural' theories – for example, the notion of 'scenes' and the idea of 'neo-tribes' – that subsequently emerged.

Issues of gender and sexuality are also afforded close attention, together with the consumption practices of 'mainstream' youth. Here, attention focuses on research highlighting the way young people actively engage with the media, creatively forging their cultures and identities through their tastes and modes of consumption. While the merits of this position are acknowledged, so too are its limitations.

'Merchants eye teenagers the way stockmen eye cattle': youth, media, and theories of mass culture

After 1945 the social profile of American youth was accentuated by a combination of demographic shifts, the expansion of education and a proliferation of the commercial youth market (see Chapter 2). The increased 'cultural visibility' of young people contributed to popular anxieties about juvenile crime (see Chapter 3), but many social scientists responded positively. During the 1940s, for example, the distinguished sociologist Talcott Parsons coined the phrase 'youth culture' to denote what he saw as a distinct set of values and behaviour shared by the young. Presenting this in a relatively optimistic light, Parsons stressed the positive role of youth culture as a transitionary stage between childhood and the responsibilities of adult life. 'Youth culture', Parsons explained,

> ... has important sensitive functions in easing the transition from the security of childhood in the family of orientation to that of full adult in marriage and occupational status.
>
> (Parsons, 1942: 614)

One of the most widely-known postwar studies of American adolescence also depicted youth culture as relatively benign. James Coleman's *The Adolescent Society* (1961) was nervous in its survey of Illinois high school cliques, depicting an adolescent culture with its 'own language, symbols and, even more important, system of values ... different from those established in the wider society' (Coleman, 1961: 9). Nevertheless, while Coleman depicted a youth culture increasingly divorced from the wider adult world, his view was optimistic. With prudent adult intervention, he argued, the peer culture could be steered towards socially beneficial goals.

But there were also more disconsolate voices. For some commentators, the upsurge of American youth culture after the Second World War was the nadir of the country's more general slide into a shallow, debased world of 'mass culture'. The view was constituent in a broader climate of uncertainty. Although America's postwar economic growth had brought widespread prosperity, the 1950s saw a wide body of opinion revile what was regarded as the malignant cultural fallout of the consumer boom. Historian Richard Pells (1985) shows how, across the political spectrum, authors decried the rise of a degraded 'mass culture' they saw as the corollary of trends towards cynical mass marketing and bland consumerism. And, from this perspective, the flourishing youth market seemed stark evidence of mass culture's oppressive banality. In 1950, for instance, writer David Riesman condemned a pop music industry he saw as wielding the power 'to mold popular taste and to eliminate free choice by consumers' (Riesman, 1950: 361). Cultural critic Dwight Macdonald also saw the young as falling easy prey to the wiles of commerce. 'These days', he dolefully explained in a 1958 overview of the teen market, 'merchants eye teenagers the way stockmen eye cattle, thinking in terms of how much the creatures will cut up for' (Macdonald, 1958: 63).

But the most acerbic critique of the youth market came in *Teen-age Tyranny*, a best-selling book of 1962 authored by Grace and Fred Hechinger. Denouncing popular dance crazes such as the twist as 'bump-and-grind exhibitionism' and a 'flagrant example of a teen-age fad dominating the adult world' (1962: 112–113), the Hechingers lamented the way Americans seemed to be 'growing down rather than growing up', the nation standing 'in such awe of its teen-age segment that it is in danger of becoming a teen-age society, with permanently teen-age standards of thought, culture and goals' (Hechinger and Hechinger, 1962: x).

An equally despondent 'mass culture' critique appeared in postwar Europe. The rise of teenage consumption during the 1950s and early 1960s was often celebrated as the essence of prosperous modernity (see Chapter 4) but, for some commentators, modern youth culture was indicative of a drift towards a tawdry and crudely commercial 'Americanisation'. As cultural theorist Dick Hebdige shows, for many European critics the United States – the home of monopoly capitalism and commercial culture – became a paradigm 'for the future threatening every advanced industrial democracy in the western world' (Hebdige, 1988ii: 52–53). In Britain, for example, the writer Richard Hoggart derided contemporary trends towards 'canned entertainment and packeted provision' that seemed, for him, to offer an 'unvaried diet of sensation without commitment' (1957: 246). And Hoggart singled out contemporary youth as a benchmark of this cultural paucity. Denouncing modern youth as a 'hedonistic but passive barbarian', Hoggart poured scorn on 'the juke box boys' with their 'drape suits, picture ties and American slouch', who spent their evenings in 'harshly lighted milk bars' putting 'copper after copper into the mechanical record player' – a realm of cultural experience that, Hoggart argued, represented 'a peculiarly thin and pallid form of dissipation' (1957: 248–250).

Writers such as Reisman, Macdonald and Hoggart offered a liberal version of the 'mass culture' critique. For them, modern culture was being undermined by the rise of a vulgar and inane commercialism. But a more radical version of this 'mass culture' thesis was also developed by Marxist and neo-Marxist theorists, who attacked popular culture as an oppressive apparatus serving the interests of capitalism. Significant in this tradition were writers associated with Germany's Institute for Social Research at the University of Frankfurt am Main. Writing during the 1930s and 1940s, members of what became known as the 'Frankfurt School' were deeply critical of commercial popular culture. For the Frankfurt theorists, the 'culture industry' was not only a source of profit for capitalist business, but also functioned to secure the status quo by fostering conformity, passivity, and political apathy among mass audiences.[1]

One of the most well-known versions of this critique was produced by Theodor Adorno in his analysis of popular music, originally published in 1941. Adorno had little time for the products of the commercial music industry, arguing they were characterised by two processes – standardisation and pseudo-individualisation. Standardisation referred to the substantial similarities between modern popular songs that, Adorno argued, were churned off a production-line like any other mass-produced commodity. Pseudo-individualisation referred to the incidental differences that worked to disguise this uniformity. According to Adorno, slight variations from the norm and moments of novelty (for example, the hook-line of a chorus or a catchy musical riff) made a song attractive and gave it the semblance of originality. In contrast to the creativity and intellectual depth of classical and avant-garde forms of music, then, Adorno saw popular songs as standardised products devoid of originality or meaning. His view of popular audiences was equally disparaging, seeing them as 'arrested at the infantile stage ... they are childish; their primitivism is not that of the underdeveloped, but that of the forcibly retarded' (1991: 41).

The Marxist version of the 'mass culture' thesis, then, saw popular music as a vapid, standardised product working in the service of capitalism. From this perspective, popular music (in common with other branches of the 'culture industry') was criticised for not only being part of an exploitative capitalist market, but also for fostering banal conformity among its audiences. In 1973, writing in *Marxism Today* (the journal of the Communist Party of Great Britain), John Boyd articulated the viewpoint succinctly. For Boyd, 1970s youth culture was characterised by an 'imposed alienation'. 'Platform shoes and long skirts', Boyd warned, represented 'the antipathy of freedom', while young workers were brainwashed by that most insidious instrument of capitalist domination – the 1970s disco:

> Alienation is epitomised in the discotheque – the room is darkened so that you cannot see who you are with; the 'music' is so loud that there is no possibility of conversation with others ... the mind is further clogged by flashing lights causing near hypnotic conditions; concentration is not required as the maximum playing time of one record is three minutes. Every sense is taken care of to ensure that not one thought, let alone a social idea, takes place.
>
> (Boyd, 1973: 378)

Boyd's portrayal of the 1970s disco as a cunning capitalist conspiracy now seems laughable. But comparable scorn for popular media is detectable in the work of many more recent critics. Theorists of postmodernism such as Jean Baudrillard (1983; 1985) and Frederic Jameson (1984), for instance, have viewed cultural trends in the late twentieth century with differing degrees of despair and resignation, interpreting the media-saturated age of postmodernity as marking the rise of a uniquely 'depthless' form of cultural life (see below). And, surveying youth culture of the early twenty-first century, US journalist Alissa Quart was especially pessimistic. In her book *Branded: The Buying and Selling of Teenagers* (2003), Quart lamented 'the unbearable commercialization of youth' (Quart, 2003: xxvi). In her biting critique of corporate brands, Quart argued that young people's creativity had been crushed by relentless commercial manipulation, the book's promotional blurb ominously warning readers – 'Did you know you're being brainwashed?'

Slaves to the rhythm?: A critique of mass culture theories

Critics, of course, rightly highlight the power of corporate industries. And in pursuit of optimal profit, many 'cultural industries' have adopted the economic efficiencies afforded by systems of standardised production. The history of popular music, for instance, is full of examples of success based on churning out standardised, mass-marketed products. Most famously, the assembly-line production techniques of American car companies were the inspiration for the Motown Record Corporation, established by Berry Gordy in 1960. Having spent time working in Detroit's Lincoln-Mercury car plant, Gordy was fascinated by its efficiency and subsequently applied its assembly-line procedures to the 'manufacture' of music (Smith, 1999: 71). Gordy's 'Hitsville' recording studios were kept active 22 hours a day, producing songs in a factory-like manner. And the characteristic 'Motown sound' – an accentuated back beat, melodic chord structures, and a call-and-response singing style – became a standard blueprint, while Motown's acts were methodically groomed, dressed, and choreographed by the company.

In Japan Johnny Kitagawa was equally business-like. Founding his talent agency – Johnny & Associates Inc. – in 1962, Kitagawa shaped Japan's boy band landscape for more than half a century. Propelling one act after another to the heights of Japanese pop, his stable included groups like SMAP, Arashi, KAT-TUN, and Hey! Say! JUMP, along with solo artists such as Hiromi Go. And their road to success was distinguished by Kitagawa's unashamedly formulaic approach. His protégés were all recruited, coached, and marketed in a regime of strict standardisation and uniformity – to the extent that the term 'Johnnies' became generically applied to any of Kitagawa's performers (Campion, 2005).[2]

Also systematic were the record producing trio Mike Stock, Matt Aitken, and Pete Waterman (abbreviated as SAW), who dominated British pop during the 1980s and early 1990s. Dubbed the 'Hit Factory', they developed a formulaic sound that combined Hi-NRG disco beats and Italian melodies, and (like Motown and Kitagawa) SAW adopted assembly-line techniques as they chalked-up more than 100 UK Top Forty hits and sold over 40 million records. Comparable strategies were also adopted by British TV producer Simon Cowell. Cowell's 'reality' talent shows *Pop Idol* (2001–2003) and *The X Factor* (2004–present) were distinguished by their uniform approach to recruiting, coaching, and promoting a succession of 'standardised' pop stars.

Moreover, Cowell's talent shows can, themselves, be seen as relatively uniform products that rolled off his TV assembly-line. Formats were regular and consistent, while the same basic formulae were modified and 'retooled' for repeated sale across a multitude of international markets. By 2014, for example, *Pop Idol* had sired 49 local adaptations, while *The X Factor* had spawned 45 versions worldwide (Esser et al., 2016: 297).

Clearly, then, theorists such as Adorno are right to highlight the dimensions of standardisation that characterise a large part of the media industries' output. But 'mass culture' critics' view of vulnerable consumers being gripped by an irresistible (and aesthetically debased) commercial machine is open to important criticisms. Media industries, for example, are not the ruthlessly efficient capitalist operations that mass culture theorists imply. Even a mammoth investment in advertising and promotion is no guarantee of successful sales, illustrated by the glorious commercial flops that litter the history of popular entertainment. The products of the 'culture industry', moreover, have not always worked to reproduce the ideas of the powerful.

From rock 'n' roll to gangsta rap, popular music has often been a centre for cultural conflict. Moreover, rather than simply being a 'soundtrack' playing in the background of historical events, popular music has sometimes been integral to forces bringing about social and political change.[3] Peter Wicke, for example, argues that rock music in East Germany played an important role in the collapse of the communist regime, and that '... rock musicians were instrumental in setting in motion the actual course of events which led to the destruction of the Berlin Wall and the disappearance of the GDR' (Wicke, 1992: 81). Similarly, Seth Hague and his colleagues argue that the Rock Against Racism movement that emerged in Britain during the late 1970s did not simply proclaim anti-racist politics, but also embodied it aesthetically by bringing punk and reggae musicians together on stage. In this instance, Hague et al. argue, 'the music became the object of the politics, not just a means to it' (Hague et al. 2008: 21).

And, even though Motown hits were standardised products that rolled off Berry Gordy's assembly-line, cultural theorist Paul Gilroy notes how Motown (along with other soul music of the day) was a crucial component of the civil rights movement. 'These singers', Gilroy argues, 'did not simply provide a soundtrack for the political actions of their soul sisters and brothers. They were mandated to speak on behalf of the community in elaborate, celebratory, ritual performances' (Gilroy, 1994: 88). And, while 1970s disco has been maligned by its critics for being frivolous and shallow, authors such as Alice Echols (2010) show how disco played an important part in the sexual and racial politics of the time, and was a central force in the emergence of gay cultural identities.

Perhaps the biggest criticism to be made of mass culture approaches, however, relates to their elitist attitude towards popular culture. Adorno, for example, was happy to assign prestige and 'meaning' to classical and avant-garde music and its listeners, but derided popular musical forms as standardised and banal. Such a comparison, however, is problematic since it judges popular genres against classical and avant-garde ideals of 'originality' and 'authenticity'.

As Bernard Gendron observed in his thoroughgoing appraisal of Adorno's thesis, 'standardisation' is an obvious feature of many pop music genres and artists' repertoires, but recognition of similarities among popular texts is often what provides their audiences with enjoyment. So, Gendron argues, 'we might consider standardization not only as an expression of rigidity, but also as a source of pleasure' (Gendron, 1986: 29). But mass culture theorists have little time for popular pleasure. Instead, the enlightened few are congratulated for their intellectual ability to resist the power of the culture industry and recognise the value of 'real' creativity, while popular audiences are dismissed as the passive and 'forcibly retarded' victims of the commercial machine. In contrast, however, theorists such as David Hesmondhalgh argue for the importance of emotion, experience, and pleasure. And, for Hesmondhalgh, music has particular significance in this respect. Our tastes in music, he argues, are not only intensely linked to our sense of identity and self but also provide a basis for our intimate relations with others. As Hesmondhalgh explains:

> Music ... represents a remarkable meeting point of intimate and social realms. It provides a basis of self-identity (this is who I am, this is not) and collective identity (this is who we are, this is who we're not), often in the same moment. All cultural products have this potential – films, television programmes, even shoes and cars. Yet music's seemingly special link to emotions and feeling makes it an especially powerful site for the bringing together of private and public experience.
>
> (Hesmondhalgh, 2013: 2)

Hesmondhalgh's approach is rooted in the theoretical traditions of cultural studies, an academic discipline that first took shape in Britain during the 1960s. Central to the development of this field were the ideas of the seminal theorist Raymond Williams. Whereas traditional approaches to cultural life had established a hierarchal distinction between 'high' culture (deemed worthy, creative, and meaningful) and 'low' or 'mass' culture (dismissed as worthless, commercial and banal), Williams argued that culture should instead be seen as 'a whole way of life ... which expresses certain meanings and values not only in art and learning but also in institutions and ordinary behaviour' (1961: 57). Informed by Williams' approach, researchers increasingly eschewed the elitism of 'mass culture' approaches and understood popular culture as a more complex field – one in which commercial interests certainly wielded considerable power, but where audiences and consumers were also able to carve out meaningful identities and relationships. It was an approach that became especially evident in the study of young people and their engagement with the media.

'The kids are alright': youth, style, and subcultural 'resistance'

Williams' ideas were especially influential on members of the Centre for Contemporary Cultural Studies (CCCS), established at Britain's Birmingham

University in 1964 (see Chapter 4). Led by Stuart Hall, the CCCS made many influential contributions to the fields of media and cultural studies. Particularly significant was the way they saw audiences as actively involved in making meanings from media texts. Whereas traditions of 'effects' research had tended to see audiences as passively accepting ideas 'encoded' in media texts (see Chapter 5), the CCCS team emphasised the way audiences actively participate – both cognitively and emotionally – in making sense of texts.[4] In these terms, audiences do not simply accept a media text's 'encoded' meanings, but actively interpret and sometimes reconfigure (or challenge) those meanings. Such interventions into media theory were highly influential but, so too, were the CCCS authors' analyses of culture. Drawing on Williams' view of culture as 'a whole way of life', the CCCS team saw popular texts and the practices of everyday life as being just as relevant and meaningful as the provinces of 'high' culture or 'great art'. The CCCS authors, moreover, combined these insights with a battery of ideas drawn from American and European sociological, semiotic, and political theorists as they explored areas stretching from the form and meaning of media texts, to the structures of working-class culture, gender relations, and the political dimensions of racism.

The 'CCCS approach' was never a unified set of arguments or a common analytic perspective. But issues of class-based conflict were common to much of their work. Here, the CCCS writers drew on a range of sophisticated Marxist theories. Particularly influential were the ideas of the French Marxist philosopher Louis Althusser and his view of ideology as being not simply a mechanism that inculcated an illusory 'false consciousness' among the subordinate class, but a conceptual framework 'through which men [*sic*] interpret, make sense of, experience and "live" the material conditions in which they find themselves' (Hall, 1980ii: 33). Another key influence were the ideas of the Italian Marxist, Antonio Gramsci and his view of capitalist societies as being characterised by an ongoing, class-based struggle for hegemony – or the moral, cultural, intellectual (and thereby political) leadership of society. While dominant groups were often able to secure their power through this struggle, Gramsci argued, subordinate groups were *also* active social agents who could always challenge and resist the dominant hegemony.

The CCCS authors explored these ideas in relation to a broad range of issues, but the analysis of youth culture was a prominent interest. Here, the CCCS team were influenced by Phil Cohen's earlier (1972) analysis of postwar British youth culture. Focusing on developments in London's East End, Cohen argued that the rebuilding of local neighbourhoods, combined with the collapse of traditional labour markets and changing patterns of consumption, had disrupted the material basis of working-class life. For Cohen, the various youth styles of the 1950s and 1960s – Teddy boys, mods, skinheads – could be understood as symbolic responses to this dislocation. These style-based social groups, Cohen argued, were 'magical' attempts by working-class youth to bridge the gap between traditional patterns of working-class life and the new cultural landscape of postwar Britain. By fusing together key concerns of their working-class 'parent' culture (for example, an emphasis on local identities and collective loyalties) with the new products of the flourishing media and culture industries (most obviously fashion and pop music), young people produced *sub*cultural movements such as the mods and skinheads. According to Cohen, then, subcultures served to:

> ... express and resolve, albeit 'magically', the contradictions which remain hidden and unresolved in the parent culture ... [each subculture attempts] to retrieve some of the socially cohesive elements destroyed in their parent culture and to combine these with other class fractions symbolising one or other of the options confronting it.
>
> (Cohen 1972: 23)

Instead of dismissing youth styles as trivial fads, then, Cohen presented them as important purveyors of social meaning, intrinsically linked to wider patterns of social change. This approach was extended by the CCCS team. In *Resistance through Rituals* (Hall and Jefferson, 1976) the CCCS authors presented a range of different studies that, collectively, suggested subcultural styles represented a symbolic, or 'ritualistic' expression of working-class youth's social experiences. Like Cohen, the CCCS team argued that working-class youth constructed a cultural, or *sub*cultural, response pertinent to their life experiences by fusing together elements of their 'parent' culture (for example, working-class argot, neighbourhood ties and particular notions of masculinity and femininity) with elements derived from other cultural sources – in particular, music and fashion. Crucially, however, the CCCS introduced a neo-Marxist, 'Gramscian' account of young people as locked into class-based struggles and conflicts. So, whereas Cohen had seen subcultural style as an 'ideological *solution*' to contradictions assailing the parent culture, the CCCS were more forthright – interpreting youth subcultures as symbolic (or 'ritualistic') strategies of *resistance* to ruling-class power structures. In what became known as 'subcultural theory',[5] the CCCS authors argued that young people's distinctive styles (those of Teddy boys, mods, and skinheads, for example) were strategies of symbolic resistance to a dominant, class-based social order. From this perspective, then, youth subcultures were seen as forms of cultural insubordination, expressions of defiant rebellion in which working-class youths appropriated the articles, artefacts, and icons generated by the commercial media, and symbolically reworked them to take on new, threatening, and subversive meanings.

For the CCCS theorists, moreover, it was possible to differentiate fairly precisely between *sub*cultural groups of working-class youth and the *counter*-cultures of their middle-class peers (Clarke et al., 1976: 60–61). According to the CCCS authors, subcultures (Teddy boys, mods, skinheads etc.) generally reproduced traditional working-class values and tended to be leisure-oriented, fairly temporary episodes in young people's lives. In contrast, countercultures (beats, hippies, etc.) placed more emphasis on individual experience, while the stark polarity between work and leisure characteristic of subcultures was much less pronounced in the countercultures' bohemian, non-conformist milieu. More fundamentally, the CCCS authors contended, while working-class sub-cultures represented a revolt against the status quo from 'below', the middle-class countercultures were a more politically-conscious attack from 'within' (Clarke et al., 1976: 62–63).

The emphasis the CCCS model placed on the *symbolic* dimensions to these struggles was important. The approach effectively turned subcultural styles into 'texts', and strategies of semiotic analysis were keenly deployed in attempts to 'read' the subversive meanings seen as ingrained in the skinhead's boots and braces or the punk's bondage trousers and spiky hairstyle. Here, two concepts (both derived from the French anthropologist, Claude Lévi-Strauss) emerged as especially important – bricolage and homology. 'Bricolage' referred to the way the meanings of particular objects were transformed as they were adopted and recontextualised by subcultural groups. According to Dick Hebdige, for example, the 1960s mods appropriated the motor scooter ('a formerly ultra-respectable means of transport') and transformed it into 'a weapon and a symbol of solidarity' (Hebdige 1976: 93). 'Homology', meanwhile, denoted the way disparate stylistic elements – music, clothes, and leisure activities – coalesced to form a coherent symbolic expression of a subcultural group's identity. Using the example of British bikers, for instance, Paul Willis identified a 'homo-logical' relationship between the physical qualities of the motorcycle and the subcultural ethos of the biker gang. The 'solidity, responsiveness, inevitableness [*sic*], the strength of the motorcycle', Willis argued, corresponded with 'the concrete, secure nature of the bikeboys' world' (Willis, 1978: 53). Developing this approach, Hebdige produced an especially deft analysis of punk rock in *Subculture: The Meaning of Style* (1979). For Hebdige, British punk style of the 1970s was akin to 'semiotic guerrilla warfare' (1979: 105), an exercise in sar-torial defiance that went 'against the grain of a mainstream culture' and trans-formed the 'naturalized' meanings of everyday cultural artefacts and media texts into something alien, spectacular and threatening (1979: 100–101):

> Objects borrowed from the most sordid of contexts found a place in punks' ensembles; lavatory chains were draped in graceful arcs across chests in plastic bin liners. Safety pins were taken out of their domestic 'utility' context and worn as gruesome ornaments through the cheek, ear or lip … fragments of school uniform (white bri-nylon shirts, school ties) were symbolically defiled (the shirts covered in graffiti, or fake blood; the ties left undone) and juxta-posed against leather drains or shocking pink mohair tops.
>
> (Hebdige, 1979: 112)

The limits of subcultural theory

The emphasis the CCCS writers placed on style as a site of class-based struggle was indebted to their historical context. Britain during the 1970s was a society beset by social, economic and political conflict, and the rise of youth subcultures like punk made it seem like the wider sense of crisis was being played out in the music and fashions of the time. And, generally, subcultural theory made a major contribution to the study of young people's lives. Its importance lies not only in the way it established style and music as important realms of cultural meaning, and worthy of scholarly analysis. Subcultural theory also made a valuable challenge to assumptions that young people shared a common, generationally-based 'youth culture'. Crucially, the CCCS authors highlighted the way socio-economic inequalities and relations of power had a major impact on youngster's cultural experiences. Understandably, therefore, subcultural theory has been a major influence on a wide body of researchers worldwide. But, while many have taken up the themes and perspectives originally formulated by the CCCS, this has not been done uncritically. Many theorists have pointed to the shortcomings and oversights of the approach. Indeed, many of the CCCS team have, themselves, critically reflected on subcultural theory's limitations.

The CCCS authors, for example, always acknowledged the limits to subcultural 'resistance'. Confined to specific realms of social life – leisure, style, and media consumption – the subcultural challenge was always partial and tangential and, as Hebdige himself put it, 'no amount of stylistic incantation can alter the oppressive mode in which the commodities used in subculture have been produced' (1979: 130). For some, however, the heavy attention given to symbolic meanings was problematic. According to Hebdige, style could be analysed as an autonomous text, with 'resistance' taking place at a level independent of the consciousness of subcultural participants – and Hebdige conceded that it was 'highly unlikely' that members of any subcultures would recognise themselves in his account (Hebdige 1979: 139). But this lack of attention to the actual intentions behind young people's creation of style provoked criticism. 'It seems to me', Stanley Cohen conjectured, 'that somewhere along the line, symbolic language implies a knowing subject, a subject at least dimly aware of what the symbols are supposed to mean' (2002: lvii–lviii). In relying on an 'aesthetics which may work for art, but not equally well for life', Cohen warned, subcultural theory risked 'getting lost in the forest of symbols' (Cohen 2002: lx).

The CCCS theorists' focus on issues of social class also drew criticism. The polarity constructed between working-class *subcultures* and middle-class *counter-cultures*, for example, could oversimplify groups whose composition was often complex and varied. According to Peter Clecak, for instance, the 1960s counterculture was composed of diverse movements and ideas that allowed people from a mixture of social backgrounds 'to find symbolic shapes for their social and spiritual discontents and hopes' (Clecak, 1983: 18). Gary Clarke, meanwhile, pointed to the contradictions between Hebdige's emphasis on punk's 'working-class creativity' and the movement's origins among London's art-school avant-garde (Clarke, 1990: 86); and Sheryl Garratt highlighted the heterogeneity of Britain's late 1980s acid house scene, arguing there was a degree of truth to the oft-repeated cliché that 'bankers were dancing next to barrow boys' (Garratt 1998, 160).

The CCCS model was also criticised for allowing social class to overshadow other systems of power relations. Angela McRobbie (1981), for example, was quick to draw attention to the gendered assumptions of much subcultural theory. McRobbie was, herself, affiliated with the Birmingham group, but she was critical of the way some of her colleagues' work rendered the category of 'youth' as unproblematically masculine. Indeed, the studies produced by many subcultural theorists seemed to marginalise young women, concentrating almost exclusively on male experience. Subsequently, it was an omission addressed in a wide body of research focused on girls and young women (see below).

For many critics, the CCCS view of subcultures as 'authentic', unmediated expressions of identity was also flawed. Focusing their analysis on what they saw as the creative '"moment" of originality in the formation of style' (Clarke and Jefferson, 1976: 148), the CCCS theorists tended to equate intervention by commercial business with the 'neutralisation' of an authentic subculture – so that market intercession was seen as returning once meaningful and 'oppositional' subcultural styles to the fold of bland consumerism. As John Clarke and Tony Jefferson put it:

> The 'main stream' youth cultural response represents ... the 'incorporated' version of the 'deviant' style: the version that has been bought up, sanitized, 'made safe' and resold to the wider youth market: the 'deviant' lifestyle become consumption style: the commercial version of the 'real'.
>
> (Clarke and Jefferson, 1976: 148)

This model of 'commercial incorporation', however, has been seen as problematic. For some theorists, the relationship between subcultures and the commercial media is not a simple, linear progression that begins with 'grass-roots authenticity' and ends with 'sanitised product'. Instead, it can be seen as a more 'circuitous', symbiotic process of mutual interaction. The account of subcultures offered by the CCCS is analogous to a 'biological' narrative that starts out with 'birth' (authentic innovation) and concludes in 'death' (commercial incorporation). But, in reality, the 'lives' of subcultural styles are more complex and multifaceted – they are endlessly recycled, regenerated, and re-embedded in new temporal and geographic contexts. Moreover, from their outset, the crystallisation and dissemination of youth subcultures relies on intervention from the media industries. Cohen's (2002) study of British mods and rockers during the 1960s, for instance, highlighted the way media coverage gave greater form and definition to subcultural formations that were initially vague and indistinct (see Chapter 4). The theme was developed in Sarah Thornton's (1995) analysis of Britain's 1980s rave culture. Like Cohen, Thornton argued that the representational power of the media was crucial in shaping the rave scene's identity and its members' sense of themselves. Subcultures, Thornton explained:

> ... do not germinate from a seed and grow by force of their own energy into mysterious 'movements' only to be belatedly digested by the media.

Rather, media, and other cultural industries are there and effective right from the start.

(Thornton, 1995: 117)

While acknowledging the media's role in the development of rave culture, however, Thornton still emphasised how ravers, themselves, had been 'active and creative participants in the formation of club cultures' (Thornton, 1995: 161). Although 'authentic' subcultures were, in essence, media constructions, Thornton argued they remained powerful sources of meaning and self-identity for their participants. Here, Thornton borrowed from French theorist Pierre Bourdieu's notion of 'cultural capital'. For Bourdieu (1986) 'cultural capital' denoted the forms of knowledge, artefacts, and modes of behaviour that bestowed prestige and social advantage on those social groups that possessed them. Adapting the concept, Thornton argued that '*sub*cultural capital' represented the knowledge, tastes, and artefacts that conferred status in the eyes of subcultural members. 'Just as books and paintings display cultural capital in the family home', Thornton explained:

... so subcultural capital is objectified in the form of fashionable haircuts and well assembled record collections ... Just as cultural capital is personified in 'good' manners, so subcultural capital is embodied in the form of being 'in the know', using (but not over-using) current slang and looking as if you were born to perform the current dance styles.

(Thornton, 1995: 11–12)

Generally, distinctions between 'meaningful' subcultures and 'incorporated' media fabrications have been difficult to sustain. As cultural theorist Simon Frith noted in an early critique, attempts to elaborate a clear-cut divide between the 'subcultural' and the 'mainstream' have invariably led to a 'false freezing of the world into deviants and the rest' (1978: 53). Moreover, relatively few youngsters ever enter the 'authentic' subcultural scenes described by the CCCS team. As Gary Clarke pointed out, subcultural theory was preoccupied with the spectacular and focused only on the 'stylistic deviance of a few' (Clarke, 1990: 75). And the CCCS theorists, themselves, conceded that 'the great majority of working-class youth never enters a tight or coherent subculture at all' (Clarke et al., 1976: 16). Indeed, rather than making a wholehearted commitment to a subcultural lifestyle, most youngsters adopt only a limited range of subcultural trappings or insignia (perhaps wearing a 'mod' jacket, or buying a 'punk' record). As social theorist Steve Redhead wryly observed, '"authentic" subcultures were produced by subcultural theories, not the other way around' (Redhead, 1990: 25).

The 'post-subcultural' turn: translocal scenes and eclectic neo-tribes

The perceived weaknesses of subcultural theory (combined with changes in the form of subcultures themselves) prompted the emergence of alternative perspectives. For some theorists, for example, the growing plurality and mutability of youth styles during the 1980s and 1990s evoked wider cultural trends towards 'postmodern' fragmentation and intertextuality. 'Postmodernism' is a notoriously nebulous concept. Generally, it denotes a set of cultural characteristics that, according to some commentators, were generated in tandem with the profound social, economic, and cultural changes of the late twentieth century. According to postmodern theorists such as Jean François Lyotard (1984), a succession of global shifts – the transformation of world political orders; major industrial restructuring and economic realignment; rapid developments in technology and media; and significant shifts in family and community relationships – had brought about a new 'postmodern condition' in which all overarching claims to knowledge and 'truth' were subject to growing scepticism and doubt. Alongside this crisis in the status of knowledge, some writers argued, there had also emerged a distinctive set of cultural trends and aesthetic sensibilities. Jean Baudrillard (1985), for example, argued that the proliferation of media and information technologies had engendered an 'ecstasy of communication', a condition in which boundaries between formerly discrete areas of cultural life were erased and people were immersed in a 'hyperreal' media world where borders between the real and the imaginary had become blurred and indistinct.

Postmodern aesthetics were, for some observers, especially evident in the kaleidoscope of shifting, intermingling youth styles and pop music prevalent at the end of the twentieth century. These developments were explored in a series of 'club cultures' studies of British dance music produced during the 1990s by authors affiliated to the Manchester Institute of Popular Culture (based at Manchester Metropolitan University). Drawn together by Steve Redhead, this research was varied in focus but generally pointed to the way (post)modern club cultures seemed to defy attempts at uncovering a concrete sense of 'meaning' behind their styles and appeared, instead, to be 'free-floating' and not locked into any specific historical moment or location.[6] Other research, too, developed new critical perspectives in what Rupert Weinzierl and David Muggleton (2003) dubbed a move towards 'post-subcultural studies' – a diverse field of work that encompassed both fundamental challenges to subcultural theory and attempts to revise and update the CCCS authors' original approaches.[7]

Rather than ideas of subculture, the concept of 'scene' became influential in the study of popular music. Musicians and music journalists had long used the word 'scene' as a loose description of distinctive genres or groups of artists, but it was developed as an analytic term by Will Straw. For Straw, 'scenes' were modes of connection that 'actualiz[ed] a particular state of relations between various populations and social groups, as these coalesce around specific coalitions of musical style' (1991: 379). That is to say, scenes were associations and communities based on specific forms of music and which, Straw argued, could crystallise around either spatial locations or common sets of musical sensibility, potentially cutting across factors such as class, gender, or ethnicity.

For its proponents, the concept of the 'scene' recognised a broader and more dynamic set of social relationships than those encompassed in sub-cultural theory. The idea of 'scenes', it was argued, offered a means to ana-lyse the myriad ways music was both produced and consumed across local and transglobal settings. In local terms, for example, Barry Shank's (1994) study of Austin, Texas highlighted the way social networks and relationships took shape based around a local music scene which, Shank argued, was comprised of a plurality of distinctive but overlapping genre groups. A more translocal approach was taken by Keith Kahn-Harris (2007) in his study of 'extreme' heavy metal. For Harris, 'extreme metal' was constituted by a series of local scenes – stretching from Britain and the US to Israel and Sweden – that were bonded globally through a vibrant exchange of musical influences and styles.[8]

Critics, however, saw the concept of 'scene' as flawed by its haziness. David Hesmondhalgh, for instance, found much to commend in individual 'scene' studies, but argued the term had been used 'for too long in too many different and imprecise ways' (2007: 43). Writers such as Straw, for example, had used the term 'scene' to denote a cultural space transcending locality, whereas figures such as Shank had used the same term to term denote music practices within a particular town or city. According to its advocates, such variation demonstrated the inherent flexibility of 'scene' as a tool of analysis, Straw defending 'the term's efficiency as a default label for cultural unities whose precise boundaries are invisible and elastic' (Straw, 2001: 248). Hesmondhalgh, however, was more dubious, arguing that the discrepancies and disparities made for con-ceptual weakness and a lack of analytic precision.

Alongside the notion of 'scenes', the idea of the 'neo-tribe' was also deployed as an alternative to subcultural theory. Originating in the work of Michel Maffesoli (1996), the concept of the neo-tribe denoted the way indi-viduals were, during the late twentieth century, seen as increasingly expressing collective identities through distinctive rituals and consumption practices. According to Maffesoli, these 'neo-tribal' groups were not formed according to 'traditional' structural determinants – for example, class, gender, or religion – but through diverse, dynamic, and often ephemeral consumption patterns. Moreover, the fluid boundaries of 'neo-tribes' allowed members to wander through multiple group attachments, so that collective identity was 'less a question of belonging to a gang, a family or a community, than of switching from one group to another' (Maffesoli, 1996: 76). Both Andy Bennett (1999i) and Ben Malbon (1999) drew on these ideas in their analyses of modern dance music. For both authors, the apparently fluid membership of various dance music factions was indicative of a 'neo-tribal' sensibility. This was seen as a product of both the increasingly diverse universe of youth style, and the 'frag-mented' texture of dance music itself – characterized by DJs' techniques of digital sampling, mixing, and 'mashing'. The implication of these arguments was that young people's consumption of popular music was no longer deter-mined by conformity to rigid subcultural genres, but by changing individual repertoires of taste rooted in the 'unstable and shifting cultural affiliations which characterize late modern consumer-based identities' (Bennett, 1999i: 605).

According to critics, however, the emphasis post-subcultural theories placed on fluid tastes and individual consumption obscured the continued relevance of socio-economic class and structural inequality in young people's lives. David Hesmondhalgh, for instance, contended that Bennett's model of neo-tribes was effectively a 'celebration of consumerism' that glossed over the way structural inequalities constrain both people's access to cultural commodities and the ways such commodities were ultimately used to fashion identities' (Hesmondhalgh, 2007: 39). Christine Griffin concurred, arguing that much 'post-subcultural' work missed (or actively avoided) any engagement with issues of class. Griffin was especially critical of the notions of 'individualisation' and 'self-reflexivity' that had underpinned much post-subcultural theorising. Such approaches had interpreted shifts in advanced industrial societies as eroding traditional anchors for social and personal identities; but, according to Griffin, there was 'little evidence that the macro-economic structurations of class have changed substantially since the 1960s and 1970s', while in Britain there had actually been 'a dramatic increase in social and economic inequalities around health, employment and education' (Griffin, 2011: 255).[9]

Arguments that post-subcultural approaches had 'evacuated' issues of social inequality from their terms of analysis were, to be fair, somewhat overstated. Moreover, many post-subcultural studies effectively brought out the complexities of style, taste, and attitude in an increasingly media-saturated, commodity-driven cultural landscape. Furthermore, the rich ethnography in some post-subcultural research offered much fuller accounts of 'lived experience' than had often been the case with subcultural theory. Greater dimensions of 'post-subcultural' flux and fusion were also clearly more evident in many young people's styles and cultural sensibilities.

That said, any sense that distinctive, relatively cohesive subcultural groups had slipped into the past was probably premature. Ethnogaphic research produced in Britain by David Muggleton (2000), for example, showed that many young people still consciously identified themselves as punks, goths, or skinheads and, Muggleton argued, saw their tastes in style and music as a bohemian-like expression of *'freedom* – freedom from rules, structures, controls and from the predictability of conventional lifestyles' (Muggleton, 2000: 167). Paul Hodkinson's (2002) study of British goths also challenged claims that distinctive subcultural styles had fallen by the postmodern wayside. Hodkinson acknowledged that, amid the frenetic media flows of contemporary culture, stylistic boundaries had become less clear-cut; but he insisted that goths were still 'characterized more by their substance than by their fluidity' (2002, 196; 62). Undoubtedly, subcultural theory's original emphasis on class-based 'resistance' as the *raison d'être* of subcultural style fails to capture the diversity, dynamism, and complexity inherent to young people's cultural expressions. But, as J. Patrick Williams argues, not all young people have been subsumed into an eclectic bazaar of 'hedonism, individualism and consumerism', and distinct subcultures still exist insofar as many youngsters 'continue to collectively distinguish themselves from an undifferentiated mainstream' (Williams, 2018: 16).

And, for some participants, subcultural involvement has been extended over a longer period of life. Ethnographic research across a range of subcultural groups – including punk (Bennett, 2006), goth (Hodkinson, 2011), and Britain's northern soul enthusiasts (Smith, 2009) – has suggested that many people continue to invest heavily in subcultural practices well beyond their 'youth'. This apparent increase in the longevity of subcultural involvement is partly rooted in a general extension of transitions into 'adulthood' (see Chapter 3). But, as Bennett and Hodkinson (2012) argue, it is also constituent in broader shifts in modern lifestyles and practices of consumption. The notion of subcultures as characteristically 'youthful', therefore, has become less the case as ageing subcultural affiliates 'keep on a-rockin''.

Grrrl power: subcultures, gender, and sexuality

One of the biggest problems with subcultural theory had been the way it marginalised young women. Girls had either been ignored altogether, or appeared as an adjunct in studies that chiefly examined young men. In response, feminist researchers sought to foreground the lives of girls and young women. Rather than seeing girls' experience as a mere footnote to male subcultures, authors such as Angela McRobbie argued that young women's cultural activities were qualitatively different to those of young men. As McRobbie (writing with Jenny Garber) explained, the crucial issue was not 'the absence or presence of girls in male sub-cultures', but 'the complementary ways in which young girls interact among themselves and with each other to form a distinctive culture of their own' (McRobbie and Garber, 1976: 219).

Writing in Britain during the 1970s, McRobbie observed how young women were more socially and culturally constrained than their male peers (McRobbie, 1978). Girls' activities and behaviour, she noted, were subject to much greater levels of societal and parental regulation. Furthermore, McRobbie observed, young women's disposable income has generally been less than that of young men, while (especially for working-class girls) childcare and domestic responsibilities have been considerably greater. And, 50 years later, much the same is true across the world. A report released by UNICEF in 2016, for instance, showed that, globally, 10–14-year-old girls spend 50 per cent more time doing unpaid household work than boys their age (UNICEF, 2016). And, in many local contexts, social norms and cultural traditions work oppressively to regulate and restrict young women's lives.

As a result, some theorists have suggested that, in contrast to male-oriented subcultures (which have primarily existed in 'public' spaces), girls' cultural spaces have been concentrated in the 'private' realm of the home. In economically developed countries, the bedroom (especially) has been cited as a key site where girls socialise and elaborate their sense of identity (McRobbie and Garber, 1976). Indeed, ethnographic research by Sarah Baker (2004) and Siân

Lincoln (2012) highlights the importance of 'bedroom culture' for both young women *and* young men; this work demonstrating not only how young people use décor and possessions in their bedrooms to explore and express their sense of self, but also how the more general use of physical and virtual spaces is a crucial dimension in young people's elaboration of identities and cultures.

While some researchers have explored the 'private' dimensions to young women's cultures, others have challenged the idea that women have been absent from, or marginal to, the more 'public' world of subcultures and countercultures. Gretchen Lemke-Santangelo (2009), for instance, has demonstrated how women played a significant part in the US counterculture of the 1960s and 1970s. Similarly, Helen Reddington (2007) reveals the centrality of women in the rise of British punk during the 1970s and 1980s, while Lauraine Leblanc shows how the punk subculture continued to be drawn upon by many young women 'to resist the prescriptions of femininity, [and] to carve out a space where they can define their own sense of self' (Leblanc, 1999, 219–220). An array of commentators, meanwhile, have championed the 'riot-grrrl' movement of the 1990s (an offshoot of American punk) as a powerfully defiant example of young women's cultural agency.[10] Britain's club scene of the late 1980s and 1990s has also been seen as a site for expressions of rebellious femininity. For instance, in contrast to views that club culture was 'dominated by the lads' (Thornton 1995: 25), Maria Pini has argued that the club circuit afforded women the 'possibility for ... adventure, exploration and discovery' through the opportunities it offered for 'taking drugs, going "mental" and dancing through the night without sexual harassment' (2001: 13; 34).

The late 1990s and early 2000s also saw an increased prominence of girls across North American and European popular culture (see Chapter 4). Noticeable was the growing centrality of confident, independent and relatively complex female characters in movies such as *Clueless* (1995), *Bring It On* (2000) and *Mean Girls* (2004), along with TV series such as *My So-Called Life* (1994–1995) and *Buffy the Vampire Slayer* (1997–2003) (see Chapter 3). These developments were partly a consequence of commercial industries' attempts to tap into new consumer markets but, as Mary Celeste Kearney observes, they were also indebted to an influx of women and feminist ideas into the world of media production which, in filmmaking, spawned a spate of movies that 'broadened the spectrum of female adolescence beyond the white, middle-class, suburban stereotype of teenage girlhood consistently reproduced by the Hollywood studios' (2002: 131).

The growing profile of girls in popular culture, combined with the increasing academic research that focused on young women, prompted the emergence of 'girls studies' as a distinct sphere of scholarship – signposted by the launch of a dedicated academic journal, *Girlhood Studies*, in 2008. The field, however, initially attracted a degree of criticism for its apparent ethnocentrism. Kearney, for instance, noted how 'non-white, non-Western girls remain vastly understudied as a result of such research being conducted primarily in Canada, Australia, Great Britain, Northern Europe, and the United States' (Kearney, 2009: 19).

Subsequently, however, the scope of girls studies has diversified. In the US, for instance, notable ethnographic research by (among others) Ruth Nicole Brown (2009), Aimee Cox (2015) and Oneka LaBennett (2011) has explored the representations, experiences, and expressions of Black girlhood. Other authors, meanwhile have contributed to an expanding range of studies dealing with the experience of girls and young women in a variety of global contexts.[11]

Early studies of youth culture and subculture were not only marked by their scant attention to young women. They also gave limited attention to issues of masculinity. Of course, many of the initial subculture studies were preoccupied with male interests and activities. But they rarely considered the precise nature of 'masculine' identities. Indeed, across the social sciences and humanities, the analysis of masculinity was relatively underdeveloped until the 1980s when an increasing body of research began to interrogate the nature of masculine identities and their associated power relations across a wide variety of cultures, historical periods, and institutional settings. In this respect, the work of US theorist R.W. Connell (1995) was especially influential. Connell highlighted the way issues of class, 'race' and sexuality shape 'multiple masculinities' that are structured in a hierarchy of dominance and subordination. And, subsequently, a wealth of research has explored constructions and articulations of masculinity. In the analysis of youth culture, the trend was reflected in studies of representations of young masculinities in film and TV, such as those provided by both Murray Pomerance and Frances Gatewa (2004) and Annette Wannamaker (2011). Analyses of young masculine identities, meanwhile, featured in studies such as Nancy Macdonald's (2001) examination of young men's search for respect and status in the graffiti subcultures of London and New York, Karen Lumsden's (2013) account of Scottish 'boy racers' and Sherene Idriss's (2018) exploration of the creative career aspirations of young Arab-Australian men. And, more generally, Anoop Nayak and Mary Jane Kehily (2013) have integrated research on masculinity and femininity in their examination of the various ways young people define themselves across national and local cultures.

Along with questions of gender, issues of sexual identity were also peripheral in early subcultural studies. As Judith Halberstam (2003; 2005) observed, subcultural theory's presumed heterosexual framework meant that consideration of sexuality and sexual styles was either omitted altogether, or was relegated to the fringes of analysis. From the late 1980s, however, such assumptions were challenged by a burgeoning body of work inspired by, and constituent in, the rise of 'queer studies'. Informed by such theorists as Michel Foucault (1978) and Judith Butler (1988; 1990), queer perspectives deconstruct the 'traditional' conceptual binaries of man/woman, heterosexual/homosexual, normal/abnormal and critique these dualisms as social and cultural constructs (see Chapter 9). 'Queer' subcultures and identities, therefore, have deconstructed and subverted conventional notions of gender and sexuality, challenging their hierarchies and associated systems of power.

While Halberstam did not do away with the term 'subculture', she argued that studies of queer subcultures demanded recognition of their distinctive features. Queer subcultures, Halberstam argued, were not simply 'spin-offs' of wider formations like punk or hip-hop.[12] But neither were they simply taste cultures allied with those lesbian and gay movements that sought assimilation within a heteronormative culture rooted in home and family. Instead, queer subcultures offered a potent critique of *both* hetero- *and* homo-normativity. Queer subcultures like riot dyke and queercore bands, drag kings, and queer slam poets were, Halberstam contended, 'alternative temporalities' that allowed participants 'to believe that their futures can be imagined according to logics that lie outside the conventional forward-moving narratives of birth, marriage, reproduction and death' (Halberstam, 2003: 314). Halberstam's arguments set the tone for a range of subsequent research on queer subcultures. Studies charted, for example, the distinctive identities and expressive styles of queercore (Ciminelli and Knox, 2005; Nault, 2017), dykecore (Shoemaker, 2010) and homo-hop (Wilson, 2007). But other researchers also highlighted the fluidity of queer sub-cultural practice. Susan Driver, for instance, pointed to the way queer-girl sub-cultures were characterised not by the consistency of their tastes and sensibilities, but by 'a mobility and heterogeneity that constitutes group affiliations and self transformations' (Driver, 2007: 215). And, similarly, Jodie Taylor's (2012) eth-nographic research on a variety of queer music scenes also highlighted distinct dimensions of 'aesthetic heterogeneity' in which punk, pop, rock, and other music genres were borrowed, blended, and reconstituted.[13]

Additionally, Driver (2007) – along with authors such as Jeffrey Dennis (2006) and Mareike Jenner (2014) – has highlighted the way young lesbian, gay, bisexual, and transgender (LGBT) characters have, since the 1990s, increasingly featured in mainstream film and TV. Despite such trends, however, it must be remembered that homophobia is still a prevalent force in many contexts. Indeed, in 2019 same-sex relations were still criminalised in 70 United Nations member states, and carried a possible death penalty in 13 countries (ILGA: 2019). Under the theocratic regime of the Islamic Republic of Iran, for example, Elam Golpushnezhad shows how an underground gay rap scene faces a dual challenge – hip-hop itself is officially viewed as 'deviant' and deplorably 'Westernized', while homosexuality is reviled. For a gay rapper operating in this climate of hostility, therefore, 'One's life is literally at stake' (Golpushnezhad, 2015: 124).

All-consuming passions: youth as 'creative' consumers

During the 1970s subcultural theory had focused on the spectacular styles of groups such as skinheads and punks. But during the late 1980s and early 1990s many researchers turned attention to young people's everyday practices of media consumption. In *Common Culture* (1990), for example, Paul Willis (for-merly a member of the Birmingham CCCS) highlighted young people's cul-tural production across a range of media and cultural forms. Rather than conceiving 'creativity' simply in terms of economic production and exchange, however, Willis gave attention to more general dimensions of identity formation, in which 'young people are all the time expressing or attempting to express something about their actual or potential cultural significance' (1990: 1). Invoking Raymond Williams' notion of culture as 'a whole way of life' (see above), Willis sought to reveal the elements of agency in young people's day-to-day cultural activities. Seeing commodities as cultural catalysts rather than as ends in themselves, Willis used the term 'grounded aesthetics' to denote the ways young people manipulated the goods and resources made available by the media and other commercial industries, youngsters re-articulating products' meanings in the creation of their own cultures and forms of self-representation.

For Willis, then, meanings were not intrinsic to cultural artefacts but were generated through the ways people used of them. Young people's acts of commodity consumption and media use were, according to Willis, not passive and indiscriminate but active practices of 'symbolic creativity'. Drawing illustrative examples from a range of rich (British-based) ethnographic studies, Willis argued that a variety of cultural activities and media forms (TV soap operas and advertisements, cinemagoing, teen magazines, pop music, fashion, and hairstyles) were used by young people as raw materials for creative expression, youth's patterns of consumption representing 'a kind of self-creation – of identities, of space, of cultural forms – with its own kind of cultural empowerment' (Willis, 1990: 82). Fashion, for instance, was seen by Willis as offering many creative and disruptive opportunities. Young people, he argued 'don't just buy passively or uncritically', instead they 'make their own sense of what is commercially available, make their own aesthetic judgements, and sometimes reject the normative definitions and categories of "fashion" promoted by the clothing industry' (Willis, 1990: 85). From this perspective, young people did not consume commercial goods and media texts unthinkingly, but actively appropriated the products available in the market, recontextualising, and transforming their meanings. This emphasis on young people as active agents in the creation of cultural meanings, therefore, starkly differs to the image of bovine consumer conformity presented by mass culture theorists (see above). It also markedly contrasts with the notions of passive, uncritical audiences underpinning much media 'effects' research (see Chapter 5).

The stress Willis put on the creative dimensions to young people's consumption pointed to the wider changes in media and cultural studies during the 1980s and 1990s. His emphasis on concrete fieldwork was indicative of a more general 'ethnographic turn' that saw researchers move away from theoretical approaches that privileged the 'power' of the text, and instead give greater attention to people's own understandings of their cultural practices and media use. But Willis's accent on the creative dimensions to media consumption was also part of the wider attention given to audiences as active participants in the processes of meaning-making. Rather than seeing audiences as helpless puppets that danced to the tune of media producers, researchers increasingly focused on the way people engaged actively with texts, their diverse responses influenced by factors of class, gender, sexual, and ethnic identity, along with the wider cultural contexts in which the media were encountered.

Attention to the 'creativity' of media audiences became an especially strong theme in the study of fan cultures. Fans have long been popularly regarded as rather sad creatures, invariably pathologised as socially dysfunctional outsiders or maligned as irrational obsessives. But during the 1990s several theorists drew attention to the way fans engaged actively and meaningfully with the objects of their passion. In this respect the work of US theorist Henry Jenkins (1992) was especially influential. Rejecting stereotypical depictions of fans as silly social misfits, Jenkins argued that fans of pop stars, films, and TV shows were actually skilled manipulators of media texts. Here, Jenkins drew on Michel de Certeau's (1984) concept of 'textual poaching'. For de Certeau, 'textual poaching' denoted the way subordinate groups subverted the meanings of dominant cultural forms. Oppressed social groups, he argued, fashioned a cultural environment for themselves by appropriating resources made available by the socially dominant forms of cultural production. And, according to Jenkins, fans were 'textual poachers' *par excellence*. Offering an ethnographic account of fans of TV shows such as *Star Trek* and *Beauty and the Beast*, Jenkins showed how they used the programmes as the basis for their own stories, songs, videos, and social exchanges in a rich and creative cultural network. Distinguishing fans from the general audience, Jenkins emphasised the distinctive interpretations and alternative identities generated in the texts fans produced for themselves (for example, fanzines and fanfiction). In these terms, fandom represented 'a participatory culture which transforms the experience of media consumption into the production of new texts, indeed of a new culture and a new community' (Jenkins, 1992: 46).

John Fiske was also impressed by fans' cultural creativity. Like Jenkins, Fiske saw fans as artfully appropriating cultural forms made available in the commercial market. Fiske contended that *all* popular audiences were (to some extent) creative in the ways they consumed and made sense of media texts, but he argued that fans took this creativity one step further by actually engaging in some form of textual production themselves (for example, by organising clubs and events, writing their own fanzines and fiction, or amassing splendid collections of ephemera). According to Fiske, fan cultures operated their own systems of production and distribution, forming a 'shadow cultural economy' that lay outside the 'official' media industries and offered fans 'opportunities to make meanings of their social identities and social experiences that are self-interested and functional' (Fiske, 1992: 35). At times, Fiske conceded, this process remained at the level of a compensatory fantasy life, but at others it was translated into 'empowered social behaviour' that could 'enhance the fan's power over, and participation in, the original, industrial text' (Fiske, 1992: 43).[14]

Notions of 'creative consumption' were also evident in theories of 'lifestyle'. The idea of lifestyle was originally developed during the early twentieth century in the work of Max Weber (1978), who argued that social stratification depended not solely on patterns of economic relation, but also on the degree of 'status' attached to the cultures and tastes of different social groups. During the 1990s notions of lifestyle attracted renewed interest amid an explosion of research dealing with consumption and identity. Here, the work of British theorist Anthony Giddens (1991) was especially influential. Like Maffesoli (see above), Giddens suggested that many of the beliefs and practices that defined identities in traditional societies (organised religion, for instance) wielded less influence in the modern, 'posttraditional' age. Instead, he argued, people were faced with a cavalcade of choices in their lives – not just about things like appearance and lifestyle, but more broadly about their life destinations and relationships. As a result, Giddens contended, modern individuals had become constantly 'self-reflexive', continually making decisions about what they should do and who they should be. In this context, 'the self' became a kind of project that individuals constantly worked upon, people engaging in continuous processes of lifestyle choice as they elaborated a coherent biographical 'narrative'.

Such perspectives informed a number of studies of youth culture. In Sweden, for example, Bo Reimer's fieldwork appeared to show that young people's tastes in entertainment were affected by factors such as 'class, gender, education, income and civil status', but none of these appeared to be as significant as a common lifestyle oriented around leisure, entertainment and media consumption which existed 'almost independent of socio-economic background' (Reimer 1995, 135). In Britain, the work of Steven Miles (2000) was also influenced by concepts of lifestyle. Drawing on Ulrich Beck's (1992) notion of the 'risk society' (see Chapter 4), Miles argued that young people faced a world in which their life experiences – in terms of family structure, educational opportunities, and routes to employment – were becoming increasingly tenuous. In response, they sought a sense of stability by drawing on the symbolic values of the products they consumed. Young people, Miles suggested, used their practices of consumption to develop a lifestyle they felt 'fitted in' with their peer group, but which also gave them a sense of distinctive individuality in a world characterised by instability and change. Like Willis, Miles saw young people as active agents who forged their identities and cultures through the appropriation, transformation, and recontextualisation of media texts – but Miles also emphasised the way these practices took place within a broader field of economic power. Characterising the relationship between youth culture and the commercial market as 'mutually exploitative', Miles observed how young people are 'liberated and constrained by the mass media at one and the same time – it provides them with the canvass, but the only oils they can use to paint that canvass are consumerist ones' (Miles 2000, 85).

For some critics, however, claims for the 'creative' possibilities of consumer practice could be over celebratory. Jim McGuigan (1992) offered an especially scathing critique, giving short shrift to ideas that, in his assessment, amounted to little more than an 'uncritical endorsement of popular taste and pleasure' (McGuigan, 1992: 6). While he was happy to accept that people were active agents in the formation of their own culture, McGuigan was critical of what he saw as a drift towards a 'cultural populism' that gave inadequate regard to the economic conditions under which these processes took place. And these debates were set to continue in relation to the new world of 'participatory culture' that, some theorists argued, was inaugurated by the proliferation of digital technology (see Chapter 9). More generally, while cultural studies theorists justifiably highlighted the importance of audience reception/creativity, the early twenty-first century saw issues of power, ownership and control became more poignant as processes of globalisation and business integration strengthened the economic hand of multi-national corporations. These issues are considered in more depth in the following chapter.

Notes

1 As both Driscoll (2002) and Gonick (2006) observe, there has frequently been a misogynistic undercurrent to this critique, with young women's interests and tastes often presented as the model of 'mass cultural' conformism.
2 Kitagawa, whose career saw several allegations of sexual misconduct, died in 2019 (*Japan Times*, 10 July, 2019).
3 An overview of debates about the relation between popular music and politics can be found in Street (2012).
4 In this respect, an especially important contribution was Hall's (1980i) foundational essay, 'Encoding/Decoding'.
5 British 'subcultural theory' of the 1970s should not be confused with the 'subcultural theory' of deviance associated with the American 'Chicago School' of sociology during the 1920s and 1930s, where researchers such as Thrasher (1927) saw juvenile gangs as a product of environmental tensions.
6 The main 'club cultures' studies are collected in Redhead (ed.) (1993) and Redhead, Wynne and O'Connor (eds) (1997).
7 Contributions to 'post-subcultural' theory are brought together in Bennett and Kahn-Harris (eds) (2004), Hodkinson and Deicke (eds) (2007) and Muggleton and Weinzierl (eds) (2003).
8 Bennett and Peterson (eds) (2004) collect a variety of studies of local and translocal music scenes.
9 See also the critiques presented by Blackman (2005) and Shildrick and MacDonald (2006).
10 Accounts of the riot grrrl movement can be found in Bock (2008), Marcus, (2010) and Monem (2007).
11 Studies of girlhoods in different global contexts include Helgren and Vasconcellos (eds) (2010), Hussain (2019), Muhonja (2017) and Soto (2018).
12 Other authors highlight the queer elements that are often pronounced in wider subcultures. See, for example, Healy's (1996) study of gay skinheads and Westengard's (2019) account of queer gothic culture.
13 A range of studies of queer youth cultures are collected in Driver (ed.) (2008).
14 Subsequently, 'fan studies' developed into a distinct field of analysis. Notable contributions include Barton and Lampley (eds) (2013), Busse (2017), Gray, Harrington and Sandvoss (eds) (2007), Hills (2002) and Sandvoss (2005).

7 Media industries, globalisation, and the international youth market

A star rising in the East: Tencent and global shifts in the youth market

Based in two gleaming skyscrapers in the city of Shenzhen, the Chinese corporation Tencent Holdings Ltd. had, by 2020, become the world's biggest video game company. Tencent was founded in 1998 by Ma Huateng (better known as Pony Ma) and his business colleagues, and during the early twenty-first century it grew into a billion-dollar technology behemoth. Controlling hundreds of subsidiary companies, Tencent's interests stretched across a spectrum of industries. Tencent Music Entertainment, for example, controlled the majority of China's online music services, with more than 652 million active users in 2019 (Dredge, 2019). Tencent also owned two of China's biggest social media platforms, QQ and WeChat – the latter's number of monthly active users passing the 1 billion mark in 2018 (Jao, 2018). The Tencent stable also included a legion of apps and web services such as the TenPay mobile payment system, the Weiyun cloud storage service and even a movie studio, Tencent Pictures, launched in 2015.

Tencent's video games empire, meanwhile, became colossal. By 2020, for instance, it owned Riot Games, the Los Angeles-based company responsible for two of the world's biggest games – *League of Legends* and *Teamfight Tactics*. Tencent also owned a 40 per cent stake in Epic Games, the North Carolina-based company behind the successful *Fortnite* game, along with the Epic Games Store and the Unreal Engine (software that underlies a multitude of popular games). Additionally, Tencent owned 84 per cent of Supercell, the Finnish company behind mobile games such as *Clash of Clans* and *Brawl Stars*, as well as boasting significant stakes in *Call of Duty* publisher Activision and *Assassin's Creed* publisher Ubisoft. It was hardly surprising, then, that in 2018 Tencent became the first Asian technology company with a market value that surpassed $500 billion, propelling it past Facebook to become the fifth largest corporation in the world.

Tencent's exponential growth was indicative of both the rapid proliferation of digital media and China's rise as a major economic power. But Tencent's success also represented broad trends in business organisation. The corporation's burgeoning portfolio of diverse commercial interests was indicative of wider trends towards business integration and transmedia conglomeration. Moreover, Tencent's strategy of buying-up and investing in the world's major game-makers – along with its tactic of developing international collaborations and partnerships – exemplified the increased globalisation of the media industries. Indeed, given that Tencent is incorporated in the Cayman Islands and also trades the New York Stock Exchange, it becomes hard to call it simply a 'Chinese' company. Rather, it is a trans-global media conglomerate.

This chapter explores issues of globalisation and business conglomeration in relation to media industries geared to the youth market. It begins by consider-ing the nature of globalisation and the way a range of technological, economic, and political developments intensified the impact of globalising forces during the late twentieth and early twenty-first centuries. One of the consequences of these trends has been the rise of transnational, transmedia business corporations, and this development is explored in the specific context of media industries geared to young consumers. The chapter also assesses critical interpretations of these shifts. Particular consideration is given to theories of 'cultural imperialism' that see the international circulation of media as being dominated by a Wes-tern – or specifically American – worldview, one that serves to promulgate capitalist values and homogenise global culture. While significant inequalities characterise the ownership and control of the world's media, the chapter shows how notions of cultural imperialism fail to capture the complexity of global flows of media and culture. With particular regard to the youth market, the chapter demonstrates how 'global' products are invariably reconfigured, or 'glocalised', in local contexts. Attention is also given to the way flows of international media – or 'mediascapes' – have become many faceted, multi-directional, and open-ended. In these terms, Western media control has been increasingly cross-cut by the emergence of many non-Western communication interests, while local youth audiences have actively appropriated and inscribed new meanings into global media forms. The chapter concludes by considering the way youth cultures have been mobilised by countries such as Japan and South Korea in exercises of 'nation branding' that attempt to extend the countries' 'soft power' through boosting the global appeal of their national media and popular culture.

A world of business integration: globalisation, conglomeration, and the media

Theories of globalisation have, since the late 1980s, impacted across a range of academic disciplines. For the media theorist Roland Robertson, globalisation was 'a concept [that] refers to both the compression of the world and the intensification of our consciousness of the world as a whole' (1995i: 8), but there exist a wide variety of accounts of globalisation's precise nature and sig-nificance. Central to the general concept of globalisation is the notion that the late twentieth century saw the firm boundaries of nations increasingly bypassed by new forms of 'global' economic and political relations, with the result that individual lives and local communities became more deeply affected by economic and cultural forces that operate worldwide. According to Anthony Giddens (1990), for example, globalisation was marked by trends towards greater 'time-space distanciation', with a stretching of connections across the globe that dissolved fixed links between 'time' and 'place', so that long-distance relationships can be experienced as close, even when the parties seldom (if ever) occupy the same space at the same time. Distanciation, Giddens argued, had also set in motion a process of 'disembedding', with social relationships increasingly lifted out from their local contexts and restructured across global spans of time and space. This intensification of worldwide social relations, Giddens suggested, had linked distant locations in such a way that local events were increasingly shaped by phenomena occurring many miles away and vice-versa.

A different interpretation of globalisation was offered by David Harvey (1989). Like Giddens, Harvey's analysis highlighted transformations in the planes of time and space, but Harvey explained globalisation as a process of 'time-space compression' – with the dimensions of time and space squeezed together, so that the world has come to seem both smaller and faster-moving. Despite their differences, however, both Giddens and Harvey saw globalisation as a stretching of relations across the world. For both, global contacts had been deepened, or intensified, so that people's local lives and experiences had become increasingly interpenetrated by globalising forces. Yet, whereas Harvey saw globalisation as the outcome of recent shifts in the organisation of capitalism, Giddens argued it was a continuation of trends set in motion by the processes of modernity that first took shape in eighteenth-century Europe. For Giddens, moreover, globalisation was a contradictory and uneven process. On one hand, he argued, globalisation 'pulled away' from 'local' communities – supra-national political organisations, for example, assuming some of the powers and capacities of nation-states. But, at the same time, Giddens observed how processes of globalisation could also give a renewed importance to local identities and institutions. And, indeed, the upsurge in nationalist movements (from Scotland to Serbia) during the 1990s and beyond seems to highlight profound contradictions in the character and effects of globalisation.

Of course, worldwide connections are hardly new. Over many centuries, for example, the Catholic Church bound people together across national boundaries through shared beliefs and rituals, while the development of the telegraph in mid-nineteenth-century America helped fuse together widely divergent geographic regions into federal unity.[1] But, while globalising tendencies can be identified in earlier periods, commentators such as Jan Aart Scholte (2005) argue that the late twentieth century saw a combination of factors give added impetus to processes of global interconnection and interdependency. Scholte cites a variety of inter-linked factors as being a cause (and, in turn, a consequence) of this trend. Significant was the increased movement – or what can be termed 'diasporic' dispersion – of different groups of people around the world. Also crucial was the rise of global agencies of governance such as the United Nations and the European Union, along with major trends towards the globalisation of finance in the form of foreign exchange dealings, banking securities markets, derivatives, and the insurance industry. And of fundamental importance were a collection of interrelated trends – advances in media and communications technologies, the rise of governments with a neoliberal political outlook, and the trans-global conglomeration of business organisations.

Developments in communications technology clearly played an important role in the acceleration of globalising trends. During the 1960s the influential media theorist Marshall McLuhan had already highlighted the emergence of what he termed the 'global village', as developments in electronic and satellite communications seemed to draw the world together into a united media community (McLuhan, 1964). Subsequent advances in the fields of telecommunications and information technology – especially the growth of digital and fibre optic technologies – further increased the speed and scope of global communication and, as a consequence, contributed to a proliferation of transnational commerce. These trends, in turn, were galvanised by political and economic shifts.

From the late 1970s governments in the US, Europe, and an increasing number of other countries embraced what has been dubbed 'neoliberal' policies of 'marketisation' – that is to say, policies that favour shifts away from state intervention in the economy and towards principles of free market competition. In the context of the media industries, proponents of such a move often termed it a process of 'deregulation' or 'liberalisation' that boosted innovation and enterprise, and (through the competition encouraged by a free market) ensured economic advantage for consumers. As Graham Murdock (1990) has pointed out, however, the moves might more aptly be termed a process of *re*-regulation, since the changes did not actually remove legislation or controls but introduced a *new* set of market regulations. For critics, moreover, this new, neoliberal market environment offered the greatest advantages to large, privately-owned corporations who were best able to exploit the market system and, as a result, steadily expanded the scope and scale of their business.[2]

Accompanying the rise of neoliberal governments, fundamental economic shifts also spurred (and, themselves, reflected) trends towards greater globalisation. This was manifest in the rise of massive, transnational, business conglomerates. That is to say, companies whose business interests span multiple industries and business sectors, and whose operations are worldwide in scale. Partly, trends towards business conglomeration were driven by the emergence of a new, more volatile world market. The change was already detectable by the late 1960s, but became more pronounced during the 1970s and 1980s as a consequence of saturated Western markets, increased competition from Japan and newly industrialised nations (such as Taiwan, Korea and Singapore), together with a rise in international oil prices. In response to these pressures, business sought to adapt and realign. As David Hesmondhalgh (2019) shows, to secure their economic survival companies adopted strategies of horizontal integration (buying-up rivals who operated in the same industrial sector), vertical integration (taking control of companies involved at different stages of production and circulation), multi-sector integration (buying into related industries to ensure a cross-promotion of products), and internationalisation (buying or partnering companies abroad) (2019: 201–260).[3] By the beginning of the twenty-first century, therefore, a combination of market deregulation and intensified economic competition had led to the emergence of huge, multi-interest business conglomerates whose corporate strategies straddled national boundaries in an increasingly interconnected world economy.

These processes are exemplified by the rise of video games giant Tencent (see above). But, more generally, processes of business integration and conglomeration (or, as some theorists term it, 'convergence') saw media industries increasingly dominated by a coterie of massive, global companies.[4] The US-based conglomerate AT&T, for instance, is the world's largest telecommunications company and, in 2018, became the world's largest media and entertainment business when it acquired WarnerMedia. Itself a huge conglomerate, by 2020 WarnerMedia boasted control of an array of media companies, including the Warner Bros. film and TV studio, TV networks such as HBO, CNN, and the Cartoon Network, publishing concerns such as DC Comics, along with a host of other entertainment and sports interests. Disney also emerged as a global media conglomerate through not only ownership of its film studios, theme parks, and resorts; but through its acquisition of other major media interests, including the ABC TV network (bought in 1995), Marvel Entertainment (the comics empire, bought in 2009), Lucasfilm (the makers of the *Star Wars* movies, bought in 2012) and 21st Century Fox (itself a multinational media corporation, bought in 2019). ViacomCBS Inc was another global media Titan. Formed in 2019 through the merger of the CBS Corporation and Viacom (both, in themselves, major media conglomerates), ViacomCBS Inc boasted control of not only the CBS Entertainment Group and Paramount Pictures (along with their subsidiaries), but an array of business interests that spanned film, TV, publishing, and digital media.

By the early twenty-first century, the ownership of online media was also heavily concentrated among a handful of global conglomerates. Apple was particularly dominant. Founded in 1976 as a manufacturer of personal computers, it subsequently grew into a major multinational operation with interests across consumer electronics, online services, and software. And its reach was boosted by several major acquisitions, including the audio company Beats Electronics (bought in 2014) and the music-identifying app Shazam (bought in 2017). The search engine company Google was also an online giant. Itself reorganised (in 2015) into a subsidiary of the holding company Alphabet Inc., Google's growth had been characterised by innumerable business acquisitions, most notably that of the mobile operating system Android (in 2005), the video-sharing platform YouTube (in 2006) and the mobile device manufacturer Motorola (in 2011). Amazon was another major player. Originally founded by Jeff Bezos in 1994 as an online marketplace for books, by 2019 it had expanded to include e-commerce, cloud computing, artificial intelligence, and digital streaming services and, worth $810 billion, it represented the world's most valuable public company (La Monica, 2019). Facebook also became a huge conglomerate through a series of major business acquisitions – most notably the purchase of social media apps Instagram (in 2012) and WhatsApp (in 2014) – and, while its value was surpassed by that of Tencent in 2018, Facebook still had a net worth of around $479 billion in 2019.

Processes of integration and concentration of ownership, however, were possibly best illustrated by developments in the music industry. Through merger and acquisition a 'Big Three' labels – Sony Music Entertainment, Warner Music Group, and Universal Music Group – had, during the early twenty-first century, come to dominate the field, and by 2016 they accounted for over 62 per cent of all music sold, downloaded and streamed throughout the world (Resinkoff, 2016).

For some critics, this kind of concentration of media ownership among a cabal of global companies had a dire impact on culture and democracy. In their book *The Global Media* (1997), for example, US theorists Edward Herman and Robert McChesney saw these trends as representing an extension and intensification of 'the commercial model of communication' that delivered power and influence into the hands of small number of capitalist, multinational businesses (1997: 9). Continuing the theme, McChesney (1999) argued that the rise of new communication technologies and the deregulation of national media industries during the 1990s had laid the way for a world where news coverage was constrained, cultural expression was suffocated and democracy smothered by huge media empires driven solely by their hunger for profit. This perspective can be seen as part of a critical tradition characterised by notions of 'cultural imperialism'.

Working for the Yankee dollar: globalisation, cultural imperialism, and Americanisation

Theories of 'cultural imperialism' were a facet of the fierce criticisms that, during the late twentieth century, were being aimed at aspects of globalisation. According to some observers, neoliberalism and global moves towards market deregulation brought an intensification of international inequalities, a more exploitative treatment of workers and a devastation of the environment. During the 1990s this critique was articulated by a broadly-based (though often quite young) movement that sought to challenge the grip of transnational corporations. In November 1999, for example, a conference of the World Trade Organisation in Seattle was confronted by 50,000 demonstrators, while 2001 saw further protests at the World Economic Forum in Salzburg and the G-8 Summit in Genoa.[5] The movement found an unofficial spokeswoman in Canadian journalist, Naomi Klein. In her best-selling book, *No Logo* (2000), Klein launched a broadside against the power of multinational companies. According to Klein, processes of economic deregulation had allowed huge

companies to seize the reins of the global economy, with business conglomerates able to manipulate world markets to their own advantage. For some critics,
moreover, these negative *economic* dimensions to globalisation were accompanied by *cultural* trends that also facilitated the extension of international
inequality and exploitation.

This critique of the cultural consequences of globalisation – sometimes
dubbed theories of 'cultural imperialism' – has its roots in critical communication scholarship that emerged during the Cold War. According to critics, as
America competed against the Soviet Union for global dominance, US communications and media corporations worked to boost America's influence in
the developing world by spreading US values through the export of media and
culture. The classic articulation of the thesis was made by American theorist
Herbert Schiller, who suggested the concept of cultural imperialism denoted:

> … the sum of the processes by which a society is brought into the modern
> world system and how its dominating stratum is attracted, pressured,
> forced, and sometimes bribed into shaping social institutions to correspond
> to, or even promote, the values and structures of the dominating centre of
> the system.
>
> (Schiller, 1976: 9)[6]

From this perspective, the US represented a new kind of empire. While it had
no formal territorial colonies, critics argued, America's systems of mass communication were used to impose its influence around the globe. The US media
were seen as promulgating capitalist values in developing nations, thereby
strengthening the position of America as a world power and generating markets
for its businesses. Theories of cultural imperialism were especially influential
during the 1960s and 1970s, when the right to develop sovereign media systems was often seen as an important aspect of national liberation struggles
against colonial powers. But the approach subsequently retained influence in
the work of scholars such as McChesney (see above) and Oliver Boyd-Barrett
(1998; 2014), who argued that, with the accelerated pace of globalising trends,
such perspectives were still key to understanding the ways culture and media
worked to sustain global economic relationships.

And, along with growing concerns about an intensification of economic
inequalities, the acceleration of globalising trends also gave renewed impetus to
anxieties about the impact of commercialism on social and cultural life. During
the 1950s and 1960s 'mass culture' perspectives had been critical of 'Americanised' popular culture, and the rise of what was seen as a world dominated
by shallow consumerism (see Chapter 6). And, in a similar fashion, the
increasingly global reach of Western TV, film, and music during the late
twentieth century was seen by some theorists as spawning a homogenised – or
'Americanised' – commercial culture that steamrollered over indigenous 'folk'
cultures, values, and ways of life. US sociologist George Ritzer (1993), for
instance, argued that global societies were becoming 'McDonaldized'. Using

McDonald's (the international chain of hamburger restaurants) as his paradigmatic example, Ritzer contended that modern businesses' quest for greater efficiency and cost-effectiveness had brought about strictly regimented methods of production characterised by an intense degree of rationalisation and standardisation. While 'McDonaldization' was an efficient form of production, however, Ritzer argued it had destructive social and cultural consequences. 'McDonaldization', Ritzer argued, had a 'dehumanising' effect on workers who lost their sense of freedom and creativity in an environment dominated by controls, calculation, and bureaucracy. Moreover, cultural life was steadily impoverished as 'McDonaldized' industries spawned a world of uniformity and homogenisation.

And, for some commentators, trends towards homogenisation were especially pronounced in the rise of a 'global' youth culture. Jo Langham Brown and her associates, for example, saw the rise of the Internet, MTV, and transnational brands as providing a common menu of media and entertainment for young consumers worldwide. As they explained:

> The commercial media have promoted the emergence of a global community of young people free from the values and preferences of any particular social and geographical location and embedded in the ethic of consumerism, preoccupied, it seems, by celebrities, fashion and the demands of an ad-oriented lifestyle.
>
> (Langham, Brown, Ralph and Lees, 1999: xi)

Naomi Klein was also despondent. Surveying modern youth culture, Klein argued that global corporations like Nike and Tommy Hilfiger had turned young consumers into brand-obsessed 'walking, talking, life-sized Tommy [Hilfiger] dolls' (2000: 28). For Klein, the grip of big business had blunted the radical edge of youth subcultures, so that even 'street styles' had been seamlessly absorbed into the corporate brands' relentless pursuit of global sales. 'Gathering tips from the graffiti artists of old', Klein contended, 'the superbrands have tagged everyone – including the graffiti writers themselves' (2000: 73).

And, certainly, there is much validity to the view that multinational corporations dominate contemporary media systems. Moreover, the global scale of advertising and marketing has ensured that Western products – and, with them, Western cultures and lifestyles – have diffused to all corners of the world. The international availability of Western film, music, and TV, for example, has allowed the styles and consumption practices of teenage America to circulate globally. As Claire Wallace and Sijka Kovatcheva have argued, Western configurations of 'youthfulness' have now taken root in regions that hitherto had little experience of a commercial youth market (Wallace and Kovatcheva, 1998: 153). Nevertheless, while inequalities of power and control have to be acknowledged, notions of a linear and unilateral 'cultural imperialism' – or, for that matter, 'Americanisation' – oversimplify and distort the flows of media production, distribution, and consumption. Instead, researchers have increasingly drawn attention to the complex, multi-faceted nature of trans-global media flows – and the complexity of these processes has been especially evident in the field of youth culture.

'Think globally, act locally': youth culture, glocalisation, and mediascapes

For many theorists, ideas of cultural homogenisation fail to capture the complexity of global flows of media and culture. 'Global' products, for instance, often have to be adapted and reconfigured for local markets. Originally coined by Japanese economists to describe their country's marketing strategies, the term 'glocalisation' – a neologism of 'global and 'local' – was popularised by Roland Robertson (1995ii) to describe the way trans-national media corporations adapt their production to meet the specific tastes and demands of local contexts. For Robertson, global processes did not happen against or outside local forces. Rather, he argued, both the global and the local were mutually constituent concepts. As Victor Roudometof explains, the notion of 'glocalisation' is used:

> … to highlight the extent to which the global cannot be conceived of in opposition to or in isolation from the local, that both global and local are participants in contemporary social life, and that the future is not determined solely by macro-level forces but also by groups, organizations, and individuals operating at the micro level (or what is usually meant by the term *agency*).
>
> (Roudometof, 2016: 12)

Practices of 'glocalisation' have become commonplace in the media and culture industries.[7] Even McDonald's – a brand Ritzer sees as synonymous with processes of standardisation (see above) – has to make 'glocal' concessions in its international marketing strategies. So, while McDonald's operates with worldwide standards and branding, its local systems of franchising use locally-sourced foods and offer menus tailored to local tastes (Crawford, Humphries and Geddy, 2015). In modern TV production, particularly, issues of glocalisation have often figured prominently. Albert Moran (2009), for example, has shown how a TV show made in one national market is often sold overseas as a template or set of 'franchised knowledges', which allow it to be remade for transmission in another market. Sometimes, as in the case of the game shows *Who Wants to Be a Millionaire* and *The Weakest Link*, the franchise arrangements stipulate a high degree of fidelity to the initial programme, so the local version seems to be a 'lookalike' version of the original. But this form of 'closed' TV franchise is relatively uncommon. According to Moran, more flexible, 'glocalised' approaches are the norm, with TV companies generally happy to countenance adaptations that make allowance for local sensitivities and sensibilities.

Dimensions of 'glocalisation' loomed especially large in the history of MTV. During the 1990s the TV music network (originally based in the US) steadily expanded overseas with the launch of successive international TV stations – for instance, MTV Asia, Australia, Brasil, Europe, Latin America, and Russia. Crucially, this expansion was underpinned by a 'think globally, act locally' philosophy in which each new station adhered to an overall style of programming, but configured this around local tastes and musical talent. In itself, for example, MTV Asia comprised three regional channels – MTV Mandarin, MTV Southeast Asia, and MTV India. Launched in 1995, the Chinese-language station MTV Mandarin broadcast to viewers in China, Hong Kong, Taiwan, and Singapore, with 60 per cent of its playlist consisting of Mandarin music videos. MTV Southeast Asia, also launched in 1995, was available throughout Asia, offering a mix of music from Indonesia, Malaysia, and Thailand. And, in 1996, MTV Southeast Asia was split into a third channel, MTV India. Available in India, Pakistan, Bangladesh, and Sri Lanka, 70 per cent of MTV India's programming was made up of Indian pop music and films, with the balance made up of international music videos. In 2000, meanwhile, the MTV stable expanded further, with the launch of MTV Japan – a 24-hour, Japanese-language station with programming largely composed of Japanese material. MTV Korea followed in 2001 and, again, featured original, locally-produced content as its mainstay. As SeungHo Cho and Jee Young Chung have observed (2009), therefore, MTVs strategies of transnational expansion were distinguished by distinct elements of glocalisation.

Concepts of a one-way 'cultural imperialism', meanwhile, have been further undermined by changing patterns of media production and distribution. Since the 1970s, these have seen developing nations emerge as major players in the media environment, with Western media control increasingly cross-cut by an elaborate syncopation of non-Western communication systems and business interests. The success of TikTok was a case in point. Within two years of its beginnings in China in 2016, the video app was available in 75 different languages and had become hugely popular worldwide (see Chapter 3). The rise of Tencent as a video game colossus was another example. Indeed, as Philip Penix-Tadsen (2019) shows, the games industry of the early twenty-first century was characterised by myriad international links in which countries of the Global South – in the Indian subcontinent, the Middle East, and Asia – were pivotal.

'Bollywood', meanwhile, has long been one of the major hubs of the global film industry. In 2018–19, for instance, the Indian film industry produced 2,446 films (Film Federation of India, 2019); and, while these won a huge domestic following, they also attracted major overseas audiences among not only diasporic communities but also international cinemagoers more generally. Indeed, *Dangal* (2016), the highest-grossing Bollywood film outside India, scooped worldwide box office revenues of $340 million (Statistica, 2018i). India's music industry is, perhaps, less well-known, but nonetheless burgeoned during the early twenty-first century. Indicative was the rise of T-Series, the music and film production company founded by Gulshan Kumar in 1983. Initially best known for its Bollywood soundtracks, T-Series developed into

India's largest selling music label before branching into film. But T-Series also owned and operated the most popular channel on YouTube. Indeed, in May 2019 it became the first YouTube channel to boast 100 million subscribers (Bhushan, 2019),[8] and by 2020 it was YouTube's most viewed channel, clocking-up a staggering 3.23 billion monthly views (Statistica, 2020).

Such developments were indicative of the way the basis of the global music industry shifted during the early twenty-first century. During the 1990s the US share of the international market for popular music was already shrinking as the relatively low cost of making and distributing recordings (compared to films and TV shows) made it possible for a wide range of national music industries to prosper. In some instances indigenous output came to overshadow American products. Luciana Mendonca (2002), for example, has shown how sales of American pop music in Brazil declined significantly during the 1990s, while Brazilian music came to constitute around 80 per cent of recordings broadcast on the country's radio. And in 2014 the annual report of the International Federation of the Phonographic Industry (IFPI) lauded the way local artists accounted for many top selling albums in local markets:

> In France, for example, 17 of the top 20 selling albums of 2013 were local repertoire ... In Germany, seven of the top 10 selling albums in 2013 were local repertoire, a trend reflected in 13 selected non-English language markets.
>
> (IFPI, 2014: 15)

Of course, as the organisation that officially represents the international recording industry, the IFPI might have a vested interest in presenting the music business as a world of happy plurality. Nevertheless, the early twenty-first century saw many indications that international flows of music were becoming more multi-faceted, and artists from places once considered the periphery of the music business were better able to break into global markets. The shift was partly indebted to technological developments, especially the rise of streaming services. In 2017, for example, 'Despacito' by Puerto Rican artist Luis Fonsi became just the 35th single to top America's *Billboard* Hot 100' for at least ten weeks – a popularity indebted to its success on streaming services, where 'Despacito' had become the most-streamed song of all time, receiving 4.6 billion plays worldwide within six months. As Lucian Grainge, CEO of Universal Music Group observed:

> Streaming has opened up the possibility of a song with a different beat, from a different culture and in a different language to become a juggernaut of success around the world.
>
> (cited in Brandle, 2017)

Other 'local' artists also found international success. The 1990s, for instance, saw the rise of 'J-Pop' – a fusion of Japanese music and 1960s-style Western pop – which not only dominated music charts in Japan and many other Asian countries, but also enjoyed success (along with Japanese *anime* cartoons and *manga* comics) worldwide. The triumphs of J-Pop, however, were overshadowed by the subsequent success of 'K-Pop'. South Korean popular culture, like that of Japan, expanded its international influence during the 1990s. The growth of satellite and cable television, for example, saw Korean TV shows pull in big audiences in Japan, China, Taiwan, and Vietnam. But during the early twenty-first century it was pop music – or K-Pop – that became South Korea's most notable cultural export. Indicative was the runaway popularity of K-Pop boy band BTS (*Bangtan Sonyeondan*, or Beyond the Scene). Originally formed in Seoul in 2010, by the end of the decade BTS were one of the most successful pop acts in history. In 2019 they became the first ever group to spend five weeks at No. 1 in the '*Billboard* Artist 100', and the same year they joined The Beatles and The Monkees to become the third group in 50 years to have three No. 1 albums in the '*Billboard* 200' across a twelve-month period.

Critics may argue that K-Pop groups like BTS essentially reproduce Western music styles. But, as JungBong Choi and Roald Maliangkay observe, this view overlooks the way K-Pop fans see the music as 'reprocessing' Western influences, 'giving peculiar Korean "spins" to the mode of presentation' (Choi and Maliangkay, 2015: 3). And, more generally, 'globalisation' itself should be seen as more complex than a simple drive towards a Western- (or American-) dominated homogenisation. Instead, as the cultural theorist Arjun Appadurai (1990; 1996) has suggested, globalisation is better seen as an aggregation of flows composed of media, technology, ideologies, and ethnicities that move in many different directions. This model moves away from accounts that see globalisation as a coherent, unitary process, in which a few Western corporations possess overpowering strength. Instead, it sees globalisation as a network of cultural flows that have no clearly defined centre or periphery.

For Appadurai, processes of globalisation were a fluid, ever-changing landscape that he saw as being, itself, composed of five overlapping and mutually-constituted 'scapes'. 'Ethnoscapes' were, according to Appadurai, the worldwide 'diasporic' movement of people as tourists, immigrants, refugees, exiles, and guest-workers. 'Financescapes', meanwhile, denoted the volatile and increasingly complicated global movement of capital and currency. The 'technoscape' was the unequal and shifting worldwide distribution of technologies that provided the infrastructure for global connections. And 'ideoscapes' were the realm of beliefs, values, and 'grand narratives' that were, Appadurai argued, 'often directly political and frequently have to do with the ideologies of states and the counter ideologies of movements explicitly oriented to capturing state power or a piece of it' (1990: 299). But the media were also fundamental to the flowing landscapes of globalisation. And, for Appadurai, the 'mediascape' denoted both 'the distribution of the electronic capabilities to produce and disseminate information' and 'the images of the world created by these media' (1990: 298).

In mediascapes, Appadurai contended, information and images are distributed through communication technologies in evermore complex ways to increasingly diverse audiences. As a consequence, he argued, 'many audiences throughout the world experience the media themselves as a complicated and interconnected repertoire of print, celluloid, electronic screens, and billboards. The lines between the "realistic" and the fictional landscapes they see are blurred ...' (Appadurai, 1990: 299). Here, Appadurai's spatial 'scape' metaphor is important because it highlights the way people's fluid and fragmented experiences of the media are a consequence of intensified global flows. Appadurai's account still acknowledges the vast power wielded by large corporations in media production and circulation, but it lays stress on the way the production, circulation, and consumption of media texts is always many faceted, multi-directional, and open-ended. From this perspective, therefore, young consumers around the world do not unthinkingly buy into a homogenised (or Westernised/Americanised) cultural diet of burgers, blue jeans, and Bon Jovi albums. Instead, the complex transnational streams of media feed into the development of a diversity of cultures and identities as different groups of young people actively draw upon 'global' media forms and creatively 're-embed' them in local cultures and contexts.

'Glocal' youth cultures and the appropriation of 'mythic' America

For cultural theorists Sunaina Maira and Elisabeth Soep (2005) young people occupy a central place in processes of globalisation. Adopting Appadurai's phraseology, Maira and Soep coin the term 'youthscapes' to denote the ways modern youth cultures are spawned through 'the intersections between popular culture practices, national ideologies, and global markets' (Maira and Soep, 2005: xv). The importance of youth to globalisation, they argue, lies in the way young people figure in all five of the 'scapes' comprising Appadurai's model of globalised cultural flows. 'Youth', they explain, 'is a social category that belongs to all five of his units of analysis':

> Young people participate in social relations; use and invent technology; earn, spend, need; desire, and despise money; comprise target markets while producing their own original media; and formulate modes of citizenship out of the various ideologies they create, sustain and disrupt.
>
> (Maira and Soep, 2005: xvi)

The notion of youthscapes is suggestive of the way local youth cultures are not formed in isolation. Rather, they are generated through complex processes of international connection and young people's active engagement with global media. Indeed, for critics of the cultural imperialism thesis, one of its greatest weaknesses was its failure to take adequate account of the agency of local audiences, and their capacity to appropriate, adapt, and 'indigenise' globally circulating media. Theorists such as James Lull (1995) and John Thompson (1995), for example, highlighted the way local audiences inscribe new meaning into global media forms, reworking them to take on fresh cultural significance. As Thompson explained, the way media products are understood and used 'is always a localized phenomenon':

> ... it always involves specific individuals who are situated in particular socio-historical contexts, and who draw on the resources available to them in order to make sense of media messages and incorporate them into their lives. And messages are often transformed in the process of appropriation as individuals adapt them to the contexts of everyday life.
>
> (Thompson, 1995: 174)

Ethnographic and reception studies have drawn attention to the way local patterns of media interpretation and use are invariably diverse. For example, research by Tamar Liebes and Elihu Katz (1990) and Daniel Miller (1992) on different national audiences for TV soap operas suggested the meanings of transnational media were relatively 'open', and this allowed for a range of divergent – in some instances even 'resistant' – readings by indigenous audiences. And similar elements of media 'reinterpretation' and 're-embedding' have also been prominent in the history of international youth cultures. US popular culture, especially, has often figured in these processes.

American texts and images have been a conspicuous presence in the cultures and subcultures forged by young people worldwide. Partly this is a consequence of the way US economic power has ensured the historical prominence of American culture in global media. But it is also indebted to the way US media offer a relatively 'open' set of cultural signifiers. As Dick Hebdige argued:

> American popular culture – Hollywood films, advertising images, packaging, clothes and music – offers a rich iconography, a set of symbols, objects and artefacts which can be assembled and re-assembled by different groups in a literally limitless number of combinations.
>
> (Hebdige, 1988ii: 74)

Like 'youth', 'America' is, in Roland Barthes' terms (see Chapter 4), a repository of rich 'mythologies' and symbolic connotations. As Rob Kroes argues, in modern popular culture 'America' represents 'a construct, an image, a fantasma' (2006: 92):

> America's national symbols and myths have been translated into an international iconographic language, a visual lingua franca. They have been turned into free-floating signifiers, internationally understood, free for everyone to use.
>
> (Kroes, 2006: 96–97)

Obviously, the mythic American Dream of untrammelled freedom and boundless opportunity bears scant relation to the realities experienced by vast numbers of people living in the US. But, as Kroes suggests, young people around the world who embrace US music, films, and fashion effectively 're-contextualize and remsemanticize American culture', and 'make it function within expressive settings entirely of their own making' (Kroes, 2006: 94). In fact, rather than being resented as an instrument of US cultural imperialism, American goods and media have often been championed by local audiences as positive symbols of freedom and modernity. As Steve Chibnall has observed, for many young people around the world, buying Levi's jeans or Coca-Cola 'can take on the status of a personal political statement because the symbolic association of these objects with freedom, individuality and the "American way" is underwritten in countless cinematic and televisual texts which relate product aesthetics to social attitudes, personal aspirations and nationality' (Chibnall, 1996: 150). For many audiences around the world, then, American goods and media have become symbolic tokens of autonomy and emancipation. And, possibly because American style has been such an emotionally-charged carrier of individuality and freedom, it has frequently been the target of conservative criticism and authoritarian control.

In Nazi Germany, for example, American music and style was a site of cultural struggle. The Nazi government of the 1930s favoured German classical or folk music, while American jazz and Big Band swing (performed by the likes of Glenn Miller, Duke Ellington, and Benny Goodman) was maligned as 'degenerate'. But the music still boasted many German enthusiasts. It had particular appeal among what were termed '*Swing Jugend*' or 'Swing Youth' – groups of young people from mainly liberal-minded, middle-class families who eschewed the ideals of 'youthfulness' promoted by Nazi youth movements such as the *Hitler-Jugend* (Hitler Youth), and instead enthused over American music and style.[9] Beginning during the late 1930s, Germany's major cities – Berlin, Stuttgart, Frankfurt, Hamburg – saw distinctively dressed youngsters gather in bars and cafés, enjoying jazz music at dances characterised by what one Gestapo report described as 'an uninhibited indulgence in swing' (Noakes, 1998: 452). Swing youth were never a formally organised group, and did not oppose the Nazis in any self-conscious way, but there was a latent sense of defiance in their devotion to 'American' hedonism and their refusal to conform to Nazi ideals. As Claire Wallace and Raimund Alt suggest, they stood as 'an example of everyday resistance that, while not being an overtly political struggle, seemed to represent a rejection of the dominance of the regime' (Wallace and Alt, 2001: 278). It was an insolence, moreover, that infuriated the Nazis. Heinrich Himmler – head of the SS – took the view that all young people who listened to jazz music should be 'beaten, given the severest exercise, and then put to hard labour' (Gill, 1994: 195). And during the early 1940s the suppression of swing youth intensified; with raids on clubs, arrests, and even imprisonments in concentration camps.

In the Soviet Union, too, American style became a vehicle for anti-authoritarian dissent. As Hilary Pilkington (1994) shows, during the Cold War the *stilagi* were a particular topic of controversy. Groups of relatively well-to-do urban youngsters, the *stilagi* showed little interest in official forms of Soviet culture and instead adopted Western forms of music and fashion, developing their own distinctive image – *stil'* – a (re)interpretation of American rock 'n' roll style. Reviled as ideologically subversive and unacceptably bourgeois by the Soviet establishment, the *stilagi* faced concerted opposition from state institutions and the press. Brigades of *Kosmosol* (the official Soviet youth movement) were formed to campaign against the influence of *stil'* and, in the cities of Sverdlovsk and Ul'ianovsk, *Kosmosol* patrols were reported to have cut both the trousers and hair of local *stilagi* (Pilkington, 1994: 226).

The mythologies of US popular culture have also exerted strong appeal in Britain. Against the drab backdrop of the postwar years, especially, visions of America offered a taste of excitement.[10] This appeal was felt especially keenly, Chibnall argues, by working-class youth, for whom 'Yankee style offered a sense of worth, individuality and empowerment' (Chibnall, 1996: 155). According to Chibnall, the zoot suit was a preeminent example of the way cultural forms transplanted from America took on new meanings in the context of postwar Britain. The broad, draped jackets and pegged trousers of the zoot suit had originally been sported by young Mexican-American *Pachucos* and black hustlers in US cities during the early 1940s. Brash and flamboyant, the style seemed an insolent defiance of dominant conventions. The swaggering gesture was not lost on white society and, in 1943, gangs of off-duty servicemen roamed the streets of Los Angeles brutally beating zoot-suited Mexican-Americans in a series of racist attacks.[11] By the end of the 1940s, however, the violence dissipated as zoot style crept into mainstream American fashion. But in Britain, Chibnall (1985) argues, the zoot suit retained its rebellious aura. Imported with the arrival of GIs during the war, the zoot suit was adopted by British 'spivs' (flashy petty villains), though by the late 1940s the style had become more firmly equated with working-class youth. In this context, Chibnall suggests, the original, 'racial' significance of the zoot suit was lost. Filtered through indigenous conceptions of style, 'the impenetrable argot and defiant machismo of the *Pachuco* and Harlem hipsters were cut away and replaced with the familiar rhyming slang and quick-witted banter of the artful dodger, the rascally opportunist' (Chibnall, 1985: 66). Gradually evolving into the distinctive dress of the 1950s Teddy boy (see Chapter 4), the style represented a 'blasphemous mixture of orthodox British dandyism and Yank style' and, among both working-class youth and officialdom, was recognised as 'a symptom of a fundamental disrespect for the old class modes and manners – a disrespect born of a romance with an alien culture' (Chibnall, 1985: 74; 69).

In a similar vein, Andrew Blake (2010) has highlighted the history of interplay between American and British popular music. From rock 'n' roll and R'n'B, to hip-hop and techno, American music has exerted a strong influence in Britain. But, as Blake argues, this relationship is 'not a one-way traffic but *cultural exchange*' (155, orig. emphasis) that has been characterised by 'dialogue, differentiation and diversion' (151). Rather than simply imitating American 'originals', then, British musicians have reinterpreted and reconfigured musical genres, feeding the new result back into the global flow of culture. The explosion of Beatlemania is illustrative. Admittedly, the success of The Beatles and the British pop 'invasion' of the US during the 1960s could be seen as a by-product of 'Americanisation' – with the British music industry remaking and re-marketing music genres imported from the US. But this would over-look the way British musicians (like K-Pop bands 50 years later) appropriated and reinterpreted the American idioms, and combined them with local cultural elements. As a consequence, the end-product was a distinctly 'British' cultural form that in turn, fed into the development of music and style not only in the US but worldwide.

Other British contributions have also loomed large in the global 'youths-cape'. Christine Feldman-Barrett (2009), for example, shows how the mod subculture that originated in London's dimly lit clubs of the early 1960s (see Chapter 4) subsequently took root as a variety of 'glocalised' incarnations in the US, Germany, and Japan. Punk, too, spilled out from its foundational scenes in 1970s London and New York, and developed 'glocal' expressions across the world. Moreover, as Russ Bestley and his colleagues argue, these local punk scenes have not simply mimicked the Anglo-American originals, but have developed as distinctive milieu that 'hybridise and assimilate, and in turn reflect national, regional, and local identities' (Bestley et al., 2019: 11).

In this respect, punk is not alone. As styles and music circulate around the world, processes of glocalisation invariably take place as they are taken up and reworked by local audiences. Some cultural forms, however, may especially lend themselves to such processes. Andy Bennett, for example, has argued that hip-hop possesses certain characteristics that make it particularly suited to glo-calisation and local reconfiguration. The commercial packaging of hip-hop as a global commodity, Bennett suggests, has facilitated its easy access by young people worldwide (Bennett, 2000: 137). But also important is the distinctive 'hands on' nature of the genre, which has meant that audiences and performers become essentially interchangeable. Thus, while hip-hop existed as a huge commercial industry, Bennett contends, it could still win numerous local audiences because it retained 'a strong identification with the street and with the ethos of grass roots expression' (Bennett, 1999ii: 86).

Other authors have supported Bennett's account of hip-hop's 'glocalisation'. Tony Mitchell's (1996; (ed.) 2001) research in particular, testified to the wide-ranging uses of rap music and hip-hop style across the world – with French[12] and Italian hip-hop functioning as a vehicle of protest against racism and police har-assment, while Maori rap groups in New Zealand have campaigned for the rights of indigenous peoples around the world. And similar themes of glocalised adap-tation emerge from studies of hip-hop in Japan (Condry, 2006), Latin America (Catillo-Garsow and Nichols, 2016), Africa (Clark, 2018) and South Korea (Song, 2019). So, rather than spawning a legion of inferior imitations of the African-American original, the global flow of hip-hop has seen the genre reworked and reconfigured as new, identifiably local, forms of cultural expression (see Chapter 8). Local hip-hop scenes, therefore, are part of a 'transnational hip-hop community' but, as Russell White succinctly puts it, each scene also has 'its own identity, addresses nationally specific issues and employs its own culturally and linguistically specific markers' (White, 2010: 169).

Riding the waves of global cool: youth culture, soft power, and 'nation branding'

The modern flows of media and culture, however, have never been free-floating and independent. Issues of power and control have always determined which cultures get circulated, the specific ways they are disseminated, and exactly how they are received and take root. Trans-global conglomerates have obviously wielded significant influence in this respect, but governments have also played a part. And the role of government policy in the global circulation of youth culture increased during the early twenty-first century as many countries attempted to use national popular culture as a 'soft power' that enhanced their international standing and influence.

The concept of 'soft power' was originally developed by the US diplomat and political scientist Joseph Nye. In his book *Bound to Lead* (1990), Nye distinguished between 'hard' forms of power associated with economic and military dominance, and the 'soft' power of persuasion and 'setting the agenda and determining the framework of a debate' (Nye, 1990: 32). According to Nye, soft power was a realm of influence rather than compulsion. It was, he argued, 'the ability to get what you want through attraction rather than coercion or payments' (Nye, 2004: x). In the exercise of soft power, Nye explained, 'what the target thinks is particularly important, and the targets matter as much as the agents. Attraction and persuasion are socially constructed. Soft power is a dance that requires partners' (Nye, 2011: 84). For Nye, soft power had three key pillars. Political values and foreign policies, he contended, were two important avenues through which countries could persuade others to see them as legitimate and as having moral authority. But boosting the reach and reputation of their national culture was also, Nye suggested, a crucial means through which countries could strengthen their leverage.

As Terry Flew (2016) notes, there are some striking parallels between Nye's notion of soft power and the concept of cultural imperialism developed by theorists such as Herbert Schiller (see above). Both perspectives identify exposure to another country's media content as serving to shape the values, beliefs, and ideas of people in the recipient culture. But, for the likes of Schiller, US cultural imperialism was a *negative* force that mitigated against more organic and locally based notions of cultural sovereignty. In contrast, Flew observes, Nye identifies exposure to the soft power of American culture as 'a positive influence in world affairs' (Flew, 2016: 286). Indeed, Nye originally formulated the concept of soft power as a response to fears that, during the 1990s, the US was declining as a world power. Primarily addressed to foreign policy decision-makers, Nye's ideas were intended to demonstrate routes through which America's global influence could be maintained. And, subsequently, the concept of soft power was taken up in discussions of the way a broad range of other countries were attempting to secure their national interests through promoting their media and cultural industries. In some of these strategies, youth culture and music figured prominently, as countries sought to 'brand' themselves as enviably 'cool'.

Of course, in some senses, youth culture has long figured in the informal exercise of soft power. Most obviously, for instance, US and British music and style have exerted worldwide influence since the 1950s, Adrian Athique observing how the rise of rock 'n' roll 'constitutes a classic case of American "soft power"' (2016: 137). But the place of youth culture in foreign policy has become more explicit as many countries become more conscious of their 'brand' image. Authors such as Melissa Aronczyk (2013) and Keith Dinnie (2016) have drawn attention to the way that, during the early twenty-first century, countries began to invest more time and energy in conscious processes of 'nation branding'. Much like commercial companies (see Chapter 3), countries have sought to gain market advantage by fostering symbolic associations between their 'national brand' and particular values and identities. And, in doing so, some countries have eschewed their traditional 'folk' cultures in favour of promoting their more commercially-oriented popular cultures. This, Katja Valaskiivi (2013; 2016) argues, is because the consumerist and youth-oriented associations of popular culture give it an enticing allure. In particular, Valaskiivi contends, popular culture lends itself to the cultivation of a sense of national 'cool' – the notion of 'cool' denoting the attractive (and eminently saleable) traits of 'youthfulness, authenticity, trendiness, and creativity … [along with] a rebellious attitude towards authorities' (2013: 492). And, Valaskiivi suggests, Japan was a pioneer in this practice of 'cool' nation branding.

During the 1970s Japan was already developing strategies of cultural diplomacy. The country, for example, sought to enhance its international standing through educational exchange programmes and the promotion of traditional culture. During the 1980s and 1990s, however, it was the country's popular culture – films, TV shows, animation, and pop music – that increasingly gained international appeal; first in neighbouring Asian countries, and then in the US (and, to a lesser extent, Europe). In 2002 the trend gained attention when American journalist Douglas McGray highlighted 'Japan's Gross National Cool' in an article for the journal *Foreign Policy*. Hailing the success of Japanese popular culture (*manga* comics, *anime* films, pop music, films, and so on), McGray argued that the trend not only created a new, 'cool' image for Japan but also brought the country economic and political gains. The lessons were not lost on the Japanese government who, Valaskiivi suggests, increasingly sought to capitalise on the 'Cool Japan' phenomenon as a form of soft power (2013: 488). These efforts, as Michal Daliot-Bul (2009) notes, were also partly inspired by the British government's championing of 'Cool Britannia' during the 1990s (see Chapter 4). Encouraged by such ideas, Japan sought to develop its global interests through the promotion of its popular culture. Under the governments of Junichiro Koizumi (2001–2006), especially, the expression 'Cool Japan' gained currency for a variety of policies geared to developing the country's media and cultural industries. An array of government ministries, for instance, were involved in promotional projects such as 2003's J-Brand initiative, along with the creation of the Cool Japan Office in 2010 and the launch of the Council for the Promotion of Cool Japan in 2013. 'Pop-culture diplomacy', therefore, became a key feature of Japan's approach to foreign relations as the country sought to extend its soft power through the appeal of its 'cool' media.

In South Korea similar strategies also developed. During the late 1990s the country emerged as a centre for the production of transnational media. This spread of Korean popular culture has been termed '*Hallyu*' or the 'Korean Wave' (a term coined by Chinese journalists to describe local youngsters' sudden craze for Korean products), and its development was indebted to government policy. Between the 1960s and 1980s South Korea's authoritarian military governments had promoted labour-intensive, low-cost, and low-wage manufacturing as the country's economic mainstay. The media and creative industries, meanwhile, were strictly regulated and remained relatively undeveloped. But a series of large-scale pro-democracy protests brought an end to the military regime in 1993, and subsequent governments shifted South Korea's economic direction. Facing stiff manufacturing competition from China, the South Korean government aggressively promoted its media and cultural industries as new drivers of economic growth. A deregulation of financial industries and trade also brought a flow of capital into South Korean media, and this was buttressed by government loans and investment funds. Moreover, as Seung Kwon and Joseph Kim (2014) show, this support for the culture industries was part of an integrated policy framework that also developed the country's technological infrastructure, along with its electronics, mobile communication, and multimedia industries. The ensuing flood of new media products found a ready market among South Korea's growing middle-class. But even greater success was scored in neighbouring East and Southeast Asian countries where, as Youna Kim argues, Korean Wave media targeted a growing 'culturally cosmopolitan and technologically literate' market composed of 'younger generations under 30, "urban-middle, rural-rich classes"' (Kim, 2013: 5).

The Korean Wave initially broke during the late 1990s with the export of TV dramas to countries such as China, Japan, and Singapore. This was followed by successes for South Korean films, fashion, and pop music. But these moves were eclipsed by even greater success after 2008 as a 'New Korean Wave' gathered momentum. Whereas the original Korean Wave had been founded on technologies such as satellite broadcasting, what Dal Yong Jin (2016) dubs '*Hallyu* 2.0' was more squarely based on Internet platforms, social media, and online marketing. Moreover, along with Asia, *Hallyu* 2.0 was also heavily pitched towards markets in the US and Europe. Indeed, a benchmark of its success was Bong Joon-ho's dark comedy, *Parasite* (2019), a box office hit that became the first non-English-language film to win an Oscar for Best Picture. But, compared to the original Korean Wave, *Hallyu* 2.0 was also more specifically targeted at young audiences – with the lead taken by South

Korea's games and pop music industries. And, whereas the games industries of Japan and the West had concentrated on consul-based games, South Korea's companies focused on the development of online and mobile gaming, and this secured them a major slice of this developing global market. Meanwhile, the spread of social media sites and video platforms such as YouTube helped push K-Pop into an international spotlight, and brought major audiences for acts such as Rain (*Bi*), Super Junior, Girls Generation (*Sonyosidae*) and, of course, BTS.[13]

Along with Japan and South Korea, China has also been seen by some commentators as trying to extend its soft power by promoting its culture and media industries. The strategy has, for instance, seen China host major international events such as the Beijing Olympics in 2008 and the Shanghai World Expo in 2010. China has also funded hundreds of Confucius Institutes in universities worldwide to promote Chinese languages and culture. The international reach of China Central Television (CCTV) has also been extended through the launch of foreign-language services, while the Chinese government has assisted the international co-production of films and TV series, and has supported the growth of entertainment media conglomerates such as Tencent. The authoritarian character of China's government, however, can mitigate against the success of such initiatives. As Yanling Yang (2016) argues, China's strict regulation of film content effectively undermines any desire the government may have to present China in a positive light in the country's movies. International film audiences, Yang observes, will inevitably be wary of anything that hints at state propaganda. And, more generally, the Chinese government's record of censorship, surveillance and brutal political repression would pose problems for any attempt at a worldwide promotion of 'Chinese Cool'. In a global youth market that puts great store by myths of youthful individualism and independence, media products produced by a disciplinarian state would obviously struggle to find a foothold. As a consequence, it is perhaps understandable that, as Hesmondhalgh suggests, China's bid for cultural soft power has been steadily superseded by an emphasis on its 'Belt and Road Initiative' (BRI), geared towards building a transport infrastructure linking China to Central Asia and Europe (2019: 407).

A global vogue for 'Chinese Cool', therefore, seems an unlikely prospect for the immediate future. But youth culture has clearly figured prominently in the attempts of countries such as Japan and South Korea to develop a 'national brand' and extend their soft power. Yet, for some theorists, the whole concept of 'soft power' is flawed. Terry Flew, for instance, points out that notions of soft power rest on 'transmission-based' accounts of the media and popular culture that ignore the active agency of audiences. The tendency, he argues, is 'to view the transmission of such cultural forms into other countries as an end in itself, with far less attention being given to questions of engagement with these cultural forms in other countries' (2016: 285). So, simply because local audiences enjoy *manga* comics or K-Pop, this is no guarantee they will enthuse over

Japan or Korea. Notwithstanding his undertones of Islamophobia, the argument is made pithily by the historian Niall Ferguson:

> ... the trouble with soft power is that it's, well, soft. All over the Islamic world kids enjoy (or would like to enjoy) bottles of Coke, Big Macs, cds by Britney Spears and DVDs starring Tom Cruise. Do any of these things make them love the United States more? Strangely not.
>
> (Ferguson, 2009)

Notions of soft power, then, may be unduly naïve in their assumptions about the impact of media texts on their audiences. Nonetheless, there can be little doubt that, for countries like South Korea, the worldwide promotion of their 'cool' popular culture has been an economic boon. Indeed, in 2012 the value of the Korean Wave was estimated to be around $10 billion, and was expected to grow to $57 billion in 2020 (Kim, 2013: 6).

Successes like BTS, moreover, demonstrate how the international circulation of media and culture is not simply a one-way barrage from 'the West to the rest', but is a complex set of multi-directional and interconnected flows. Within these currents of media and culture, moreover, issues of hybridity figure prominently. Woongjae Roo, for instance, shows how the initial success of the Korean Wave in Asia was partly indebted to the 'in-between' character of South Korea's popular culture – its mix of cultural influences enabling it 'to retain broader cultural affinities with China and other Asian countries while also being just Westernized enough to mediate information from [the] West to Asia' (2009: 146). Roo also highlights the important processes of cultural hybridisation that occurred as *Hallyu* surged onto international shores, and South Korean film, TV and music became 'resources through which local peoples construct their own cultural spaces' (ibid). In these terms, Roo contends, the transnational appeal of the Korean Wave exemplifies the way 'globalization, particularly in the realm of popular culture, engenders an unpredictable, fluid, and creative form of *hybridization* that works to sustain local identities in the global context' (144, orig. emphasis). The next chapter focuses in more detail on these issues of identity and hybridity in the realm of youth cultures.

Notes

1 Overviews of the history of globalising trends can be found in Holton (2005), Hopkins (ed.) (2002), Martell (2010: 41–66), and Osterhammel and Peterson (2005).

2 More detailed surveys of the impact of neoliberalism and market de-regulation on the media industries can be found in Berry (2019) and Hesmondhalgh (2019: 133–166).

3 Effective summaries of these developments also appear in Hardy (2014: 79–108) and Jin (2020: 72–86).

4 Convergence was a key trend among communications companies during the early twenty-first century. For some commentators, however, a shift towards 'de-convergence' was also increasingly evidenced, with a splintering of companies

through 'spin-offs' and 'split-offs'. An example would be the CBS Corporation's spin-off from Viacom in 2005. These developments, however, are usually seen as taking place in parallel to (rather than replacing) trends towards convergence. See Jin (2015) and Sparviero and Peil (eds) (2018).

5 Accounts of what was sometimes dubbed the 'anti-globalisation movement' can be found in Martell (2010) and Moghadam (2009).

6 Other notable contributions to the tradition came from the Belgian theorist Armand Mattelart and the Canadian scholar Dallas Smythe. A valuable review of theories of cultural imperialism is provided in Tomlinson (1991).

7 Sigismondi (2012) highlights the growing role of glocalisation in the operation of modern media industries, while Roberts (ed.) (2016) furnishes a collection of studies considering the place of European media in processes of glocalisation.

8 In doing so, T-Series toppled Swedish Internet celebrity PewDiePie's five-year reign as owner of the most subscribed channel on YouTube (see Chapter 3).

9 During the 1980s and 1990s there was a surge of interest in the history of swing youth, with the publication of a number of popular and academic accounts. See, for example, Beck (1985), Breyvogel (ed.) (1991), Polster (ed.) (1989), and Willett (1989). In 1992 there even appeared a movie produced by Disney – *Swing Kids*.

10 Horn (2009) provides an overview of the influence of American popular culture on British youth during the 1950s and 1960s.

11 Similar incidents were reported from as far afield as Detroit, New York and Philadelphia. Full accounts of the history of the zoot suit and the responses it elicited can be found in Alvarez (2008), Escobar (1996) and Peiss (2011).

12 France has boasted an especially prolific hip-hop culture. French hip-hop first took root during the early 1980s, while the 1990s saw MC Solaar emerge as one of the country's foremost rap pioneers – his debut album, *Qui Sème le Vent Récolte le Tempo* (1991), becoming one of the biggest-selling rap albums outside the US. During the 1990s, harder-edged artists such as NTM (*Nique Ta Mère*) and IAM (Imperial Asiatic Men) also came to the fore. For accounts of the growth of French hip-hop, see Bocquet and Pierre-Adolphe (2017) and McCarren (2013).

13 The importance of online media to the success of K-Pop was demonstrated in 2012 when 1.6 billion hits on YouTube turned South Korean singer Psy's hit song 'Gangnam Style' (along with its horse-riding dance) into a global phenomenon.

8 Global media, local youth cultures, and hybridity

'Somewhere in America': youth culture, ethnicity, and identity

The Mipsterz triggered an international debate in 2013. 'Mipsterz' was a tongue-in-cheek neologism that combined the words 'Muslim' and 'hipster' (the latter being widely used to denote hip, young urbanites), and it was adopted as a jocular name-tag by a collection of young, US-born Muslims. The Mipsterz group began in 2012 as an online community where young, creative Muslims shared interests, discussed ideas and planned artistic collaboration. But in 2013 the group sparked controversy when they produced a short video entitled *Somewhere in America #Mipsterz*.[1] The two–and-half minute film was a montage of sequences featuring around 20 young, American, Muslim women wearing the *hijab* (the traditional Islamic veil, or headscarf) in their daily lives.

Donning the *hijab* in a variety of styles (from a turban to the traditional wrap), the Mipsterz women were all trendily dressed in Western fashions, and the film featured them hanging out, skateboarding, jogging through the park and posing for photographs. The video attempted to show what it meant to be a Muslim woman *hijabi* (someone who wears the *hijab*) who was born, and lived in, the US. The Mipsterz women were represented as confident, independent, fashionable, and fun. And the positive theme was underscored by the video's soundtrack – 'Somewhere in America' by Jay-Z – a song whose anti-racist themes celebrate the rise of a new generation of integrated Americans. Uploaded onto YouTube, within days the film had attracted over 500,000 viewers and had sparked international discussions via social media about both the politics of the veil and the representation of Muslim women. Some audiences applauded the video, seeing it as a bold and refreshing challenge to stereotypical representations of Muslim *hijabi* women as passive and austere. Others, however, were more critical and slated the film for objectifying the women it featured, for being a shallow and consumption-fixated portrayal of femininity, and/or for misrepresenting Islam and presenting unacceptably immodest and over-sexualised images of Muslim women.

The worldwide dimension to the *Mipsterz* controversy illustrated how the connections of the modern media were increasingly bringing together global audiences. Beyond this, however, it also demonstrated the pronounced conflicts surrounding issues of ethnicity, religion, gender, and identity. In particular, some of the more conservative critiques of *Mipsterz* highlighted the way Muslim women are, as Golnaz Golnaraghi and Sumayya Daghar put it, 'caught between Orientalist and traditionalist discourses' (2017: 120). That is to say, on one hand, Muslim women are confronted by a Western, Orientalist discourse that constructs them as an alien and (increasingly since the events of 9/11) dangerous 'Other' (see Chapter 4). But, on the other hand, they also face a traditionalist Islamic discourse that 'attempts to contain their bodies with patriarchal and rigid structures informed by politicized anti-colonial and anti-West movements' (Golnaraghi and Daghar, 2017: 105).

Additionally, the themes of *Mipsterz* pointed to the way some young, Muslim women were navigating their way through the complex discourses of religion, ethnicity, and gender. The *Mipsterz* women were, proponents suggested, elaborating new and distinctive identities that *both* pushed past traditionalist understandings of modesty and Islamic fashion, *and* resisted simple 'assimilation' into dominant Western ideals. As journalist Hajer Naili (who participated in the video) later explained:

> We do not try to fit into Western society. We are women who were born in the West ... [but] I don't try to fit into society, this is who I am. And besides that, I'm a Muslim woman. So why wouldn't it be compatible to express this double culture; this double identity. We are women with multifacets [sic], and this is who we are.
>
> (quoted in Hafiz, 2014)

This chapter explores the issues and debates thrown into relief by the *Mipsterz* controversy. It considers the changing elaborations of ethnicity and identity that – as a consequence of the flows of globalisation – have increasingly characterised modern youth cultures. The chapter begins by highlighting the way local youth cultures cannot be considered in isolation, but have to be understood as part of a 'global tapestry' woven from a wealth of connected 'threads'. Growing numbers of young people, for example, have experienced global migration, while many use media technologies to form and sustain transnational dialogues and worldwide connections. The chapter also gives close attention to the 'hybrid' cultures and identities that emerge from what Jan Nederveen Pieterse terms the 'global mélange' – a trend towards the mixing of cultural categories, forms, and beliefs drawn from different locales (2020: 91). The chapter explores the way these processes of cultural hybridisation have been especially evident in the realms of youth culture and music; and it considers the way such developments may be constituent in the emergence of a new plurality of negotiated and dynamic identities. At the same time, however, the continued prevalence of global inequalities is underscored. And, while fluidity and fusion have become major features of contemporary youth culture, the chapter highlights how local places, institutions, and material cultures remain significant forces in the lives of many young people around the world.

'*Routes* rather than *Roots*': diaspora, youth cultures, and hybridity

Modern youth cultures are not formed in isolation, but through processes of interconnection, fusion and amalgamation in what Arjun Appadurai (1990) sees as the 'landscape' of globalisation (see Chapter 7). For Appadurai, processes of globalisation are constituted through interrelated, worldwide flows of capital, technology, media, beliefs, and peoples. And, for some theorists, the international flow of peoples – or what Appadurai terms 'ethnoscapes' – has been a particularly important aspect of modern globalisation. Using the concept of 'diaspora' (from the Greek phrase meaning 'to disperse'), many researchers have analysed the nature and consequences of different people's travels across borders, and dispersion around the world. According to Avtar Brah, for example, the process of diasporic movement generates new forms of cultural identity that 'are at once local and global', being composed of 'networks of trans-national identifications encompassing "imagined" and "encountered" communities' (Brah, 1996: 196). Such cultures are not tied down to particular places, but are better conceptualised in terms of motion and contingency. Or, as Paul Gilroy puts it, they are a matter of *routes* rather than *roots* – that is to say, they are patterns of movement and diffusion that involve the formation of 'creolized, syncretized, hybridized and chronically impure cultural forms' (Gilroy, 1993i: 335). Moreover, Gilroy emphasises the issues of power and conflict that have been central to the development of these 'diasporic identities', arguing they are generated through 'forced dispersal and reluctant scattering', so that 'diaspora identity is focused less on the equalising, proto-democratic force of common territory and more on the social dynamics of remembrance and commemoration defined by a strong sense of the dangers involved in forgetting the location of origin and the process of dispersal' (Gilroy, 1993i: 318).

During the 1980s Gilroy had been a member of Birmingham University's Centre for Contemporary Cultural Studies (CCCS) (see Chapters 4 and 6). His early research represented a multi-layered analysis of the complex struggles around 'race', class and nation in modern Britain,[2] but his later work gave particular attention to black 'expressive culture' and its relation to processes of diaspora and political struggle. For Gilroy, black culture and experience could only be understood in terms of its trans-Atlantic connections. In his analysis of these relationships, Gilroy eschewed notions of a pan-global, homogeneous 'Black identity', but he also resisted notions of distinctly British, American, or Caribbean black culture. Instead, Gilroy introduced the concept of the 'Black Atlantic' to denote the history of intercultural connections linking globally dispersed black peoples (Gilroy, 1993i). In these terms, Gilroy argued, a series of forced and voluntary migrations (including the slave trade, but also the free movement of people and cultural forms back and forth across the Atlantic) had spread black people across the globe, though they remained linked by a long history of cultural connection and exchange. In these terms, no one part of the Black Atlantic could be understood without considering its relation to the others. Moreover, Gilroy suggested, this process of cultural dialogue had created a plurality of hybrid identities and cultural forms that emerged between (and within) the various locales of the black diaspora.

These dimensions of cultural dialogue and hybridity have long been highlighted by Caribbean historians. During the eighteenth and nineteenth centuries, Kamau Brathwaite (1971) has argued, the violent uprooting and re-grounding of African peoples in the slave-based colonies of the New World generated new cultures and identities known as 'creole' (a term derived from linguistics). Creole cultures were not merely poor imitations of a European original. Instead, they drew on both European and African influences to forge new, distinctive cultural formations. These formations, moreover, were often marked by a growing sense of self-possession and self-definition that fed into the development of an anti-colonial national consciousness. Indeed, for many postcolonial theorists, this kind of 'destabilising' effect is an important feature of 'creolised' or 'hybrid' cultures.

Cultural hybridity can take many forms, and is interpreted in a number of different ways. For Jan Nederveen Pieterse, hybridy exists on a continuum stretching from an 'assimilationist hybridity' to a 'destabilising hybridity'. An assimilationist form of hybridity, is one in which 'the centre' predominates – it 'leans over towards the center, adopts the canon and mimics hegemony' (2020: 96). A destabilising form of hybridity, however, has more radical potential; it 'blurs the canon, reverses the current, subverts the center' (ibid.). From this perspective, colonial societies – which were based on a binary discourse that defined a dominant Western culture against an inferior 'Other' – felt challenged by 'in-between', hybrid entities because their existence defied claims that the binary distinctions were fixed, immutable and somehow 'natural'. Instead, dimensions of hybridity highlighted the way the binary distinctions were social constructs whose boundaries were always contingent and fluid. Hybridity, then, disrupted the dominant cultural discourse by engendering diversity, heterogeneity, and multiplicity. And, for postcolonial theorists such as Homi Bhabha (1990; 1994), these qualities of hybridity are fundamental to the cultural identities forged through modern processes of globalisation.

For postcolonial theorists, the importance of cultural hybridity lies in its potential to question and subvert dominant notions of the world. According to Bhabha, cultures are never fixed or complete, but exist in a continuous process of collision, interaction, and reinvention. These processes of intersection, he argued, created a distinctive 'Third Space' – a metaphorical space in which two or more disparate social or cultural forces interacted to form new, hybrid ways of thinking or being. As Bhabha explained:

> This third space displaces the histories that constitute it, and sets up new
> structures of authority, new political initiatives, which are inadequately

understood through received wisdom. The process of cultural hybridity gives rise to something different, something new and unrecognisable, a new area of meaning and representation.

(Bhabha, 1990: 211)

Bhabha's Third Space, then, denoted the way that – through processes of interface and fusion – new, hybrid cultural identities are formed, reformed, and in a constant state of becoming. From this perspective, hybridity is not merely a blending of cultural elements, nor the simple fashioning of 'glocal' products to appeal to a local market. Rather, hybridity is a Third Space, or an in-between zone where new forms of cultural meaning and production occur, blurring the limitations of existing boundaries and calling into question the established classifications of culture and identity. The video *Somewhere in America #Mipsterz* (see above) can be seen as an apt illustration of Bhabha's arguments.

In a widely circulated critique of the *Mipsterz* film, journalist Sana Saeed argued it was a shallow attempt to assimilate young Muslim women into mainstream US culture. The video, Saeed suggested, seemed to have little purpose 'aside from showing well-dressed, put together Muslim women in poses perfect for a magazine spread' (Saeed, 2013). Others, however, contended the video was a meaningful attempt to blur the lines between the cultures of 'traditional' Islam and the contemporary West, and construct an identity that – in Bhabha's terms – was 'a new area of meaning and representation'. Golnaraghi and Daghar, for instance, argued that the women featured in *Mipsterz* were 'claiming power and agency' in the way they 'attempted to discursively construct their own identities and resist binary oppositional frames informed by Orientalist and traditionalist discourses' (2017: 121). Drawing on Bhabha's ideas, they argued that the *Mipsterz* women were carving out a new, distinctively 'hybrid' cultural space:

> … the Mipsterz women exist in the third space, and have attempted to transcend the dichotomies by resisting the oppressive and romanticized ideals often imposed on them, that serve to 'other'.
>
> (2017: 120–121)

Communications theorist Kristin Peterson took a similar view. According to Peterson, the women in the *Mipsterz* video were using fashion to 'communicate something about their identities and their membership within a cultural group':

> These young women create an innovative, hybrid style that blends Islamic modesty and piety, hip and fashionable styles, and the creativity and anti-commercialism of the hipster movement. Through the visual display of fashion, the Mipsterz video provides the opportunity for young Muslims to subtly critique other Islamic fashion movements – such as social media fashion gurus and online Islamic fashion magazines that focus mainly on

consumption – and to more forcibly overthrow mainstream stereotypes of Muslim women as submissive and oppressed.

(Peterson, 2018)

More broadly, Imene Ajala (2017) points to the way fashion trends among young Muslims living in the West are also indicative of their heterogeneous, hybrid cultural identifications. As Ajala observes, Muslim youth represent a huge and growing global market that has spurred the growth of a burgeoning fashion industry that was valued at around $266 billion in 2013 (Ajala 2017: 4). 'Modest' women's fashions, for example, are geared to consumers who enjoy elements of Western style, but who also want to observe Islamic religious practice – and it is catered for by a coterie of online 'modest fashion influencers', sometimes dubbed '*hijabistas*' (a phrase formed through fusing the words '*hijab*' and '*fashionista*') (4). 'Cool' Muslim streetwear, meanwhile, is promoted by brands such as the German-based Styleislam and the France-based LSA (*Le Savoir est une Arme*) and is, Ajala explains, 'a style of urban clothing which takes into account Islamic prescriptions in terms of dress and occasionally conveys Islamic messages' (6).

Appealing to youngsters from Europe, and also Middle Eastern countries like Saudi Arabia, Egypt, and the United Arab Emirates, the success of such brands testifies to the economic significance of Muslim youth as an international market. But, more than this, Ajala argues that the rise of Islamic Dress and 'Cool Islam' challenges any essentialist view of Islam as 'a homogeneous sphere immune to change and to any external global dynamic' (Ajala, 2017: 2). Instead, while such styles appeal to young people keen to self-identify as Muslim, they are also influenced by the forces of global consumerism and growing individualisation. The result, Ajala contends, is a fusion of cultural influences that 'deconstructs and makes explicit the assertion of young Muslims in Europe adopting these products: the pride of being Muslim, but also [of being] Western, modern and cool' (7). In these terms, then, the popularity of Islamic fashion and Muslim streetwear points towards young, Muslim identities that are not immutable and 'closed', but are complex, heterogeneous, and dynamic. These are qualities, moreover, embodied in global youth cultures more generally. Through the social, economic, and cultural flows of globalisation, youth cultures have become characteristically fluid, multi-layered, and hybrid.

'Cut 'n' Mix' music: the sounds of syncretism

For some authors, however, the expression 'hybridity' is problematic, given its history within the racist discourses of colonialism. Instead, the 1990s saw the term 'syncretic' (derived from anthropology) – which has more positive, dynamic connotations – sometimes preferred as a way of describing the processes through which new cultural forms and identities are constituted at the intersection of different places, histories, and experiences. According to theorists such as Paul Gilroy and Stuart Hall, attention to this 'syncretic' criss-crossing of cultural discourses opened up new ways of theorising ethnicity and identity – an approach that moved away from notions of ethnic identities as essential and fixed, and instead conceived them as constructed, multiple, and dynamic. Both Hall and Gilroy used the term 'diasporic culture' to explore the complex intercultural exchanges and transnational linkages through which ethnic identities are translated and transmitted, and in which 'new ethnicities' are made and remade (Gilroy, 1993i; Hall, 1992i).

In some respects, this attention to processes of cultural exchange and the hybridity of identities was anticipated by Dick Hebdige's (1987) historical survey of Caribbean music. Tracing the development of calypso and ska, through reggae and Jamaican club culture, to New York rap and hip-hop, Hebdige emphasised the dynamism of Caribbean musical forms, their histories, and associated identities. Instead of attempting to trace the roots of these genres to their historical source, Hebdige argued that the 'roots' themselves were in a constant state of flux. 'The roots', Hebdige explained, 'don't stay in one place. They change shape. They change colour and they grow' (Hebdige, 1987: 10). Hence, Hebdige drew attention to the way Caribbean music had developed through ongoing 'cut 'n' mix' processes of fusion and interconnection – a 'splicing together' of sounds and identities that addressed communities stretching from Africa to Western Europe and the US.

This 'splicing together' of dynamic and 'hybridised' cultural forms has been a core trait of modern youth culture, style, and music. Indeed, with its fusion of black R'n'B and white country and western music, 1950s rock 'n' roll was the 'granddaddy' of hybridised youth cultures. Rock 'n' roll was, itself, a syncretric phenomenon; but it also spawned a host of other hybrid forms as it became re-articulated and re-embedded across the world. Eric Zolov (1999), for example, shows how the popularity of rock 'n' roll among Mexican youth fed into the country's shifting cultural and political relations during the 1950s and 1960s. As in Europe, the 1950s saw conservative opinion in Mexico condemn American rock 'n' roll and US youth style as harbingers of cultural decline. In public debate, Zolov argues, rock 'n' roll became associated with notions of *desmadre* – a slang term denoting a condition of social chaos that springs from the literal 'unmothering' of a person or situation. The controversy continued into the 1960s and, as many Mexican youngsters embraced the music and values of the Western counterculture, critics feared their interest undermined indigenous culture and 'reinforced subservience to foreign values' (Zolov 1999: 111). But, according to Zolov, the American texts did not simply bulldoze their way across Mexican cultural life. Instead, elements of US youth culture were combined with local cultural forms in a configuration that, Zolov argues, 'allowed youth to invent new ways of *being* Mexican, ways that ran counter to the dominant ideology of state-sponsored nationalism' (Zolov 1999: 111).

The development of *raï* music in Algeria stands as another example of a creative blending between Western media and indigenous culture. Originally an Algerian acoustic folk music, *raï* was transformed during the 1980s as local popular songs and rhythms were increasingly mixed with Western instruments (electric guitars, synthesisers, and drum machines), and influences from American disco and Europop. As a consequence, Marc Schade-Poulsen has observed, modern *raï* became a fusion that expressed the 'ambivalent or fundamental duality in the identity of Algerian youth' (Schade-Poulsen, 1995: 85). According to Schade-Poulsen, *raï* music's popularity lay in the way its melding of different musical idioms addressed Algerian youth's own attempts to negotiate the tensions between their interest in Western lifestyles and their commitment to traditional institutions of family and religious life.

Hybridity is also, Deborah Hernandez (2010) suggests, a characteristic of Latino musical practice. The music cultures of Latin Americans living in the US, Hernandez argues, have always been characterised by 'multiple origins and intersecting pathways' (2) that have blended the music of their homelands with genres from the US and the wider world. And the fusion, she contends, has become increasingly complex as new waves of immigrants have introduced additional musical styles, such as *merengue* and *bachata* (from the Dominican Republic), and *cumbia* (from Columbia). The result, Hernandez contends, has been:

> ... a dazzling variety of musical practices – many of them not usually identified as Latino – each with its own intricate genealogy and each giving voice to the quintessentially blended and layered qualities that characterize the experience of being Latino in the United States.
>
> (Hernandez, 2010: 2)

For some theorists, reggaeton (or *reggaetón*, or *reguetón*) also stands as a quintessential musical hybrid. Originating in the clubs of San Juan, Puerto Rico during the 1990s, reggaeton combined the rhythms of hip-hop and reggae with Spanish rapping and singing. Beginning as an 'underground' music, it was associated with poor, urban, non-white youth and many of its songs dealt with the troubles of inner-city life, along with themes of violence, drugs, sex, and friendship. Initially demonised and censored by the Puerto Rican authorities, reggaeton nevertheless became one of the most popular music genres in the Spanish-speaking Caribbean. And, during the early twenty-first century – partly through social media and Internet platforms such as YouTube – reggaeton found audiences in North America, Europe, and Asia as artists such as Daddy Yankee and Ivy Queen broke into the commercial mainstream.[3]

But, for Petra Rivera-Rideau (2015), what makes reggaeton significant is not just its transnational popularity, nor simply its fusion of hip-hop and reggae. Rather, Rivera-Rideau points to the way reggaeton created a new space for the negotiation of black identities in Puerto Rico. While Puerto Rico likes to think of itself as a harmonious 'racial democracy', dominant definitions of Puerto Rican national identity have privileged whiteness and Spanish cultures, and have marginalised poor, non-white communities. In this context, Rivera-Rideau argues, reggaeton has served as a space for expressing a '"race-based cultural politics'" (1). By drawing on aesthetics and signifiers from other sites in the African diaspora, she argues, reggaeton has provided a new language to speak about the black presence in Puerto Rico and has 'produced new understandings of Puerto Riccanness that center blackness and diasporic belonging and ... [that] articulate Afro-Latino identities on the island and elsewhere' (2).

Oher music genres also stand out as examples of the way new, hybrid identities are created through diasporic interconnections. For Paul Gilroy, the history of hip-hop culture and rap music was especially emblematic of the processes. As Gilroy explained:

> Rap is a hybrid form rooted in the syncretic social relations of the South Bronx where Jamaican sound-system culture, transplanted during the 1970s, put down new roots and in conjunction with specific technological innovations, set in train a process that was to transform black America's sense of itself and a large proportion of the popular music industry as well.
>
> (Gilroy, 1993ii: 125)

Indeed, from its beginnings, rap was characterised by processes of fusion and the creation of new cultural spaces.[4] Its antecedents lie in the vernacular poetry that has long been a central feature of the oral traditions of African-American culture, but its more immediate precursors were politicised, black poets such as Gil Scott Heron, Amiri Baraka, and The Last Poets who, during the late 1960s and early 1970s, experimented with a blending of music and poetic verse. During the mid-1970s rap was further developed in New York's South Bronx, where Jamaican émigré DJ Kool Herc introduced American dancefloors to the Jamaican practice of 'toasting' – improvised, syncopated wordplay laid over dub versions of records – while artists such as Afrika Bambaataa and Grandmaster Flash exploited technological developments in mixing, dubbing, and sampling as they cut-up and reassembled fragments of music, lyrics, and soundbites in an eclectic, rhythmic soundscape. For Tricia Rose (1994) this distinctive mix emerged from the context of deindustrialisation, economic decline, and racial tensions that characterised New York during the late 1970s. Rap and the associated culture of hip-hop (graffiti, dance, style), Rose argued, were spaces in which young African- and Caribbean-Americans won a sense of status through forging new identities and by symbolically re-appropriating the urban environment.

In 1979 the success of the Sugarhill Gang's single, 'Rapper's Delight', brought rap wider commercial attention, and during the 1980s artists such as Run DMC, Eric B. & Rakim, Boogie Down Productions, and Public Enemy established rap as an integral part of the US music industry. But, as rap was taken up and re-articulated by different social groups, it spawned new cultural expressions and identities. Young Mexican-Americans and Latin Americans, for example, were involved in hip-hop culture since its inception, and during the 1980s and 1990s artists such as Cypress Hill created a distinctive sound by fusing hip-hop beats with Latino rhythms.

Transformation and translation also took place as rap and hip-hop took root on the West Coast, the 1980s seeing the rise of Los Angeles 'gangsta' rappers such as Ice-T and N.W.A (Niggaz Wit Attitudes), who rewrote the hip-hop agenda in visceral anthems to LA gang life.[5] But hip-hop has also resonated with many audiences outside the US. As George Lipsitz argues, while hip-hop 'circulates as a commodity marketed by highly centralized monopolies from metropolitan countries', it also 'serves as a conduit for ideas and images articulating subaltern sensibilities' (Lipsitz, 1994: 36).[6] Indeed, for Lipsitz, the global popularity of rap and hip-hop has been 'perhaps the most important manifestation of postcolonial culture on a global scale':

> Hip hop expresses a form of politics perfectly suited to the postcolonial era. It brings a community into being through performance, and it maps out real and imagined relations between people that speak to the realities of displacement, disillusion and despair created by the austerity economy of post-industrial capitalism.
>
> (Lipsitz, 1994: 36)

'Repping the ends': locality and hybridised hip-hop

The cultural mixing and blending that characterised the worldwide circulation of rap and hip-hop generated a host of reconfigured, 'glocalised' incarnations (see Chapter 7). And, for many postcolonial theorists, these global flows have been especially significant for their role in – as Lipsitz puts it – 'articulating subaltern sensibilities'. Adopted by a diversity of migrant and minority ethnic youngsters around the world, rap has become an avenue for the creation of new cultures, politics, and identities. Invoking Bhabha's 'spatial' metaphor, for example, P. Khalil Saucier and Kumarini Silva argue that the performance of hip-hop artists in war-torn Sri Lanka represents a hybrid 'Third Space', one forged 'between competing cultural traditions' that 'articulates the realities, frustrations, and hopes of younger Sri Lanka' (2014: 297). For Saucier and Silva, the internationally renowned British-Sri Lankan performer M.I.A – along with locally popular Sri Lankan hip-hop artists, like Krishan, Iraj, and Gajan – draw on the symbolic universe of African-American hip-hop. These influences are then integrated in a new sensibility that articulates Sri Lanka's complex relationship with the British empire, globalised popular culture and a nationalist, postcolonial identity. In these terms, hip-hop offers Sri Lankan youth 'a springboard for the formulation of positive and contemporary forms of identity and cultural practices':

> In short, hip-hop provides a space for the articulation of group solidarity, for it allows Sri Lankan youth, especially those in the diaspora, to reconnect and identify with their ethnic and cultural heritage, to speak of shared values and goals (of peace), and loyalty to the group.
>
> (Saucier and Silva, 2014: 299)

In a similar fashion J. Griffith Rollefson argues that hip-hop has come to 'express the dreams and frustrations of postcolonial Europeans' (2017: 2). Analysing the appeal of hip-hop among Senegalese Parisians, Turkish Berliners, and South Asian Londoners, Rollefson suggests that hip-hop resonates with the children and grandchildren of migrants from the former colonies and peripheries because it offers an avenue for 'syncretic expressions that are at once wholly local and definitely global' (2). As Rollefson explains:

> ... hip hop artists in postcolonial Europe seize on the commercialized forms of black American culture to elaborate their own affiliations with the lived realities and mediatized images of African American struggle, gain visibility in their own local and national contexts, and ultimately reterritorialize the music and politics to suit their own exigencies.
>
> (Rollefson, 2017: 5)

This process of 'reterritorialization' was especially clear in Britain. During the 1980s, Andy Wood (2009) argues, hip-hop was an important resource for black British youths who were seeking a sense of identity and representation. Drawing on Gilroy's idea of the Black Atlantic, Wood suggests that hip-hop was traded across the different points of the Atlantic diaspora, so that British rap artists drew inspiration from US hip-hop but merged its influence with strands of their own cultural heritage. Especially important in this respect were reggae sound systems. Initially brought to Britain by Jamaican immigrant communities during the 1950s and 1960s, sound systems combined instrumental reggae records with live vocals, played through towering speaker stacks, and their legacy gave British hip-hop its distinctive character. As Wood argues, early British hip-hop artists such as London Posse had grown up immersed in the traditions of reggae and sound systems, and they formulated a unique oeuvre by 'merging their reggae influences with Hip Hop's beats and breaks and rapping in a mixture of cockney and patois, often with a Ragga tinge' (198). The result of this 'multi-directional dialogue', Wood concludes, was 'not the sound of an essentialized black America, but a curious, compelling hybrid style' (187).

This kind of fusion of diasporic influences, Casper Melville (2020) argues, characterised a continuum of music cultures that emerged in Britain – and particularly London – from the late twentieth century. During the early 1990s, for example, there surfaced a music scene variously known as jungle, breakbeat or drum 'n' bass which plundered from a variety of sources and styles. Jungle first emerged as a chiefly black dance music spearheaded by DJs such as Fabio and Grooverider, and was subsequently popularised by performers such as Goldie – a former graffiti artist who became the face of jungle through the success of his debut album, *Timeless*, in 1995. Rattling along at 160 beats per minute, jungle was dominated by a thumping reggae bassline, but was also characterised by its fusion of ragga, hip-hop, hard-core, and house musical styles. It was an eclectic mix of sound that laid the way for the development of an urban dance music scene that was distinctly 'hybridised' in the way it drew together diverse elements of African-Caribbean, American, and British cultural influence.

Dimensions of cultural blending were also a key feature of grime. First emerging in East London during the early 2000s, grime began as an underground club scene and spread via pirate radio stations like Rinse FM. Grime's stripped-down, jagged-edged sounds drew on elements of jungle and hip-hop, while its quick-fire rap vocals offered gritty tableaux of its 'scuzzy' street origins. As Ruth Adams (2019) argues, much like hip-hop and jungle, grime was a 'combination of post-colonial diversity and hybridity', though she also highlights the intense localism that characterised early grime:

> Grime's geographic origins are emphasized explicitly in handles, song titles and lyrical content with MCs often identifying themselves not just by city, but also by their specific home area (Newham Generals), by postcode (Wiley's 'Bow E3' 2007), housing estate, or other local landmarks (The Square's 'Lewisham McDeez' 2015).
>
> (443)

As Adams observes, this emphasis on geographic origins and local identity – or, in grime argot, 'repping the ends' (i.e. determinedly representing one's community, or 'end', to the wider world) – is a long-established tradition in black music cultures. This, Dick Hebdige explains, is a practice in which 'the namer pays tribute in the "name check" to the community from which (s)he has sprung and without which (s)he would be unable to survive' (Hebdige, 1987: 8). For Adams, however, the practice has particular resonance in grime because it 'reflects the reality of many young working-class people' (444). Grime developed as polyglot of musical and lyrical influences, but 'repping the ends' underscored the way it was rooted in the local realities of its young performers and fans. For Adams, therefore, grime was distinctive in the way it 'articulate[d] new types of identity, novel manifestations of being a Londoner, of being English' (438–439).

By the late 2010s artists such as Dizzee Rascal, Stormzy, and Skepta had taken grime into the commercial mainstream. But many of grime's key features resurfaced in UK drill. Drill music first developed in Chicago's South Side (where 'drill' was slang for firing an automatic weapon). Rappers such as Chief Keef and his cousin, Fredo Santana, exemplified drill's characteristic sound – a slow tempo, matched with a deadpan delivery of dark lyrics that chronicled a life of hustling on the streets. The music found its counterpart in UK drill, which emerged around Brixton (in south London) during the mid-2010s and was largely distributed through the Internet – especially via YouTube platforms such as Link Up TV, GRM Daily, and Mixtape Madness. Raw and angry, and offering a bleak view of inner-city life, UK drill drew much influence from its US precursor. But, like other cultures forged in the diaspora of the Black Atlantic, UK drill was also firmly rooted in distinctly local identities and affiliations.

The rise of 'Asian kool': youth and 'transcultural' identities

The international reach of hip-hop, and the proliferation of its off-shoots, exemplifies the dynamic interplay between global media and young people's local identities. And, for theorists such as Hall and Gilroy, these processes of interconnection and hybridisation had created spaces where 'new ethnicities' took shape and developed (see above). These ideas were taken up by Les Back (1996) in his analysis of the syncretic forms of music and culture that emerged in Britain during the 1990s. Drum 'n' bass, for instance, was seen by Back as a preeminent example of a cultural sphere where 'the aesthetics of the nation [were] recomposed, resulting in more inclusive translocal notions of what it means to reside within UK boundaries' (1996: 233). In his survey of these processes, Back also underlined the importance of the Asian[7] diaspora. For Back, the coming together of Asian and African diasporic cultures in Britain represented an important intersection in the creation of new, syncretic identities. As Back observed, the development of new, 'translocal' cultures took on additional nuances:

> … when South Asian lexical and cultural elements are introduced into these syncretic processes. The modes of expression that are produced possess a kind of triple consciousness that is simultaneously the child of Africa, Asia and Europe.
>
> (Back, 1996: 185)

While some theorists – for example, George Lipsitz – have used the analogy of the crossroads to represent this conjunction of identities and cultural expressions, Back argued that such a metaphor oversimplifies processes of cultural interaction and development. Instead, he drew upon the idea of the 'rhizome' deployed in the work of the critical philosophers Gilles Deleuze and Felix Guattari. With its connotations of continuous growth and lateral roots, Back suggested, the notion of the rhizome provided a more useful way of conceiving the various 'forms of cultural inter-being' (1996: 185). And, following on from this, he offered the concept of the 'intermezzo' to denote spaces where cultural sensibilities merge and new identities are generated.

This kind of 'multiple consciousness' has been highlighted in many accounts of young British-Asians' 'homegrown' cultural identities. Indeed, a significant body of work has pointed to the way British-Asian youngsters have negotiated within – and between – not only differences of age, gender and class but also the discourses of 'Britishness' and 'Asianness'. While British-born Asians were once characterised as being caught 'between two cultures' (Watson, 1977), during the 1990s increasing attention focused on the way second and third generation British-Asians had actually configured *their own* 'transcultural' identities. The negotiation of generational, gendered, and ethnic identities were, for example, themes compellingly explored by filmmaker Gurinder Chadha (in her movies *Bhaji on the Beach* (1993) and *Bend It Like Beckham* (2002)), and authors such as Hanif Kureishi (most notably in his screenplay for the film *My Beautiful Laundrette* (1985), and his novels *The Buddha of Suburbia* (1990) and *The Black Album* (1995)).

Issues of cross-cultural identity formation were also underscored in academic research. Chris Barker's (1999) study of British-Asian girls' everyday discussion of TV soaps, for instance, suggested the young women were well aware of the way their identities were informed by a variety of cultural discourses, and used their engagement with TV soaps as a way of enunciating themselves as Asian, while at the same time reworking the meanings of 'Asianness' to encompass their own, syncretic British-Asian culture. Similarly, Marie Gillespie's (1995; 2000) research on British-Asian youth in south London found the youngsters used an array of international media (British TV soaps, videos of Indian films and so on) as a forum to evaluate and experiment with a variety of different cultural identities. In some respects, Gillespie argued, British-Asian youth's media consumption prompted discussion around issues common to most young people – fashion, friends and family, growing up, dating – but, along with this, she found the diversity of international media consumed by the youngsters also encouraged distinctly 'cross-cultural, comparative analyses of media representations' (Gillespie, 2000: 165).

Popular music is also an arena in which young British-Asians have negotiated their identities. Many authors, for example, have seen bhangra as a genre of music shaped by processes of migration and diaspora. The music takes its name from a form of Punjabi folk music played on traditional drums such as the *dholak* or *dholki*, but during the mid-1980s bhangra was reconfigured by young British-Asians who fused traditional bhangra beats with a variety of Western music styles (disco, house and rap) to produce a music that Rupa Huq describes as 'at least as quintessentially "British" as it is "Asian"' (Huq, 1996: 62–63). And, blending elements of bhangra with ragga (dubbed 'bhangramuffin' by the music press), the Birmingham-born singer Apache Indian took Asian dance music to mainstream success during the early 1990s with a string of hit singles and the critically acclaimed album *No Reservations* (1992). Equally successful was the producer/performer Bally Sagoo, who interwove Bollywood film scores with pulsating Western basslines to sell over 100,000 copies of six albums during the early 1990s, and scoring Britain's first Indian-language Top-Twenty hit with 'Dil Cheez' in 1997.

With a surge of press interest in British-Asian bands, musicians, and club culture during the 1990s, music journalists hailed the rise of 'Asian Kool' (Morris, 1993). But, as Rehan Hyder (2004) has observed, the idea of a unified Asian music scene was tenuous. 'Asian Kool' actually embraced a multiplicity of bands who incorporated elements of 'Asian' music in their performance in very different ways. Asian dance music, Hyder argued, incorporated a diverse range of musical genres (including hip-hop, house, and techno), with artists such as Fun^Da^Mental, Punjabi MC, and Asian Dub Foundation fusing typically Asian sounds and samples with influences drawn from black America, Europe, and contemporary Britain. In contrast, Hyder highlighted the way 'indie guitar' bands such as the Voodoo Queens and Cornershop merged instruments such as the *sitar* and *dholki* into a guitar-oriented mix influenced by 1970s punk and 1980s 'indie' bands such as The Smiths and The Jesus and Mary Chain. 'Asian

Kool', then, actually covered a wide variety of musical styles and forms of cultural expression, Hyder arguing these represented differently nuanced articulations of a dynamic and multi-faceted British-Asian identity.

The various contributors to Sanjay Sharma et al.'s (1996) anthology, *Dis-Orienting Rhythms*, took a similar view. Asian dance music of the 1990s, Sharma and his colleagues argued, was 'a cultural form that narrates diasporas, dynamically affirming, transforming and mutating both imagined and material linkages' (Sharma et al., 1996: 9). But, they argued, the category 'British-Asian' was unable to convey the dynamism and diversity of these various, sliding subjectivities. Instead, processes of social, economic, and cultural globalisation had brought a widening of potential identities and subjectivities for young people – so there existed a *plurality* of negotiated and dynamic 'British-Asian' identities. Many of these syncretic youth cultures still had a strong link with their place of 'origin' and its cultural traditions, though they had also become 'translated' by their new cultural context – exemplified by the way the band Cornershop celebrated the veteran Hindi film songstress Asha Bhosle in their 1998 indie guitar hit, 'Brimful of Asha'.

In the US, too, researchers have pointed to the way complex interconnections of ethnicity and identity characterise the cultural experiences of 'desi' youth (youngsters with a South Asian heritage, 'desi' being a term meaning 'of the land' – from the Hindu/Urdu word 'desh', meaning 'country'). Sunaina Maira (2002), for example, shows how young, second-generation South Asians living in New York City draw upon both their own ethnic traditions and the city's vibrant popular culture to negotiate identities that respond to their racially ambiguous position in the dominant black/white paradigm of US race relations. Like many other theorists, Maira highlights the way identities are forged through dimensions of cultural fusion in sites like fashionable Bhangra Remix parties, where rap beats mix with Hindi film music, reggae, and techno. But, rather than being a hybrid or 'Third' space of the kind outlined by Bhabha, Maira argues there are pronounced tensions in the way the desi youngsters bridge notions of 'ethnic' authenticity and American 'cool' – tensions that become especially marked in the realm of gender where, Maira suggests, the performance of an 'authentic Indianness' reveals how 'the surveillance of ethnic purity is inherently about the social control of purportedly transgressive sexualities' (Maira, 2002: 16).

Nitisha Sharma (2010) also draws attention to the complex character of desi youth's negotiation of cultural identity. For Sharma, especially significant is the way some young, second-generation South Asians have drawn upon concepts of blackness – 'the most visible and salient example of a racial identity in the United States' (3). South Asian rappers, DJs, producers, and journalists, Dharma suggests, have employed hip-hop's articulation of blackness in their lyrics, lives, and worldview. This, she suggests, has crafted 'new ways of being desi, or alternative desiness ... that borrow and expand upon blackness by elaborating upon its possibilities as an empowering rather than denigrated identity' (3). In these terms, by deploying the black-centred themes of hip-hop, desi youth shift away from an insular ethnic identity and instead 'turn toward communities and expressions that speak to their sense of difference, injustice and artistic expression' (x). For Sharma, therefore, desi youth's embrace of hip-hop 'privileges the cultivation of positive and progressive interracial relationships in an increasingly diverse world' (36). This may certainly be true of the relationship between desi youngsters and African-American cultural forms. Matters, however, are more conflicted when black cultural forms are drawn upon by white youth.

Cultural voyeurs and mavericks of ethnicity: white youth consuming black culture

Though seldom acknowledged as such, 'whiteness' – like all 'racial' categories – is a cultural construct. As British theorist Richard Dyer (1997) has argued, the power and authority of white culture has afforded 'whiteness' a quality of virtual invisibility, with images and representations of white culture naturalising themselves as a norm from which all others diverge. In reality, however, 'white' has been a historically fabricated racial category, Dyer arguing that 'whiteness' has often been associated with the 'mind over body' qualities of 'tightness … self control [and] self-consciousness' (Dyer, 1997: 6). But, like any other identity, 'whiteness' has also been dynamic and multi-faceted, often drawing on 'Other' cultures as a source of exciting 'difference'. Black subcultures, for example, have been a perennial influence on the styles of white youth, the two engaging in an ongoing process of aesthetic dialogue. Indeed, for Dick Hebdige, 'race' was a key 'organising principle' in British youth culture, and the development of subcultural styles could be read as 'a phantom history of race relations since the War' (Hebdige, 1979: 45). Britain's mods and skinheads of the 1960s, for example, obliquely reproduced what they saw as the effortless cool of the Jamaican rude boy, while 1970s punks often lionised Rastafarians as 'authentic' and rebellious outsiders.[8]

In the US, a similar white embrace of black cultural forms was also a distinctive feature of early youth cultures – from the jazz clubs of the roaring 1920s, through to the 1950s rock 'n' roll boom and the beat generation's veneration of black hustlers. Indeed, Norman Mailer provided the classic exposition of white youth's reverence for black street style in his (1961) essay, 'The White Negro'. White hipsters, Mailer argued, had 'absorbed the existentialist synapses of the Negro' and had come to represent a new breed of 'urban adventurers who drifted out at night looking for action with a black man's code to fit their facts' (Mailer, 1961: 273). And a white embrace of black culture has continued to be a feature of subcultural styles and musical genres down to the present day. For some critics, however, this is problematic. As Lipsitz observes, 'white' appropriations of African-American culture:

> … have a long and disreputable history [and] … their consequences are no less poisonous when well-intentioned … identification with otherness has become an essential element in the construction of 'whiteness'.
>
> (Lipsitz, 1994: 53)

Indeed, since the eighteenth century, colonial stereotypes of the murderous primitive have been paralleled by the romantic (and equally essentialist) myth of the 'Noble Savage' as an embodiment of spiritual freedom and exhilarating 'difference'. And this highly selective mythologising of 'exotic' Otherness is a theme that has run through the history of Western youth culture. In the late 1960s, for example, writer Tom Wolfe coined the phrase 'radical chic' to denote the countercultural avant-garde's attempts to garner a rebellious cachet through flirting with black radical movements such as the Black Panthers (Wolfe: 1970). And, in his study of working-class youth in 1990s Britain, Anoop Nayak found a similar strain of infatuation among white youngsters for whom the embrace of African-American music and style amounted to 'little more than cultural voyeurism, a symbolic tour through the shadowy recesses of an imagined Other' (Nayak, 2003: 120).

Essentialist stereotyping, then, has sometimes characterised white youth's encounters with the cultures of 'Others'. But, at the same time, more positive dimensions have also existed to the relationship. Alongside the 'cultural voyeurs', for example, Nayak also identified white, working-class youths for whom engagement with rap and hip-hop 'could entail a deeper race con-sciousness and, at times, a flickering recognition of their own whiteness' (Nayak, 2003: 121).[9] For Nayak, these youngsters represented 'white maver-icks, individuals who subvert the acceptable boundaries of white, English eth-nicity through hybrid interactions with global cultures' (134).

And, in a similar vein, David Roediger underscores the potentially radi-cal processes of 'racial' exchange in his (1998) taxonomy of the epithet 'wigger' (or 'wigga'). An abbreviation of the phrase 'white nigger', the term 'wigger' initially existed as a white-on-white slur, but during the 1980s and 1990s it developed more complex meanings. Roediger argues that the original, derogatory connotations of the word persisted, but it was also adopted by African-American youth as a phrase that derided the deemed inauthenticity of white attempts to affect hip-hop style. But, according to Roediger, the phrase could *also* be used approvingly by white hip-hoppers who proudly asserted they '"wished they were black"' (Roediger, 1998: 361). Roediger acknowledges the naïvety and romantic essentialism that underlay such sentiments. But he also speculates that listening to explicit critiques of 'white' society might have a radicalising impact on white rap fans' processes of identity formation. From this persepctive, the elaboration of cultural hybridity has clear transgressive potential and offers, as Pnina Werbner puts it, 'the possibility of new, positive ethnic anti-racist identity fusions' (Werbner, 2015: 16).

'Happy we are from Tehran'?: The resilience of the local

For many postcolonial theorists, then, cultural hybridity is celebrated for its radical potential to disrupt dominant binary distinctions between black/white, East/West and coloniser/colonised. And youth cultures have often been in the forefront of hybridising trends. As Pam Nilan and Carles Feixa put it, young people are 'laboratories of hybrid cultures' (2006: 2). Growing numbers of youngsters, for example, have figured in patterns of diasporic migration, and live in communities where a wide range of global cultures connect and mix. Moreover, many young people have greater access to globalised media and communications, and this has facilitated greater dimensions of transnational dialogue and interaction. Instead of being pure, fixed or 'authentic', then, many young people's subject positions have come to operate across, and within, multiple cultural sites – their identities constituted by the intersection of criss-crossing discourses of age, ethnicity, gender, class, sexuality, and so on. At the same time, however, it is important to recognise the limits to these relations.

Generally, some of the grander claims made for the impact of globalising trends need to be qualified. Kai Hafez, for example, has pointed out how the influence of globalised, cross-border communication has, in many contexts, been much less than frequently assumed. 'Major population groups', Hafez argues, 'have often been reinforced in their local, national, or at best regional communicative habits, rather than encouraged to obtain information via the media, or even exchange views, across borders' (Hafez, 2007: 168). And, while Hafez was writing in 2007, his words still stand as a valuable caution against overrating the extent of global media interconnection and integration. Indeed, as the 'Great Firewall of China' demonstrates, nation states have often been adept at maintaining their grip on the international flow of media.

And, while some young people are able to enjoy global flows of media that open up new expressive cultures and identities, the persistence of inequalities – both globally and within nations – ensures there remain many others for whom global cultures remain distant and remote. Adam Cooper and his associates, for instance, recognise the way youngsters in the Global South 'negotiate identities out of complex mixtures between local and Euro-American contexts, between binaries like tradition and modernity' (Cooper, Swartz and Mahali, 2019: 33). But they also highlight the way these processes are invariably governed by pronounced disparities. In India, for example, research by Peter DeSouza and his colleagues shows how many young people's lives are characterised by unemployment and poverty, which creates distinctions between 'youth' and 'adulthood' very different to those in the Global North (DeSouza, Kumar and Shastri, 2009). Similarly, Leonie Backeberg and Jochen Tholen demonstrate how the growing youth populations of Arab Mediterranean countries – Algeria, Egypt, Lebanon, and Tunisia – struggle with poverty and unemployment levels of up to 42 per cent (Backeberg and Tholen: 2018: 517). While the 'youth revolts' of the Arab Spring of 2011 saw major protests against oppressive regimes and low standards of living across much of the Islamic world, these often met with violent repression and left large numbers of youngsters with little faith in their countries' political systems and facing a life of 'instability, ethnic fragmentation, sectarianism, and limitations in civil rights' (Backeberg and Tholen, 2018: 520).

The position of a particular nation state in systems of international relations, moreover, inevitably shapes the way young people make sense of
globalising processes. Hilary Pilkington and her colleagues, for example,
have shown how young people in post-Soviet Russia responded to global
media with distinct ambivalence. On one hand, the revolutions of 1989 that
swept through Eastern Europe and precipitated the collapse of state socialism across the region brought a positive sense of liberation. Post-Soviet
youth, Pilkington and her colleagues argue, welcomed being included and
engaged in a 'global' information world, and drew on the new flows of
Western goods and media to 'imagine and construct new selves' (Pilkington,
2002: 217). At the same time, however, this engagement was reined in by
both a residue of 'communist' hostility to consumerism and Western culture, and by a precarious economic situation that impacted on incomes and
standards of living. As a consequence, Pilkington and her colleagues found,
young Russians were 'acutely aware of the "core-periphery" model struc-
turing contemporary cultural exchange, and they well understood Russia's
place as a "receiver" rather than a "producer" of "global culture"' (Pilkington: 2002: 224). So, while post-Soviet youth were 'looking West' insofar
as they were happy to consume Western culture, they still maintained a firm
distinction between the global and the local. As Pilkington and Ul'iana
Bliudina put it, while Russian youth 'aspire to Western standards of
living ... they do not seek to emulate Western standards of "being"; and
where spiritual life is concerned, young people remain firmly rooted to the
local' (Pilkington and Bliudina, 2002: 20).

Ten years later, Charles Walker and Svetlana Stephenson found that locally-
rooted identities were still a principal facet to the lives of East European and
post-Soviet youth. For some youngsters, especially the more affluent, the world
of new choices and pathways to 'individualized "biographical projects"' was
welcomed (Walker and Stephenson, 2012: 6). Generally, however, Walker and
Stephenson observed how most young people's aspirations were quite traditional. Furthermore, in the face of an insecure economic environment, familial
and local networks had become increasingly significant in youngsters' lives. In
an uncertain world, Walker and Stephenson concluded, ethnic, regional and
local affiliations had become more important (ibid.).

And, as Stefan Kirmse (2012) shows, in the predominantly Muslim parts of
the former Soviet South, local attachments and constraints have played an
especially significant role in mediating young people's engagement with processes of cultural globalisation. In Central Asia and the Caucasus, Kirmse argues,
young people's lives have been characterised by a complex mixture of 'experimentation and regulation'. Some youngsters, especially university students,
have been keen to experiment with the different styles and identities made
available by the transnational media. This, Kirmse observes, can lead to a
questioning of traditional hierarchies and loyalties. As in Eastern Europe,
however, the decline of state provision and the marketisation of economies has
increased many young people's dependency on their families and local

communities. Moreover, in some contexts, the flow of global media and goods has been significantly regulated by the government. In Kyrgyzstan, Kirmse suggests, state intervention has been relatively slight, but in more authoritarian states such as Turkmenistan and Uzbekistan, cultural life has been subject to more rigorous control by authorities that see processes of globalisation as either unacceptably exploitative, or as 'a flood of detrimental goods and ideas designed to alienate youth from "traditional culture"' (Kirmse, 2012: 5).

A similar set of conflicts and contradictions has also featured in the lives of youngsters in the Islamic Republic of Iran. Flows of international media and culture, Mahmood Shahbi, argues, have meant that Iran 'constitutes one of the most extreme cases of Third World post-modern cultural bricolage' (2006: 111). But, at the same time, young people face a theocratic regime whose constraints can be brutal. In 2014, for example, six young Iranians faced harsh punishment after they appeared in a video featuring three men and three unveiled women dancing on the streets and rooftops of Tehran to the sound-track of 'Happy', by American singer Pharrell Williams. Within six months the film – titled *Happy We Are From Tehran* – had been viewed by over a million people on YouTube. But Iranian authorities ruled that the video violated Islamic laws, and the participants were sentenced to a year in prison and 91 lashes (*BBC News*, 19 September 2014).[10]

Globalised flows of media and culture, then, may well have engendered new processes of interconnection and fusion. And these may have potential to generate new, hybrid identities that challenge dominant hegemonies and essentialist traditions. But, at the same time, local identities, attachments, and constraints often remain pronounced. The process of innovation and 'hybridisation', moreover, is invariably underpinned by an uneven and unequal distribution of power and, as Jan Nederveen Pieterse argues, analyses of 'cultural hybridity' must always give close attention to the terms under which cultural interplay and crossover takes place:

> Relations of power and hegemony are reproduced in hybridity, for wherever one looks closely enough, one finds the traces of asymmetry in culture, place, and descent. Hence, hybridity raises, rather than erases, the question of the terms and conditions of mixing. Meanwhile, it is also important to note the ways in which the relations of power are not merely reproduced but refigured in the process of hybridization.
>
> (Pieterse, 2012: 329)

According to some critics, furthermore, the evocation of 'hybridity' sometimes sees the concept's political edge blunted. Marwan Kraidy (2005), for example, points to the way theories of cultural hybridity originally developed in radical critiques of colonialism and racism, but subsequently diffused into a simple celebration of 'global multiculturalism' curated by the West. In this context, 'hybridty' loses its radical, disruptive potential and becomes simply a descriptive category for 'Westernised' ethnicities, 'glocalized' cultures or 'blended' styles.

Indeed, the history of white, Western youth culture bulges with occasions in which 'ethnic' sensibilities have been appropriated not as an act of cultural radicalism, but as a bid for 'exotic' charisma. In its penchant for sitars, kaftans, and 'Eastern mysticism', for example, the late 1960s counterculture can be seen as simply exploiting superficial signifiers of 'Otherness'. Equally, John Hutnyk (2000) points out how British passions for 'Asian Kool' during the late 1990s (see above) often smacked of a 'trinketisation' that repackaged and trivialised South Asian culture.

Generally, however, debates about hybridity highlight the way youngsters' identities are formed through a complex interaction of global and local cultural influences. These processes, moreover, might be seen as symptomatic of a much wider condition of identity 'dislocation', perhaps exemplifying Stuart Hall's (1992ii) notion of a generalised 'crisis of identity' in which the frameworks that once gave individuals a stable anchorage in the cultural world have been ruptured by the profound social, economic, and political upheavals that began during late twentieth century. As a consequence of these disruptions, Hall argued, the autonomous and self-sufficient identity of the Enlightenment – 'the Individual' – had increasingly given way to a new universe of subjectivities that produced 'a variety of possibilities and new positions of identification … making identities more positional, more political, more plural and diverse; less fixed, unified or trans-historical' (Hall, 1992ii: 309). In these terms, the flux and fluidity that characterise young people's processes of identity formation might epitomise the wider diversity of subject positions that Hall saw as a distinctive feature of late modern societies. The following chapter explores these issues in relation to youth culture, especially young people's complex expressions of identity in the online world.

Notes

1 At the time of writing (2020) *Somewhere in America #Mipsterz* can be viewed (without its Jay-Z soundtrack, which was removed for copyright reasons) at https://www.youtube.com/watch?v=68sMkDKMias
2 See, in particular, Gilroy (1987) and his contributions to Centre for Contemporary Cultural Studies (1982).
3 In 2017 Daddy Yankee's international success was boosted when he appeared in the video for 'Despacito', Luis Fonsi's international hit (see Chapter 7).
4 Informed histories of rap music and hip-hop culture can be found in Chang (2007), George (2005), and Toop (2000).
5 Cross (1992) provides a full account of the rise of rap in Los Angeles.
6 In postcolonial theory, the term 'subaltern' denotes subordinated populations who exist outside colonialism's hierarchies of power.
7 In Britain, the term 'Asian' is usually used to denote peoples originating from the South Asian subcontinent (primarily India, Pakistan, and Bangladesh). In North America, however, the term 'Asian' generally denotes peoples from East and Southeast Asia (principally Japan, Korea, and Vietnam).
8 Leading 1970s punk band The Clash, for example, were candid in the way they drew influence from African-Caribbean youth culture and (along with many other punk bands of the period) added cover versions of reggae classics to their set-list.

9 In a similar vein, Jones's (1988) account of youth culture in Birmingham during the 1980s emphasised the way white youths' adoption of African-Caribbean music and style had provided a sense of identity between many local black and white youngsters.
10 The sentences were subsequently suspended for three years, meaning the convicted youngsters would not go to prison unless they reoffended.

9 Youth culture, identity, and creativity in the age of digital media

The online Directioners: virtual spaces for identity and cultural production

One Direction were, by any measure, a major pop music success. The English-Irish boy band originally formed in 2010 for the British TV talent show *The X Factor*, subsequently signing to Simon Cowell's record label, Syco Records. Worldwide tours followed, along with scores of international hits, before the band began a hiatus in 2016. One Direction's commercial achievements were impressive, but also significant was the role of social networks in the band's career. One Direction's record label was adept at using social media to generate and maintain a strong emotional bond between the band and their fanbase – dubbed 'Directioners' – who became famous for their fervour for the tousle-haired songsters.

Equally significant, however, was the way the Directioners, themselves, played an active part in propelling the band to success. A wealth of fan activity boosted One Direction's rise, with legions of Directioners using Internet plat-forms like Tumblr and Twitter to promote the band and its members. As Pilar Lacasa (2016) and her colleagues argue, this involvement was an invaluable marketing tool for the band but it was also a meaningful experience for the Directioners, who used the fandom as a basis for global interaction, friendships, and communal solidarity. Beyond this, some Directioners also used their fandom to explore new dimensions of identity and expression. One sub-section of the fanbase, for instance, promoted the (probably erroneous) idea that two members of One Direction – Louis Tomlinson and Harry Styles – had a romantic relationship or 'ship'. Promoted largely through Instagram, Tumblr, and Twitter, this unlikely liaison was referred to by the portmanteau of 'Larry Stylinson', or simply 'Larry', and was configured by the press as evidence of a delusional fan pathology. More accurately, however, the 'Larries' exemplified the practice of 'shipping' (derived from the word 'relationship') in which fans explore the realms of gender, sexuality, and desire through playful fantasies of erotic encounters between fictional characters or celebrities.[1]

This was just one facet of the wealth of cultural production and creative activity undertaken by Directioners. Indeed, alongside the social networks, websites, and blogs, One Direction also elicited voluminous fanfiction, as fans conjured-up fantasy lives for their favourite band members. And sometimes their endeavours crossed over into mainstream success. In 2013, for example, Anna Todd was inspired by her passion for One Direction to begin writing an erotic novel – *After* – based on Harry Styles and the other band members. The 25-year-old Texan wrote the novel's 239 chapters on her smartphone, uploading them onto the free storytelling website Wattpad. The book was chiefly written for Todd's own enjoyment, but within a year it garnered more than a million readers and landed the author a lucrative publishing deal with Simon & Schuster (Michaels, 2014). The *After* series of novels were duly released in 2014 (with the lead character's name changed from Harry Styles to Hardin Scott) and hit the *New York Times* bestseller list – a popularity that saw Paramount Pictures pick up the books' film rights and release a movie adaptation of *After* in 2019.

The Directioners' various forms of online expression exemplified the more general way digital media and online networks have become pivotal spaces for young people. This chapter examines the increasing role of digital media in the way youngsters develop their sense of self, manage their social relationships and engage in processes of cultural creativity. It begins by considering how developments in cyberspace may have fed into a wider 'decentring' of identity in contemporary society, with individuals articulating an ever-wider range of identities and selves. For queer theorists, this fluidity has been especially pronounced in the realms of gender and sexuality, and the chapter considers the way essentialist views of stable, binary identities have been challenged by sensibilities that destabilise conventional boundaries of sex and gender. Arguably, youth culture and its associated media have been especially fertile spaces for such challenges, and the chapter examines the way a succession of pop artists – from Little Richard to Lady Gaga – have elaborated a queer 'performance' that questions the binaries of gender and sexuality. For some critics, social media also afford important spaces for identities that challenge traditional notions of gender and sexuality, and the chapter examines the way groups of young people – One Direction's Larries, for instance – explore gendered and sexual identities that flow across conventional boundaries.

The chapter continues by considering the way technologies such as Web 2.0 and smartphones increased the role of online communication and social media in young people's lives. The chapter highlights both the broad global similarities and the distinctive local differences that characterise young people's use of social media. And, while the negative dimensions to social media are acknowledged – for example, cyber-bullying and sexual harassment – recognition is also given to social media's capacity for building connections, communities, and friendships. The chapter concludes by considering young people's wealth of online creativity and cultural production, and assesses how far this surge of cultural expression represents a sea-change in the nature of young people's media engagement.

'Shifting the world's perspective on what's beautiful': identity, youth cultures, and queer 'performance'

Traditional views of identity have seen it as a unified and coherent essence, a relatively straightforward expression of 'the Individual'. This essentialist model of identity is rooted in ideas that emerged from the European Enlightenment – the period of rigorous scientific, political, and philosophical discourse that characterised European society from the late seventeenth century to the early nineteenth century. In this tradition of thought, notions of rationality and reason are sovereign, and an onus is placed on the value of certitude and 'truth'. Many of the assumptions that underpin this mode of thought, however, have subsequently attracted criticism. Postcolonial theorists, for example, have challenged the binary oppositions that underpinned colonialist thought, and have pointed to the destabilising potential of cultural hybridity (see Chapter 8). And, more broadly, poststructuralist theorists have challenged many of the Enlightenment's certainties. Poststructuralism is a broad theoretical church, though its advocates share a general rejection of the totalising and essentialist concepts associated with Enlightenment epistemologies. Influenced by the ideas of Jacques Derrida and Michel Foucault, poststructuralist theorists have challenged claims to order and 'truth', arguing that such discourses have invariably been related to systems of power in which some voices are given authority and status while others are silenced and marginalised. In these terms, the Enlightenment's view of 'the Individual' as a stable and coherent essence is also challenged. Instead, poststructuralist theorists have seen people as composed of manifold identities that are discursively created – and continuously re-created – through cultural meanings and practices. As Stuart Hall explained:

> Within us are contradictory identities, pulling in different directions, so that our identifications are continually being shifted about. If we feel that we have a unified identity from birth to death, it is only because we construct a comforting story or 'narrative' of the self about ourselves.
>
> (Hall, 1992ii: 277)

From this perspective, the social, economic and political dislocations that began during the late twentieth century may have brought what Hall (1987) saw as a 'decentring' of identity. That is to say, amid the destabilisation of traditional assumptions and securities, potentially liberating spaces may have opened up for the articulation of identities once confined to the periphery of cultural systems. And theorists of ethnicity, gender, and sexuality have all been keen to explore the multiple subjectivities that may have sprouted through the fissures and disjunctions of late modern societies. Perhaps, though, it is the sphere of youth culture that most readily exemplifies this 'decentring' of identity. Indeed, with their unstable fusion of fragmented identities and cultural reference points, modern youth cultures – especially the spectacular styles of subcultures – have always encompassed fluid and dynamic subjectivities. Rather than being fixed and coherent, youth cultures have invariably been mutable and transient, youngsters often cruising across a range of cultural affiliations, constantly forming and reforming their identities according to social context.

Anti-essentialist views of identity have been especially pronounced in queer theory.[2] 'Queer' was originally a term commonly used to deride and vilify same-sex desire, but since the late twentieth century it has been appropriated to celebrate (rather than castigate) difference from the dominant 'norms' of gender and sexuality. In analytic terms, queer theory encompasses a wide range of perspectives, though they share an anti-essentialist view of sexual identity and challenge notions of sexuality as being underpinned by intrinsic, innate sets of binary oppositions – masculinity/femininity and heterosexuality/homosexuality – that are universally 'fixed' across time and place. Such claims to unity and coherence, it is argued, are constantly undermined by the incoherencies of sex and gender, and queer theorists work to highlight and celebrate this fluidity of sexual identity. From this perspective, gender, and sexual identity are understood as enactments, creations, or – as Judith Butler has argued – a 'performance'.

For Butler, a leading queer theorist, masculinity and femininity are not a monolithic and timelessly fixed set of binary categories. Rather, they are multiform, fluid, and historically variable. Gender, Butler contends, should not be conceived as a stable identity or an 'agency from which various acts follow', but instead should be recognised as 'an identity tenuously constituted in time, instituted in an exterior space through a stylized repetition of acts' (Butler, 1990: 140). According to Butler, then, gender should be understood as a historically dynamic 'performance' – a system of cultural conventions that is fabricated and sustained through 'a process of iterability, a regularized and constrained repetition of norms' (Butler, 1993: 95). 'There is', Butler contended, 'no gender identity behind the expressions of gender; that identity is performatively constituted by the very "expressions" that are said to be its results' (Butler, 1990: 24–25).

For queer theorists, therefore, gender and sexual identities are not established on stable sets of essential binary identities, but are constituted through the repetitive performance of behaviours and physical expressions. And, in this sense, the process of 'queering', as Robert Corber and Stephen Valocchi explain, refers to 'identities and practices that foreground the instability inherent in the supposedly stable relationship between anatomical sex, gender and sexual desire' (Corber and Valocchi, 2003: 1). Butler (1991), for example, argued that cross-dressing 'drag' artists caused 'gender trouble' because their performance spotlighted the social, imitative character of gender. For Butler, the drag queen effectively 'queers' gender – that is to say, it exposes gender as a cultural code which relies on imitation and reappearance, and lacks any intrinsic, essential 'truth'. The elements of parody in the drag performance, therefore, expose, accentuate, and ultimately ridicule dominant assumptions about the 'essential' qualities of gender and sexuality.

Queer elements have also been a pronounced feature in youth subcultures – for example, mods, punks, or goths. Their spectacular styles have often conjured with different notions of gender and sexuality, and called into question dominant constructions of masculinity and femininity. Often, the history of popular music has also been characteristically 'queer'. As Jon Savage agrues:

> Pop's relationship to different ideas of sexuality and gender is ... deep and intricate: although it frequently denies it, it is from the milieux and sensibilities of the sexually divergent that pop culture draws much of its sustenance.
>
> (Savage, 1990: 155)

Of course, the history of popular music features innumerable examples where hegemonic 'performances' of gender and sexuality predominate. During the 1980s and 1990s, for instance, swaggering machismo was a prevalent theme in hip-hop, and the songs of artists such as 2 Live Crew and N.W.A were often excruciatingly misogynistic. The history of heavy metal, too, is replete with representations of heterosexual 'hypermasculinity' and 'hyperfemininity'. Robert Wasler (1993), for example, highlighted the way a wide variety of masculine archetypes were 'performed' by leading heavy metal bands of the 1980s. Guns 'n' Roses, for instance, embodied a free-wheeling, non-conformism, Bon Jovi were constructed as romantic heroes, while Poison adopted an androgynous 'glam' style. For Wasler, however, they all, in different ways, represented a spectacle of heterosexual masculine power. More broadly, however, theorists such as Susan Fast and Craig Jennex (2019) suggest that popular music has also been a site where performers and fans have challenged dominant ideas of stable, unified subjectivities, and have instead elaborated more fluid expressions of gender and sexuality.[3]

Indeed, Vincent Stephens (2019) shows how 1950s performers such as Johnnie Ray and Little Richard effectively 'queered' rock 'n' roll through presenting stage personae that challenged prevailing notions of manhood and masculinity. Disco, meanwhile was decried by critics of all political hues for being vapid and crassly commercial (see Chapter 6); but Richard Dyer (1979) shows how the eroticism, romanticism, and lavish escapism of disco offered experiences that could be the basis for a questioning of sexual and economic authority. Even heavy metal, Amber Clifford-Napoleone (2017) argues, has had spaces of 'pervasive queerness', where performers and fans have explored a diversity of gendered and sexual identities.

Artists such as David Bowie, Prince, and Marilyn Manson can also be seen as subverting traditional notions of gender and sexuality through androgynous, sexually ambiguous performances that deliberately blurred masculine and feminine conventions. And, in a similar fashion, E. Ann Kaplan (1993) has argued that the singer Madonna undermined essentialist notions of femininity through adopting a series of 'performative' masquerades in her videos and stage shows. Artists such as Annie Lennox and k.d. lang might equally be seen as 'queering' gender conventions through their adoption of a variety of masculine, androgynous and (occasionally) lesbian guises. Similarly, Lady Gaga has also underscored the 'performative' character of gender through the recurrent reinventions of her stage persona and, especially, through the creation of Jo Calderone – an exercise in 'gender manipulation' that saw Lady Gaga develop a male alter-ego to 'fuck with the malleable minds of onlookers and shift the world's perspective on what's beautiful' (2011: 34).

Alongside popular music, online communities have also been seen as rich spaces for the expression and exploration of identities that destabilise binary constructions of gender and sexuality. From the earliest days of the Internet, theorists such as Howard Rheingold (2000) and Sherry Turkle (1995) were proselytes for the liberating potential of digital communication networks. The disembodied spaces of online communication, they suggested, brought a 'postmodern' blurring of distinctions between reality and simulation that dissolved the boundaries of the self and created spaces for new, experimental, and multiple forms of identity. And, in some respects at least, the contingent, fluid character of online relations has undoubtedly leant itself to individuals and groups looking to stake out new terms of identification and belonging.

Susan Driver (2006), for example, shows how an expansive range of online sites – groups, ezines, chatrooms, live discussions, blogs, and so on – have been created by, for, and about LGBT youth. Often designed, developed, and moderated by young people themselves, these online communities have, Driver argues, put LGBT youth at the forefront of do-it-yourself digital media. Connecting online, Driver suggests, has been especially important for LGBT youth as it provides a way for young people, who may be isolated and marginalised in their everyday lives, to access and sustain links with supportive mentors, friends, and acquaintances. Alongside providing friendship and a sense of belonging, however, online networks are also sites for performative practices of self-presentation. And, while there is much variation between the gendered and sexual identities associated with different LGBT networks, Driver highlights their capacity to offer spaces where 'queer youth actively challenge fixed notions of girl/boy, male/female, and heterosexual/homosexual that proscribe diverse desire and identifications' (2006: 232).[4] In this way, then, online social networks are spaces where queer youth perform gendered and sexual identities that often flow across conventional boundaries, confounding dominant constructions of masculinity and femininity. As Driver explains:

> Queer youth cyber-communities challenge simplistic divisions between the virtual and the real, the imaginary and the physical, the textual and the embodied, the experiential and the fictional. They provide insights into the in-between spaces where youth work out the unique contours of their sexualities and genders, as they communicate their identifications and desires in words and images shared with others across diverse contexts.
>
> (Driver, 2006: 244)

'Queerness', moreover, does not simply relate to the sexual identities of individuals or groups. For queer theorists such as Eve Sedgwick (1985), it was also possible to produce 'queer' readings of the cultural world. According to

Sedgwick, for instance, a 'queer lens' could be applied in the analysis of literary texts, thereby highlighting discursive spaces that existed outside the binary identities of heterosexuality and homosexuality. This 'queer' reading of texts made evident their fissures of instability and gaps where alternative interpretations could emerge. And this 'queer lens' is, in many respects, exemplified by the young One Direction fans who imagined a 'ship' between the band members (see above).

As Hannah McCann and Clare Southern found from their (2019) digital ethnography of the One Direction 'Larries', whether the fans really believed a relationship existed between Styles and Tomlinson (or simply pretended this, as a source of their own pleasure) was relatively unimportant. More significant was the way the fans (who positioned themselves in a variety of sexual identities) deployed queer reading practices to develop a subtext that ruptured dominant expectations about gender and sexuality. The Larries, McCann and Southern suggest, were adopting a queer gaze 'that reads "against the grain" of a heteronormative framing' (54). In these terms, through their celebration of the One Direction 'ship', the fans challenged dominant heterosexual narratives and opened space for queer identities and desires. As McCann and Southern observed:

> For many Larries the online intimate community surrounding the ship serves as a space for the creation of queer possibility, collectively created and reaffirmed through the sharing of queer digital objects.
>
> (McCann and Southern, 2019: 61)

McCann and Southern's analysis of Larries highlights the 'the queer affordances of social media' (51), and the way online platforms provide young people with opportunities for the elaboration of identities and textual readings that transgress dominant boundaries. This affordance, however, is just one of the myriad ways communications technologies have transformed the means through which young people structure their social relationships and negotiate their sense of identity.

'Writing themselves into being': youth, identity, and social media

Digital technologies have had a significant impact on the ways young people perceive themselves and interact with others. Before the rise of social media, it was the use of mobile phones that drew researchers' attention to the way technological developments were playing a bigger part in youngsters' identities and relationships. During the mid-1990s, ownership of mobile phones proliferated in economically developed countries, and they became an integral part of youngsters' lives. In particular, use of mobile phones seemed to increase the importance of peer groups. Australian-based research by Patricia Gillard and her colleagues, for example, showed how possession of mobile phones made it possible for young people to 'carry' their friends around with them – not only into public spaces like the school but also into the private spaces of the home, so that for teenagers 'the combination of a private space at home and intimate talk with friends may mean that friends become more influential in their emotional development and well-being' (Gillard, Wale and Bow, 1998: 150).

SMS (Short Message Service) or 'texting' also developed into an important medium of communication. Originally conceived as a new paging system for busy professionals, SMS was rapidly laid claim to by young people and became a prevalent medium for establishing and maintaining peer group relations. In Britain, for example, fieldwork conducted by Alexander Taylor and Richard Harper (2001) found that mobile phones had become *de rigeur* among teenagers – and use of SMS was universal, with the exchange of text messages representing a ritualised form of 'gift-giving' that worked to express and cement young people's friendships. In the new millennium, however, digital communication became even more central to young people's lives as a consequence of interrelated developments in the technologies of the Internet and mobile phones.

Most obviously, the beginning of the twenty-first century saw changes in the structure of Internet sites that laid the way for the growth of 'Web 2.0'. The term 'Web 2.0' was originally coined in 2005 by Tim O'Reilly (founder of the publishing house O'Reilly Media) to describe what he saw as a new generation of platforms on the World Wide Web. When the Web first emerged during the 1990s, it had enabled essentially a one-way flow of information. That is to say, its pages were generally static and, while they could be read by viewers, elements of interaction were limited. In contrast, O'Reilly highlighted what he saw as the rise of a radically new kind of Web. This was characterised by websites with a much higher degree of dynamism and interactivity. In Web 2.0 the two-way flow of information was more pronounced, and users' experience was enhanced through a greater ability to collaborate and share information. Web 2.0, therefore, was marked by the rise of digital platforms that relied on material contributed by their users (known as 'user-generated content') and/or allowed users to create, share, collaborate, and communicate information with others – features embodied in platforms like Facebook, YouTube, Twitter, and TikTok (see Chapter 3).

Alongside the rise of a more interactive Internet, important changes also occurred in mobile phone technology. Originally, the functionality of mobile phones – known as cellular or 'cell' phones – was limited to audio calls and texting. But this changed in 2007 when Apple introduced the iPhone, the first smartphone. Performing many of the functions of a computer, smartphones allow the storage of data and, compared to cell phones, have much stronger hardware capabilities and extensive mobile operating systems. This facilitates the use of a wide range of software and Internet applications (including access to music, video, cameras, and gaming). The technologies of Web 2.0 and the smartphone, therefore, were complementary, and the convergence of the two laid the way for a boom in mobile digital media and communications.

As has been the case with many new forms of communication (see Chapter 3), youth was in the forefront of these developments, and smartphone ownership became virtually ubiquitous among young people across the economically developed world. In the US, for example, 96 per cent of young people aged between 18 and 29 owned a smartphone by 2018 (Statistica, 2019ix). Elsewhere, the picture was similar. In China, for instance, 94 per cent of people aged between 18 and 34 owned a smartphone in 2016 (Statistica, 2018ii). And, by 2018, 99 per cent of German youngsters aged between 18 and 19 had a smartphone (Statistica, 2018iii), and in the UK they were owned by 93 per cent of 15-year-olds (Statistica, 2019x). At the same time, however, global inequalities were still pronounced in access to the new technologies. In India, for example, only 24 per cent of the entire population possessed a smartphone in 2018, and 35 per cent had no phone at all (Statistica, 2019xi).[5] Moreover, economic inequalities ensured that even many youngsters with access to a smartphone were still excluded from using its more sophisticated functions (see Chapter 3).

Nevertheless, the social lives of young people with access to the full functionality of smartphones were profoundly transformed. The convergence of Web 2.0 interactivity and the technologies of mobile devices ensured that online social networks became the warp and weft of social relations for many young people. In 2018, for example, a study undertaken by the Pew Research Center, suggested the growth of mobile connections was fuelling more persistent online activity by young people. Of US youngsters aged between 13 and 17, the Pew researchers found that 44 per cent reported they went online several times a day, while some 45 per cent stated they were online 'almost constantly' – meaning that around nine in ten US teenagers were online multiple times daily (Anderson and Jiang, 2018: 8). Moreover, the youngsters' online activity was revolving less around a single platform. Most significantly, while 71 per cent of teenagers said they used Facebook in 2014–15, this had declined to 51 per cent in 2018, and only 15 per cent said it was the site they used most often. Instead, platforms such as YouTube and social media sites like Instagram and Snapchat had leapt in popularity. Of their sample of youngsters, the Pew researchers reported that 85 per cent used YouTube, 72 per cent used Instagram and 69 per cent used Snapchat (Anderson and Jiang, 2018: 2). The popularity of Facebook among young people, then, was ebbing. Instead, youngsters' online activity was increasingly taking place across multiple Internet sites and platforms.

Social media networks have become integral to young people's lives because they represent a valuable arena in which to elaborate identity and build social relationships. As the US theorist danah boyd explains, the popularity of social networks lies in the way they allow youngsters to 'write themselves and their community into being' (boyd, 2008: 120). However, whereas earlier Internet researchers such as Rheingold and Turkle had celebrated the new possibilities for multiple, fluid online identities (see above), for most young people the reality of everyday use of the Internet is more prosaic. Most research suggests, for example, that young people's online lives are deeply embedded in their offline experience. During the late 1990s, for instance, Chris Abbott argued that the Internet promoted 'complementarity rather than alterity' (1998: 97). That is to say, for most young users, the Web did not represent an 'alternative world' but a setting where they connected with their peers, swapping opinions and comparing experiences. Undoubtedly, some young people engage playfully and creatively with different identities in contexts such as online games and virtual worlds. But, for the most part, empirical research suggests that young people's online and offline lives are mutually constituted rather than separate and distinct.

In her study of young people in Bermuda, for example, Katie Davis shows how youngsters strive for consistency and coherence (rather than multiplicity) in their online and offline identities. Pre-existing, offline friendships, she argues, underpin the way young people make use of the Internet and 'adolescents tend to present themselves online in a manner that is consistent with their offline identities' (Davis, 2014: 17). As boyd points out, social media networks are akin to 1950s drive-in cinemas or 1980s shopping malls in the way they provide young people with a public space to socialise and build relationships. 'Collectively', boyd argues, the significance of social media lies in the way they 'provide teens with a space to hang out and connect with friends' (boyd, 2014: 5).

The importance of social networks in the lives of young people was underscored by a large, US-based study undertaken by Mizuko Ito and her associates in the first decade of the new millennium (Ito et al., 2009). Drawing together 23 case-studies, the three-year ethnographic investigation revealed how youngsters used social media for a wide variety of reasons – for socialising with friends, swapping information, gossiping, or just having fun. In some senses, then, social networks are very much akin to traditional 'teen hangouts' in the way they provide spaces for socialising and building friendships. At the same time, however, many theorists have also pointed to the way social media networks have complicated traditional boundaries dividing the 'public' and 'private' realms. Sonia Livingstone (2009), for example, has highlighted how young people's increased use of social media networks like Facebook has meant that many 'private' interactions now take place in public domains, so that youngsters' social lives have become a blurred intersection of private and public realms – new forms of online space that danah boyd terms 'networked publics' (boyd, 2011).

In her analysis of the way young people navigate their way through these blurry public/private online spaces, Erika Pearson offers the metaphor of 'a bedroom with walls made of glass'. Inside this 'glass bedroom', Pearson argues,

> ... private conversations and intimate exchanges occur, each with varying awareness of distant friends and strangers moving past transparent walls that separate groups from more deliberate and constructed 'outside' displays. The glass bedroom itself is not an entirely private space ... it is a bridge that is partially private and public, constructed online through signs and language.
>
> (Pearson, 2009)

In these terms, then, communication through social media networks is a fuzzy mixture of the private and the public. On one level, young people have a sense that their online dialogues take place separate from – or 'walled off' from – the outside world. At the same time, however, the 'walls' are made from glass, so they afford a level of visibility that may be beyond the control of the occupant (unless, that is, they consciously decide to adjust the platform's privacy settings – i.e. draw the 'curtains'). In this way, then, Pearson suggests young people's use of social media can be seen as a performance of identity that takes place in a blurred amalgamation of public and private realms. Drawing on such ideas, theorists such as Siân Lincoln (2014) argue that, rather than being lost and confused in hazy distinctions between public and private spheres, young people are often adept at organising their use of social networks – so that the virtual spaces of social media become almost an extension of the physical spaces of youngsters' bedrooms. From this perspective, while social networks like Facebook or Instagram are a way for young people to reach out and make social relationships in a variety of public contexts, they *also* serve as a way of demarcating personal identities, individual tastes and private spaces.

Online youth in a networked era

Outside North America, Europe, and Australia, less research has been undertaken on young people's use of social networks. That which exists, however, suggests that young people around the world use online media for largely similar purposes – to chat with friends, listen to music, play games, browse the news, exchange information, express intimate feelings, or generally goof about. Alongside these broad similarities, however, there are also characteristics particular to specific local and national contexts. Comparing the ways girls from Thailand and the US elaborated their online identities, for example, Narissra Punyanunt-Carter and Jason Smith found the girls' practices 'were more similar than different', though they observed how some notable cultural differences surfaced in the way the young women portrayed themselves, with the Thai girls being more cautious in their degree of self-disclosure and making fewer references to fashion and brands (2010: 88).

Compared to Western youth, Chinese youngsters' use of the Internet also evidences broad similarities alongside distinctive local features. Jun Fu (2018), for instance, shows how the online practices of Chinese youngsters exhibit many features similar to those of US, European, and Australian youth. Like their global peers, Chinese young people use social media as way of developing social relations and as a space for identity 'performance' through posting comments and sharing content. Moreover, as elsewhere, Chinese youngsters' online identities are rooted in their offline lives, Fu arguing that 'experiences of online and offline space are mutually constituted rather than a discrete dichotomy' (140). And, again like young people elsewhere, Chinese youngsters carefully negotiate between the Internet's 'private' and 'public' realms. For some

Chinese youth, however, the boundaries separating these spheres are not always the blurry realm experienced by Western youngsters.

Many Chinese youngsters, Fu observes, maintain a consistent identity across their online presence. But some, he argues, employ distinct strategies to adjust their identity performance depending on the sense of privacy afforded by specific platforms. For instance, the mobile text and voice-messaging service WeChat is designed as a private platform, and is a fairly 'closed' space where youngsters personally know most of their contacts. WeChat, Fu suggests, is mainly used by young people for sharing 'happy moments' (in the form of text, pictures and video clips) with family and friends, and for posting innocuous content suitable for public scrutiny. In contrast, Weibo is a micro-blogging site (similar to Twitter) intended to be a more public space where the majority of other participants are unknown to users in their physical lives. Fu argues, however, that Weibo's aura of relative anonymity is perceived by many young people as making it 'a safer, more private space than is available in physical life' (140). As a consequence, he suggests, Weibo has become a site where young people are more prepared to voice social and political opinions and express their personal values (including arguments for social justice, freedom, and democracy).[6] The intended uses of WeChat and Weibo, therefore, have been effectively reversed by many young users. Wechat (the 'private' platform) is used 'as a public space to record the public side of their lives' (135), while Weibo (the 'public' micro-blog) has become a site for expressing personal beliefs and values.

The experience Fu outlines, therefore, demonstrates both the degree of global consistency and the dimensions of national variation in youngsters' use of digital communication. Fu's account, moreover, also clearly illustrates how online interaction has permeated young people's lives. As he argues (quoting danah boyd), Chinese youth's negotiation of identity on social media:

> … demonstrates that in a networked era when young people are connected to the Internet at any given time, the binary between online and offline is no longer helpful, a more valid question to ask should be 'how context, audience, and identity intersect' in young people's life.
>
> (Fu, 2018: 140)

The Internet has clearly come to be a key means through which youngsters articulate their identities and maintain social relationships. As a consequence, some theorists suggest that the fabric of modern youth culture has been transformed. As Andy Bennett argues, with the prevalence of social networks and online platforms, it becomes impossible to think of youth cultures as being fixed to a specific locality, or even as being rooted in any corporeal mode of expression. As Bennett puts it:

> … we can no longer take it for granted that membership of a youth culture involves issues of stylistic unity, collective knowledge of a particular

club scene, or even face-to-face interaction. On the contrary, youth cultures may be seen increasingly as cultures of 'shared ideas', whose interactions take place not in physical spaces such as the street, club or festival field but in the virtual spaces facilitated by the Internet.

(Bennett, 2004: 163)

According to some theorists, moreover, these changes have created particularly valuable opportunities for young women. Whereas the physical spaces central to youth culture – for example, the street or the nightclub – are invariably circumscribed by a masculine presence, some researchers suggest this can be less pronounced in the virtual spaces of the Internet. As Justine Cassell and Meg Cramer have argued:

Girls in particular may thrive online where they may be more likely to explore alternate identities without the dangers associated with venturing outside of their homes alone, more likely to be able to safely explore their budding sexuality, and more likely to openly demonstrate technological prowess, without the social dangers associated with the term 'geek'.

(Cassell and Cramer, 2008: 54)

The Internet and social media may well have provided young women with new avenues for cultural experience and expression. At the same time, however, many studies also point to the way the gendered power structures of the physical world are often reproduced online. For example, British researchers Sarah Handyside and Jessica Ringrose highlight the way that, in online spaces, young women's bodies are surveilled much more heavily than those of their male peers. Analysing youngsters' use of the video-sharing app Snapchat, they found a distinct 'double-standard' in which young women were more often subjected to derogatory 'body shaming' comments, and were more often branded as 'slutty' for sharing (public or private) images of themselves (Handyside and Ringrose, 2017). And, in the US, research undertaken by the Pew Research Center demonstrated the high levels of sexual harassment experienced by young women on the Internet, with 21 per cent of women aged 18 to 29 reporting they had being sexually harassed online, and roughly half (53 per cent) reporting they had received unsolicited explicit images (Duggan, 2017: 7).

More generally, online harassment – or 'cyber-bullying' – has been identified as a significant problem for many young people. In the US, for instance, the Pew Research Center found that 59 per cent of teenagers had been bullied or harassed online, with 16 per cent reporting they had received physical threats, and 7 per cent reporting that explicit images of themselves had been shared without their consent (Anderson, 2018: 2). Additionally, some studies suggest social media networks can be characterised by a hierarchical monitoring of social approval, with users competing for popularity and self-affirmation by accruing 'likes', 'friends' and 'followers'. As Adriana Manago and her colleagues observe, this can lead to envy and disappointment – or 'FoMO' (Fear of Missing Out) – when individuals overlook that others may intentionally publicise or enhance the 'good' and 'flattering' parts of their lives (Manago et al., 2015). Concern has also surrounded the relationship between social media use and levels of anxiety and depression among young people. In Britain for example, several high-profile cases sparked alarm about the possible links between social media and incidents of self-harm and suicide by young people. In response, critics called for companies such as Instagram and Facebook to regulate their content more effectively, while 2020 saw the Royal College of Psychiatrists argue that companies should be forced to release data on how young people were using social media networks (*BBC News*, 2020).

There may, however, be elements of 'media panic' to some of these concerns (see Chapter 5). And, overall, research on the relationship between social media use and mental health among young people has been equivocal. In an overview of existing studies of the issue, Betul Keles and her colleagues concluded that, although existing research suggested an association between significant use of social media and levels of depression and anxiety among young people, further investigation was required. Any relationship that existed, they argued, would inevitably be complex; and the apparent association between social media use and young people's mental problems was, they stressed, 'correlational but not conclusively causative' (Betul et al., 2020: 90). Moreover, while there may be some negative facets to young people's use of social media, many researchers are at pains to stress the potential benefits. Alice Marwick (2013), for instance, explains how online social spaces can afford feelings of intimacy and friendship, while danah boyd (2014) stresses the feelings of friendship and connectedness young people can derive from being involved in online social networks. And, while Britain's Royal Society for Public Health (RSPH) acknowledged problems such as cyber-bullying, its research also highlighted the many positive experiences youngsters could derive from social media. The society, for example, observed how many young people improved their health literacy through reading blogs or watching vlogs, while social media could be a valuable source of counsel and comfort:

> Sharing problems or issues with friends, peers and broader social networks can be met with positive reaction. Nearly seven in 10 teens report receiving support on social media during tough or challenging times.
>
> (RSPH, 2017: 14)

'They're doers. They're participators. They're creators': youth, digital media, and 'convergence culture'

As well as offering spaces for the elaboration of identity and social relations, digital technologies and social media networks have also afforded young people new avenues for creative expression. As the abundant online activities of One Direction fans demonstrates (see above), the rise of the Internet and social media has brought an outpouring of youngsters' imaginative creativity. For Mary Celeste Kearney (2006), these developments have had particularly important consequences for young women, who have exploited the newly available arenas of cultural production – music, videos, 'zines, and so on – to explore their identities and connect with others. In doing so, Kearney argues, 'a highly cultural productive generation of female youth' have not only challenged traditional assumptions about media production as a world dominated by adult men, they have also subverted the restrictive roles and practices long associated with femininity. As Kearney explains:

> ... by engaging with the technologies and practices of media production, [girls] are actively subverting the traditional sex/gender system that has kept female cultural practices confined to consumerism, beauty, and the domestic sphere for decades.
>
> (Kearney, 2006: 12)

Geraldine Bloustein and Margaret Peters (2011) also draw attention to the way digital production and communication technologies have provided young people with new vistas of creativity. From their ethnographic fieldwork, Bloustein and Peters show how networks of music fans, performers, and promoters stretching from Adelaide to London, Berlin, and Boston have allowed youngsters to teach and learn from one another, developing sophisticated skills in Web design, turntable mixing, sound engineering, and entrepreneurialism. Emphasising the agency and creativity of the young people in their study, Bloustein and Peters saw them as analogous to the concept of the 'produser'.

The term 'produser' was popularised by Australian media theorist Axel Bruns to describe what he saw as a merging of the roles of producer and consumer in the interactive environment of Web 2.0.[7] For Bruns, the new dimensions of involvement and exchange made possible by the technologies of Web 2.0 had reconfigured the nature of media audiences and consumers. Where once they had been essentially passive receivers of media content, Bruns contended, they had now become actively involved in collaborating on the processes of media production. As Bruns argued, 'produser' was a term that:

> ... highlights that within communities that engage in the collaborative creation and extension of information and knowledge ... the role of 'consumer' and even that of 'end user' have long disappeared and the distinctions between producers and users of content have faded into comparative insignificance.
>
> (2008: 2)

Other theorists, too, have seen the development of digital media and communications as heralding a new age of empowered audiences and consumers. Henry Jenkins, in particular, has argued that technologies like Web 2.0 have opened up an increasing range of participatory spaces and sites for creative activity whose existence annuls 'the old rhetoric of opposition and co-optation [that] assumed a world where consumers had little direct power to shape media content and where there were enormous barriers to entry in the marketplace' (Jenkins, 2003). Instead, Jenkins contends, new media technologies have brought a more participatory and actively creative culture in which consumers have greater ability to 'archive, annotate, and recirculate media products' (Jenkins, 2003).

Coining the phrase 'convergence culture', Jenkins – like many theorists (see Chapter 3) – highlights contemporary trends towards integration and inter-connection between media format, content, and platforms of distribution. But, alongside these forms of convergence, Jenkins also identifies a merger of the realms of production and consumption. This he sees as creating new, enhanced modes of interactive participation for audiences. In this respect, Jenkins extends his earlier (1992) work on fan cultures in which he saw fans as active and creative manipulators of media texts (see Chapter 6). For Jenkins, advances in media technologies have generalised the dimensions of engagement and crea-tivity that he saw as characteristic of fan cultures, so that fans could be seen as 'preparing the way for a more meaningful public culture' (Jenkins, 2008: 239). From this perspective, developments such as Web 2.0 and the rise of social media have allowed for a greater degree of convergence between processes of production and consumption, and between commercial and amateur media enterprise. 'Relations between producers and consumers are breaking down', Jenkins argues, 'as consumers seek to act upon the invitation to participate in the life of the franchises' (Jenkins, 2008: 20). As he explains:

> Rather than talking about media producers and consumers as occupying separate roles, we might now see them as participants who interact with each other according to a new set of rules that none of us fully understands.
>
> (Jenkins, 2006: 3)

A range of researchers have adopted such perspectives in their analyses of modern youth culture. Leisha Jones (2011), for example, uses the concept of 'prosumption' in her analysis of the flurry of fan activity that surrounded Ste-phanie Meyers' series of *Twilight* romantic-fantasy novels for young adults (first published in 2005) and the ensuing movie franchise, *The Twilight Saga* (begun in 2008). *Twilight* itself was a major commercial success but, for Jones, what was especially significant was the ensuing proliferation of texts created by 'girl pro-sumers' who 'deploy technological savvy and critical aesthetic acumen to gen-erate a host of responses to *Twilight*, which they then publish on the Internet' (Jones, 2011: 439). According to Jones, this wealth of fiction and other fan-generated material was 'taking reader response to a whole new level of self-actualization', and represented a hub of creativity 'through which girls *enculture*, and produce one another, actualizing one or any number of selves online' (ibid.). And the same might also be said of the outpouring of cultural production undertaken by One Direction fans. Indeed, author Anna Todd could be considered a personification of the 'prosumer' ideal in the way she transformed her passion for Harry Styles and co. into a wildly popular fanfiction series, followed by a money-spinning media franchise (see above).

A convergence between the roles of production and consumption has also long been a pronounced feature of the video games industry. Since the 1990s players have tinkered with commercial video games, freely adding to them, reconfiguring them, and extending their degree of sophistication. Through these processes of 'modding' (short for 'modifying'), players have developed new 'skins' for avatar characters, configured new storylines, game levels, and scenarios, and even crafted entirely new games – all disseminated via online fan sites and communities. But players have also been increasingly incorporated into processes of game design and development, so they are no longer simple consumers of a 'completed' end product. It has, for example, become commonplace for games manufacturers to involve fans in the testing of games prior to their commercial release. To trial new products and prolong the shelf-life of existing games, firms have also enthusiastically provided 'modders' with a host of 'shareware' resources and open-source editing tools to assist their creative endeavours. And, for some commentators, these dimensions of audience participation have represented a new direction in relations between producers and consumers. Sue Morris, for instance, suggested that many video games should now be understood as a form of 'co-creative media'. 'Neither developers nor player creators can be solely responsible for production of the final assemblage regarded as "the game"', Morris argued, 'it requires input from both' (Morris, 2003: 345).

Undoubtedly, digital media and Web 2.0 technologies have provided young people with a wealth of new, accessible avenues for producing and publishing texts, images, and all manner of audio-visual material. And, as cultural theorists have long demonstrated, youth are not simply the passive dupes of manipulative commercial media, but are active agents who generate their own cultures and identities (see Chapter 6). Nevertheless, some critics are circumspect about the grander claims made for media interaction, collaborative production and the 'empowering' dimensions of prosumption. Jenkins' work, particularly, has been criticised for using the very engaged world of fandom as a model for understanding the behaviour of media audiences more generally. As Elizabeth Bird observes, this tends to lose sight of 'the more mundane, internalized, even passive articulation with media that characterizes a great deal of media consumption' (Bird, 2011: 504). Indeed, José van Dijck cites 'an emerging rule of thumb' that suggests only one in a hundred people will be active online content producers – with 10 'interacting' by commenting, and the remaining 89 simply viewing (van Dijck, 2009). Moreover, as Bird succinctly puts it, 'much online activity is simply inconsequential banter' (Bird, 2011: 504).

Furthermore, while audiences certainly actively engage with media texts, this should not overshadow the way media producers can still inscribe representations of the world that influence audiences' attitudes and behaviour. Andy

Ruddock (2008), for example, analyses a successful advertising campaign in Britain that – through the use of hip imagery and viral media – transformed cider drinking (once a woefully unfashionable preference) into a cool and trendy lifestyle choice. Working with young audiences, Ruddock found that they were undoubtedly active, informed, and 'media-savvy' but, at the same time, they were also very aware of (even irritated by) their own realisation they had been successfully manipulated.

Issues of power, ownership and control are also downplayed in notions of 'prosumption' and collaborative production. Media companies, for example, have become adept at deploying 'terms of service' on online activity, so that anything users post effectively becomes the property of the company. Such terms and conditions, Christian Fuchs argues, 'are totalitarian mechanisms that are necessarily not democratically controlled by the users, but under the control of corporations' (Fuchs, 2011: 303). And many theorists have pointed to the exploitative way many companies have minimised their costs by harnessing the input and expertise of amateur fans. Variously dubbed 'free labor' (Terranova, 2000), 'invisible labour' (Downey, 2001) or 'playlabour' (Kücklich, 2005), the practice is pronounced in the world of video games but has also become a feature across the field of media production. Moreover, as their online data is harvested and traded through the practices of 'surveillance capitalism', audiences are themselves turned into commodities. As Fuchs explains:

> … web 2.0 is largely a commercial, profit-oriented machine that exploits users by commodifying their personal data and usage behaviour … and subjects these data to economic surveillance so that capital is accumulated with the help of targeted personal advertising.
>
> (Fuchs, 2011: 304)

Commercial companies, moreover, have become adept at co-opting fan activities and viral media into marketing campaigns that foster consumers' emotional commitment to brands by cultivating a sense of dialogue, involvement, and active participation. In this respect marketing consultants C.K. Prahalad and Venkat Ramaswamy have promoted the concept of 'co-creation', arguing that commercial success lies not in an old view of consumers as passive recipients of goods and services, but in a new embrace of 'joint creation of value by the company and the customer; allowing the customer to co-construct the service experience to suit their context' (Prahalad and Ramaswamy, 2004i: 8). In their book *The Future of Competition* (2004ii), Prahalad and Ramaswamy argue that brands are best able to compete if they can draw their customers into a relationship of active collaboration and 'co-creation' which, they contend, not only improves businesses' ability to respond to consumer demand; but also fosters consumers' loyalty and emotional commitment to brands. In the youth market such strategies have been especially pronounced, spurred by widespread assumptions that 'millennial' youngsters are characterised by their creativity and technological proficiency (see Chapter 3). As the marketing agency Tongal explained to prospective clients in 2016, millennials were 'the perfect partners for co-creation'. 'They're doers. They're participators. They're creators'. As Tongal enthused:

> Millennials love to create content. They make it by themselves and they make it with friends. What smart marketers are realizing is that by giving Millennials the opportunity to create projects with them, they can become their friends too.
>
> (Tongal, 2016)

The genial language, however, disguises the fact that the 'friendship' is patently not an equal one. While young consumers may interact with companies online, they have no meaningful power in terms of ownership or control. As Fuchs argues, audiences may 'participate' in the production of cultural goods, but the wealth accrued is retained by industry, and authority remains firmly in the hands of big business:

> Corporate platforms owned by Facebook, Google and other large companies strongly mediate the cultural expressions of Internet users. Neither the users nor the waged employees of Facebook, Google and others determine the business decisions of these companies. They do not 'participate' in economic decision-making, but are excluded from it.
>
> (Fuchs, 2014: 56)

Rather than marking a shift into a radically new era of 'prosumption' and 'co-creation', young people's prolific engagement with social media and Web 2.0 technologies might be better seen as a facet to what the Australian cultural theorist Graeme Turner (2010) sees as a wider 'demotic turn' in contemporary cultural life. For Turner, this 'demotic' (meaning 'of, or for, the common people') trend is marked by 'the increasing number of opportunities for ordinary people to appear in the media' (Turner, 2010: 2). In these terms, developments in media technology and format have given ordinary people both greater levels of media access and a greater degree of visibility as they turn themselves into media content through the proliferation of reality TV, confessional talk shows, social media, Internet influencers, and so on.

A positive aspect to this demotic trend is that it can give exposure to issues previously ignored in media coverage. An example might be the US Black Lives Matter movement that, in 2013, began using online media in its mass protest against police violence and racial injustice. Similarly, in 2017 the international #MeToo campaign used social media networks to involve millions of women in a challenge to sexual harassment.[8] And, more generally, there is evidence to suggest the Internet has played a part in extending some young people's level of civic and political engagement. For instance, a major study funded by the European Commission between 2007 and 2011 found that, across six European countries, young people were largely alienated from, or at least felt dissatisfied with, traditional political institutions (Banaji and Buckingham, 2013). But, for those already involved in politics, the Internet represented 'an important mobilization tool' (155). And (perhaps more importantly), for young people from minority communities – political, sexual, ethnic, regional, or religious – the online world represented 'a space to enact diverse identities, to question notions of tradition, to discuss the meaning of culture and citizenship, or to develop methods of participation and protest' (ibid.).

The 'demotic turn', then, is not without positive features. But, as Turner points out, growing participation does not necessarily equate with increased power and authority. Indeed, as Turner rather ruefully explains, while 'ordinary people' may feature more prominently in media representations and communication, the symbolic economy remains resolutely controlled by huge, transnational media companies:

> Notwithstanding the webcam girls, the trading of music on the Internet, the availability of digital production technologies in all kinds of media forms, this is still in the same hands it has always been. It might be seductive to think of the Internet as an alternative, counter-public sphere and in many ways its chaotic contents would support such a view. But, it is a system that is dominated by white, middle class American men and increasingly integrated into the major corporate structures of the traditional media conglomerates.
>
> (Turner, 2004: 82)

An appreciation of the continuing power of market institutions, however, should not slide us back into theories of a dissolute 'mass culture' in which commercial Svengalis lead passive and undiscriminating young consumers by the nose. Young people are undoubtedly creative and innovative users of the media; appropriating, transforming, and re-contextualising texts as they engineer their identities and sense of self. But notions of a new generation of creative and digitally 'empowered' millennials overlooks the way inequalities of wealth, power, and control continue to frame young people's engagement with the media. Indeed, casting youngsters as 'doers', 'participators' and 'creators' can be seen as just the latest instalment in a long history of 'generational symbolism' (see Chapter 4) in which stereotypical representations of youth are used to elaborate a very particular – and ideologically loaded – view of society and the character of social change.

Notes

1 The practice of 'shipping' has its roots in 'slash fiction' – fan-generated erotic fiction, initially published in fanzines, that focused on same-sex pairings of heterosexual characters from popular fiction. The term 'slash fiction' derives from the way an oblique stroke (or slash) is used to separate the names of the two protagonists. For example, Penley (1997) analysed 'Kirk/Spock' stories, an early example of slash fiction in which fans imagined a sexual relationship between the two leading characters

in *Star Trek*, the 1960s TV show. The term 'shipping' developed during the 1990s and was used by fans of TV shows such as *The X-Files*, who envisioned how the lead characters might be in a romantic relationship. Name blending (such as 'Larry Stylinson') or compound names (like 'Larry') have become increasingly used both to abbreviate character pairings and to create a name for the 'ship' itself. Discussion of slash fiction, with particular attention to the way it often represents a space for queer cultural practice, can be found in Busse (2017).

2 Overviews of the genealogies and applications of queer theory can be found in McCann (2020) and Sullivan (2003).

3 Along with Fast and Jennex (eds) (2019), studies of the queer dimensions to popular music are collected in Brett, Wood and Thomas (eds) (2006), Lee (2018), and Whiteley and Rycenga (eds) (2006).

4 Alexander (2006: 229–292) also provides a critical analysis of the way queer youth use the Internet to configure their identities and relationships.

5 This was, however, set to change. In 2018 the technology conglomerate Cisco projected that by 2022 there would be 829 million smartphone users in India, accounting for 60 per cent of the population (Bhattacharya, 2018).

6 As Wallis observes, there are often tensions between the way the Chinese government uses digital communication platforms to secure social control and maintain its legitimacy, and the way these same platforms 'create opportunities for other social forces to push their own agenda and promote social change' (2011: 420).

7 In turn, the concept of the 'produser' evolved from the idea of the 'prosumer' – a term coined by the American futurist Alvin Toffler to describe the way he thought developments in electronic communication would lead to 'the progressive blurring of the line that separates producer from consumer' (1980: 267). This shift, Toffler conjectured, was set to transform passive, consumer society into a world where many people provided home-grown services to themselves and others, selectively producing or consuming depending on their expertise and interests. Tapscott and Williams (2006) developed similar ideas in their account of the Internet's capacity to engender 'mass collaboration'.

8 It must be remembered, however that 'participatory culture' is not intrinsically progressive. As Fuchs points out, Anders Brevik – the fascist terrorist who murdered 77 people in the Norwegian terror attacks of 2011 – was known as a keen participant in his online communities (Fuchs, 2014: 59).

10 Conclusion

Youth, media, and 'circuits of culture'

Young people and the media: a 'circuit of youth culture'?

Despite the economic recessions and industrial restructuring of the 1980s and 1990s, and the global financial crisis of 2007–8, the youth market retained its economic significance. Certainly, the labour markets that had underpinned the explosion of 'teenage' consumption in Europe and North America during the 1950s and 1960s had changed, and young people's routes into full-time work had become more protracted and diverse. But during the early twenty-first century the youth market remained a cornerstone of the world's media, consumer, and entertainment industries. Moreover, expanding well beyond its 'generational base', the youth market had come to include groups of adults who staked out their cultural identities through lifestyles associated with the hip cachet of youth – expressive, independent, and hedonistic. Effectively, then, 'youth culture' was no longer confined to the young but had come to denote a particular set of consumer attitudes and outlooks.

The relationship between youth, consumption, and the commercial market, however, has remained an area of debate. While theorists have generally moved away from mass culture perspectives that see young people as the passive victims of exploitative cultural industries, tensions have continued between approaches associated with political economy and those informed by the traditions of cultural studies. From a cultural studies perspective, the onus tends to be on the agency of audiences and consumers, and their capacity to construct their own identities and cultures from commercial resources. Political economists such as Graham Murdock (1997) and Nicholas Garnham (1998), however, have argued that cultural studies' close attention to audience's meanings and practices has sometimes 'exaggerated the freedoms of consumption in daily life' (Garnham, 1998: 603), and requires a more thorough engagement with 'the ways that these grounded processes are structured by wider economic and ideological formations' (Murdock, 1997: 63). And Christian Fuchs has criticised what he sees as a 'celebratory' tradition in cultural studies that 'focuses on worshipping TV audiences (and other audiences) as "rebelling" and constantly "resisting" in order to consume ever more' (Fuchs, 2014: 65). Political economists, in contrast, have tended to emphasise dimensions of power and control within the media, occasionally – critics argue – sliding into overly pessimistic notions of a relatively passive, easily manipulated audience. Attempts to bridge this theoretical divide have been notoriously problematic but, in an attempt to transcend the dualism, some theorists have turned to the concept of 'circuits of culture'. This approach sees the meanings of media texts as being produced through a confluence of mutually constitutive processes – a 'circuit of culture' – in which social and cultural influences *are* important; but *also* significant is the way these factors interact with developments in other realms, especially the fields of production, demand, reception, and regulation.

The concept of a 'circuit of culture' was originally developed in the mid-1980s by Richard Johnson. According to Johnson, to understand the way media forms develop, circulate, and generate meaning, attention must be given to the way they move through a 'circuit' consisting of three main stages – production, textuality, and reception. Each stage, he argued, was distinct and involved 'characteristic changes of form', but were linked together in processes of interdependence and interaction so that '(e)ach moment or aspect depends upon the others and is indispensable to the whole' (Johnson, 1997: 83). Analytic perspectives that failed to acknowledge each stage of the circuit and its relation to the others, Johnson contended, could not adequately account for the form and meaning of media texts. In these terms, then, approaches that dwelt exclusively on issues of (for example) authorial intent or textual character were insufficient. Instead, other aspects of the 'cultural circuit' – for instance, the organisation of production and the readings generated by audiences – also demanded attention, along with the dimensions of influence and interplay that invariably existed between the various points of the 'circuit'.

Taking up from Johnson's original model, Paul Du Gay and his colleagues (1997) also argued that media texts and cultural artefacts developed their meanings through a number of mutually constitutive processes. Refining Johnson's approach, Du Gay's analysis saw meanings as being continuously re-worked through a cultural circuit that consisted of five distinct processes – production, identity formation, representation, consumption, and regulation. A full analysis of a cultural phenomenon, Du Gay argued, demanded adequate attention to each aspect of this circuit. Moreover, rather than seeing the circuit as following a linear path from production to consumption, Du Gay (like Johnson), emphasised the connections that existed between each stage. In these terms, the different parts of the circuit continually overlapped and interacted in complex and contingent ways that varied over time and between different contexts. So, rather than privileging any one key factor (such as production or consumption), Du Gay argued that meanings were formed through the way the different elements of the cultural circuit came together in particular circumstances.

Other authors have deployed a similar model. Julie D'Acci, for example, has advocated a comparable approach in her concept of the 'circuit of media' though, for her, cultural meanings are generated through the interaction of four key sites – the moment of production, the cultural artefact itself, processes of reception, and the broader socio-historical context in which these processes take place (D'Acci, 2004). Gerald Goggin (2006), meanwhile, adopts a 'circuit' model broadly similar to Du Gay's in his study of mobile phones – though Goggin seeks to extend and reframe the approach by giving additional emphasis to the changing attributes and configurations of technology. There are, then, different inflections of the 'circuit of culture' model, but they share a common interest in highlighting the way cultural meanings are produced and circulate throughout a series of inter-linked, mutually constituted sites. As Du Gay and his associates explained, the cultural meanings of texts and artefacts are always 'constructed through a dialogue – albeit rarely an equal one in terms of power relations – between production and consumption' (Du Gay et al., 1997: 103).

A 'circuitous' approach can also be productively applied to the analysis of youth culture and its relation to the media. Drawing on the ideas of authors such as Johnson and Du Gay, it is possible to see commercial media and young people's cultural formations as co-dependent sites within an inter-linked 'circuit of culture' – or, perhaps, a 'circuit of youth culture' – where meanings are not generated in any one sovereign sphere (for example, production or consumption), but through the articulation of a number of processes whose interplay leads to variable and contingent outcomes.

Within this circuit, questions of political economy are undoubtedly crucial. Indeed, in any analysis of texts and artefacts (TV shows, films, popular music, fashion, social media), it is imperative to consider their systems of production. Attention to issues such as business organisation, ownership, and control highlights the (rarely equal) power relationships that underpin the production and circulation of media texts and cultural goods geared to young people. A focus on the realm of political economy also reveals the underlying links between patterns of economic development and political ideology. The rise of transnational media giants such as Facebook and Tencent, for example, did not take place in a political vacuum, but was indebted to the ascension of political forces that championed economic liberalisation and the deregulation of global markets. Indeed, political policies have also impacted upon the character of 'youth' as a distinct life stage. In both North America and Europe, for instance, young people's prolonged and less predictable passage into the 'adult' world of full-time employment has not been born out of the ether, but has been a consequence of the transformation of traditional labour markets and governments' drive towards free-market economics.

Issues of political economy also draw attention to the importance of technological developments within the shifting relations of production – the rise of global business conglomerates relying on (and, in turn, further stimulating) the development of new communication technologies that have allowed for quicker and more efficient international flows of information and finance. Technological developments have also had an impact on the structures of production and the cultures of business organisation. Flexible, automated electronic technologies have allowed for the development of more specialised goods and services targeted not at a monolithic mass market, but at a series of distinctive consumer groups. In the youth market, for instance, this shift towards segmentation has been marked by the rise of 'niche' media forms, the burgeoning number of YouTube channels, and the rise of fashion brands geared to particular attitudes and lifestyles.

Alongside these shifts, issues of meaning and representation have also become more economically significant. In their attempt to address particular markets and lifestyle groups, producers have increasingly called upon the skills of designers, advertisers, and marketers. These 'cultural intermediaries' have come to occupy a pivotal economic role, their expertise in signifying practices increasingly drawn upon by manufacturers in their efforts to invest products with desirable meanings and cultural associations. Effectively, then, the growing importance of cultural intermediaries lies in their ability to connect the sites of cultural production and cultural consumption. This has been especially apparent in the youth market, marked by the increased use of social media and Internet 'influencers' to connect producers with the attitudes and aspirations of a lucrative – but notoriously elusive – consumer group.

Questions of production, then, are inseparable from issues of representation and cultural identity. But processes of consumption also play a major role in the 'circuit of youth culture'. An exclusive focus on producers' attempts to invest their goods and services with particular meanings reveals little about what those products actually signify for the young people using them. The appropriation and use of texts by audiences and consumers is always a crucial link in the chain. Cultures of consumption, moreover, 'feed back into' sites of production and representation in an ongoing cycle of commodifcation. In the youth market, for example, producers draw on the 'symbolic expertise' of their army of cultural intermediaries (market researchers, analysts, and influencers) in their attempts to track the cultural tastes of young consumers, allowing them to develop texts and products inscribed with meanings attuned as closely as possible to youngsters' tastes and values.

In these terms, any attempt to understand contemporary youth cultures and their relation to the commercial media demands attention to the way meanings are produced and circulate *throughout* the mutually constitutive sites of the cultural circuit. Unless adequate attention is given to all its dimensions – production, identity formation, representation, consumption, and regulation – it is impossible to grasp the full cultural meanings and significance of young people's engagement with the media.

Global perspectives and portents of change

One of the key themes of this book has been highlighting the way modern youth cultures are forged through global flows of media, cultures, and peoples. While global connections have long been a feature of many young people's lives, by the beginning of the twenty-first century these had become more pronounced as a consequence of the intensification of 'globalising' trends in technology, politics, and economics. Increasingly, however, world events seemed to point to a slowing down, even a reversal, of globalisation as there unfolded an era of religious extremism, ethnic conflict, right-wing populism, and heightened nationalism. In 2016, for example, the UK 'Brexit' vote to leave the European Union and 'take back control', along with the election of Donald Trump as US President on the promise to put 'America First', seemed to signal a broad shift towards a rejection of transnational trade pacts, a disengagement from global cooperation, and a putting up of walls and fences (both figuratively and literally). The rise of far-right politics in Hungary, Poland, and the Czech Republic, meanwhile, testified to Europe's growing levels of hostility to immigrants, a survey in 2017 suggesting that 55 per cent of Europeans wanted to ban Muslim immigrants from entering the continent (Goodwin et al., 2017).

At the same time, however, these events need to be seen in context. As Jan Nederveen Pieterse (2020) argues, the worldwide 'tide' of right-wing populist politics is actually complex and diverse. Despite superficial similarities, he argues, local populist movements range widely in their ideas and agendas. Moreover, while the US and UK might be moving towards policies of economic nationalism, not everyone is taking this path. 'Widen the horizon', Pieterse suggests, 'and many trends look quite different' (2020: 193). For example, while the US withdrew from the Trans-Pacific Partnership (TPP) – a trade agreement drafted in 2015 – the other signatories proceeded regardless, enacting the Comprehensive and Progressive Agreement for Trans-Pacific Partnership (CPTPP) in 2018. And the Asian Infrastructure Investment Bank (AIIB), set up in 2015 as multilateral development bank to support the building of infrastructure in the Indo-Pacific region, boasted 78 member states worldwide by 2020, while a further 24 states were prospective members (AIIB, 2020). As countries like the US and the UK retreated, therefore, China and India (the leading shareholders in the AIIB), together with other emerging economies, have become the vanguard of globalisation. Indeed, China's 'Belt and Road Initiative' (BRI) promises to be a '21st Century Silk Road', providing infrastructures connecting Asia, Africa, and Europe. As Pieterse argues, therefore:

> Worldwide, there is no reversal of globalization: there is, rather, a shift of the powerhouse of globalization from the Atlantic to the Pacific economies, while the previously leading economies turn to cultivating sour grapes and opt for 'economic nationalism'.
>
> (Pieterse, 2020: 196)

Furthermore – and perhaps with more direct impact on the world's youth cultures – global flows of media, entertainment, consumption, and ideas remain pronounced. As a consequence, despite the inward-looking character of some governments, young people's cultures and identities will continue to be generated through processes of connection, interaction, and hybridisation.

Nevertheless, at the time of writing (April 2020), world events give the future a marked sense of uncertainty. Just as the financial crisis of 2007–8 was spread through the hubs of global banks and money markets, the coronavirus (or Covid-19) spread through the international travel hubs of airports and transport networks. And, as hundreds of thousands died, a large portion of the world's population were 'locked-down' in quarantine or isolation, and the world's economy spluttered to a virtual standstill. The pandemic gave a poignancy to the work of authors who, decades earlier, had written of the rise of a 'risk society' and a growing 'culture of fear'. For some commentators, it also spelled an end to the era of high globalisation. Writing in the journal *Foreign Policy*, for instance, Philippe Legrain pointed to the way the crisis might pave the way for greater immigration controls and protectionism worldwide. 'The coronavirus', Legrain conjectured, had 'highlighted the downsides of extensive international integration while fanning the fears of foreigners and providing legitimacy for national restrictions on global trade and flows of people' (Legrain, 2020). On the other hand, however, the British journalist and political economist Will Hutton saw more hopeful possibilities. The coronavirus emergency, he speculated, might be occasion for a fundamental change in international relations, and the 'unregulated, free-market globalisation with its propensity for crises and pandemics' could give way to 'another form that recognises interdependence and the primacy of evidence-based collective action' (Hutton, 2020). The likelihood of such a radical shift, however, seemed moot.

What was more certain was that huge economic dislocation was set to follow the crisis. And, as in the past, the likely recession and rises in unemployment would register their biggest impact on the young. The economic position of many young people (already precarious) would worsen, and transitions from childhood to adulthood would become even more insecure. And, almost inevitably, the 'young generation' would be configured by the media and politicians as a symbolic focus for debates about the social and economic turmoil. At the same time, however, youth cultures would endure. And young people would continue to draw on the world's media as raw materials for the elaboration of identities that were meaningful, expressive and – sometimes – inspiring.

References

Aarseth, E., Bean, A., Boonen, H., Carras, M. et al. (2017) 'Scholars' Open Debate Paper on the World Health Organization ICD-11 Gaming Disorder Proposal', *Journal of Behavioral Addictions*, Vol. 6, No. 3, pp. 267–270.

Abbott, C. (1998) 'Making Connections: Young People and the Internet', in Sefton-Green, J. (ed.), *Digital Diversions: Youth Culture in the Age of Multimedia*, London: UCL Press, pp. 84–105.

Abrams, M. (1959) *The Teenage Consumer*, London: Press Exchange.

Abrams, M. (1961) *Teenage Consumer Spending in 1959*, London: Press Exchange.

Adams, M. (1994) *The Best War Ever: America and World War II*, Baltimore, MD: Johns Hopkins University Press.

Adams, R. (2019) '"Home Sweet Home, That's Where I Come From, Where I Got My Knowledge of the Road and the Flow From" (Kano, "Home Sweet Home"): Grime Music as an Expression of Identity in Postcolonial London', *Popular Music and Society*, Vol. 42, No. 4, pp. 438–455.

Adamski, W. and Grootings, P. (eds) (1989) *Youth, Education and Work in Europe*, London: Routledge.

Adorno, T. (1991) (orig. pub. 1941) 'On Popular Music', in Adorno, T., *The Culture Industry: Selected Essays on Mass Culture*, London: Routledge.

Advertising Age (1951) 'Everybody Talks about Youth Advertising …', 26 February, p. 1.

Aglietta, M. (1979) *A Theory of Capitalist Regulation: The US Experience*, London: Verso.

Ahmed, S. and Matthes, J. (2017) 'Media Representation of Muslims and Islam from 2000 to 2015: A Meta-Analysis', *International Communication Gazette*, Vol. 79, No. 3, pp. 219–244.

Ajala, I. (2017) 'From Islamic Dress and Islamic Fashion to Cool Islam: An Exploration of Muslim Youth Hybrid Identities in the West', *The International Journal of Interdisciplinary Cultural Studies*, Vol. 12, No. 3, pp. 1–11.

Alanen, L. (2001) 'Explorations in Generational Analysis', in Alanen, L. and Mayall, B. (eds), *Conceptualising Child-Adult Relations*, London: Routledge, pp. 11–22.

Alexander, J. (2006) *Digital Youth: Emerging Literacies on the World Wide Web*, Cresskill, NJ: Hampton Press.

Altheide, D. (2009) 'Moral Panic: From Sociological Concept to Public Discourse', *Crime, Media, Culture*, Vol. 5, No. 1, pp. 79–99.

Alvarez, L. (2008) *The Power of the Zoot: Youth Culture and Resistance during World War II*, Berkeley, CA: University of California Press.

American Psychological Association (APA) (2005) 'Resolution on Violence in Video Games and Interactive Media', American Psychological Association, online, https://www.apa.org/about/policy/interactive-media.pdf (accessed 13 January 2020).

American Psychological Association (APA) (2015) 'Resolution on Violent Video Games', American Psychological Association, online, www.apa.org/about/policy/violent-video-games.aspx (accessed 13 January 2020).

Anderson, C. and Ford, C. (1986) 'Affect of the Game Player: Short-Term Effects of Highly and Mildly Aggressive Video Games', *Personality and Social Psychology Bulletin*, Vol. 12, No. 4, pp. 390–402.

Anderson, C., Berkowitz, L., Donnerstein, E.et al. (2003) 'The Influence of Violent Media on Youth', *Psychological Science in the Public Interest*, Vol. 4, No. 3, pp. 81–110.

Anderson, C., Nobuko, I., Bushman, B., Rothstein, H.et al. (2010) 'Violent Video Game Effects on Aggression, Empathy, and Prosocial Behavior in Eastern and Western Countries: A Meta-Analytic Review', *American Psychological Association*, Vol. 136, No. 2, pp. 151–173.

Anderson, M. (2018) 'A Majority of Teens Have Experienced Some Form of Cyberbullying', Pew Research Center, online, https://www.pewresearch.org/internet/2018/09/27/a-majority-of-teens-have-experienced-some-form-of-cyberbullying/ (accessed 30 April 2020).

Anderson, M. and Jiang, J. (2018) 'Teens, Social Media and Technology 2018', Pew Research Center, online, https://www.pewresearch.org/internet/2018/05/31/teens-social-media-technology-2018/ (accessed 30 April 2020).

APA Task Force on Violent Media (2015) 'Technical Report on the Review of the Violent Video Game Literature', American Psychological Association, online, www.apa.org/pi/families/violent-media.aspx (accessed 13 January 2020).

Appadurai, A. (1990) 'Disjuncture and Difference in the Global Cultural Economy', *Theory, Culture and Society*, Vol. 7, Nos. 2–3, pp. 295–310.

Appadurai, A. (1996) *Modernity at Large: Cultural Dimensions of Globalization*, Minneapolis, MN: University of Minnesota Press.

Arkoff, S. (1997) *Flying through Hollywood by the Seat of My Pants*, Secaucus, NJ: Carol Publishing.

Armstrong, M. (2019) 'MySpace Isn't Dead', Statistica, online, 18 March, https://www.statista.com/chart/17392/myspace-global-traffic/ (accessed 13 November, 2019).

Arnett, J. (2000) 'Emerging Adulthood: A Theory of Development from the Late Teens through the Twenties', *American Psychologist*, Vol. 55, No. 5, pp. 469–480.

Arnett, J. (2004) *Emerging Adulthood: The Winding Road from the Late teens through the Twenties*, New York: Oxford University Press.

Arnett, J. (2016) 'Emerging Adulthood in Europe: Common Themes, Diverse Paths, and Future Directions', in Žukauskienė, R. (ed.), *Emerging Adulthood in a European Context*, London: Routledge, pp. 205–216.

Arnett, J. and Hughes, M. (2012) *Adolescence and Emerging Adulthood: A Cultural Approach*, Harlow: Pearson.

Arnett, J., Kloep, M., Hendry, L. and Tanner, J. (eds) (2011) *Debating Emerging Adulthood: Stage or Process?*, New York: Oxford University Press.

Arnett, J. and Tanner, J. (eds) (2006) *Emerging Adults in America: Coming of Age in the 21st Century*, Washington, DC: American Psychological Association.

Aronczyk, M. (2013) *Branding the Nation: The Global Business of National Identity*, New York: Oxford University Press.

Ashton, D., Maguire, M. and Spilsbury, M. (1990) *Restructuring the Labour Market: The Implications for Youth*, Basingstoke: Macmillan.

Asian Infrastructure Investment Bank (AIIB) 'Members and Prospective Members of the Bank', AIIB, online, 10 March, https://www.aiib.org/en/about-aiib/governance/members-of-bank/index.html (accessed 28 March 2020).

Athique, A. (2016) *Transnational Audiences: Media Reception on a Global Scale*, Cambridge: Polity Press.

Australian Government (2010) 'Literature Review on the Impact of Playing Violent Video Games on Aggression', Attorney-General's Department, online, https://www.classification.gov.au/about-us/research-and-publications/literature-review-impact-playing-violent-video-games-aggression (accessed 13 January 2020).

Avdela, E. (2008) 'Corrupting and Uncontrollable Activities: Moral Panic about Youth in Post-Civil-War Greece', *Journal of Contemporary History*, Vol. 43, No. 1 pp. 25–44.

Baberá, P., Jost, J., Nagler, J. and Tucker, J. (2015) 'Tweeting from Left to Right: Is Online Political Communication More than an Echo Chamber?', *Psychological Science*, Vol. 26, No. 10, pp. 1531–1542.

Back, L. (1996) *New Ethnicities and Urban Culture: Racisms and Multiculture in Young Lives*, London: UCL Press.

BackeBerg, L. and Tholen, J. (2018) 'The Frustrated Generation: Youth Exclusion in Arab Mediterranean Societies', *Journal of Youth Studies*, Vol. 21, No. 4, pp. 515–534.

Baker, S.L. (2004) 'Pop in(to) the Bedroom: Popular Music in Pre-teen Girls' "Bedroom Culture"', *European Journal of Cultural Studies*, Vol. 7, No. 1, pp. 75–93.

Bakshy, E., Messing, S. and Adamic, L. (2015) 'Exposure to Ideologically Diverse News and Opinion on Facebook', *Science*, Vol. 348, No. 6239, pp. 1130–1132.

Balbi, G. and Magaudda, P. (2018) *A History of Digital Media: An Intermedia and Global Perspective*, New York: Routledge.

Banaji, S. and Buckingham, D. (2013) *The Civic Web: Young People, the Internet, and Civic Participation*, Cambridge, MA: MIT Press.

Bandura, A., Ross, D. and Ross, S.A. (1961) 'Transmission of Aggression through Imitation of Aggressive Models', *The Journal of Abnormal and Social Psychology*, Vol. 63, No. 3, pp. 575–582.

Bandura, A., Ross, D. and Ross, S.A. (1963) 'Imitation of Film-Mediated Aggressive Models', *The Journal of Abnormal and Social Psychology*, Vol. 66, No. 1, pp. 3–11.

Barker, C. (1999) *Television, Globalization and Cultural Identities*, Milton Keynes: Open University Press.

Barker, M. (ed.) (1984) *The Video Nasties: Freedom and Censorship in the Media*, London: Pluto Press.

Barker, M. (1984) *A Haunt of Fears: The Strange History of the British Horror Comics Campaign*, London: Pluto Press.

Barker, M. (1992) 'Stuart Hall: Policing the Crisis', in Barker, M. and Beezer, A. (eds), *Reading into Cultural Studies*, London: Routledge, pp. 81–99.

Barker, M. (2001) 'The Newsom Report: A Case Study in "Common Sense"', in Barker, M. and Petley, J. (eds), (2nd edn), *Ill Effects: The Media/Violence Debate*, London: Routledge, pp. 27–46.

Barker, M. and Petley, J. (2001) 'Introduction: From Bad Research to Good: A Guide for the Perplexed', in Barker, M. and Petley, J. (eds), (2nd edn), *Ill Effects: The Media/Violence Debate*, London: Routledge, pp. 1–26.

Barnard, S. (1989) *On the Radio: Music Radio in Britain*, Milton Keynes: Open University Press.

Barron, C. and Lacombe, D. (2005) 'Moral Panic and the Nasty Girl', *Canadian Review of Sociology*, Vol. 42, No. 1, pp. 51–69.

Barthes, R. (trans. Lavers, A.) (1972) *Mythologies*, London: Paladin.

Barton, K. and Lampley, J. (eds) (2013) *Fan Culture: Essays on Participatory Fandom in the 21st Century*, Durham, NC: Duke University Press.

Baudrillard, J. (1983) *Simulations*, New York: Semiotext.

Baudrillard, J. (1985) 'The Ecstasy of Communication', in Foster, H. (ed.), *Post-modern Culture*, London: Pluto Press, pp. 126–135.

Baxter, K. (2008) *The Modern Age: Turn-of-the-Century American Culture and the Invention of Adolescence*, Tuscaloosa, AL: University of Alabama Press.

BBC News (2014) 'Iran: Happy Video Dancers Sentenced to 91 Lashes and Jail', *BBC News*, online, 19 September, https://www.bbc.co.uk/news/world-middle-east-29272732/ (accessed 3 March 2020).

BBC News (2016) 'Millennials "Set to Earn Less than Generation X"', *BBC News*, online, 18 July, https://www.bbc.co.uk/news/business-36821582 (accessed 13 November, 2019).

BBC News (2020) 'Social Media Data Needed for "Harm" Research, Say Doctors', *BBC News*, online, 17 January, https://www.bbc.co.uk/news/health-51134545 (accessed 28 March 2020).

Beck, E. (1985) 'The Anti-Nazi "Swing Youth", 1942–1945', *Journal of Popular Culture*, Vol. 19, No. 3, pp. 45–53.

Beck, U. (1992) *Risk Society: Towards a New Modernity*, London: Sage.

Beck, U. (1999) *World Risk Society*, Cambridge: Polity Press.

Beckett, F. (2010) *What Did The Baby Boomers Ever Do For Us?: Why the Children of the Sixties Lived the Dream and Failed the Future*, London: Biteback.

Beer, C. (2019) 'Is TikTok Setting the Scene for Music on Social Media?', Global WebIndex, online, 3 January, https://blog.globalwebindex.com/trends/tiktok-music-social-media/ (accessed 8 December 2019).

Bell, D. and Blanchflower, D. (2011) 'Youth Employment in Europe and the United States', *Nordic Economic Policy Review*, No. 1, pp. 11–37.

Bellanta, M. (2012) *Larrikins: A History*, St Lucia, Queensland: University of Queensland Press.

Belson, W.A. (1978) *Television Violence and the Adolescent Boy*, Farnborough, Hants: Saxon House.

Benjamin, F., Brown, G., Dhaliwal, J. and Kunto, G. (2011) *The Youth Marketing Handbook*, London: MobileYouth.

Bennett, A. (1999i) 'Subcultures or Neo-Tribes?: Rethinking the Relationship Between Youth, Style and Musical Taste', *Sociology*, Vol. 33, No. 3, pp. 599–617.

Bennett, A. (1999ii) 'Hip Hop Am Main: The Localization of Rap Music and Hip Hop Culture', *Media, Culture, Society*, Vol. 21, pp. 77–91.

Bennett, A. (2000) *Popular Music and Youth Culture: Music, Identity and Place*, Basingstoke: Macmillan.

Bennett, A. (2004) '"Virtual Subculture?" Youth, Identity and the Internet', in Bennett, A. and Kahn-Harris, K. (eds), *After Subculture: Critical Studies in Contemporary Youth Culture*, Basingstoke: Palgrave Macmillan, pp. 162–172.

Bennett, A. (2006) 'Punk's Not Dead: The Continuing Significance of Punk Rock for an Older Generation of Fans', *Sociology*, Vol. 40, No. 2, pp. 219–235.

Bennett, A. and Hodkinson, P. (2012) 'Introduction', in Bennett, A. and Hodkinson, P. (eds), *Ageing and Youth Cultures: Music, Style and Identity*, London: Berg, pp. 1–8.

Bennett, A. and Kahn-Harris, K. (eds) (2004) *After Subculture: Critical Studies in Contemporary Youth Culture*, London: Palgrave Macmillan.

Bennett, A. and Peterson, R. (eds) (2004) *Music Scenes: Local, Translocal and Virtual*, Nashville, TN: Vanderbilt University Press.

Bennett, S., Marton, K., and Kervin, L. (2008) 'The "Digital Natives" Debate: A Critical Review of the Evidence', *British Journal of Educational Technology*, Vol. 39, No. 5, pp. 775–786.

Bernard, J. (1961) 'Teen-Age Culture: An Overview', *The Annals of the American Academy of Political and Social Science*, Vol. 338, November, pp. 1–12.

Berry, M. (2019) 'Neo Liberalism and the Media', in Curran, J. and Hesmondhalgh, D. (eds), *Media and Society* (6th edn), London: Bloomsbury Academic, pp. 57–82.

Bestley, R., Dines, M., Gordon, A. and Guerra, P. (2019) 'The Punk Narrative Turned Upside Down: Transmissions from the Local to the Global', in Dines, M., Gordon, A. and Guerra, P. (eds), *The Punk Reader: Research Transmissions from the Local and the Global*, Bristol: Intellect, pp. 9–28.

Betul, K., McCrae, N. and Grealish, A. (2020) 'A Systematic Review: The Influence of Social Media on Depression, Anxiety and Psychological Distress in Adolescents', *International Journal of Adolescence and Youth*, Vol. 25, No. 1, pp. 79–93.

Bhabha, H. (1990) 'The Third Space', in Rutherford, J. (ed.), *Identity: Community, Culture, Difference*, London: Lawrence & Wishart, pp. 207–221.

Bhabha, H. (1994) *The Location of Culture*, London: Routledge.

Bhattacharya, A. (2018) 'The Number of Smartphone Users in India Will More than Double in Four Years', *Quartz India*, online, 4 December, https://qz.com/india/1483368/indias-smartphone-internet-usage-will-surge-by-2022-cisco-says/ (accessed 28 March 2020).

Bhushan, N. (2019) 'India's T-Series Becomes First YouTube Channel to Hit 100 Million Subscribers', *Billboard*, online, 30 May, https://www.billboard.com/articles/business/8513683/t-series-youtube-channel-100-million-subs-guinness-world-records (accessed 13 February 2020).

Bird, E. (2011) 'Are We All Produsers Now? Convergence and Media Audience Practices', *Cultural Studies*, Vol. 25, Nos. 4–5, pp. 502–516.

Bischoff, P. (2014) 'Tencent Owns 3 of the World's Biggest Social Networks', *Tech in Asia*, online, 3 November, https://www.techinasia.com/tencent-owns-3-worlds-5-biggest-social-networks (accessed 13 November, 2019).

Blackman, S. (2005) 'Youth Subcultural Theory: A Critical Engagement with the Concept, its Origins and Politics, from the Chicago School to Postmodernism', *Journal of Youth Studies*, Vol. 8, No. 1, pp. 1–20.

Blake, A. (2010) 'Americanisation and Popular Music in Britain', in Campbell, N., Davies, J. and McKay, G. (eds), *Issues in Americanisation and Culture*, Edinburgh: Edinburgh University Press, pp. 147–162.

Blanchflower, D. and Freeman, R. (2000i) 'Introduction', in Blanchflower, D. and Freeman, R. (eds), *Youth Employment and Joblessness in Advanced Countries*, Chicago: Chicago University Press, pp. 1–18.

Blanchflower, D. and Freeman, R. (2000ii) 'The Declining Economic Status of Young Workers in OECD Countries', in Blanchflower, D. and Freeman, R. (eds), *Youth Employment and Joblessness in Advanced Countries*, Chicago: Chicago University Press, pp. 19–56.

Bloustein, G. and Peters, M. (2011) *Youth, Music and Creative Cultures: Playing for Life*, Basingstoke: Palgrave Macmillan.

Bock, J. (2008) *Riot Grrrl: A Feminist Re-Interpretation of the Punk Narrative*, Saarbrucken: VDM Verlag Dr. Muller Aktiengesellschaft & Co. KG.

Bocquet, J. and Pierre-Adolphe, P. (2017) *Rap ta France: Histoires d'un Mouvement*, Paris: La Table Ronde.

Bolin, G. (2017) *Media Generations: Experience, Identity and Mediatised Social Change*, London: Routledge.

Bolton, P. (2012) *Education: Historical Statistics*, London: House of Commons Library.

Bonn, S. (2010) *Mass Deception: Moral Panic and the U.S. War on Iraq*, New Brunswick, NJ: Rutgers University Press.

Bouabid, A. (2016) 'Riots of the Other: An Analysis of Societal Reactions to Contemporary Riots in Disadvantaged Neighbourhoods in the Netherlands', *European Journal of Criminology*, Vol. 3, No. 6, pp. 714–726.

Bourdieu, P. (1986) 'The Forms of Capital', in Richardson, J. (ed.), *Handbook of Theory and Research for the Sociology of Education*, New York: Greenwood, pp. 241–258.

Bourdieu, P. (1991) *Language and Symbolic Power*, Cambridge: Polity.

boyd, d. (2008) 'Why Youth [Heart] Social Network Sites: The Role of Networked Publics in Teenage Social Life', in Buckingham, D. (ed.), *Youth, Identity and Social Media*, Cambridge, MA: MIT Press, pp. 119–142.

boyd, d. (2011) 'Social Network Sites as Networked Publics: Affordances, Dynamics, and Implications', in Papacharissi, Z. (ed.), *A Networked Self: Identity, Community, and Culture on Social Network Sites*, New York: Routledge, pp. 39–58.

boyd, d. (2014) *It's Complicated: The Social Lives of Networked Teens*, New Haven, CT: Yale University Press.

boyd, d. and Ellison, N. (2008) 'Social Network Sites: Definition, History, and Scholarship', *Journal of Computer-Mediated Communication*, Vol. 13, No. 1, pp. 210–230.

Boyd, J. (1973) 'Trends in Youth Culture', *Marxism Today*, Vol. 17, No. 12, pp. 375–378.

Boyd-Barrett, O. (1998) 'Media Imperialism Reformulated', in Thussu, D. (ed.), *Electronic Empires: Global Media and Local Resistance*, London: Arnold, pp. 157–176.

Boyd-Barrett, O. (2014) *Media Imperialism*, London: Sage.

Brah, A. (1996) *Cartographies of Diaspora: Contesting Identities*, London, Routledge.

Brandative (2016) '#Millennials - Your Guide to Understanding Generation Y in Asia', Brandative, online, 4 July, https://www.brandtative.com/millennials-guide-understanding-generation-y-asia/ (accessed 21 November 2019).

Brandle, L. (2017) 'Luis Fonsi and Daddy Yankee's "Despacito" Sets Global Streaming Record', *Billboard*, online, 19 July, https://www.billboard.com/articles/news/7873032/despacito-breaks-record-most-streamed-song-all-time (accessed 13 February 2020).

Brathwaite, K. (1971) *The Development of Creole Society in Jamaica, 1770–1820*, Oxford: Clarendon Press.

Brett, P., Wood, E. and Thomas, G. (eds) (2006) (2nd edn) *Queering the Pitch: The New Gay and Lesbian Musicology*, London: Routledge.

Breyvogel, W. (ed.) (1991) *Piraten, Swings und Junge Garde: Jugendwiderstand im Nationalsozialismus*, Bonn: Dietz Nachf.

Brickell, C. (2017) *Teenagers: The Rise of Youth Culture in New Zealand*, Auckland: Auckland University Press.

Brierly, S. (2005) *The Advertising Handbook*, London: Routledge.

Briggs, J. (2015) *Sounds French: Globalization, Cultural Communities, and Pop Music, 1958–1980*, Oxford: Oxford University Press.

Brown, A. (2017) 'Younger Men Play Video Games, but So Do a Diverse Group of Other Americans', Pew Research Center, online, 11 September, https://www.pewresearch.org/fact-tank/2017/09/11/younger-men-play-video-games-but-so-do-a-diverse-group-of-other-americans/ (accessed 13 January 2020).

Brown, B. and Merritt, R. (2002) *No Easy Answers: The Truth behind Death at Columbine*, New York: Lantern Books.

Brown, R.N. (2009) *Black Girlhood Celebration: Toward a Hip-hop Feminist Pedagogy*, New York: Peter Lang.

Bruns, A. (2008) *Blogs, Wikipedia, Second Life and Beyond: From Production to Produsage*, New York: Peter Lang.

Buckingham, D. (1993) 'Introduction: Reading Audiences – Young People and the Media', in Buckingham, D. (ed.), *Reading Audiences: Young People and the Media*, Manchester: Manchester University Press, pp. 1–23.

Buckingham, D. (2006) 'Is There a Digital Generation?', in Buckingham, D. and Willett, R. (eds), *Digital Generations: Children, Young People, and New Media*, Mahwah, NJ: Lawrence Erlbaum Associates, pp. 1–18.

Buckingham, D. (2014) 'Selling Youth: The Paradoxical Empowerment of the Young Consumer', in Buckingham, D., Bragg, S. and Kehilly, M.J. (eds), *Youth Cultures in the Age of Global Media*, Basingstoke: Palgrave Macmillan, pp. 202–224.

Buckingham, D. and Jensen, H. (2012) 'Beyond "Media Panics": Reconceptualising Public Debates about Children and Media', *Journal of Children and Media*, Vol. 6, No. 4, pp. 413–429.

Buckingham, D. and Kehily, M.J. (2014) 'Introduction', in Buckingham, D. and Kehily, M.J. (eds), *Youth Cultures in the Age of Global Media*, Basingstoke: Palgrave Macmillan.

Buckingham, D., Whiteman, N., Willet, R. and Burn, A. (2007) *The Impact of the Media on Children and Young People with a Particular Focus on Computer Games and the Internet - Prepared for the Byron Review on Children and New Technology*, London: Department for Children, Schools and Families.

Business Week (1946) 'Teen-Age Market: It's "Terrif"', 8 June, pp. 72–73.

Business Week (2002) 'A Teen Dream for Investors', online 15 July, https://www.bloomberg.com/news/articles/2002-07-14/a-teen-dream-for-investors (accessed 16 May 2020).

Busse, K. (2017) *Framing Fan Fiction: Literary and Social Practices in Fan Fiction Communities*, Iowa City, IA: University of Iowa Press.

Butler, J. (1988) 'Performative Acts and Gender Construction: An Essay in Phenomenology and Feminist Criticism', *Theatre Journal*, Vol. 40, No. 4, pp. 519–531.

Butler, J. (1990) *Gender Trouble: Feminism and the Subversion of Identity*, London: Routledge.

Butler, J. (1991) 'Imitation and Gender Insubordination', in Fuss, D. (ed.), *Inside/Out: Lesbian Theories, Gay Theories*, New York: Routledge, pp. 13–31.

Butler, J. (1993) *Bodies That Matter*, London: Routledge.

Bynner, J. (2005) 'Rethinking the Youth Phase of the Life-course: The Case for Emerging Adulthood?', *Journal of Youth Studies*, Vol. 8, No. 4, pp. 367–384.

Cain, G. (2010) 'South Korea Cracks Down on Gaming Addiction', *Time*, online, 20 April, https://content.time.com/time/world/article/0, 8599, 1983234-2, 00.html (accessed 21 January 2020).

Cain, S. (2017) '"Youthquake" Named 2017 Word of the Year by Oxford Dictionaries', *The Guardian*, online, 15 December, https://www.theguardian.com/books/2017/dec/15/youthquake-named-2017-word-of-the-year-by-oxford-dictionaries (accessed 26 March 2020).

Campion, C. (2005) 'J-Pop's Dream Factory', *The Guardian*, online, 21 August, https://www.theguardian.com/music/2005/aug/21/popandrock3 (accessed 28 March 2020).

Cannon, D. (1994) *Generation X and the New Work Ethic*, Demos Working Paper, London: Demos.

Carey, J. and Elton, M. (2010) *When Media Are New: Understanding the Dynamics of New Media Adoption and Use*, Ann Arbor, MI: University of Michigan Press.

Carter, C. and Weaver, C.K. (eds) (2006) *Critical Readings: Violence and the Media*, Buckingham: Open University Press.

Cassell, J. and Cramer, M. (2008) 'High Tech or High Risk: Moral Panics about Girls Online', in McPherson, T. (ed.), *Digital Youth, Innovation, and the Unexpected*, Cambridge, MA: MIT Press, pp. 53–75.

Catillo-Garsow, M. and J. (eds), (2016) *La Verdad: An International Dialogue on Hip Hop Latinidades*, Columbus, OH: Ohio State University Press.

Caulfield, K. (2018) 'From the Beatles to Kanye West & Beyond: Artists with the Most No. 1 Albums on the *Billboard* 200 Chart', *Billboard*, online, 6 October, https://www.billboard.com/articles/columns/chart-beat/7873993/beatles-jay-z-artists-most-number-1s-billboard-200 (accessed 8 December 2019).

Ceislik, M. and Pollock, G. (eds) (2002) *Young People in Risk Society: The Restructuring of Youth Identities and Transitions in Late Modernity*, London: Routledge.

Centre for Contemporary Cultural Studies (1982) *The Empire Strikes Back: Race and Racism in Seventies Britain*, London: Hutchinson.

Certeau, M. de (1984) *The Practice of Everyday Life*, Berkeley, CA: University of California Press.

Chang, J. (2007) *Can't Stop, Won't Stop: A History of the Hip-Hop Generation*, New York: Ebury Press.

Charters, W.W. (1933) *Motion Pictures and Youth: A Summary*, New York: The Macmillan Company.

Chibnall, S. (1985) 'Whistle and Zoot: The Changing Meaning of a Suit of Clothes', *History Workshop*, No. 20, pp. 56–81.

Chibnall, S. (1996) 'Counterfeit Yanks: War, Austerity and Britain's American Dream', in Davies, P. (ed.), *Representing and Imagining America*, Keele: Keele University Press, pp. 150–159.

Cho, S. and Chung J.Y. (2009) 'We Want Our MTV: Glocalisation of Cable Content in China, Korea and Japan', *Critical Arts: South-North Cultural and Media Studies*, Vol. 23, No. 3, pp. 321–341.

Choi, J. and Maliangkay, R. (2015) 'Why Fandom Matters to the International Rise of K-Pop', in Choi, J. and Maliangkay, R. (eds), *K-Pop: The International Rise of the Korean Music Industry*, Abingdon: Routledge, pp. 1–18.

Chudacoff, H. (1989) *How Old Are You?: Age Consciousness in American Culture*, Princeton, NJ: Princeton University Press.

Chudacoff, H. (1999) *The Age of the Bachelor: Creating an American Subculture*, Princeton, NJ: Princeton University Press.

Ciminelli, D. and Knox, K. (2005) *Homocore: The Loud and Raucous Rise of Queer Rock*, Los Angeles: Alyson Books.

Clark, M. (2018) *Hip-Hop in Africa: Prophets of the City and Dustyfoot Philosophers*, Athens, OH: Ohio University Press.

Clarke, G. (1990) (orig. pub. 1981) 'Defending Ski-Jumpers: A Critique of Theories of Youth Subcultures', in Frith, S. and Goodwin, A. (eds), *On Record: Rock, Pop and the Written Word*, London: Routledge, pp. 68–80.

Clarke, J. and Jefferson, T. (1976) 'Working Class Youth Cultures', in Mungham, G. and Pearson, G. (eds), *Working Class Youth Culture*, London: Routledge & Kegan Paul, pp. 138–158.

Clarke, J., Hall, S., Jefferson, T. and Roberts, B. (1976) 'Subcultures, Cultures and Class: A Theoretical Overview', in Hall, S. and Jefferson, T. (eds), *Resistance through Rituals: Youth Subcultures in Post-War Britain*, London: Hutchinson, pp. 9–74.

Clecak, P. (1983) *America's Quest for the Ideal Self: Dissent and Fulfilment in the 60s and 70s*, Oxford: Oxford University Press.

Clifford-Napoleone, A. (2017) *Queerness in Heavy Metal Music*, Abingdon: Routledge.

Cohen, J. (2019) 'How Mike "The Situation" Sorrentino Plans to Make His *Jersey Shore* Return', *E! Online*, online, 12 September, https://www.eonline.com/news/1072599/how-mike-the-situation-sorrentino-plans-to-make-his-jersey-shore-return (accessed 8 December 2019).

Cohen, P. (1972) 'Subcultural Conflict and the Working Class Community', *Working Papers in Cultural Studies*, No. 2, Birmingham: University of Birmingham.

Cohen, P. and Ainley, P. (2000) 'In the Country of the Blind?: Youth Studies and Cultural Studies in Britain', *Journal of Youth Studies*, Vol. 3, No. 1, pp. 79–95.

Cohen, S. (2002) (3rd edn) *Folk Devils and Moral Panics: The Creation of the Mods and Rockers*, London: Routledge.

Colby, S. and Ortman, J. (2014) 'The Baby Boom Cohort in the United States: 2012 to 2060: Population Estimates and Projections', *Current Population Reports*, May, United States Census Bureau, Washington DC: US Department of Commerce.

Coleman, J. (1961) *The Adolescent Society: The Social Life of the Teenager and its Impact on Education*, Glencoe: Free Press.

Coleman, J.C. (1992) 'The Nature of Adolescence', in Coleman, J.C. and Warren-Adamson, C. (eds), *Youth Policy in the 1990s: The Way Forward*, London: Routledge, pp. 8–27.

Comaroff, J. and Comaroff, J. (2005) 'Reflections on Youth, from the Past to the Postcolony', in Honwana, A. and De Boeck, F. (eds), *Makers and Breakers: Children and Youth in Postcolonial Africa*, Oxford: James Currey, pp. 19–30.

Comte, A. (1854) (trans. Martineau, H.) *The Positive Philosophy of Auguste Comte*, New York: D. Appleton & Co.

Condry, I. (2006) *Hip-Hop Japan: Rap and the Paths of Cultural Globalization*, Durham, NC: Duke University Press.

Connell, R.W. (1995) *Masculinities*, Berkeley, CA: University of California Press.

Cooper, A., Swartz, S. and Mahali, A. (2019) 'Disentangled, Decentred and Democratised: Youth Studies for the Global South', *Journal of Youth Studies*, Vol. 22, No. 1, pp. 29–45.

Corber, R. and Valocchi, S. (2003) 'Introduction', in Corber, R. and Valocchi, S. (eds), *Queer Studies: An Interdisciplinary Reader*, Oxford: Blackwell, pp. 1–20.

Corner, J. (2017) 'Fake News, Post-Truth and Media-Political Change', *Media, Culture and Society*, Vol. 39, No. 7, pp. 1100–1107.

Côté, J. (2014) 'The Dangerous Myth of Emerging Adulthood: An Evidence-Based Critique of a Flawed Developmental Theory', *Applied Developmental Science*, Vol. 18, No. 4, pp. 177–188.

Côté, J. and Bynner, J. (2008) 'Changes in the Transition to Adulthood in the UK and Canada: The Role of Structure and Agency in Emerging Adulthood', *Journal of Youth Studies*, Vol. 11, No. 3, pp. 251–268.

Coupland, D. (1991) *Generation X: Tales for an Accelerated Culture*, New York: St. Martin's Press.

Cox, A. (2015) *Shapeshifters: Black Girls and the Choreography of Citizenship*, Durham, NC: Duke University Press.

Crawford, A., Humphries, S. and Geddy, M. (2015) 'McDonald's: A Case Study in Glocalization', *Journal of Global Business Issues*, Vol. 9, No. 1, pp. 11–18.

Crime Statistics Agency (2016) 'How Has Youth Crime in Victoria Changed Over the Past Ten Years?', Crime Statistics Agency, online, 19 July, https://www.crimestatistics.vic.gov.au/research-and-evaluationpublicationsyouth-crime/how-has-youth-crime-in-victoria-changed-over-the (accessed 28 March 2020).

Critcher, C. (2000) '"*Still Raving*": Social Reaction to Ecstasy', *Leisure Studies*, No. 19, pp. 145–162.

Critcher, C., Hughes, J., Petley, J. and Rohloff, A. (eds) (2013) *Moral Panics in the Contemporary World*, London: Bloomsbury.

Cronin, T. (2014) 'Historicizing the Media Effects Debate', in Conboy, M. and Steel, J. (eds), *The Routledge Companion to British Media History*, London: Routledge, pp. 85–99.

Cross, B. (1992) *It's Not about a Salary: Rap, Race and Resistance in Los Angeles*, London: Verso.

Cuevo, H. and Miranola, A. (2019) 'Youth in the Global South: An Introduction', in Cuevo, H. and Miranola, A. (eds), *Youth, Inequality and Social Change in the Global South*, Singapore: Springer, pp. 1–13.

Cumberbatch, G. (2002) 'Media Effects: Continuing Controversies', in Cobley, P. and Briggs, A. (eds), *The Media: An Introduction*, Harlow: Pearson, pp. 259–271.

Cuthbertson, A. (2019) 'Children in China Will Be Banned from Playing Video Games at Night or for More than 90 Minutes a Day', *The Independent*, online, 7 November, https://www.independent.co.uk/life-style/gadgets-and-tech/gaming/china-gaming-ban-video-game-addiction-a9188806.html (accessed 21 January 2020).

Czarnecki, S. (2019) 'Study: PewDiePie is YouTube's Highest Earner At $8m a Month', *PR Week*, online, 6 August, https://www.prweek.com/article/1593191/study-pewdiepie-youtubes-highest-earner-8m-month (accessed 8 December 2019).

D'Acci, J. (2004) 'Cultural Studies, Television Studies, and the Crisis in the Humanities', in Spigel, L. and Olsson, J. (eds), *Television after TV: Essays on a Medium in Transition*, Durham, NC: Duke University Press, pp. 418–446.

Daliot-Bul, M. (2009) 'Japan Brand Strategy: The Taming of "Cool Japan" and the Challenges of Cultural Planning in a Postmodern Age', *Social Science Japan Journal*, Vol. 12, No. 2, pp. 247–266.

Davies, H. (1978) *The Beatles: The Authorized Biography*, London: Granada.

Davis, J. (1990) *Youth and the Condition of Britain: Images of Adolescent Conflict*, London: Athlone.

Davis, K. (2014) 'Youth Identities in the Digital Age: The Anchoring Role of Friends in Young People's Approaches to Online Identity Expression', in Bennett, A. and Robards, B. (eds), *Mediated Youth Cultures: The Internet, Belonging and New Cultural Configurations*, Basingstoke: Palgrave Macmillan, pp. 11–25.

Davis, N. (1999) *Youth Crisis: Growing Up in the High-Risk Society*, Westport, CT: Praeger.

Daxue Consulting (2017) 'Chinese Millennials' Spending Behaviors: Pay for Quality, Not Necessity, Despite a Slowing Economy', Daxue Consulting, online, 27 February, http://daxueconsulting.com/chinese-millennials-spending-behaviors/ (accessed 23 November 2017).

De Silva, M. (2019) 'Spotify is Still the King of Music Streaming - For Now', *Quartz*, online, 28 October, https://qz.com/1736762/spotify-grows-monthly-active-users-and-turns-profit-shares-jump-15-percent/ (accessed 13 November, 2019).

Dennis, J. (2006) *Queering Teen Culture: All-American Boys and Same-Sex Desire in Film and Television*, Abingdon: Routledge.

Department of Health and Human Services (1998) *Trends in the Well-Being of America's Children and Youth*, Washington, DC: Department of Health and Human Services.

DeSouza, P., Kumar, S. and Shastri, S. (2009) *Indian Youth in a Transforming World: Attitudes and Perceptions*, Delhi: Sage.

Dinnie, K. (2016) (2nd edn) *Nation Branding: Concepts, Issues, Practice*, Abingdon: Routledge.

Doherty, T. (2002) (2nd edn) *Teenagers and Teenpics: The Juvenilization of American Movies in the 1950s*, Philadelphia, PA: Temple University Press.

Downes, D. (1966) *The Delinquent Solution: A Study in Subcultural Theory*, London: Routledge & Kegan Paul.

Downey, G. (2001) 'Virtual Webs, Physical Technologies, and Hidden Workers', *Technology and Culture*, Vol. 42, No. 2, pp. 209–235.

Draper, N. (2012) 'Is Your Teen at Risk?': Discourses of Adolescent Sexting in United States Television News', *Journal of Children and Media*, Vol. 6, No. 2, pp. 221–236.

Dredge, S. (2019) 'Tencent Music Now Has 31m Paying Online-Music Users', *Music:)ally*, online, 14 August, https://musically.com/2019/08/14/tencent-music-now-has-31m-paying-online-music-users/ (accessed 28 March 2020).

Driscoll, C. (2002) *Girls: Feminine Adolescence in Popular Culture and Cultural Theory*, New York: Columbia University Press.

Driver, S. (2006) 'Virtually Queer Youth Communities of Girls and Birls: Dialogical Spaces of Identity Work and Desiring Exchanges', in Buckingham, D. and Willet, R. (eds), *Digital Generations: Children, Young People, and New Media*, Mahwah, NJ: Lawrence Erlbaum Associates, pp. 229–250.

Driver, S. (2007) *Queer Girls and Popular Culture: Reading, Resisting, and Creating Media*, New York: Peter Lang.

Driver, S. (ed.) (2008) *Queer Youth Cultures*, Albany, NY: State University of New York Press.

Drotner, K. (1992) 'Modernity and Media Panics', in Skovmand, M. and Schröder, K. C. (eds), *Media Cultures: Reappraising Transnational Media*, London: Routledge, pp. 42–62.

Drotner, K. (1999) 'Dangerous Media? Panic Discourses and Dilemmas of Modernity', *Pedagogica Historica*, Vol. 35, No. 3, pp. 593–616.

Du Gay, P., Hall, S., Janes, L., Mackay, H. and Negus, K. (1997) *Doing Cultural Studies: The Story of the Sony Walkman*, London: Sage.

Dubois, E. and Blank, G. (2018) 'The Echo Chamber is Overstated: The Moderating Effect of Political Interest and Diverse Media', *Information, Communication and Society*, Vol. 21, No. 5, pp. 729–745.

Duggan, M. (2017) 'Online Harassment 2017', Pew Research Center, online, https://www.pewresearch.org/internet/2017/07/11/online-harassment-2017/ (accessed 30 April 2020).

Durkin, K. (2010) 'Videogames and Young People with Developmental Disorders', *Review of General Psychology*, Vol. 14, No.2, pp. 122–140.

Dwyer, T. (2010) *Media Convergence*, Maidenhead: Open University Press.

Dyer, R. (1979) 'In Defence of Disco', *Gay Left*, No. 9, pp. 20–23.

Dyer, R. (1997) *White*, London: Routledge.

Early, G. (2004) (2nd edn) *One Nation under a Groove: Motown and American Culture*, Ann Arbor, MI: University of Michigan Press.

Echols, A. (2010) *Hot Stuff: Disco and the Remaking of American Culture*, New York: W. W. Norton.

Edmunds, J. and Turner, B. (2002) *Generations, Culture and Society*, Buckingham: Open University Press.

Eggebean, D. and Sturgeon, S. (2006) 'Demography of the Baby Boomers', in Whitbourne, S. and Willis, S. (eds), *The Baby Boomers Grow Up: Contemporary Perspectives on Midlife*, Mahwah, NJ: Lawrence Erlbaum Associates, pp. 3–22.

Eisenstadt, S.N. (1956) *Generation to Generation: Age Groups and Social Structure*, Glencoe, IL: Free Press.

Erikson, E. (1950) *Childhood and Society*, New York: W. W. Norton.

Escobar, E. (1996) 'Zoot-Suiters and Cops: Chicano Youth and the Los Angeles Police Department during World War II', in Erenberg, L. and Hirsch, S. (eds), *The War in American Culture: Society and Consciousness during World War* II, Chicago: University of Chicago Press, pp. 284–312.

Esser, A., Jensen, P., Keinonen, H. and Lemor, A. (2016) 'The Duality of Banal Nationalism: Television Audiences and the Musical Talent Competition Genre', in Aveyard, K., Moran, A. and Jensen, P. (eds), *New Patterns in Global Television Formats*, Bristol: Intellect, pp. 295–310.

European Commission (Eurostat) (2017) 'Statistics Explained: Unemployment Statistics', http://ec.europa.eu/eurostat/statistics-explained/index.php/Unemployment_statistics, European Commission, online (accessed 23 September 2017).

Eyerman, R. and Jamison, A. (1998) *Music and Social Movements: Mobilizing Traditions in the Twentieth Century*, Cambridge: Cambridge University Press.

Facer, K., Furlong, J., Furlong, R., and Sutherland, R. (2003) *Screenplay: Children and Computing in the Home*, London: Routledge.

Farkas, J. and Schou, J. (2019) *Post-Truth, Fake News and Democracy: Mapping the Politics of Falsehood*, London: Routledge.

Fass, P. (1978) *The Damned and the Beautiful: American Youth in the 1920s*, Oxford: Oxford University Press.

Fast, S. and Jennex, C. (2019) 'Introduction', in Fast, S. and Jennex, C. (eds), *Popular Music and the Politics of Hope: Queer and Feminist Interventions*, Abingdon: Routledge, pp. 1–19.

Federal Bureau of Investigation (FBI) (2015) 'Former State Senator Leland Yee and Three Others Plead Guilty to Racketeering', U.S. Attorney's Office, online, 1 July, https://www.fbi.gov/contact-us/field-offices/sanfrancisco/news/press-releases/former-state-senator-leland-yee-and-three-others-plead-guilty-to-racketeering (accessed 21 January 2020).

Feldman-Barrett, C. (2009) *'We Are the Mods': A Transnational History of a Youth Subculture*, New York: Peter Lang.

Feldman-Barrett, C. (2018) 'Back to the Future: Mapping a Historic Turn in Youth Studies', *Journal of Youth Studies*, Vol. 21, No. 6, pp. 733–746.

Ferguson, C.J. (2007i) 'Evidence for Publication Bias in Video Game Violence Effects Literature: A Meta-Analytic Review', *Aggression and Violent Behavior*, Vol. 12, No. 4, pp. 470–482.

Ferguson, C.J. (2007ii) 'The Good, the Bad and the Ugly: A Meta-Analytic Review of Positive and Negative Effects of Violent Video Games', *Psychiatric Quarterly*, Vol. 78, No.4, pp. 309–316.

Ferguson, C.J. (2010) 'Blazing Angels or Resident Evil? Can Violent Video Games Be a Force for Good?', *Review of General Psychology*, Vol. 14, No. 2, pp. 68–81.

Ferguson, C.J. (2013i) *Adolescents, Crime, and the Media: A Critical Analysis*, New York: Springer.

Ferguson, C.J. (2013ii) 'Letter to APA on Policy Statement on Violent Media', online, 7 October, https://www.stetson.edu/today/2013/10/letter-to-apa-on-policy-statement-on-violent-media/ (accessed 13 January 2020).

Ferguson, C.J. (2013iii) 'Violent Video Games and the Supreme Court: Lessons for the Scientific Community in the Wake of Brown v. Entertainment Merchants Association', *American Psychologist*, Vol. 68, No. 2, pp. 57–74.

Ferguson, C.J. (2015) 'Do Angry Birds Make for Angry Children? A Meta-Analysis of Video Game Influences on Children's and Adolescents' Aggression, Mental Health, Prosocial Behavior, and Academic Performance', *Perspectives on Psychological Science*, Vol. 10, No. 5, pp. 646–666.

Ferguson, C.J. and Colwell, J. (2017) 'Understanding Why Scholars Hold Different Views on the Influence of Video Games on Public Health', *Journal of Communication*, Vol. 67, No. 3, pp. 305–327.

Ferguson, C.J. and Colwell, J. (2019) 'Lack of Consensus Among Scholars on the Issue of Video Game "Addiction"', *Psychology of Popular Media Culture*, advance online publication, https://doi.org/10.1037/ppm0000234 (accessed 21 January 2020).

Ferguson, C.J. and Kilburn, J. (2009) 'The Public Health Risks of Media Violence: A Meta-Analytic Review', *Journal of Pediatrics*, Vol. 154, No. 5, pp. 759–763.

Ferguson, C.J. and Kilburn, J. (2010) 'Much Ado about Nothing: The Misestimation and Over-Interpretation of Violent Video Game Effects in Eastern and Western Nations: Comment on Anderson et al. (2010)', *Psychological Bulletin*, Vol. 36, No. 2, pp. 174–178.

Ferguson, N. (2009) 'Think Again: Power', *Foreign Policy*, online, 3 November, https://foreignpolicy.com/2009/11/03/think-again-power/ (accessed 28 March 2020).

Ferrell, J., Hayward, K., Morrison, W. and Presdee, M. (2004) *Cultural Criminology Unleashed*, London: Routledge.

Ferrer, R. (2018) 'Who are the Millenials?', CaixaBank Research, online, 16 April, https://www.caixabankresearch.com/en/who-are-millennials (accessed 21 November 2019).

Film Federation of India (2019) 'Indian Feature Films Certified from 1–4-2018 to 31–33-2019', Film Federation of India, online, 31 March, www.filmfed.org/IFF2019.html (accessed 13 February 2020).

Fiske, J. (1992) 'The Cultural Economy of Fandom', in Lewis, L. (ed.), *The Adoring Audience: Fan Culture and Popular Media*, London: Routledge, pp. 30–49.

Flew, T. (2016) 'Entertainment Media, Cultural Power, and Post-Globalization: The Case of China's International Media Expansion and the Discourse of Soft Power', *Global Media and China*, Vol. 1, No. 4, pp. 278–294.

Foucault, M. (trans. Hurley, R.) (1978) *The History of Sexuality Vol. 1: An Introduction*, New York: Pantheon Books.

Fowler, D. (1995) *The First Teenagers: The Lifestyle of Young Wage-Earners in Interwar Britain*, London: Woburn.

Fox, S. (1985) *The Mirror Makers: A History of American Advertising and Its Creators*, New York: Vintage.

Frand, J. (2000) 'The Information-Age Mindset: Changes in Students and Implications for Higher Education', *EDUCAUSE Review*, No. 35, September–October, pp. 14–24.

Frank, T. (1997) *The Conquest of Cool: Business Culture, Counterculture and the Rise of Hip Consumerism*, Chicago: University of Chicago Press.

Freeman, R. and Halton, K. (1964) 'Changing Faces', *Sunday Times Magazine*, 2 August, pp. 12–19.

Frith, S. (1978) *The Sociology of Rock*. London: Constable.

Fromm, J. and Garton, C. (2013) *Marketing to Millennials: Reach the Largest and Most Influential Generation of Consumers Ever*, New York: AMACOM.

Fu, J. (2018) 'Chinese Youth Performing Identities and Navigating Belonging Online', *Journal of Youth Studies*, Vol. 21, No. 2, pp. 129–143.

Fuchs, C. (2011) 'Web 2.0, Surveillance and Prosumption', *Surveillance and Society*, Vol. 8, No. 3, pp. 288–309.

Fuchs, C. (2014) *Social Media: A Critical Introduction*, London: Sage.

Furedi, F. (2006) *Culture of Fear Revisited: Risk-Taking and the Morality of Low Expectation*, London: Continuum.

Furlong, A. (2009) 'Reconceptualizing Youth and Young Adulthood', in Furlong, A. (ed.), *Youth and Young Adulthood: New Perspectives and Agendas*, London: Routledge, pp. 1–2.

Furlong, A. (2013) *Youth Studies: An Introduction*, London: Routledge.

Furlong, A. and Cartmel, F. (1997) *Young People and Social Change: Individualization and Risk in Late Modernity*, Buckingham: Open University Press.

Furlong, A. and Cartmel, F. (2007) (2nd edn) *Young People and Social Change: New Perspectives*, Maidenhead: Open University Press.

Gabriel, T. (1995) 'A Generation's Heritage: After the Boom, a Boomlet', *New York Times*, 12 February.

Gaines, D. (1991) *Teenage Wasteland: Suburbia's Dead End Kids*, New York: Pantheon Books.

Garnham, N. (1998) 'Political Economy and Cultural Studies: Reconciliation or Divorce?', in Storey, J. (ed.), *Cultural Theory and Popular Culture: A Reader*, Harlow: Pearson, pp. 600–612.

Garofalo, R. (1999) 'From Music Publishing to MP3: Music Industry in the Twentieth Century', *American Music*, Vol. 12, No.3, pp. 318–354.

Garratt, S. (1998) *Adventures in Wonderland: A Decade of Club Culture*, London: Headline.

Gauntlett, D. (2001) 'The Worrying Influence of "Media Effects" Studies', in Barker, M. and Petley, J. (eds), *Ill Effects: The Media/Violence Debate* (2nd edn), London: Routledge, pp. 47–62.

Gauntlett, D. (2005) *Moving Experiences: Understanding Television's Influences and Effects*, Luton: John Libbey.

Gendron, B. (1986) 'Theodor Adorno Meets the Cadillacs', in Modleski, T. (ed.), *Studies in Entertainment*, Bloomington, IN: Indiana University Press, pp. 18–36.

Genova, V. (2018) 'PewDiePie Reveals His Channel Statistics After Alinity Suggested All His Fans Were 9 Year Olds', *Dexerto.com*, online, 1 July, https://www.dexerto.com/entertainment/pewdiepie-reveals-his-channel-statistics-after-alinity-suggested-all-his-fans-were-9-year-olds-110491 (accessed 8 December 2019).

George, N. (2005) (2nd edn) *Hip Hop America*, New York: Penguin.

Giddens, A. (1990) *The Consequences of Modernity*, Cambridge: Polity Press.

Giddens, A. (1991) *Modernity and Self-Identity: Self and Society in the Late Modern Age*, Stanford, CA: Stanford University Press.

Giddens, A. (1999) *Runaway World: How Globablization is Reshaping Our Lives*, London: Profile Books.

Gilbert, J. (1986) *A Cycle of Outrage: America's Reaction to the Juvenile Delinquent in the 1950s*, Oxford: Oxford University Press.

Gill, A. (1994) *An Honourable Defeat: A History of German Resistance to Hitler*, London: Heinemann.

Gillard, P., Wale, K. and Bow, A. (1998) 'The Friendly Phone', in Howard, S. (ed.), *Wired-Up: Young People and the Electronic Media*, London: UCL Press, pp. 135–152.

Gillespie, M. (1995) *Television, Ethnicity and Cultural Change*, London: Routledge.

Gillespie, M. (2000) 'Transnational Communications and Diaspora Communities', in Cottle, S. (ed.), *Ethnic Minorities and the Media*, Buckingham: Open University Press, pp. 164–178.

Gillett, C. (1996) (2nd edn) *The Sound of the City: The Rise of Rock and Roll*, London: Souvenir.

Gillis, J. (1974) *Youth and History*, New York: Academic Press.

Gilroy, P. (1987) *'There Ain't No Black in the Union Jack': The Cultural Politics of Race and Nation*, London: Hutchinson.

Gilroy, P. (1993i) *The Black Atlantic: Modernity and Double Consciousness*, London: Verso.

Gilroy, P. (1993ii) *Small Acts: Thoughts on the Politics of Black Cultures*, London: Serpent's Tail.

Gilroy, P. (1994) 'Get Up, Get Into It and Get Involved: Soul, Civil Rights and Black Power', in Storey, J. (ed.), *Cultural Theory and Popular Culture: A Reader*, London, Harvester Wheatsheaf, pp. 88–98.

Giroux, H. (1996) *Fugitive Cultures: Race, Violence and Youth*, London: Routledge.

Giroux, H. (1997) *Channel Surfing: Race Talk and the Destruction of Today's Youth*, Basingstoke: Macmillan.

Giroux, H. (2012) *Disposable Youth: Racialized Memories, and the Culture of Cruelty*, New York: Routledge.

Gladwell, M. (1997) 'Annals of Style', *New Yorker*, 17 March, pp. 77–88.

Glassner, B. (2018) (2nd edn) *The Culture of Fear: Why Americans Are Afraid of the Wrong Things*, New York: Basic Books.

Goff, D. (2013) 'A History of the Social Media Industries', in Albarran, A. (ed.), *The Social Media Industries*, London: Routledge, pp. 16–45.

Goggin, G. (2006) *Cell Phone Culture: Mobile Technology in Everyday Life*, London: Routledge.

Goggin, G. (2010) 'Official and Unofficial Mobile Media in Australia: Youth, Panics, Innovation', in Donald, S., Anderson, T. and Spry, D. (eds), *Youth, Society and Mobile Media in Asia*, London: Routledge, pp. 120–134.

Go-Globe (2013) 'Social Media in China: Statistics and Trends', *Go-Globe*, online, 12 March, https://www.go-globe.com/social-media-china/ (accessed 14 November 2019).

Golnaraghi, G. and Daghar, S. (2017) 'Feminism in the Third Space: Critical Discourse Analysis of Mipsterz Women and Grassroots Activism', in Pullen, A., Harding, N. and Philips, M. (eds), *Feminist and Queer Theorists Debate the Future of Critical Management Studies* (Dialogues in Management Studies, Vol. 3), Bingley: Emerald Publishing, pp. 103–127.

Golpushnezhad, E. (2015) 'Queering Tehran: Discovering Gay Rap in Iran', in Feldman-Barrett, C. (ed.), *Lost Histories of Youth Culture*, New York: Peter Lang, pp. 123–140.

Golub, A. and Lingley, K. (2008) '"Just *Like the Qing Empire*": Internet Addiction, MMOGs, and Moral Crisis in Contemporary China', *Games and Culture*, Vol. 31, No. 1, pp. 59–75.

Gonick, M. (2006) 'Between "Girl Power" and "Reviving Ophelia": Constituting the Neoliberal Girl Subject', *NWSA Journal*, Vol. 18, No. 2, pp. 1–23.

Goode, E. and Ben-Yehuda, N. (2011) (2nd edn) *Moral Panics: The Social Construction of Deviance*, Oxford: Wiley-Blackwell.

Goodwin, M., Raines, T. and Cutts, D. (2017) 'What Do Europeans Think about Muslim Immigration?', Chatham House, online, 7 February, https://www.chatham house.org/expert/comment/what-do-europeans-think-about-muslim-immigration (accessed 28 March 2020).

Grant, A. and Wilkinson, J. (eds), (2009) *Media Convergence: The State of the Field*, Oxford: Oxford University Press.

Gray, J., Harrington, L., and Sandvoss, C. (eds), (2007) *Fandom: Identities and Communities in a Mediated World*, New York: New York University Press.

Graziani, T. (2018) 'How Douyin Became China's Top Short-Video App in 500 Days', *WalktheChat*, online, 30 July, https://walkthechat.com/douyin-became-chinas-top -short-video-app-500-days/ (accessed 8 December 2019).

Green, C. and Bavelier, D. (2007) 'Action Video Game Experience Alters the Spatial Resolution of Vision', *Psychological Science*, Vol. 18, No. 1, pp. 88–94.

Greenwood, J., Seshadri, A. and Vandenbroucke, G. (2005) 'The Baby Boom and Baby Bust', *American Economic Review*, Vol. 95, No. 1, pp. 183–207.

Griffin A. (2019) 'Trump to Launch Crackdown on Violent Video Games after Mass Shootings', *The Independent*, online, 5 August, https://www.independent.co.uk/life-style/gadgets-and-tech/gaming/trump-video-games-toledo-shooting-8chan-el-pa so-press-conference-today-a9040066.html (accessed 13 January 2020).

Griffin, C. (2011) 'The Trouble with Class: Researching Youth, Class and Culture Beyond the "Birmingham School"', *Journal of Youth Studies*, Vol. 14, No. 3, pp. 245–259.

Griffiths, M., Kuss, D., Lopez-Fernandez, O. and Pontes, H. (2017) 'Problematic Gaming Exists and Is an Example of Disordered Gaming: Commentary on: Scholar's Open Debate Paper on the World Health Organization ICD-11 Gaming Disorder Proposal (Aarseth et al.)', *Journal of Behavioral Addictions*, Vol. 6, No. 3, pp. 296–301.

Griffiths, M., van Rooij, A., Kardefelt-Winther, D., Starcevic, V. et al. (2016) 'Working towards an International Consensus on Criteria for Assessing Internet Gaming Disorder: A Critical Commentary on Petry et al. 2014)', *Addiction*, Vol. 111, No. 1, pp. 167–175.

Grizzard, M., Lewis, R., and Tamborini, R. (2014) 'Being Bad in a Video Game Can Make Us Morally Sensitive', *Cyberpsychology, Behavior, and Social Networking*, Vol. 17, No. 8, online, https://www.liebertpub.com/doi/10.1089/cyber.2013.0658 (accessed 13 January 2020).

Grossman, D. (1995) *On Killing: The Psychological Cost of Learning to Kill in War and Society*, Boston, MA: Little, Brown & Co.

Grossman, D. and DeGaetano, G. (1999) *Stop Teaching Our Kids to Kill: A Call to Action Against TV, Movie and Video Game Violence*, New York: Crown.

Grossman, L. (2005) 'The Wander Years', *Time*, 24 January, pp. 42–53.

Grotum, T. (1994) *Die Halbstarken: Zur Geschichte einer Jugendkultur der 50er Jahre*, Frankfurt: Campus.

Guardian (2011) '*Jersey Shore*'s The Situation Offered Cash Not to Wear Abercrombie & Fitch', *The Guardian*, online, 17 August, https://www.theguardian.com/media/2011/aug/17/jersey-shore-situation-abercrombie-fitch (accessed 21 November 2019).

Guardian (2012) 'NRA: Full Statement by Wayne LaPierre in Response to Newtown Shootings', *The Guardian*, online, 21 December, https://www.theguardian.com/world/2012/dec/21/nra-full-statement-lapierre-newtown#maincontent (accessed 13 January 2020).

Guardian (2019) 'Facebook to Be Fined $5bn for Cambridge Analytica Privacy Violations', *The Guardian*, online, 12 July, https://www.theguardian.com/technology/2019/jul/12/facebook-fine-ftc-privacy-violations (accessed 21 November 2019).

Gunter, B. and Farnham, A. (1998) *Children as Consumers: A Psychological Analysis of the Young People's Market*, London: Routledge.

Hafez, K. (2007) *The Myth of Media Globalization*, Cambridge: Polity.

Hafiz, Y. (2014) 'Mipsterz' Co-Creator Abbas Rattani Speaks out on Controversial Video', *HuffPost*, online, 25 January, https://www.huffingtonpost.co.uk/entry/mipsterz-creator-abbas-rattani_n_4394578?ri18n=tru/ (accessed 3 March 2020).

Hague, S., Street, J. and Savigny, H. (2008) 'The Voice of the People?: Musicians as Political Actors', *Cultural Politics*, Vol. 4, No. 1, pp. 5–24.

Hajdu, D. (2008) *The Ten Cent Plague: The Great Comic Book Scare and How it Changed America*, New York: Farrar, Straus & Giroux.

Halberstam, J. (2003) 'What's That Smell? Queer Temporalities and Subcultural Lives', *International Journal of Cultural Studies*, Vol. 6, No 3, pp. 313–333.

Halberstam, J. (2005) *In a Queer Time and Place: Transgender Bodies and Subcultural Lives*, New York: New York University Press.

Hall, G.S. (1904) *Adolescence: Its Psychology and Its Relations to Physiology, Anthropology, Sociology, Sex, Crime and Education*, 2 Vols, New York: D. Appleton & Co.

Hall, S. (1980i) 'Encoding/Decoding', in Hall, S., Hobson, D., Lowe, A. and Willis, P. (eds), *Culture, Media, Language*, London: Hutchinson, pp. 128–138.

Hall, S. (1980ii) 'Cultural Studies and the Centre: Some Problematics and Problems', in Hall, S., Hobson, D., Lowe, A. and Willis, P. (eds), *Culture, Media, Language*, London: Hutchinson, pp. 15–47.

Hall, S. (1987) 'Minimal Selves', in Appignanesi, L. (ed.), *Identity*, ICA Documents6, London: Institute of Contemporary Arts, pp. 44–46.

Hall, S. (1992i) 'New Ethnicities', in Donald, J. and Rattansi, A. (eds), *'Race', Culture and Difference*, London: Sage, pp. 252–259.

Hall, S. (1992ii) 'The Question of Cultural Identity', in Hall, S., Held, D. and McGrew, T. (eds), *Modernity and its Futures*, Oxford: Polity Press, pp. 273–327.

Hall, S. and Jefferson, T. (eds) (1976) *Resistance through Rituals: Youth Subcultures in Post-War Britain*, London: Hutchinson.

Hall, S., Critcher, C., Jefferson, T., Clarke, J. and Roberts, B. (1978) *Policing the Crisis: Mugging, the State and Law and Order*, London: Macmillan.

Hamblett, C. and Deverson, J. (1964) *Generation X*, London: Anthony Gibbs & Phillips.

Handyside, S. and Ringrose, J. (2017) 'Snapchat Memory and Youth Digital Sexual Cultures: Mediated Temporality, Duration and Affect', *Journal of Gender Studies*, Vol. 26, No. 3, pp. 347–360.

Hardy, J. (2014) *Critical Political Economy of the Media: An Introduction*, London: Routledge.

Harris, A. (2004) *Future Girl: Young Women in the Twenty-First Century*, London: Routledge.

Harris, J. (2001) *The Effects of Computer Games on Young Children: A Review of the Research*, RDS Occasional Paper, No. 72, London: Home Office, Research, Development and Statistics Directorate.

Harvey, D. (1989) *The Condition of Postmodernity: An Enquiry into the Conditions of Cultural Change*, Oxford: Basil Blackwell.

Hasinoff, A. (2012) 'Sexting as Media Production: Rethinking Social Media and Sexuality', *New Media and Society*, Vol. 15, No. 4, pp. 449–465.

Hasinoff, A. (2015) *Sexting Panic: Rethinking Criminalization, Privacy, and Consent*, Urbana, IL: University of Illinois Press.

Healy, M. (1996) *Gay Skins: Class Masculinity and Queer Appropriation*. London: Cassell.

Hearn, A. and Schoenhoff, S. (2016) 'From Celebrity to Influencer: Tracing the Diffusion of Celebrity Value across the Data Stream', in Marshall, P.D. and Redmond, S. (eds), *A Companion to Celebrity*, Chichester: John Wiley & Sons, pp. 194–212.

Heath, J. and Potter, A. (2004) *Nation of Rebels: Why Counterculture Became Consumer Culture*, New York: HarperBusiness.

Hebdige, D. (1976) 'The Meaning of Mod', in Hall, S. and Jefferson, T. (eds), *Resistance through Rituals: Youth Subcultures in Post-war Britain*, London: Hutchinson, pp. 87–98.

Hebdige, D. (1979) *Subculture: The Meaning of Style*, London: Methuen.

Hebdige, D. (1987) *Cut 'n' Mix: Culture, Identity and Caribbean Music*, London: Comedia.

Hebdige, D. (1988i) 'Hiding in the Light: Youth Surveillance and Display', in Hebdige, D. (ed.), *Hiding in the Light: On Images and Things*, London: Routledge, pp. 17–36.

Hebdige, D. (1988ii) 'Towards a Cartography of Taste, 1935–1962', in Hebdige, D. (ed.), *Hiding in the Light: On Images and Things*, London, Routledge, pp. 45–76.

Hechinger, G. and Hechinger, F. (1962) *Teen-age Tyranny*, New York: Morrow.

Hechinger, G. and Hechinger, F. (1965) 'In the Time It Takes You to Read These Lines the American Teen-Ager Will Have Spent $2,378.22', *Esquire*, July 1965, pp. 65–68, 113.

Heggarty, M. (2008) *Victory Girls, Khaki-Wackies, and Patriotutes: The Regulation of Female Sexuality during World War II*, New York: New York University Press.

Heinz, W. (2009) 'Youth Transitions in an Age of Uncertainty', in Furlong, A. (ed.), *Handbook of Youth and Young Adulthood: New Perspectives and Agendas*, Abingdon: Routledge, pp. 3–13.

Helgren, J. and Vasconcellos C. (eds) (2010) *Girlhood: A Global History*, New Brunswick, NJ: Rutgers University Press.

Hellmann, J. (1997) *The Kennedy Obsession: The American Myth of JFK*, New York: Columbia University Press.

Helsper, J. and Eynon, R. (2010) 'Digital Natives: Where is the Evidence?', *British Educational Research Journal*, Vol. 36, No. 3, pp. 503–520.

Hendry, L. and Kloep, M. (2010) 'How Universal is Emerging Adulthood? An Empirical Example', *Journal of Youth Studies*, Vol. 13, No. 2, pp. 169–179.

Hernandez, D. (2010) *Oye Como Va!: Hybridity and Identity in Latino Popular Music*, Philadelphia, PA: Temple University Press.

Herman, E. and McChesney, R. (1997) *The Global Media: The New Missionaries of Global Capitalism*, London: Cassell Academic.

Hesmondhalgh, D. (2007) 'Recent Concepts in Youth Cultural Studies: Critical Reflections from the Sociology of Music', in Hodkinson, P. and Deicke, W. (eds), *Youth Cultures: Scenes, Subcultures and Tribes*, London: Routledge, pp. 37–50.

Hesmondhalgh, D. (2013) *Why Music Matters*, Oxford: Wiley Blackwell.

Hesmondhalgh, D. (2019) (4th edn) *The Cultural Industries*, London: Sage.

Hier, S. (ed.) (2011) *Moral Panic and the Politics of Anxiety*, London: Routledge.

Hilgard J., Engelhardt, C. and Rouder J. (2017) 'Overstated Evidence for Short-term Effects of Violent Games on Affect and Behavior: A Reanalysis of Anderson et al. 2010', *Psychological Bulletin*, Vol. 143, No. 7, pp. 757–774.

Hill, J. (1991) 'Television and Pop: The Case of the 1950s', in Corner, J. (ed.), *Popular Television in Britain: Studies in Cultural History*, London: BFI, pp. 90–107.

Hills, M. (2002) *Fan Cultures*, London: Routledge.

Hind, J. and Mosco, S. (1985) *Rebel Radio: The Full Story of British Pirate Radio*, London: Pluto Press.

Hine, T. (1999) *The Rise and Fall of the American Teenager*, New York: Avon.

Hodkinson, P. (2002) *Goth: Identity, Style and Subculture*, Oxford: Berg.

Hodkinson, P. (2011) 'Ageing in a Spectacular "Youth Culture": Continuity, Change and Community amongst Older Goths', *British Journal of Sociology*, Vol. 62, No. 2, pp. 262–282.

Hodkinson, P. and Deicke, W. (eds) (2007) *Youth Cultures: Scenes, Subcultures and Tribes*, London: Routledge.

Hoggart, R. (1957) *The Uses of Literacy*, London: Chatto & Windus.

Hollander, S.C. and Germain, R. (1993) *Was There a Pepsi Generation before Pepsi Discovered It?: Youth-Based Segmentation in Marketing*, Chicago: American Marketing Association.

Hollingshead, A. (1949) *Elmstown's Youth: The Impact of Social Classes on Adolescents*, New York: Wiley.

Holloway, S., and Valentine, G. (2003) *Cyberkids: Children in the Information Age*, London: Routledge.

Holton, R. (2005) *Making Globalization*, Basingstoke: Palgrave Macmillan.

Hopkins, A. (ed.) (2002) *Globalization in World History*, London: Pimlico.

Horn, A. (2009) *Juke Box Britain: Americanisation and Youth Culture, 1945–60*, Manchester: Manchester University Press.

Howe, N. and Strauss, W. (2000) *Millennials Rising: The Next Great Generation*, New York: Vintage Books.

Howker, E. and Malik, S. (2010) *Jilted Generation: How Britain Has Bankrupted Its Youth*, London: Icon.

Huesmann, L.R (1986) 'Psychological Processes Promoting the Relation between Media Violence and Aggressive Behavior by the Viewer', *Journal of Social Issues*, Vol. 42, No. 3, pp. 125–139.

Huesmann, L.R., Moise-Titus, J., Podolski, C. and Eron, L. (2003) 'Longitudinal Relations between Children's Exposure to TV Violence and their Aggressive and Violent Behavior in Young Adulthood, 1977–1992', *Developmental Psychology*, Vol. 39, No. 2, pp. 201–221.

Humphrey, M. (2007) 'Culturalising the Abject: Islam, Law and Moral Panic in the West', *Australian Journal of Social Issues*, Vol. 42, No. 1, pp. 9–25.

Huq, R. (1996) 'Asian Kool?: Bhangra and Beyond', in Sharma, S., Hutnyk, J. and Sharma, A. (eds), *Dis-Orienting Rhythms: The Politics of the New Asian Dance Music*, London: Zed Books, pp. 61–80.

Hussain, S. (2019) *Contemporary Muslim Girlhoods in India: A Study of Social Justice, Identity and Agency in Assam*, London: Routledge.

Hutnyk, J. (2000) 'Magical Mystical Tourism', in Hutnyk, J. (ed.), *Critique of Exotica: Music, Politics and the Culture Industry*, London: Pluto Press, pp. 87–113.

Hutton W. (2020) 'Coronavirus Won't End Globalisation, but Change It Hugely for the Better', *The Guardian*, online, 8 March, https://www.theguardian.com/commentisfree/2020/mar/08/the-coronavirus-outbreak-shows-us-that-no-one-can-take-on-this-enemy-alone (accessed 28 March 2020).

Hyder, R. (2004) *Brimful of Asia: Negotiating Ethnicity on the UK Music Scene*, Aldershot: Ashgate.

Idriss, S. (2018) *Young Migrant Identities: Creativity and Masculinity*, London: Routledge.

IFPI (2014) *IFPI Digital Music Report: Lighting Up New Markets*, IFPI.

ILGA (International Lesbian, Gay, Bisexual, Trans and Intersex Association) (2019) *State-Sponsored Homophobia*, Geneva: ILGA.

InfluencerDB (2018) 'Top 10 Gaming Influencers on Instagram', *InfluencerDB*, online, 19 January, https://influencerdb.com/blog/top-10-gaming-influencers-instagram/ (accessed 21 November 2019).

International Labour Office (1988) *Year Book of Labour Statistics*, Geneva: International Labour Office.

Iqbal, M. (2019) 'WeChat Revenue and Usage Statistics', BusinessofApps, online, 27 February, https://www.businessofapps.com/data/wechat-statistics/ (accessed 6 March 2020).

Ito, M., Baumer, S., Bittanti, M., boyd, d. et al. (2009) *Hanging Out, Messing Around and Geeking Out: Kids Living and Learning with New Media*, Cambridge, MA: MIT Press.

Iwabuchi, K. (2015) 'Pop-culture Diplomacy in Japan: Soft Power, Nation Branding and the Question of "International Cultural Exchange"', *International Journal of Cultural Policy*, Vol. 21, No. 4, pp. 419–432.

Izea (2019) 'Top Beauty Influencers of 2019', Izea, online, 1 February, https://izea.com/2019/02/01/makeup-artist/ (accessed 21 November 2019).

Jaeger, H. (1985) 'Generations in History: Reflections on a Controversial Concept', *History and Theory*, Vol. 24, No.3, pp. 273–292.

Jameson, F. (1984) 'Postmodernism or the Cultural Logic of Late Capitalism', *New Left Review*, Vol. 146, pp. 53–92.

Jao, N. (2018) 'WeChat Now Has over 1 Billion Active Monthly Users Worldwide', *Technode*, online, 5 March, https://technode.com/2018/03/05/wechat-1-billion-users/ (accessed 7 March 2020).

Jenkins, H. (1992) *Textual Poachers: Television Fans and Participatory Culture*, London: Routledge.

Jenkins, H. (2003) 'Interactive Audiences: The Collective Intelligence of Media Fans', online, http://web.mit.edu/~21fms/People/henry3/collective%20intelligence.html (accessed 28 March 2020).

Jenkins, H. (2006) 'The Chinese Columbine: How One Tragedy Ignited the Chinese Government's Simmering Fears of Youth Culture and the Internet', in Jenkins, H. (ed.), *Fans, Bloggers, and Gamers: Exploring Participatory Culture*, New York: New York University Press, pp. 222–225.

Jenkins, H. (2008) *Convergence Culture: Where Old and New Media Collide*, New York: New York University Press.

Jenner, M. (2014) 'We Need to Talk About Jack!: On the Representation of Male Homosexuality in American Teen Soaps', in Pullen, C. (ed.), *Queer Youth and Media Cultures*, Basingstoke: Palgrave Macmillan, pp. 131–144.

Jephcott, P. (1967) *A Time of One's Own*, Edinburgh: Oliver and Boyd.

Jiang, J. (2018) 'How Teens and Parents Navigate Screen Time and Device Distractions', Pew Research Center, online, https://www.pewresearch.org/internet/2018/08/22/how-teens-and-parents-navigate-screen-time-and-device-distractions/ (accessed 30 April 2020).

Jin, D.Y. (2015) *De-Convergence of Global Media*, London: Routledge.

Jin, D.Y. (2016) *New Korean Wave: Transnational Cultural Power in the Age of Social Media*, Urbana, IL: University of Illinois Press.

Jin, D.Y. (2020) *Globalization and Media in the Digital Platform Age*, London: Routledge.

Johnson, L. (2006) *Mind Your X's and Y's: Satisfying the Cravings of a New Generation of Consumers*, New York: Free Press.

Johnson, R. (1997) (orig. pub. 1986) 'What is Cultural Studies Anyway?', in Storey, J. (ed.), *What Is Cultural Studies?: A Reader*, London: Arnold, pp. 75–114.

Jones, C., Ramanau, R., Cross, S. and Healing, G. (2010) 'Net Generation or Digital Natives: Is there a Distinct New Generation Entering University?', *Computers and Education*, Vol. 54, No. 3, pp. 722–732.

Jones, L. (2011) 'Contemporary Bildungsromans and the Prosumer Girl', *Criticism*, Vol. 53, No. 3, pp. 439–469.

Jones, S. (1988) *Black Culture, White Youth: The Reggae Tradition from JA to UK*, Basingstoke: Macmillan.

Jowett, G., Jarvie, I. and Fuller K. (1996) *Children and the Movies: Media Influence and the Payne Fund Controversy*, Cambridge: Cambridge University Press.

Jowitt, T. (2017) 'Tales in Tech History: Napster', *Silicon*, 10 November, https://www.silicon.co.uk/e-marketing/ecommerce/tales-tech-history-napster-224585 (accessed 13 November, 2019).

Kahn-Harris, K. (2007) *Extreme Metal: Music and Culture on the Cutting Edge*, Oxford: Berg.

Kaplan, E.A. (1993) 'Madonna Politics: Perversion, Repression, or Subversion? Or Masks and/as Master-y', in SchwichtenBerg, C. (ed.), *The Madonna Connection: Representational Politics, Subcultural Identities, and Cultural Theory*, Boulder, CO: Westview Press, pp. 149–165.

Karp, P. (2008) 'Peter Dutton says Victorians Scared to Go Out because of "African Gang Violence"', *The Guardian*, online, 3 January, https://www.theguardian.com/australia-news/2018/jan/03/peter-dutton-says-victorians-scared-to-go-out-because-of-african-gang-violence (accessed 28 March 2020).

Katz, C. (1998) 'Disintegrating Developments: Global Economic Restructuring and the Eroding of Ecologies of Youth', in Skelton, T. and Valentine, G. (eds), *Cool Places: Geographies of Youth Cultures*, London: Routledge, pp. 130–144.

Kearney, M.C. (2002) 'Girlfriends and Girl Power: Female Adolescence in Contemporary U.S. Cinema', in Gatewood, F. and Pomerance, M. (eds), *Sugar, Spice, and Everything Nice: Cinemas of Girlhood*, Detroit, MI: Wayne State University Press, pp. 125–144.

Kearney, M.C. (2006) *Girls Make Media*, Abingdon: Routledge.

Kearney, M.C. (2009) 'Coalescing: The Development of Girls' Studies', *NWSA Journal*, Vol. 21, No. 1, pp. 1–28.

Kearney, M.C. (2014) 'Historicize This! Contextualism in Youth Media Studies', in Buckingham, D. and Kehilly, M.J. (eds), *Youth Cultures in the Age of Global Media*, Basingstoke: Palgrave Macmillan, pp. 53–70.

Kellner, D. (1995) *Media Culture: Cultural Studies, Identity and Politics Between the Modern and the Postmodern*, Routledge: London, 1995.

Kellner, D. (1997) 'Overcoming the Divide: Cultural Studies and Political Economy', in Ferguson, M. and Golding, P. (eds), *Cultural Studies in Question*, London: Sage, pp. 102–119.

Kennedy, G, Krause, K., Judd, T., Churchward, A. and Gray, K. (2006) 'First Year Students' Experiences with Technology: Are They Really Digital Natives?', *Australasian Journal of Educational Technology*, Vol. 24, No. 1, pp. 108–122.

Kim, M. (2019) 'Video Games Are Dividing South Korea', *MIT Technology Review*, online, 23 December, https://www.technologyreview.com/s/614933/video-games-national-crisis-addiction-south-korea/ (accessed 28 March 2020).

Kim, Y. (2013) 'Introduction: Korean Media in a Digital Cosmopolitan World', in Kim, Y. (ed.), *Korean Media Go Global*, London: Routledge, pp. 1–28.

Kirmse, S. (ed.) (2012) 'Bridging the Gap: The Concept of "Youth" and the Study of Central Asia and the Caucasus', in Kirmse, S. (ed.), *Youth in the Former Soviet South: Everyday Lives between Experimentation and Regulation*, London: Routledge, pp. 1–8.

Klein, N. (2000) *No Logo: No Space, No Choice, No Jobs – Taking Aim at the Brand Bullies*, London: Flamingo.

Kocha, N. (ed.) (1996) *The World's Greatest Brands*, Basingstoke: Macmillan Business.

Koffman, O. and Gill, R. (2014) '"I Matter and So Does She": Girl Power (Post)feminism and the Girl Effect', in Buckingham, D., Bragg, S. and Kehily, M.J. (eds), *Youth Cultures in the Age of Global Media*, London: Palgrave Macmillan, pp. 242–257.

Kottasova, I. (2014) 'Swedish Police Shut Down Pirate Bay', *CNN Business*, online, 29 December, https://money.cnn.com/2014/12/10/technology/pirate-bay-shut/index.html (accessed 13 November 2019).

Kowert, R. and Quandt, T. (eds) (2016) *The Video Game Debate: Unravelling the Physical, Social, and Psychological Effects of Digital Games*, New York: Routledge.

Krahé, B. and Möller, I. (2004) 'Playing Violent Electronic Games, Hostile Attributional Style, and Aggression-related Norms in German Adolescents', *Journal of Adolescence*, Vol. 27, No. 1, pp. 53–69.

Krahé, B., Möller, I., Huesmann, L.R, Kirwil, Let al. (2011) 'Desensitization to Media Violence: Links with Habitual Media Violence Exposure, Aggressive Cognitions, and Aggressive Behavior', *Journal of Personality and Social Psychology*, Vol. 100, No. 4, pp. 630–646.

Kraidy, M. (2005) *Hybridity, or the Cultural Logic of Globalization*, Philadelphia, PA: Temple University Press.

Krinsky, C. (ed.) (2008) *Moral Panics over Contemporary Children and Youth*, Aldershot: Ashgate.

Krinsky, C. (ed.) (2013) *The Ashgate Research Companion to Moral Panics*, Farnham: Ashgate.

Kroes, R. (2006) 'American Mass Culture and European Youth Culture', in Schildt, A. and Detlef, S. (eds), *Between Marx and Coca-Cola: Youth Cultures in Changing European Societies, 1960–1980*, New York: Berghahn Books, pp. 82–109.

Krotz, J. (2010) 'Tap into the Lucrative Tween Market', *Fox Business*, online, December 8, http://www.foxbusiness.com/features/2010/12/08/tap-lucrative-tween-market.html (accessed 23 September 2017).

Kücklich, J. (2005) 'Precarious Playbour: Modders and the Digital Games Industry', *Fibreculture*, No. 5, online, five.fibreculturejournal.org/fcj-025-precarious-playbour-modders-and-the-digital-games-industry/ (accessed 28 March 2020).

Kühne, R. and Baumgartner, S. (2018) 'Youth and Media: An Outline of Key Developments', in Kühne, R., Baumgartner, S., Koch, T. and Hofer, M. (eds), *Youth and Media: Current Perspectives on Media Use and Effects*, Baden-Baden: Momos, pp. 7–18.

Kumar, V. and Mirchandani, R. (2012) 'Increasing the ROI of Social Media Marketing', *MIT Sloan Management Review*, Vol. 54, No. 1, pp. 55–61.

Kundu, V. (2018) 'Tencent Beats Facebook to Become World's 5th Most Valuable Company!', *Trak.in*, online, 26 January, https://trak.in/tags/business/2017/11/22/tencent-beats-facebook-becomes-worlds-5th-valuable-company/ (accessed 13 February 2020).

Kvavik, R., Caruso, J. and Morgan, G. (2004) *ECAR Study of Students and Information Technology 2004: Convenience, Connection, and Control*, Boulder, CO: EDUCAUSE Center for Applied Research.

Kwon, S. and Kim, J. (2014) 'The Cultural Industry Policies of the Korean Government and the Korean Wave', *International Journal of Cultural Policy*, Vol. 20, No. 4, pp. 422–439.

La Monica, P. (2019) 'Amazon is Now the Most Valuable Company on the Planet', *CNN Business*, online, 8 January, https://edition.cnn.com/2019/01/08/investing/amazon-most-valuable-company-microsoft-google-apple/index.html (accessed 13 February 2020).

LaBennett, O. (2011) *She's Mad Real: Popular Culture and West Indian Girls in Brooklyn*, New York: New York University Press.

Lacasa, P., Zaballos, L. and Prieto, J. (2016) 'Fandom, Music and Personal Relationships through Media: How Teenagers Use Social Networks', *Journal of the International Association for the Study of Popular Music*, Vol. 6, No. 1, pp. 44–67.

Lady Gaga (2011) 'From the Desk of Lady Gaga', *V Magazine*, No. 74, Winter, pp. 34–37.

Langham Brown, J., Ralph, S. and Lees, T. (1999) 'Foreword', in Ralph, S., Brown, J. and Lees, T. (eds), *Youth and the Global Media*, Luton: University of Luton Press, pp. ix–xiv.

Larkin, R. (2007) *Comprehending Columbine*, Philadelphia PA: Temple University Press.

Laurie, P. (1965) *The Teenage Revolution*, London: Anthony Blond.

Lawrence, E., Sides, J. and Farrell, H. (2010) 'Self-Segregation or Deliberation? Blog Readership, Participation, and Polarization in American Politics', *Perspectives on Politics*, Vol. 8, No. 1, pp. 141–157.

Leblanc, L. (1999) *Pretty in Punk: Girls' Gender Resistance in a Boys' Subculture*, New Brunswick, NJ: Rutgers University Press.

Lee, C., Kim, H., and Hong, A. (2017) 'Ex-Post Evaluation of Illegalizing Juvenile Online Games after Midnight: A Case of Shutdown Policy in South Korea', *Telematics and Informatics*, Vol. 34, No. 8, pp. 1597–1606.

Lee, G. (ed.) (2018) *Rethinking Difference in Gender, Sexuality and Popular Music*, Abingdon: Routledge.

Leech, K. (1973) *Youthquake: Spirituality and the Growth of a Counter-culture*, London: Sheldon Press.

Legrain, P. (2020) 'The Coronavirus Is Killing Globalization as We Know It', *Foreign Policy*, online, 12 March, https://foreignpolicy.com/2020/03/12/coronavirus-killing-globalization-nationalism-protectionism-trump/ (accessed 28 March 2020).

Lemke-Santangelo, G. (2009) *Daughters of Aquarius: Women of the Sixties Counterculture*, Lawrence, KS: University of Kansas Press.

Lenhart, A., Kahne, J., Middaugh, E., MacGill, A.et al. (2008) 'Teens, Video Games and Civics: Teens Gaming Experiences are Diverse and Include Significant Social Interaction and Civic Engagement', Pew Internet & American Life Project, online, https://eric.ed.gov/?id=ED525058 (accessed 13 January 2020).

Lent, J. (ed.) (1999) *Pulp Demons: International Dimensions of the Postwar Anti-Comics Campaign*, Madison: Fairleigh Dickinson University Press.

Lesko, N. (2001) *Act Your Age!: A Cultural Constriction of Adolescence*, New York: Routledge.

Levinson, J.C. (1984) *Guerrilla Marketing: Secrets for Making Big Profits from Small Businesses*, Boston, MA: Houghton Mifflin.

Lewis, P. (1978) *The Fifties*, London: Heinemann.

Li, Y. and Ranier, M. (2010) 'Are "Digital Natives" Really Digitally Competent?: A Study on Chinese Teenagers', *British Journal of Educational Technology*, Vol. 41, No. 6, pp. 1029–1042.

Liebes, T. and Katz, E. (1990) *The Export of Meaning: Cross-cultural Readings of 'Dallas'*, Oxford: Oxford University Press.

Life (1959) 'A New $10-Billion Power: The US Teenage Consumer', 31 August, pp. 78–85.

Lincoln, S. (2012) *Youth Culture and Private Space*, Basingstoke: Palgrave Macmillan.

Lincoln, S. (2014) 'Young People and Mediated Private Space', in Bennett, A. and Robards, B. (eds), *Mediated Youth Cultures: The Internet, Belonging and New Cultural Configurations*, Basingstoke: Palgrave Macmillan, pp. 42–58.

Lipsitz, G. (1994) *Dangerous Crossroads: Popular Music, Postmodernism and the Poetics of Place*, New York: Verso.

Liquid Telecom (2018) 'African.Gen Z Report 2018', Liquid Telecom, online, https://www.liquidtelecom.com/information-centre/whitepapers/african-generation-z-report (accessed 21 November 2019).

Littauer, A. (2003) 'The B-Girl Evil: Bureaucracy, Sexuality, and the Menace of Bar-room Vice in Postwar California', *Journal of the History of Sexuality*, Vol. 12, No. 2, pp. 171–204.

Livingston, A. (2010) *The Secrets of Advertising to Gen Y Consumers*, Bellingham, WA: Self-Counsel Press.

Livingstone, S. (2002) *Young People and New Media: Childhood and the Changing Media Environment*, London: Sage.

Livingstone, S. (2009) 'In Defence of Privacy: Mediating the Public/Private Boundary at Home', London: LSE Research Online, online, http://eprints.lse.ac.uk/archive/00000505 (accessed 28 March 2020).

Livingstone, S. and Bober, M. (2005) *UK Children Go Online: Listening to Young People's Experiences*, London: London School of Economics and Political Science.

Livingstone, S. and Haddon, L. (eds) (2009) *Kids Online: Opportunities and Risks for Children*, Bristol: Policy Press.

Lloyd, A. (1995) *Doubly Deviant, Doubly Damned: Society's Treatment of Violent Women*, Harmondsworth: Penguin.

Look (1967) *Youthquake*, New York: Cowles Educational Books.

LSE (2017) 'Social Media Platforms and Demographics', London School of Economics and Political Science, online, https://info.lse.ac.uk/staff/divisions/communications-division/digital-communications-team/assets/documents/guides/A-Guide-To-Social-Media-Platforms-and-Demographics.pdf (accessed 14 November 2019).

Lull, J. (1995) *Media, Communication, Culture: A Global Approach*, Cambridge: Polity.

Lumsden, K. (2013) *Boy Racer Culture: Youth, Masculinity and Deviance*, London: Routledge.

Lyotard, J.F. (1984) *The Postmodern Condition: A Report on Knowledge*, Manchester: Manchester University Press.

Macdonald, D. (1958) 'A Caste, a Culture, a Market', *New Yorker*, 22 November, pp. 57–94.

MacDonald, F. (2017) 'Positioning Young Refugees in Australia: Media Discourse and Social Exclusion', *International Journal of Inclusive Education*, Vol. 21, No. 11, pp. 1182–1195.

Macdonald, N. (2001) *The Graffiti Subculture: Youth, Masculinity and Identity in London and New York*, Basingstoke: Palgrave.

MacDonald, R. (ed.) (1997) *Youth, the 'Underclass' and Social Exclusion*, London: Routledge.

Mackay, H. (2018) 'Instagram: How Much do Social Influencers Earn?', *BBC News*, online, 3 October, https://www.bbc.co.uk/news/uk-45735861 (accessed 21 November 2019).

Maffesoli, M. (trans. Smith, D.) (1996) *The Time of the Tribes: The Decline of Individualism in Mass Society*, London: Sage.

Mailer, N. (1961) 'The White Negro', in Mailer, N., *Advertisements for Myself*, London: Andre Deutsch, pp. 269–289.

Maira, S. (2002) *Desis in the House: Indian American Youth Culture in New York City*, Philadelphia, PA: Temple University Press.

Maira, S. and Soep, E. (2005) 'Introduction', in Maira, S. and Soep, E. (eds), *Youthscapes: The Popular, the National, the Global*, Philadelphia, PA: University of Pennsylvania Press, pp. xv–xxxv.

Majavu, M. (2018) 'The "African Gangs" Narrative: Associating Blackness with Criminality and Other Anti-Black Racist Tropes in Australia', *African and Black Diaspora*, Vol. 12, No. 1, pp. 27–39.

Malbon, B. (1999) *Clubbing: Dancing, Ecstasy and Vitality*, London: Routledge.

Manago, A., Ward, L., Lemm, K., Reed, L. and Seabrook, R. (2015) 'Facebook Involvement, Objectified Body Consciousness, Body Shame and Sexual Assertiveness in College Women and Men', *Sex Roles*, Vol. 72, No. 1, pp. 1–14.

Mannheim, K. (1952) 'The Problem of Generations', in Kecskemeti, P. (ed.), *Essays on the Sociology of Knowledge*, London: Routledge & Kegan Paul, pp. 276–322.

Marcus, S. (2010) *Girls to the Front: The True Story of the Riot Grrrl Revolution*, New York: HarperPerennial.

Margaryana, A., Littlejohn, A. and Vojtb, G. (2011) 'Are Digital Natives a Myth or Reality?: University Students' Use of Digital Technologies', *Computers and Education*, Vol. 56, No. 2, pp. 429–440.

Market Assessment International (1999) *Millennium Youth 1999*, London: Market Assessment Publications.

Markey, P. and Ferguson, C.J. (2017) 'Internet Gaming Addiction: Disorder or Moral Panic?', *American Journal of Psychiatry*, Vol. 174, No. 3, pp. 195–196.

Martell, L. (2010) *The Sociology of Globalisation*, Cambridge: Polity.

Marwick, A. (2013) *Status Update: Celebrity, Publicity and Branding in the Social Media Age*, New Haven CT: Yale University Press.

May, K. (2002) *Golden State, Golden Youth: The California Image in Popular Culture, 1955–1966*, Chapel Hill: University of North Carolina Press.

Mazzarella, S. (2020) *Girls, Moral Panic and News Media: Troublesome Bodies*, New York: Routledge.

McCann, H. (2020) *Queer Theory Now: From Foundations to Futures*, London: Red Globe Press.

McCann, H. and Southern, C. (2019) 'Repetitions of Desire: Queering the One Direction Fangirl', *Girlhood Studies*, Vol. 12, No. 1, pp. 49–65.

McCann-Erickson Worldwide (1989) *The New Generation: The McCann-Erickson European Youth Study, 1977–87*, London: McCann-Erickson.

McCarren, F. (2013) *French Moves: The Cultural Politics of le Hip Hop*, Oxford: Oxford University Press.

McChesney, R. (1999) *Rich Media, Poor Democracy: Communication Politics in Dubious Times*, Urbana, IL: University of Illinois Press.

McCrindle, M. and Wolfinger, E. (2010) *The ABC of XYZ: Understanding the Global Generations*, Sydney: University of New South Wales Press.

McGray, D. (2002) 'Japan's Gross National Cool', *Foreign Policy*, May/June, pp. 44–54.

McGuigan, J. (1992) *Cultural Populism*, London: Routledge.

McIntyre, H. (2018) 'The Top 10 Streaming Music Services by Number of Users', *Forbes*, online, 25 May, https://www.forbes.com/sites/hughmcintyre/2018/05/25/the-top-10-streaming-music-services-by-number-of-users/#7503f9465178 (accessed 13 November, 2019).

McIntyre, L. (2018) *Post-Truth*, Cambridge, MA: MIT Press.

McLaughlin, E. (2008) 'Hitting the Panic Button: Policing/ "Mugging"/Media /Crisis', *Crime Media Culture*, Vol. 4, No. 1, pp. 145–154.

McLuhan, M. (1964) *Understanding Media*, New York: McGraw-Hill.

McRobbie, A. (1978) 'Working Class Girls and the Culture of Femininity', in Women's Studies Group (eds), *Women Take Issue*, London: Hutchinson, pp. 96–108.

McRobbie, A. (1981) 'Settling Accounts with Subcultures', in Bennett, T., Martin, G., Mercer, C. and Woollacott, J. (eds), *Culture, Ideology and Social Process: A Reader*, London: Batsford Academic/Open University Press, pp. 111–124.

McRobbie, A. (1994) 'The Moral Panic in the Age of the Postmodern Mass Media', in McRobbie, A. (ed.), *Postmodernism and Popular Culture*, London: Routledge, pp. 198–219.

McRobbie, A. (2000) (2nd edn) 'Sweet Smell of Success?': New Ways of Being Young Women', in McRobbie, A. (ed.), *Feminism and Youth Culture*, London: Macmillan, pp. 198–214.

McRobbie, A. (2004) 'Notes on Postfeminism and Popular Culture: Bridget Jones and the New Gender Regime', in Harris, A. (ed.), *All about the Girl: Culture, Power and Identity*, New York: Routledge, pp. 3–4.

McRobbie, A. (2008) *The Aftermath of Feminism: Gender, Culture and Social Change*, London: Sage.

McRobbie, A. and Garber, J. (1976) 'Girls and Subcultures: An Exploration', in Hall, S. and Jefferson, T. (eds), *Resistance through Rituals: Youth Subcultures in Post-War Britain*, London: Hutchinson, pp. 209–222.

McRobbie, A. and Thornton, S. (1995) 'Rethinking "Moral Panic" for Multi-Mediated Social Worlds', *British Journal of Sociology*, Vol. 46, No. 4, pp. 559–574.

Medhurst, A. (1995) 'It Sort of Happened Here: The Strange, Brief Life of the British Pop Film', in Romney, J. and Wootton, A. (eds), *Celluloid Jukebox: Popular Music and the Movies since the 1950s*, London: BFI, pp. 60–71.

Melville, C. (2020) *It's a London Thing: How Rare Groove, Acid House and Jungle Remapped the City*, Manchester: Manchester University Press.

Mendonca, L. (2002) 'The Local and the Global in Popular Music: The Brazilian Music Industry, Local Culture, and Public Policies', in Crane, D., Kawashima, N. and Kawasaki, K. (eds), *Global Culture: Media Arts, Policy and Globalization*, London: Routledge, pp. 105–117.

Michaels, S. (2014) 'One Direction Fanfic Author Inks Worldwide Book Deal', *The Guardian*, online, 4 June, https://www.theguardian.com/music/2014/jun/04/one-direction-fanfic-anna-todd-inks-worldwide-book-deal (accessed 28 March 2020).

Milavsky, J.R, Kessler, R., Stipp, H. and Rubens, W. (1982) *Television and Aggression: A Panel Study*, London: Academic Press.

Miles, S. (2000) *Youth Lifestyles in a Changing World*, Buckingham: Open University Press.

Miles, S. (2002) 'Consuming Youth: Consuming Lifestyles', in Miles, S., Anderson, A. and Meethan, K. (eds), *The Changing Consumer: Markets and Meanings*London: Routledge, pp. 131–145.

Miller, D. (1992) 'The Young and the Restless in Trinidad: A Case of the Local and the Global in Mass Consumption', in Hirsch, E. and Silverstone, R. (eds), *Consuming Technologies: Media and Information in Domestic Spaces*, London: Routledge, pp. 163–182.

Mintel Publications (1988) *Youth Lifestyle*, London: Mintel.

Mitchell, C. and Reid-Walsh, J. (eds), (2005) *Seven Going on Seventeen: Tween Culture in Girlhood Studies*, Oxford: Peter Lang.

Mitchell, T. (1996) *Popular Music and Local Identity: Rock, Pop and Rap in Europe and Oceania*, London: Leicester University Press.

Mitchell, T. (ed.) (2001) *Global Noise: Rap and Hip-Hop outside the USA*, Middletown, CT: Wesleyan University Press.

Mitteraurer, M. (1992) *A History of Youth*, Oxford: Blackwell.

Modell, J. (1989) *Into One's Own: From Youth to Adulthood in the United States 1920–1975*, Berkeley, CA: University of California Press.

Moghadam, V. (2009) *Globalization and Social Movements: Islamism, Feminism, and the Global Justice Movement*, Plymouth: Rowman & Littlefield.

Monem, N. (2007) *Riot Grrrl: Revolution Girl Style Now!*, London: Black Dog.

Mooney, K. (2005) 'Identities in the Ducktail Youth Subculture in Post-World-War-Two South Africa', *Journal of Youth Studies*, Vol. 8, No. 1, pp. 41–57.

Moran, A. (2009) 'When TV Formats are Translated', in Moran, A. (ed.), *TV Formats Worldwide: Localizing Global Programs*, Bristol: Intellect, pp. 41–54.

Morgan, G. and Poynting, S. (2012) 'Introduction: The Transnational Folk Devil', in Morgan, G. and Poynting, S. (eds), *Global Islamophobia: Muslims and Moral Panic in the West*, London: Ashgate, pp. 1–14.

Morgan Stanley (2017) 'India's Millennials to Drive Growth in Four Key Sectors', *Forbes' Brand Voice*, online, June 23, https://www.forbes.com/sites/morganstanley/2017/06/23/indias-millennials-to-drive-growth-in-four-key-sectors/#1d091c8c4f27 (accessed 23 September 2017).

Morris, G. (1993) '... So What Is This Asian Kool?', *Select*, August, p. 46.

Morris, S. (2003) 'Wads, Bots and Mods: Multiplayer FPS Games as Co-Creative Media', in Copier, M. and Raessens, J. (eds), *Level Up: Digital Games Research Conference Proceedings*, Utrecht, University of Utrecht, pp. 338–349.

Morrison, D. and Millwood, A. (2007) 'The Meaning and Definition of Violence', *International Journal of Media and Cultural Politics*, Vol. 3, No. 3, pp. 289–305.

Mosco, V. (2009) (2nd edn) *The Political Economy of Communication*, London: Sage.

Muggleton, D. (2000) *Inside Subculture: The Postmodern Meaning of Style*, Oxford: Berg.

Muggleton, D. and Weinzierl, R. (eds), (2003) *The Post-Subcultures Reader*, Oxford: Berg.

Muhonja, B.B. (2017) *Womanhood and Girlhood in Twenty-First Century Middle Class Kenya: Disrupting Patri-centered Frameworks*, Lanham, MD: Lexington Books.

Murdock, G. (1990) 'Redrawing the Map of the Communications Industries: Concentration and Ownership in the Era of Privatisation', in Ferguson, M. (ed.), *Public Communication*, London: Sage, pp. 1–15.

Murdock, G. (1997) 'Cultural Studies at the Crossroads', in McRobbie, A. (ed.), *Back to Reality? Social Experience and Cultural Studies*, Manchester: Manchester University Press, pp. 58–73.

Murdock, G. and McCron, R. (1973) 'Scoobies, Skins and Contemporary Pop', *New Society*, Vol. 23, No. 547, pp. 690–692.

Murray, J. and Arnett, J. (eds) (2019) *Emerging Adulthood and Higher Education: A New Student Development Paradigm*, London: Routledge.

Murray, R. (1990) 'Fordism and Post-Fordism', in Hall, S. and Jacques, M. (eds), *New Times: The Changing Face of Politics in the 1990s*, London: Lawrence & Wishart, pp. 38–53.

Nanjing Marketing Group (2018) 'How to Use Short-Video App, Douyin, for Your China Marketing', Nanjing Marketing Group, online, 13 June, https://www.nanjingmarketinggroup.com/blog/How-To-Use-Douyin-For-China-Marketing (accessed 8 December 2019).

Nault, C. (2017) *Queercore: Queer Punk Media Subculture*, London: Routledge.

Nayak, A. (2003) *Race, Place and Globalization: Youth Cultures in a Changing World*, Oxford: Berg.

Nayak, A. and Kehily, M.J. (2013) (2nd edn) *Gender, Youth and Culture: Global Masculinities and Femininities*, Basingstoke: Palgrave Macmillan.

Negus, K. (1998) 'Cultural Production and the Corporation: Musical Genres and the Strategic Management of Creativity in the US Recording Industry', *Media, Culture and Society*, Vol. 20, pp. 359–379.

Negus, K. (1999) *Music Genres and Corporate Cultures*, London: Routledge.

Nelson, L., Badger, S. and Wu, B. (2004) 'The Influence of Culture in Emerging Adulthood: Perspectives of Chinese College Students', *International Journal of Behavioural Development*, Vol. 28, No. 1, pp. 26–36.

Neville, R. (1970) *Playpower*, London: Jonathan Cape.

New York Times (2018) 'Facebook Says Cambridge Analytica Harvested Data of up to 87 Million Users', *New York Times*, online, 4 April, https://www.nytimes.com/2018/04/04/technology/mark-zuckerBerg-testify-congress.html (accessed 21 November 2019).

Newbourne, E. and Kerwin, K. (1999) 'Generation Y: Marketing Changes', *Business Week*, 15 February, pp. 80–86.

Newsom, E. (1994) *Video Violence and the Protection of Children, Report of the Home Affairs Committee*, London: HMSO.

Newsweek (1957) 'The Colossal Drive-In', 22 July, pp. 50, 85.

Nilan, P. and Feixa, C. (2006) 'Introduction: Youth Hybridity and Plural Worlds', in Nilan, P. and Feixa, C. (eds), *Global Youth? Hybrid Identities, Plural Worlds*, Abingdon: Routledge, pp. 1–13.

Nixon, S. (1997) 'Circulating Culture', in du Gay, P. (ed.), *Production of Culture: Cultures of Production*, London: Sage/Open University, pp. 177–220.

Noakes, J. (ed.), (1998) *Nazism 1919–1945 Vol. 4: The German Home Front in World War II*, Exeter: Exeter University Press.

Nolan, D., Burgin, A., Farquharson, K. and Marjoribanks, T. (2016) 'Media and the Politics of Belonging: Sudanese Australians, Letters to the Editor and the New Integration', *Patterns of Prejudice*, Vol. 50, No. 3, pp. 253–275.

Noxon, C. (2006) *Rejuvenile: Kickball, Cartoons, Cupcakes, and the Reinvention of the American Grown-Up*, New York: Crown.

Nye, J. (1990) *Bound to Lead: The Changing Nature of American Power*, New York: Basic Books.

Nye, J. (2004) *Soft Power: The Means to Success in World Politics*, New York: Public Affairs.

Nye, J. (2011) *The Future of Power: Its Changing Nature and Use in the Twenty-first Century*, New York: Public Affairs.

Oblinger, D. and Oblinger, J. (2005) 'Is It Age or IT: First Steps towards Understanding the Net Generation', in Oblinger, D. and Oblinger, J. (eds), *Educating the Net Generation*, Boulder, CO: EDUCAUSE, pp. 2.1–2.20.

Ofcom (2016) *Communications Market Report 2016*, London: Office of Communications.

Office of National Statistics (ONS) (2015) 'Overview of the UK Population', online, https://www.ons.gov.uk/peoplepopulationandcommunity/populationandmigration/populationestimates/articles/overviewoftheukpopulation/2015-11-05 (accessed 8 December 2019).

Office of National Statistics (ONS) (2019) 'Families and Households in the UK: 2019', Office of National Statistics, online, https://www.ons.gov.uk/peoplepopulationand community/birthsdeathsandmarriages/families/bulletins/familiesandhouseholds/2019 (accessed 8 December 2019).

Office of the State's Attorney Judicial District of Danbury (2013) *Report of the State's Attorney for the Judicial District of Danbury on the Shootings at Sandy Hook Elementary School and 36 Yogananda Street, Newtown Connecticut on December 14, 2012*, Danbury: State of Connecticut, Division of Criminal Justice.

Oliver, B. and Goerke, V. (2007) 'Australian Undergraduates' Use and Ownership of Emerging Technologies: Implications and Opportunities for Creating Engaging Learning Experiences for the Net Generation', *Australasian Journal of Educational Technology*, Vol. 23, No. 2, pp. 171–186.

Oliver, M.B., Raney, A. and Bryant J. (eds), (2020) (4th edn) *Media Effects: Advances in Theory and Research*, London: Routledge.

O'Malley Greenburg, Z. (2019) 'Artist, Icon, Billionaire: How Jay-Z Created His $1 Billion Fortune', *Forbes*, online, 3 June, https://www.forbes.com/sites/zackomalley greenburg/2019/06/03/jay-z-billionaire-worth/#182393ee3a5f (accessed 8 December 2019).

O'Reilly, T. (2005) 'What Is Web 2.0: Design Patterns and Business Models for the Next Generation of Software', 30 September, https://www.oreilly.com/pub/a/web2/archive/what-is-web-20.html

Osgerby, B. (2020) (forthcoming) '"Bad to the Bone": The Myth and Mystique of the Motorcycle Gang', in van der Steen, B. and Verburgh, T. (eds), *Researching Subcultures, Myth and Memory*, London: Palgrave Macmillan.

Osgood, D.W., Ruth, G., Eccles, J., Jacobs, J., and Barber, B. (2005) 'Six Paths to Adulthood: Fast Starters, Parents without Careers, Educated Partners, Educated Singles, Working Singles, and Slow Starters', in Settersten, R., FurstenBerg, F. and Rumbaut, R. (eds), *On the Frontier of Adulthood: Theory, Research, and Public Policy*, Chicago: University of Chicago Press, pp. 320–355.

Osterhammel, J. and Peterson, N. (2005) *Globalization: A Short History*, Princeton, NJ: Princeton University Press.

Palladino, G. (1996) *Teenagers: An American History*, New York: Basic Books.

Pardee, T. (2010) 'Media-Savvy Gen Y Finds Smart and Funny Is "New Rock 'n' Roll"', *Advertising Age*, online, 11 October, http://adage.com/article/news/marketing-media-savvy-gen-y-transparency-authenticity/146388/ (accessed 28 March 2020).

Parekh, R. (2018) 'Internet Gaming', American Psychiatric Association, online, June, https://www.psychiatry.org/patients-families/internet-gaming (accessed 21 January 2020).

Parsons, T. (1942) 'Age and Sex in the Social Structure of the United States', *American Sociological Review*, Vol. 7, No. 5, pp. 604–616.

Parsons, T. (1943) 'The Kinship System of the Contemporary United States', *American Anthropologist*, Vol. 45, pp. 22–38.

Pearson, E. (2009) 'All the World Wide Web's a Stage: The Performance of Identity in Online Social Networks', *First Monday*, Vol. 4, No. 3, online, http://firstmonday.org/htbin/cgiwrap/bin/ojs/index.php/fm/article/view/2162/2127 (accessed 28 March 2020).

Pearson, G. (1983) *Hooligan: A History of Respectable Fears*, London: Macmillan.

Pearson, G. (1984) 'Falling Standards: A Short, Sharp History of Moral Decline', in Barker, M. (ed.), *The Video Nasties: Freedom and Censorship in the Media*, London: Pluto Press, pp. 88–103.

Pearson, J. (1999) *Women's Reading in Britain 1750–1835: A Dangerous Recreation*, Cambridge: Cambridge University Press.

Peiss, K. (1987) *Cheap Amusements: Working Women and Leisure in Turn-of-the-Century*, New York: Temple University Press.

Peiss, K. (2011) *Zoot Suit: The Enigmatic Career of an Extreme Style*, Philadelphia, PA: University of Pennsylvania Press.

Pells, R. (1985) *The Liberal Mind in a Conservative Age: American Intellectuals in the 1940s and 1950s*, New York: Harper Row.

Penix-Tadsen, P. (ed.) (2019) *Video Games and the Global South*, Pittsburgh PA: Carnegie Mellon University / ETC Press.

Penley, C. (1997) *NASA/TREK: Popular Science and Sex in America*, London: Verso.

Peters, J. (2017) 'Banon's Views Can Be Traced to a Book That Warns, "Winter Is Coming"', *New York Times*, online, 8 April, https://www.nytimes.com/2017/04/08/us/politics/stephen-bannon-book-fourth-turning.html (accessed 8 December 2019).

Peterson, K. (2018) 'Cultural Expressions and Criticisms in the US Mipsterz Fashion Video', *Recherches Sociologiques et Anthropologiques*, Vol. 49, No. 1, pp. 79–97, online, https://journals.openedition.org/rsa/2421?lang=en/ (accessed 3 March 2020).

Petley, J. (2013) '"Are We Insane?" The "Video Nasty" Moral Panic', in Critcher, C., Hughes, J., Petley, J. and Rohloff, A. (eds), *Moral Panics in the Contemporary World*, London: Bloomsbury, pp. 73–100.

Petry, N., Rehbein, F., Gentile, D., Lemmen, J.et al. (2014) 'An International Consensus for Assessing Internet Gaming Disorder Using the New DSM-5 Approach', *Addiction*, Vol. 109, No. 9, pp. 1399–1406.

Pieterse, J.N. (2012) 'Cultural Hybridity', in Anheier, H. and Juergensmeyer, M. (eds), *Encyclopedia of Global Studies*, Thousand Oaks, CA: Sage, pp. 327–330.

Pieterse, J.N. (2020) (4th edn) *Globalization and Culture: Global Mélange*, Oxford: Rowman & Littlefield.

Pilkington, H. (1994) *Russia's Youth and Its Culture: A Nation's Constructors and Constructed*, London: Routledge.

Pilkington, H. (2002) 'Conclusion', in Pilkington, H., Omel'chenko, E., Flynn, M., Bliudina, U. and Starkova, E. (eds), *Looking West?: Cultural Globalization and Russian Youth Cultures*, University Park: Pennsylvania State University Press, pp. 216–226.

Pilkington, H. and Bliudina, U. (2002) 'Cultural Globalization: A Peripheral Perspective', in Pilkington, H., Omel'chenko, E., Flynn, M., Bliudina, U. and Starkova, E. (eds), *Looking West?: Cultural Globalization and Russian Youth Cultures*, University Park: Pennsylvania State University Press, pp. 1–20.

Pini, M. (2001) *Club Cultures and Female Subjectivity: The Move from Home to House*, London: Palgrave.

Pipher, M. (1994) *Reviving Ophelia: Saving the Selves of Adolescent Girls*, New York: G.P. Putnam and Sons.

PMYB (2017) 'Discover the Earning Power of Vloggers PewDiePie and Zoella', PMYB, online, 26 July, https://pmyb.co.uk/youtubers-pewdiepie-zoella-earn/ (accessed 8 December 2019).

Poiger, U. (2000) *Jazz, Rock and Rebels: Cold War Politics and American Culture in a Divided Germany*, Berkeley, CA: University of California Press.

Polster, B. (ed.) (1989) *Swing Heil! Jazz im Nationalsozialismus*, Berlin: Transit.

Pomerance, M. and Gateward, F. (eds), (2004) *Where the Boys Are: Cinemas of Masculinity and Youth*, Detroit, MI: Wayne State University Press.

Poole, E. and Richardson, J. (eds), (2006) *Muslims and the News Media*, London: I.B. Tauris.

Potter, W.J. (2012) *Media Effects*, London: Sage.

Poynting, S., Noble, G., Tabar, P. and Collins, J. (2004) *Bin Laden in the Suburbs: Criminalising the Arab Other*, Sydney: Institute of Criminology.

Prahalad, C.K. and Ramaswamy, V. (2004i) 'Co-creation Experiences: The Next Practice in Value Creation', *Journal of Interactive Marketing*, Vol. 18, No. 3, pp. 5–14.

Prahalad, C.K. and Ramaswamy, V. (2004ii) *The Future of Competition: Co-Creating Unique Value with Customers*, Boston, MA: Harvard Business Press.

Prensky, M. (2001) 'Digital Natives, Digital Immigrants', *On the Horizon*, Vol. 9, No. 5, pp. 1–6.

Przybylski, A. (2014) 'Who Believes Electronic Games Cause Real World Aggression?', *Cyberpsychology, Behavior, and Social Networking*, Vol. 17, No. 4, pp. 228–234.

Przybylski, A. and Weinstein, N. (2019) 'Violent Video Game Engagement Is Not Associated with Adolescents' Aggressive Behaviour: Evidence from a Registered Report', *Royal Society Open Science*, No. 6, 171474, online, http://dx.doi.org/10.1098/rsos.171474 (accessed 13 January 2020).

Przybylski, A., Weinstein, N. and Murayama, K. (2017.) 'Internet Gaming Disorder: Investigating the Clinical Relevance of a New Phenomenon', *American Journal of Psychiatry*, Vol. 174, No.3, pp. 230–236.

Punyanunt-Carter, N. and Smith, J. (2010) 'East Meets West: Is There a Difference between Thai and American Girls' Use of the Internet and Negotiation of Identity?', in Mazzarella, S. (ed.), *Girl Wide Web 2.0: Revisiting Girls, The Internet, and the Negotiation of Identity*, New York: Peter Lang, pp. 69–90.

Quart, A. (2003) *Branded: The Buying and Selling of Teenagers*, Cambridge, MA: Perseus Publishing.

Reddington, H. (2007) *The Lost Women of Rock Music: Female Musicians of the Punk Era*, Aldershot: Ashgate.

Redhead, S. (1990) *The End of the Century Party: Youth and Pop Towards 2000*, Manchester: Manchester University Press.

Redhead, S. (ed.) (1993) *Rave Off: Politics and Deviance in Contemporary Youth Culture*, Aldershot: Avebury.

Redhead, S., Wynne, D. and O'Connor, J. (eds), (1997) *The Clubcultures Reader: Readings in Cultural Studies*, Oxford: Blackwell.

Reeves, J. and Campbell, R. (1994) *Cracked Coverage: Television News, the Anti-Cocaine Crusade and the Reagan Legacy*, Durham, NC: Duke University Press.

Reher, D. and Requena, M. (2015) 'The Mid-Twentieth Century Fertility Boom from a Global Perspective', *The History of the Family*, Vol. 20, No. 3, pp. 420–445.

Reimer, B. (1995) 'Youth and Modern Lifestyles', in Fornäs, J. and Bolin, G. (eds), *Youth Culture in Late Modernity*, London: Sage, pp. 120–144.

Reinarman, C. and Levine, H. (1989i) 'Crack in Context: Politics and Media in the Making of a Drug Scare', *Contemporary Drug Problems*, No. 16, pp. 535–577.

Reinarman, C. and Levine, H. (1989ii) 'The Crack Attack: America's Latest Drug Scare, 1986–1992', in Best, J. (ed.), *Images of Issues: Typifying Contemporary Social Problems*, New York: Aldine de Gruyter, pp. 251–289.

Reinarman, C. and Levine, H. (eds), (1997) *Crack in America: Demon Drugs and Social Justice*, Berkeley, CA: University of California Press.

Resinkoff, P. (2016) 'Two Thirds of All Music Sold Comes from Just Three Companies', *Digital Music News*, online, 3 August, https://www.digitalmusicnews.com/2016/08/03/two-thirds-music-sales-come-three-major-labels/ (accessed 28 March 2020).

Rheingold, H. (2000) (2nd edn) *The Virtual Community: Homesteading on the Electronic Frontier*, Cambridge, MA: MIT Press.

Rideout, V. and Robb, M. (2019) *The Common Sense Census: Media Use by Tweens and Teens*, Common Sense Media.

Riesman, D. (1950) 'Listening to Popular Music', *American Quarterly*, Vol. 2, Winter, pp. 359–371.

Ritchie, K. (1995) *Marketing to Generation X*, New York: Lexington.

Ritzer, G. (1993) *The McDonaldization of Society: An Investigation into the Changing Character of Contemporary Social Life*, Thousand Oaks, CA: Pine Forge Press.

Rivera-Rideau, P. (2015) *Remixing Reggaetón: The Cultural Politics of Race in Puerto Rico*, Durham, NC: Duke University Press.

Roberts, K. (1995) *Youth and Employment in Modern Britain*, Oxford: Oxford University Press.

Roberts, R. (ed.) (2016) *European Glocalization in Global Context*, New York: Springer.

Robertson, R. (1995i) 'Mapping the Global Condition: Globalization as the Central Concept', in Featherstone, M. (ed.), *Global Culture: Nationalism, Globalization and Modernity*, London: Sage, pp. 15–30.

Robertson, R. (1995ii) 'Glocalization: Time-Space and Homogeneity-Heterogeneity', in Featherstone, M., Lash, S. and Robertson, R. (eds), *Global Modernities*, London: Sage, pp. 25–43.

Rock, P. and Cohen, S. (1970) 'The Teddy Boy', in Bogdanor, V. and Skidelsky, R. (eds), *The Age of Affluence, 1951–1964*, London: Macmillan, pp. 288–318.

Roediger, D. (1998) 'What to Make of Wiggers: A Work in Progress', in Austin, J. and Willard, M. (eds) *Generations of Youth: Youth Cultures and History in Twentieth-Century America*, New York: New York University Press, pp. 358–366.

Rollefson, J.G. (2017) *Flip the Script: European Hip Hop and the Politics of Postcoloniality*, Chicago: University of Chicago Press.

Roo, W. (2009) 'Globalization, Or the Logic of Cultural Hybridization: The Case of the Korean Wave', *Asian Journal of Communication*, Vol. 19, No. 2, pp. 137–151.

Rose, T. (1994) *Black Noise: Rap Music and Black Culture in Contemporary America*, Hanover, NH: Wesleyan University Press.

Roudometof, V. (2016) *Glocalization: A Critical Introduction*, London: Routledge.

Rowntree, J. and Rowntree, M. (1968) 'Youth as Social Class', *International Socialist Journal*, No. 25, February, pp. 25–58.

Royal Society for Public Health (RSPH) (2017) *#StatusOfMind*, London: Royal Society for Public Health.

Ruddock, A. (2008) 'Media Studies 2.0? Binge Drinking and Why Audiences Still Matter', *Sociology Compass*, Vol. 2. No. 1, pp. 1–15.

Rutter, M., Graham, P., Chadwick, O.F.D. and Yule, W. (1976) 'Adolescent Turmoil: Fact or Fiction?', *Journal of Child Psychology and Psychiatry*, Vol. 17, No. 1, pp. 35–56.

Saeed, S. (2013) 'Somewhere in America, Muslim Women are "Cool"', *The Islamic Monthly*, online, 2 December, https://www.theislamicmonthly.com/somewhere-in-america-muslim-women-are-cool// (accessed 3 March 2020).

Said, E. (1978) *Orientalism*, New York: Pantheon Books.

Said, E. (1981) *Covering Islam: How the Media and the Experts Determine How We See the Rest of the World*, New York: Pantheon Books.

Sandvoss, C. (2005) *Fans: The Mirror of Consumption*, Cambridge, MA: Polity.

Sanjek, R. (1988) *American Popular Music and Its Business: The First Four Hundred Years*, Vol. 3: *From 1900–1984*, Oxford: Oxford University Press.

Saucier, P.K. and Silva, K. (2014) 'Keeping It Real in the Global South: Hip-Hop Comes to Sri Lanka', *Critical Sociology*, Vol. 40, No. 2, pp. 295–300.

Saunders, J., Hao, W., Long, J., King, D.et al. (2017) 'Gaming Disorder: Its Delineation as an Important Condition for Diagnosis, Management, and Prevention', *Journal of Behavioral Addictions*, Vol. 6, No. 3, pp. 271–279.

Savage, J. (1990) 'Tainted Love: The Influence of Male Homosexuality and Sexual Divergence on Pop Music and Culture since the War', in Tomlinson, A. (ed.), *Consumption, Identity and Style*, London: Routledge, pp. 103–115.

Savage, J. (2007) *Teenage: The Creation of Youth 1875–1945*, London: Chatto & Windus.

Schade-Poulsen, M. (1995) 'The Power of Love: Raï Music and Youth in Algeria', in Amit-Talai, V. and Wulff, H. (eds), *Youth Cultures: A Cross-Cultural Perspective*, London: Routledge, pp. 114–143.

Schiller, H. (1976) *Communication and Cultural Domination*, New York: International Arts and Sciences Press.

Schlesinger, P., Tumbler, H. and Murdock, G. (1991) 'The Media Politics of Crime and Criminal Justice', *British Journal of Sociology*, Vol. 42, No. 3, pp. 397–420.

Scholte, J.A. (2005) *Globalization: A Critical Introduction*, Basingstoke: Palgrave Macmillan.

Schoon, I. and Schulenberg, J. (2013) 'The Assumption of Adult Roles in the UK, the USA, and Finland: Antecedents and Associated Levels of Well-being and Health', in Helve, H. and Evans, K. (eds), *Youth and Work Transitions in Changing Social Landscapes*, London: Tufnell Press, pp. 45–57.

Schrum, K. (1998) '"Teena Means Business": Teenage Girls' Culture and Seventeen Magazine, 1944–1950', in Inness, S. (ed.), *Delinquents and Debutantes: Twentieth Century American Girls' Cultures*, New York: New York University Press, pp. 134–163.

Schrum, K. (2004) *Some Wore Bobby Sox: The Emergence of Teenage Girls' Culture, 1920–1945*, New York: Palgrave Macmillan.

Schutte, N., Malouff, J., Post-Gorden, J. and Rodasta, A. (1988) 'Effects of Playing Videogames on Children's Aggressive and Other Behaviors', *Journal of Applied Social Psychology*, Vol. 18, No. 5, pp. 454–460.

Scopelliti, R. (2018) *Youthquake 4.0: A Whole Generation and the Industrial Revolution*, Tarrytown, NY: Marshall Cavendish Business.

Sedgwick, E. (1985) *Between Men: English Literature and Male Homosocial Desire*, New York: Columbia University Press.

Segrave, K. (2006) (2nd edn) *Drive-In Theaters: A History from Their Inception in 1933*, Jefferson, NC: McFarland & Co.

Shahbi, M. (2006) 'Youth Subcultures in Post-Revolution Iran: An Alternative Reading', in Nilan, P. and Feixa, C. (eds), *Global Youth? Hybrid Identities, Plural Worlds*, Abingdon: Routledge, pp. 111–129.

Shank, B. (1994) *Dissonant Identities: The Rock 'n' Roll Scene in Austin, Texas*. Hanover, CT: Wesleyan University Press.

Sharma, N. (2010) *Hip Hop Desis: South Asian Americans, Blackness, and a Global Race Consciousness*, Durham, NC: Duke University Press.

Sharma, S., Hutnyk, J. and Sharma, A. (eds), (1996) *Dis-Orienting Rhythms: The Politics of the New Asian Dance Music*, London: Zed Books.

Shary, T. (2014) (2nd edn) *Generation Multiplex: The Image of Youth in American Cinema Since 1980*, Austin: University of Texas Press.

Sherry, J. (2001) 'The Effects of Violent Video Games on Aggression: A Meta-Analysis', *Human Communication Research*, Vol 27, No. 3, pp. 409–431.

Shildrick, T. and MacDonald, R. (2006)) 'In Defence of Subculture: Young People, Leisure and Social Divisions', *Journal of Youth Studies*, Vol. 9, No. 2, pp. 125–140.

Shinal, J. (2017) 'YouTube Claims 1.5 Billion Monthly Users as it Races to Boost Video-Ad Business', *CNBC*, online, 22 June, https://www.cnbc.com/2017/06/22/youtube-claims-1-point-5-billion-monthly-users.html (accessed 13 November, 2019).

Shoemaker, D. (2010) 'Queer Punk Macha Femme: Leslie Mah's Musical Performance in Tribe 8', *Cultural Studies, Critical Methodologies*, Vol. 10, No. 4, pp. 295–306.

Shultz, E.J. (2012) 'How Millennials Are Spending Their Precious Dollars on CPGs', *Advertising Age*, online, July 12, http://adage.com/article/news/millennials-spending-precious-dollars-cpgs/235960/ (accessed 23 September 2017).

Sibley, D. (1995) *Geographies of Exclusion*, London: Routledge.

Sigismondi, P. (2012) *The Digital Glocalization of Entertainment: New Paradigms in the 21st Century Global Mediascape*, New York: Springer.

Silva, J. (2012) 'Constructing Adulthood in an Age of Uncertainty', *American Sociological Review*, Vol. 77, No. 4, pp. 505–522.

SimilarWeb (2019) 'VK.Com October 2019 Overview', SimilarWeb, online, https://www.similarweb.com/website/vk.com (accessed 13 November, 2019).

Smahel, D., Machackova, H., Mascheroni, G., Dedkova, L., Staksrud, E., Ólafsson, K., Livingstone, S. and Hasebrink, U. (2020) *EU Kids Online 2020: Survey Results From 19 Countries*, EU Kids Online, https://www.eukidsonline.ch/files/Eu-kids-online-2020-international-report.pdf (accessed 28 March 2020).

Smith, A.C.H., Immirizi, E. and Blackwell, T. (1975) *Paper Voices: The Popular Press and Social Change, 1935–65*, London: Chatto & Windus.

Smith, C. (1966) *Young People: A Report on Bury*, Manchester: University of Manchester.

Smith, D. (1994) *The Sleep of Reason: The James Bulger Case*, London: Century.

Smith, N. (2009) 'Beyond the Master Narrative of Youth: Researching Ageing Popular Music Scenes', in Scott, D. (ed.), *The Ashgate Research Companion to Popular Musicology*, Aldershot: Ashgate, pp. 427–448.

Smith, P. (1997) 'Tommy Hilfiger in the Age of Mass Customization', in Ross, A. (ed.), *No Sweat: Fashion, Free Trade and the Rights of Garment Workers*, London: Verso, pp. 249–262.

Smith, S. (1999) *Dancing in the Street: Motown and the Cultural Politics of Detroit*, Cambridge, MA: Harvard University Press.

Smith, S. (2005) *Children, Cinema and Censorship: From Dracula to the Dead End Kids*, London: I.B.Tauris.

Solomon, M. (2014) '2015 is the Year of the Millennial Customer: 5 Key Traits These 80 Million Consumers Share', *Forbes*, online, December 29, https://www.forbes.com/sites/micahsolomon/2014/12/29/5-traits-that-define-the-80-million-millennial-customers-coming-your-way/#53c7568d25e5 (accessed 23 September 2017).

Solon, O. (2017) 'Disney Severs Tie with YouTube Star PewDiePie over Antisemitic Videos', *The Guardian*, online, 14 February, https://www.theguardian.com/technology/2017/feb/13/pewdiepie-youtube-star-disney-antisemitic-videos (accessed 8 December 2019).

Song, M. (2019) *Hanguk Hip Hop: Global Rap in South Korea*, Basingstoke: Palgrave Macmillan.

Soto, L. (2018) *Girlhood in the Borderlands: Mexican Teens Caught in the Crossroads of Migration*, New York: New York University Press.

Spangler, T. (2019) 'PewDiePie is the Most-Watched YouTube Creator of 2019 With 4 Billion Views', *Variety*, online, 5 December, https://variety.com/2019/digital/news/pewdiepie-youtube-most-viewed-youtube-creator-2019-1203425951/ (accessed 8 December 2019).

Sparviero, S. and Peil, C. (eds) (2018) *Media Convergence and Deconvergence*, Basingstoke: Palgrave Macmillan.

Spence, I. and Feng, J. (2010) 'Video Games and Spatial Cognition', *Review of General Psychology*, Vol. 14, No. 2, pp. 92–104.

Springhall, J. (1980) *Coming of Age: Adolescence in Britain, 1860–1960*, Dublin: Gill and Macmillan.

Springhall, J. (1998) *Youth, Popular Culture and Moral Panics: Penny Gaffs to Gangsta-Rap, 1830–1996*, Basingstoke: Macmillan.

Statistica (2014) 'Age Distribution of Active Social Media Users Worldwide as of 3rd Quarter 2014, By Platform', Statistica, online, 17 November, https://www.statista.com/statistics/274829/age-distribution-of-active-social-media-users-worldwide-by-platform/ (accessed 14 November 2019).

Statistica (2017) 'Youth Unemployment Rate in Europe (EU Member States) as of May 2017 (Seasonally Adjusted)', Statistica, online, https://www.statista.com/statistics/266228/youth-unemployment-rate-in-eu-countries/ (accessed 23 September 2017).

Statistica (2018i) 'Leading Bollywood Movies of All Time as of March 2018, by Non-India Box Office Revenue', Statistica, online, March 2018, https://www.statista.com/statistics/311921/highest-grossing-bollywood-movies-non-india/ (accessed 13 February 2020).

Statistica (2018ii) 'Share of Adults in China who Own a Smartphone in 2016, by Age Group', Statistica, online, March, https://www.statista.com/statistics/896512/china-share-of-adults-owning-a-smartphone-by-age-group/ (accessed 28 March 2020).

Statistica (2018iii) 'Share of Teenagers Owning Smartphones in Germany in 2018, by Age Group', Statistica, online, November, https://www.statista.com/statistics/828431/smartphone-ownership-teenagers-by-age-germany/ (accessed 28 March 2020).

Statistica (2019i) 'Most Famous Social Network Sites Worldwide as of July 2019, Ranked by Number of Active Users (in Millions)', Statistica, online, 6 September, https://www.statista.com/statistics/272014/global-social-networks-ranked-by-number-of-users/ (accessed 13 November, 2019).

Statistica (2019ii) 'Twitter – Statistics & Facts', Statistica, online, 22 February, https://www.statista.com/topics/737/twitter/ (accessed 13 November, 2019).

Statistica (2019iii) 'WhatsApp – Statistics & Facts', Statistica, online, 18 September, https://www.statista.com/topics/2018/whatsapp/ (accessed 13 November, 2019).

Statistica (2019iv) 'Instagram – Statistics & Facts', Statistica, online, 8 March, https://www.statista.com/topics/1882/instagram/ (accessed 13 November, 2019).

Statistica (2019ix) 'Smartphone Ownership in the U.S. 2015–2018, by Age Group', Statistica, June, online, https://www.statista.com/statistics/489255/percentage-of-us-smartphone-owners-by-age-group/ (accessed 28 March 2020).

Statistica (2019v) 'Snapchat – Statistics & Facts', Statistica, online, 11 February, https://www.statista.com/topics/2882/snapchat/ (accessed 13 November, 2019).

Statistica (2019vi) 'Number of Renren.com Users in China from 2009 to 2017 (in Millions)', Statistica, online, 15 October, https://www.statista.com/statistics/227059/number-of-renren-com-users-in-china/ (accessed 13 November, 2019).

Statistica (2019vii) 'Penetration Rate of Social Media in China in 2017, by Age Group', Statistica, online, 23 September, https://www.statista.com/statistics/793922/china-social-media-penetration-rate-by-age-group/ (accessed 14 November 2019).

Statistica (2019viii) 'Age Distribution of Vk.com Social Network Users in Russia in 2018', Statistica, online, 29 October, https://www.statista.com/statistics/990462/vk-users-age-distribution-russia/ (accessed 14 November 2019).

Statistica (2019ix) 'Share of adults in the United States Who Owned a Smartphone from 2015 to 2018, by Age', Statistica, online, June, statistica.com/statistics/489255/percentage-ofous-smartphone-owners-by-age-group/ (accessed 28 March 2020).

Statistica (2019x) 'Share of Children Owning Tablets and Smartphones in the United Kingdom (UK) from 2018, by Age', Statistica, online, January, https://www.statista.com/statistics/805397/children-ownership-of-tablets-smartphones-by-age-uk/ (accessed 28 March 2020).

Statistica (2019xi) 'Smartphone Ownership Rate by Country 2018', Statistica, online, February, https://www.statista.com/statistics/539395/smartphone-penetration-world wide-by-country/ (accessed 28 March 2020).

Statistica (2020) 'Most Viewed YouTube Channels Worldwide as of January 2020, by Monthly Views', Statistica, online, January2020, https://www.statista.com/statistics/373729/most-viewed-youtube-channels/ (accessed 13 February 2020).

Stephens V. (2019) *Rocking the Closet: How Little Richard, Johnnie Ray, Liberace and Johnny Mathis Queered Pop Music*, Urbana, IL: University of Illinois Press.

Stern, D., Finkelstein, N., Latting, J. and Dornsife, C. (1995) *School to Work: Research on Programs in the United States*, Bristol, PA: Falmer Press.

Stewart, F. (1992) 'The Adolescent as Consumer', in Coleman, J. and Warren-Adamson, C. (eds), *Youth Policy in the 1990s: The Way Forward*, London: Routledge, pp. 202–226.

Stratton, J. (1992) *The Young Ones: Working-class Culture, Consumption, and the Category of Youth*, Perth: Black Swan Press.

Strauss, W. and Howe, N. (1991) *Generations: The History of America's Future, 1584 to 2069*, New York: Perennial.

Strauss, W. and Howe, N. (1997) *The Fourth Turning: What the Cycles of History Tell Us about America's Next Rendezvous with Destiny*, New York: Broadway Books.

Strauss, W. and Howe, N. (2000) *Millennials Rising: The Next Great Generation*, New York: Vintage Books.

Straw, W. (1991) 'Systems of Articulation, Logics of Change: Communities and Scenes in Popular Music', *Cultural Studies*, Vol. 5, No. 3, pp. 368–388.

Straw, W. (2001) 'Scenes and Sensibilities', *Public*, No. 22/23, pp. 245–257.

Street, J. (2012) *Music and Politics*, Cambridge: Polity.

Stuessy, J. and Lipscomb, S. (2009) (6th edn) *Rock and Roll: Its History and Stylistic Development*, Upper Saddle River, NJ: Pearson Prentice Hall.

Sukarieh, M. and Tannock, S. (2015) *Youth Rising?: The Politics of Youth in the Global Economy*, London: Routledge.

Sullivan, N. (2003) *A Critical Introduction to Queer Theory*, Edinburgh: Edinburgh University Press.

Swedish Media Council (2011) 'Summary of Violent Computer Games and Aggression: An Overview of the Research 2000–2011', Swedish Media Council, online, https://www.statensmedierad.se/download/18.1957a5a61500017241926afc/1443447391701/Violent-Computer-Games.pdf (accessed 13 January 2020).

Swiencicki, M. (1998) 'Consuming Brotherhood: Men's Culture, Style and Recreation as Consumer Culture, 1880–1930', *Social History*, Vol. 31, No. 4, Summer, pp. 773–808.

Syed, M. (2016) 'Emerging Adulthood: Developmental Stage, Theory or Nonsense?', in Arnett, J. (ed.), *The Oxford Handbook of Emerging Adulthood*, New York: Oxford University Press, pp. 11–25.

Szablewicz, M. (2010) 'The Ill Effects of "Opium for the Spirit": A Critical Cultural Analysis of China's Internet Addiction Moral Panic', *Chinese Journal of Communication*, Vol. 3, No. 4, pp. 453–470.

Tanner, J. and Arnett, J. (2011) 'Presenting "Emerging Adulthood": What Makes it Developmentally Distinctive?', in Arnett, J., Kloep, M., Hendry, L. and Tanner, J. (eds), *Debating Emerging Adulthood: Stage or Process?*, New York: Oxford University Press, pp. 13–30.

Tapscott, D. (1998) *Growing Up Digital: The Rise of the Net Generation*, New York: McGraw-Hill.

Tapscott, D. and Williams, A.D. (2006) *Wikinomics: How Mass Collaboration Changes Everything*, London: Penguin.

Taylor, A. and Harper, R. (2001) *The Gift of the Gab?: A Design Oriented Sociology of Young People's Use of 'MobilZe!'*, Guildford: Digital World Research Centre, University of Surrey.

Taylor, I. (1981) *Law and Order: Arguments for Socialism*, London: Macmillan, 1981.

Taylor, J. (2012) *Playing it Queer: Popular Music, Identity and Queer World-Making*, Bern: Peter Lang.

Terranova, T. (2000) 'Free Labor: Producing Culture for the Digital Economy', *Social Text*, Vol. 18, No. 2, pp. 33–58.

The Age (2016) 'Crack Down Hard on the Hoods and Hooligans', *The Age*, online, 15 March, https://www.theage.com.au/national/victoria/crack-down-hard-on-hoods-and-hooligans-20160314-gnibdq.html (accessed 28 March 2020).

Thiel-Stern, S. (2014) *From the Dance Hall to Facebook: Teen Girls, Mass Media, and Moral Panic in the United States, 1905–2010*, Amherst, MA: University of Massachusetts Press.

Thinyane, H. (2010) 'Are Digital Natives a World-Wide Phenomenon?: An Investigation into South African First Year Students' Use and Experience with Technology', *Computers and Education*, Vol. 55, No. 1, pp. 406–414.

Thompson, J. (1995) *The Media and Modernity: A Social Theory of Modernity*, Cambridge: Polity Press.

Thompson, K. (1998) *Moral Panics*, London: Routledge.

Thornton, S. (1994) 'Moral Panic, the Media and British Rave Culture', in Ross, A. and Rose, T. (eds), *Microphone Fiends: Youth Music and Youth Culture*, London: Routledge, pp. 176–192.

Thornton, S. (1995) *Club Cultures: Music, Media and Subcultural Capital*, London: Polity.

Thrasher, F. (1927) *The Gang: A Study of 1,313 Gangs in Chicago*, Chicago: University of Chicago Press.

Time (1964) 'The Teen-Age Tide', 9 October, pp. 58–59.

Time (1966) 'Oh, to Be in London', 15 April, pp. 31–34.

Toffler, A. (1980) *The Third Wave*, New York: Bantam.

Tomlinson, J. (1991) *Cultural Imperialism: A Critical Introduction*, London: Continuum.

Tongal (2016) 'Millennials and Co-Creation: A Match Made in … Marketing', online, 6 January, https://tongal.com/blog/business/millennials-and-co-creation-a-match-made-inmarketing/ (accessed 20 March 2020).

Toop, D. (2000) *Rap Attack 3: African Rap to Global Hip Hop*, London: Serpent's Tail.

Tootelian, D. and Gaedeke, R. (1992) 'The Teen Market: An Exploratory Analysis of Income, Spending and Shopping Patterns', *Journal of Consumer Marketing*, No. 9, pp. 35–45.

TRU (2002) 'Teen Research Unlimited', TRU, online, 14 October, www/.teenresearch.com/home.cfm, www.teenresearch.com/home.cfm (accessed 8 December 2019).

Turkle, S. (1995) *Life on the Screen: Identity in the Age of the Internet*, London: Weidenfeld & Nicolson.

Turner, G. (2004) *Understanding Celebrity*, London: Sage.

Turner, G. (2010) *Ordinary People and the Media: The Demotic Turn*, London: Sage.

Turner, R. (1969) 'The Theme of Contemporary Social Movements', *British Journal of Sociology*, Vol. 20, No. 4, December, pp. 390–405.

Turrow, J. (2011) (4th edn) *Media Today: An Introduction to Mass Communication*, London: Routledge.

Tuten, T. (2008) *Advertising 2.0: Social Media Marketing in a Web 2.0 World*, Westport, CN: Praeger.

UNICEF (2016) *Harnessing the Power of Data for Girls: Taking Stock and Looking Ahead to 2030*, New York: UNICEF.

UNICEF (2017) *The State of the World's Children 2017: Children in a Digital World*, New York: UNICEF.

United Nations (nd) 'Youth', online, https://www.un.org/en/sections/issues-depth/youth-0/index.html (accessed 28 March 2020).

US Census Bureau (2001) *Census 2000*, Washington, DC: US Department of Commerce, Economics and Statistics Administration.

Valaskiivi, K. (2013) 'A Brand New Future? Cool Japan and the Social Imaginary of the Branded Nation', *Japan Forum*, Vol. 25, No. 4, pp. 485–504.

Valaskiivi, K. (2016) *Cool Nations: Media and the Social Imaginary of the Branded Country*, Abingdon: Routledge.

van Dijck, J. (2009) 'Users Like You? Theorizing Agency in User-generated Content', *Media, Culture and Society*, Vol. 31, No. 1, pp. 41–58.

van Rooij, A., Ferguson, C.J., Carras, M., Kardfelt-Winther, D.et al. (2018) 'A Weak Scientific Basis for Gaming Disorder: Let Us Err on the Side of Caution', *Journal of Behavioral Addictions*, Vol. 7, No. 1, pp. 1–9.

Viacom Brand Solutions International (2008) *The Golden Age of Youth*, New York: Viacom Brand Solutions International.

Virginia Tech Review Panel (2007) 'Mass Shootings at Virginia Tech: Report of the Review Panel Presented to Timothy M. Kaine, Governor Commonwealth of Virginia', online, https://scholar.lib.vt.edu/prevail/docs/VTReviewPanelReport.pdf (accessed 13 January 2020).

Vreeland, D. (1965) 'Youthquake', *Vogue*, 1 January, p. 112.

Waddington, P.A.J. (1986) 'Mugging as a Moral Panic: A Question of Proportion', *British Journal of Sociology*, Vol. 37, No. 2, pp. 245–259.

Walker, C. and Stephenson, S. (2012) 'Youth and Social Change in Eastern Europe and the Former Soviet Union', in Walker, C. and Stephenson, S. (eds), *Youth and Social Change in Eastern Europe and the Former Soviet Union*, London: Routledge, pp. 1–13.

Wallace, C. and Alt, R. (2001) 'Youth Cultures under Authoritarian Regimes: The Case of the Swings against the Nazis', *Youth and Society*, Vol. 23, No. 3, pp. 275–302.

Wallace, C. and Kovatcheva, S. (1998) *Youth in Society: The Construction and Deconstruction of Youth in East and West Europe*, Basingstoke: Macmillan.

Wallis, C. (2011) 'New Media Practices in China: Youth Patterns, Processes, and Politics', *International Journal of Communication*, Vol. 5, pp. 406–436.

Wannamaker, A. (2011) *Mediated Boyhoods: Boys, Teens, and Young Men in Popular Media and Culture*, New York: Peter Lang.

Warne, Chris (2006) 'Music, Youth and Moral Panics in France, 1960 to the Present', *Historia Actual Online*, No. 11, pp. 51–64.

Washington Post (1953) 'Fifth Horseman', 12 April.

Wasler, R. (1993) *Running with the Devil: Power, Gender and Madness in Heavy Metal Music*, Hannover, NH: University Press of New England.

Watson, J. (ed.) (1977) *Between Two Cultures: Migrants and Minorities in Britain*, Oxford: Blackwell.

Weber, M. (1978) 'The Distribution of Power within the Political Community: Class, Status, Party', in Roth, G. and Wittich, C. (eds), *Economy and Society: An Outline of Interpretive Sociology*, Berkeley, CA: University of California Press, pp. 926–940.

Weiner, S. (2001) *Enfants Terribles: Youth and Femininity in the Mass Media in France, 1945–1968*, Baltimore, MD: Johns Hopkins University Press.

Weinzierl, R. and Muggleton, D. (2003) 'What Is Post-Subcultural Studies Anyway?', in Muggleton, D. and Weinzierl, R. (eds), *The Post-Subcultures Reader*, Oxford: Berg, pp. 3–26.

Welch, M. (2006) *Scapegoats of September 11th: Hate Crimes and State Crimes in the War on Terror*, New Brunswick, NJ: Rutgers University Press.

Wells, T. (2011) *Chasing Youth Culture and Getting it Right: How Your Business Can Profit by Tapping Today's Most Powerful Trendsetters and Tastemakers*, Hoboken NJ: John Wiley.

Werbner, P. (2015) 'Introduction: The Dialectics of Cultural Hybridity', in Werbner, P. and Mahood, T. (eds), *Debating Cultural Hybridity: Multicultural Identities and the Politics of Anti-Racism* (2nd edn), London: Zed Books, pp. 1–28.

Wertham, F. (1954) *Seduction of the Innocent*, New York: Rinehart.

West, E. (1996) *Growing Up in Twentieth Century America: A History and Reference Guide*, Westport, CT: Greenwood Press.

West, M. (1988) *Children, Culture and Controversy*, Hamden, CT: Archon Books.

Westengard, L. (2019) *Gothic Queer Culture*, Lincoln, NE: University of Nebraska Press.

Whalquist, C. (2018) 'Is Melbourne in the Grip of African Crime Gangs?: The Facts Behind the Lurid Headlines', *The Guardian*, online, 2 January, https://www.thegua rdian.com/australia-news/2018/jan/03/is-melbourne-in-the-grip-of-african-ga ngs-the-facts-behind-the-lurid-headlines (accessed 28 March 2020).

White, J. (2013) 'Thinking Generations', *British Journal of Sociology*, Vol. 64, No. 2, pp. 216–247.

White, R. (2010) 'Sign of a Black Planet: Hip-Hop and Globalisation', in Cambell, N., Davies, J. and McKay, G. (eds), *Issues in Americanisation and Culture*, Edinburgh: Edinburgh University Press, pp. 163–180.

Whiteley, S. and Rycenga, J. (eds), (2006) *Queering the Popular Pitch*, Abingdon: Routledge.

Wicke, P. (1992) '"The Times They Are A-Changing": Rock Music and Political Change in East Germany', in Garofalo, R. (ed.), *Rockin' the Boat: Mass Music and Mass Movements*, Boston: South End Press, pp. 81–93.

Wijetunga, D. (2014) 'The Digital Divide Objectified in the Design: Use of the Mobile Telephone By Underprivileged Youth in Sri Lanka', *Journal of Computer-Mediated Communication*, Vol. 19, No. 3, pp. 712–726.

Wijman, T. (2019) 'The Global Games Market Will Generate $152.1 Billion in 2019 as the U.S. Overtakes China as the Biggest Market', *Newzoo*, online, 18 June, https:// newzoo.com/insights/articles/the-global-games-market-will-generate-152-1-billio n-in-2019-as-the-u-s-overtakes-china-as-the-biggest-market/ (accessed 13 November 2019).

Willett, R. (1989) 'Hot Swing and the Dissolute Life: Youth, Style and Popular Music in Europe 1939–49', *Popular Music*, Vol. 8, No. 2, May, pp. 157–163.

Willets, D. (2010) *The Pinch: How the Baby Boomers Took Their Children's Future – And Why They Should Give It Back*: London: Atlantic.

Williams, A. (2015) 'Meet Alpha: The Next "Next Generation"', *New York Times*, online, 19 September, https://www.nytimes.com/2015/09/19/fashion/meet-alpha-the-next-next-generation.html (accessed 21 November 2019).

Williams, C., Chuprove, V. and Zubock, J. (2003) *Youth, Risk and Russian Modernity*, Aldershot: Ashgate.

Williams, P. (2018) 'Subculture's Not Dead!: Checking the Pulse of Subculture Studies through a Review of *Subcultures, Popular Music and Social Change* and *Youth Cultures and Subcultures: Australian Perspectives*', *Young*, Vol. 27, No. 1, pp. 1–17.

Williams, R. (1961) *The Long Revolution*, Harmondsworth: Pelican.

Williams, R. (1974) *Television: Technology and Cultural Form*, London: Fontana.

Willis, P. (1978) *Profane Culture*, London: Routledge and Kegan Paul.

Willis, P. (1990) *Common Culture: Symbolic Work at Play in the Everyday Cultures of the Young*, Milton Keynes: Open University Press.

Wilson, M. (2007) 'Post-Pomo Hip-hop Homos: Hip-hop Art, Gay Rappers, and Social Change', *Social Justice*, Vol. 34, No. 1, pp. 117–140.

Wolfe, T. (1970) *Radical Chic & Mau-Mauing the Flak Catchers*, New York: Farrar, Straus & Giroux.

Wood, A. (2009) '"*Original London Style*": London Posse and the Birth of British Hip Hop', *Atlantic Studies*, Vol. 6, No. 2, pp. 175–190.

World Health Organization (1960) *New Forms of Juvenile Delinquency: Their Origin, Prevention and Treatment* (Report of the World Health Organization to the Second United Nations Congress on the Prevention of Crime and Treatment of Offenders), London: World Health Organization.

World Health Organization (2018) '6C51 Gaming Disorder', *ICD-11: International Classification of Diseases*, 11th Revision, World Health Organisation, online, https://icd.who.int/dev11/l-m/en#/http://id.who.int/icd/entity/1448597234 (accessed 21 January 2020).

Wright, R. (2000) 'I'd Sell You Suicide: Pop Music and Moral Panic in the Age of Marilyn Manson', *Popular Music*, Vol. 19, No. 3, pp. 365–385.

Wyatt, J. (1994) *High Concept: Movies, Marketing and Hollywood*, Austin: University of Texas Press.

Yang, Y. (2016) 'Film Policy, the Chinese Government and Soft Power', *New Cinemas: Journal of Contemporary Film*, Vol. 14, No. 1, pp. 71–91.

Yarrow, K. and O'Donnell, J. (2009) *Gen Buy: How Tweens, Teens, and Twenty-Somethings are Revolutionizing Retail*, San Francisco, CA: Jossey-Bass.

Yurieff, K. (2018) 'TikTok is the Latest Social Network Sensation', *CNN Business*, online, 21 November, https://edition.cnn.com/2018/11/21/tech/tiktok-app/index.html (accessed 8 December 2019).

Zarabadi, S. and Ringrose, J. (2018) 'The Affective Birth of "Jihadi Bride" as New Risky Sexualized "Other": Muslim Schoolgirls and Media Panic in an Age of Counter-Terrorism', in Talburt, S. (ed.), *Youth Sexualities: Public Feelings and Contemporary Cultural Politics Vol. 1*, Santa Barbara, CA: Praeger, pp. 83–106.

Zhang, L. (2013) 'Productive vs. Pathological: The Contested Space of Video Games in Post-Reform China (1980s-2012)', *International Journal of Communication*, No. 7, pp. 2391–2411.

Zolov, E. (1999) *Refried Elvis: The Rise of the Mexican Counterculture*, Berkeley: University of California Press.

Zuboff, S. (2019) *The Age of Surveillance Capitalism: The Fight for a Human Future at the New Frontier of Power*, London: Profile Books.

Žukauskienė, R. (2016) 'The Experience of Being an Emerging Adult in Europe', in Žukauskienė, R. (ed.), *Emerging Adulthood in a European Context*, London: Routledge, pp. 3–16.

Index

Pop Idol 110–11
'post-feminism' 80
post-Fordism 52–3, 59n17 *see also* market
	segments; niche marketing
post-subcultural theory 14, 106, 118–121,
	19n6; critiques of 121–2 *see also* neo-
	tribes; 'scenes'
postcolonial theory 68, 156, 162–3, 169,
	173n6, 177 *see also* hybridisation,
	hybridity; Orientalism; 'Otherness'
postmodernism 109–10, 119, 121, 180
poststructuralism 8, 117
Poynting, S. 68, 70, 72
Prahalad, C.K. 192
Prensky, M. 43–4
Presley, E. 22, 26–8
Prince, 179
Production Code ('Hays Code', 1930) 88
'produser' 189–92, 195n7 *see also* 'con-
	vergence culture'; co-creation
Przybylski, A. 93, 97, 101
Psy (singer) 152n13
Puerto Rico 140, 160–1
punk 107, 116, 118, 122, 125; global cir-
	culation of 146; and 'race' 111, 166,
	173n8; style 115–16; and women 123
Pussy Riot 106

queer subcultures 124–125, 129n12,
	129n13, 178 *see also* LGBT youth
queer theory 8, 124, 176–8, 195n2 ; and
	'performance' 178–80; 'queering' 180–1
Qzone 41

R'n'B (rhythm and blues) 21–2, 33n4,
	159
racism 20, 29, 66–7, 111, 113, 146, 172
	see also essentialism; Orientalism;
	'Otherness'
radio 4, 21, 27, 34n10, 44; 'pirate' stations
	27, 164
Radio Luxembourg 27
Radio One 27
Ramaswamy, V. 192
rap music: in Britain 145, 163–4, 166; as
	business, 16; and desi youth 167–8; in
	France 146, 152n12; gangsta rap 111,
	162; gay rap 125; global spread of 146–7,
	160–5; and hybridity 161–2, 167; and
	locality 162–3; and masculinity 179; ori-
	gins 159, 161–2, 173n4, 173n5; in Sri
	Lanka 162; and white youth 169
Rastafarians 168
rave culture *see* 'acid house' scene

Rebel Without a Cause 22
Redhead, S. 118–19, 129n6
reggae 111, 159–60, 163, 167, 173n8
reggaeton 160–1
Reinarman, C. 67–8
Renren Network 41
Resistance Through Rituals (S. Hall and T.
	Jefferson, eds) 8, 114–15 *see also* sub-
	cultural theory
Resolution Foundation 37
Rheingold, H. 180, 183
Richard, C. 26–7
Ringrose, J. 70–1, 187
riot grrrl movement 123, 129n10
risk society 61, 73–4, 79, 128, 201
Ritzer, G. 136–8
Rivera-Rideau, P. 160
Robertson, R. 131, 138
Rock Against Racism 111
rock 'n' roll 21–2, 33n3, 148, 159, 179;
	and 'Americanisation' 145; in Britain
	26–7, 63; in France 27, 65; and hybrid
	culture 159; in Mexico 159; and poli-
	tics 111
Rock Around the Clock 22
Roedigeer, D. 169
Rollefson, J.G. 163
Rolling Stones, The 26; drugs trial (1967)
	77
Roo, W. 151
Rooney, M. 21
Rose, T. 161
Roudometof, V. 138
Ruddock, A. 191–2
rude boys 168
Russia: and Cold War 136, 144; and global
	media, 171–2; Pussy Riot 106–7; social
	media in 41–2; *stilagi* 144–5

Saeed, S. 157
Said, E. 68 *see also* Orientalism
Salut les Copains 27
Sandy Hook shooting (2012) 87
Santana, F. 164
Saudi Arabia 158
Savage, J. 17, 179
SAW (Stock, Aitken and Waterman) 110
'scenes' 119–20, 129n8 *see also* post-sub-
	cultural theory
Schade-Poulsen, M. 160
Schiller, H. 136, 147
Scholte, J.A. 132
Schrum, K. 21
Scopelleti, R. 2